WAR
and
Peace in
WESTERN AUSTRALIA

THE SOCIAL AND POLITICAL IMPACT
OF THE GREAT WAR
1914–1926

Bobbie Oliver

University of Western Australia Press

First published in 1995 by
University of Western Australia Press
Nedlands, Western Australia 6709

National Library of Australia
Cataloguing-in-Publication entry:

Oliver, Bobbie, 1951–.
    War and peace in Western Australia:
    the social and political impact of the
    Great War, 1914–1926.
    Bibliography.
    ISBN 1 875560 57 2. ✓
    1. World War, 1914–1918 — Western
    Australia. 2. Western Australia —
    Social conditions — 1901–1945.
    3. Western Australia — Politics and
    government — 1901–1945. I. Title.

994.104

Consultant editor Amanda Curtin,
Curtin Communications, Perth
Designed by Derrick I Stone Design
Printed by Frank Daniels Pty Ltd,Perth.

FOREWORD

In the year of the eightieth anniversary of the landing of the Australian soldiers at Gallipoli, *War and Peace in Western Australia* is a timely publication. Thousands of Western Australian men were killed at Anzac Cove, in the desert, and in the mud at Flanders. Many more were maimed physically and emotionally. As late as 1939, the year of the commencement of World War II, the Australian people were still paying for the Great War of 1914–1918. The memory of the sacrifice of these men has never been forgotten and should not be so even in an Australian republic.

Bobbie Oliver's book, subtitled 'The Social and Political Impact of the Great War 1914–1926', does not follow the soldiers into the trenches. Rather it focuses on the society they sailed from and to which some returned. This emphasis, too, is timely. A generation of Western Australian historians believed that major issues in society were resolved through consensus and shared community spirit, and without the overt tensions and conflicts so apparent in the history of Eastern Australia and overseas. That comfortable and comforting view of Western Australian history served only the big winners in society and left the vast majority of people with an interpretation outside their lived experience of struggle and conflict. It is only in the last twenty years that the voices of the many have been heard again, making Western Australia's history look less one-dimensional, more humanly complex and rich, and socially fair.

War and Peace in Western Australia is a powerful contribution to this process of understanding the Westralian past. Bobbie Oliver has a keen sense of the ideologies behind the practice of politics and an equally keen appreciation of the role of individuals; and she has extended the range of sources used to interpret the period of the Great War. In her story the rich and relentlessly aggressive conservatives, usually controlling the coercive power of the State, do battle with new unionists and radicals and ordinary families. The terminology is significant, giving a double meaning to the book's Chapter 4 title, 'Grains Crushed by the Mill'. The men of 1914–1918, in 'war' and at 'home', fought for better lives for their families and for justice in society. In *War and Peace in Western Australia*, their lives and their struggles are saved from the enormous condescension of posterity — a big book about men with big hearts and iron in the soul.

Bobbie Oliver's book is also a cautionary tale, on the need for Western Australian men and women to keep attempting to put some restraint on the gross exercise of conservative power. Here indeed is a tough historian for tough historical and historiographical times. Bobbie Oliver serves Western Australia well, as did the people she honours in *War and Peace in Western Australia: The Social and Political Impact of the Great War 1914–1926*.

Dr C.T. Stannage,
Associate Professor of History,
University of Western Australia,
June 1995

WAR
and
Peace in
WESTERN AUSTRALIA

CONTENTS

ACKNOWLEDGMENTS

I wish to thank the following people and institutions for their assistance in the research, writing and publication of *War and Peace in Western Australia*: my editor Amanda Curtin; Ian Drakeford, Janine Drakeford and the staff of the University of Western Australia Press; the Australian Labor Party, Western Australian Branch; the Australian Workers Union; the Maritime Union of Australia (formerly the Waterside Workers Federation); the Seamen's Union; the Australian National Maritime Association; the Principal Registrar of the Supreme Court of Western Australia; Dalgety Australia Limited; the Department of Health (Western Australia); the Commonwealth Department of Veterans' Affairs; Mrs June Healy OAM, National Secretary of the Returned and Services League of Australia; Mr Des Gibbs, State Secretary of the Returned and Services League of Australia (WA); Sister Mary Raphael, St Mary's Roman Catholic Church Archives, Perth; the J.S. Battye Library of Western Australian History, Perth; the Australian Archives, Canberra, Perth and Melbourne; the State Archives of Western Australia; the N.G. Butlin Archives of Business and Labour, Australian National University, Canberra; the National Library, Canberra; the Mitchell Library, Sydney; the Reid Library, University of Western Australia; the Australian War Memorial, Canberra. Mr Vic Williams granted permission for me to reproduce verses from his poem 'For May Day 1952', and to quote from his book *Eureka and Beyond*. The J.S. Battye Library of Western Australian History, the Australian War Memorial, the Maritime Union of Australia, the *Australian Worker* and West Australian Newspapers Limited granted permission to use the illustrations. I especially wish to thank Joanna Sassoon and Carmel McRobert of the Battye Library's Pictorial section, and Muriel

Mahony, Department of History, University of Western Australia, for their kind assistance in obtaining photographs.

I am grateful, too, for the support, interest, and encouragement shown by colleagues and friends around Australia. *War and Peace in Western Australia* was originally a doctoral thesis, which was completed in the Department of History at The University of Western Australia in 1990, under the supervision of Associate Professor Tom Stannage, with assistance by Dr Charlie Fox. Other colleagues and fellow graduates in the History Departments of The University of Western Australia and Murdoch University generously gave material, comments and encouragement. Where possible, their contributions have been acknowledged individually. My examiners, Professors Stuart Macintyre, Ray Evans and Brian de Garis, all offered constructive comments that were most helpful in revising the thesis for publication as a book.

My doctoral research was funded by a Commonwealth Postgraduate Research Award and a travel grant from the Department of History. A research grant from the Western Australian History Foundation assisted me in preparing the book for publication.

My husband, Peter, provided much-needed support and encouragement during the years in which I was engaged in researching and writing the thesis, and revising it into the present book. During the latter task, our son, Nicholas, has been a delight and a distraction.

Lastly, I wish to acknowledge my debt to the historians whose works have been critically examined in this book, in particular four men who have all in the past been graduates and/or staff of The University of Western Australia: Professor F.K. Crowley, the late Associate Professor J.R. Robertson, Professor David Black, and Professor G.C. Bolton. Each would, I feel, agree with me that the process of history writing is an ongoing one involving constant reassessment as new material comes to light.

Bobbie Oliver

AUTHOR'S NOTES

Australian currency changed from pounds, shillings and pence to dollars and cents, in 1966. Variations in value since then make actual conversions difficult; however, at the time of the changeover, the following approximate conversions applied:

1 penny (1d)	=	2 cents
1 shilling (1s)	=	10 cents
1 pound (£1)	=	2 dollars.

Every effort has been made to obtain permission to reproduce photographs in this publication. If, for any reason, a request has not been received, the copyright-holder should contact the publisher.

LIST OF ILLUSTRATIONS

ABBREVIATIONS

ABA	All-British Association
ACL	Anti-Conscription League
AIF	Australian Imperial Force
ALF	Australian Labor Federation
ALP	Australian Labor Party
ASE	Amalgamated Society of Engineers
ASOF	Australasian Steamship Owners Federation
AWU	Australian Workers Union
CPA	Communist Party of Australia
EADC	Eastern Agricultural District Council
EGDC	Eastern Goldfields District Council
FLU	Fremantle Lumpers Union
FMU	Federated Miners Union
FSA	Farmers' and Settlers' Association
FSU	Federated Seamen's Union
IWW	Industrial Workers of the World
NSL	New Settlers League
NWWU	National Waterside Workers Union
OBU	One Big Union
PGA	Pastoralists and Graziers Association
PPA	Primary Producers Association
RSA	Returned Sailors' and Soldiers' Association of Australia
RSL	Returned Services League
SDC	State Disputes Committee
SDF	Social Democratic Federation
UMA	Ugly Men's Association
WACC	Western Australian Consultative Council
WCTU	Women's Christian Temperance Union
WIU	Workers Industrial Union of Australia
WIUWA	Workers Industrial Union of Australia, WA Section
YAL	Young Australia League

INTRODUCTION

The Great War is news again. The seventy-fifth anniversaries of its commencement, of the Anzac landing on Gallipoli, of the battles at the Western Front, and of the Armistice have been marked by pilgrimages and emotional ceremonies. World War I (1914–18) — a conflict that caused an unprecedented loss of human life on the battlefields of Europe, and which was so immense and devastating as to be referred to ever afterward as the 'Great War' — has returned from the history books to the arena of public debate and interest.

Recent years have seen reappraisals of the Australian Imperial Force, but fewer homefront studies.[1] In a Western Australian context, the need for research into the effects of the Great War has been particularly pressing. Although Suzanne Welborn's book on the battlefield experiences of Western Australian soldiers was published in 1982, *War and Peace in Western Australia* is the first comprehensive study of the homefront in this State.[2] And the impact of the Great War on Western Australia was far-reaching and devastating, its aftermath influencing the events of succeeding decades.

Western Australian society experienced deep and bitter divisions during World War I, resulting from an exacerbation of tensions already existing prior to its outbreak. Torn open during the conscription crisis of 1916 and 1917, these divisions were not healed by the coming of peace but continued to exist and to affect life during the 1920s. The problems of economic adversity, unemployment, industrial unrest, and violence were all expressions of the trauma of a society that had just passed through war — and the partisan sentiment of being 'Westralian' was not enough to overcome them.

'Labor's Battle'
Australia went to war in 1914, but the message of this contemporary cartoon is that Labor had long been at war against greedy capitalists, monopolies, employers' combinations, and appalling living and working conditions. The swordsman (symbolizing organized political and industrial Labor), protects the unionists, their wives and children. From the *Westralian Worker*, 9 October 1914.
[Courtesy Battye Library]

Yet the historical writing that emerged during the years between 1914 and the late 1920s developed themes of consensus and prosperity in Western Australia and minimized existing social divisions, tensions and inequalities. This trend was born of an influential and conservative section of society that was to determine the mainstream image of Western Australian history for the next fifty years. The WA Historical Society was formed in 1926. The papers read at the society's meetings consisted of either personal reminiscences or historical accounts of Perth and its environs in the 1800s (mostly pre-1850). They presented images of a world in which the institution of the convict system 'inspired the struggling settlers with fresh courage', the 'passing of the Bibbulmum [tribe of Aborigines]' was accepted as inevitable, the 'natives' committed 'murders and outrages', and there was no trace of class conflict, for hardships were endured by all alike.[3] The major historical work of the 1920s was Hal Colebatch's *A Story of a Hundred Years: Western Australia in 1929*, a conservative analysis of Western Australian society published for the centenary of European settlement.[4]

In 1960, Frank Crowley wrote that the 'horrible carnage of war' was soon forgotten[5]; a decade later, Geoffrey Bolton asserted that people of all classes and political and religious allegiances found consensus in 'tribal loyalties' to the State.[6] Earlier theories of economic prosperity have been tempered by research such as that of G.D. Snooks, in 1981, who showed that, owing to a series of 'severe external shocks' including two world wars and a world-wide depression, the 1913 level of real per capita income in Western Australia was not exceeded until 1950.[7] Yet despite the findings and publication of a considerable body of academic historical research during the past two or three decades, the concept of a 'prosperous 1920s' and that related myth of a peculiarly Western Australian consensus have retained much of their persuasive power.

This book attempts two major tasks. It examines the relationship between war and peace in the context of Western Australia in the years 1914 to 1926, and it challenges the concept that this State enjoyed greater social and political consensus than other areas of Australia did. Furthermore, it asserts that, by their uncritical acceptance of consensus as the dominant social and political characteristic, some historians have misinterpreted major events in Western Australian history.

In addressing these issues, conservative and labour ideologies are analysed. Conservative ideology undergirded the class structure that existed in the State throughout the 1914–26 period. Translated into repressive legislation, this ideology created divisions and sparked labour militancy. Furthermore, conservatives used postwar fears of Bolshevism in attempts to discredit the labour movement. Thus, conservative movements and political parties are interpreted as being militant and aggressive rather than as merely reacting defensively to external threats such as labour militancy.

The book also discusses the contributions of some of the chief players on both sides, who have received only a passing mention in Australian historiography; for example, labour movement figures such as Alex McCallum, Alfred and George Callanan and Cecilia Shelley, and conservatives such as Harold Boas, T.A.L. Davy and R.T. Robinson. And throughout these pages are glimpses of the lives of soldiers, lumpers and women struggling to survive on the wretched pittance allocated by the pension authorities or on scandalously low wages.

Re-creating a society that existed seventy-five years ago is no easy task. Just as a resident of the modern city of Perth has to look hard to discern traces of the town that existed in the early twentieth century, so, too, must the social historian search to discern the minds and understanding of its citizens, and those of their rural neighbours. The mid-twentieth century, in which much consensus history was written, was a time of economic prosperity that tended to foster complacency in scholars. The feminist and black consciousness movements of the 1970s and 1980s destroyed that complacency, and the historians of the 1990s expect to see social and political divisiveness. Which is the truer picture?

Undoubtedly, differences in class, ideology, gender and nationality did exist and did create divisions in pre–World War I society. Of these four factors, race and gender are discussed briefly in the ensuing chapters, while class and ideology are major themes.

Belief in racial superiority was an important principle of imperialism, and of Social Darwinism or evolutionary theory. According to the thesis of Charles Darwin, only the fittest members of a species survive; applying this to Australia, in human terms, the more 'advanced' races (and most notably the Europeans) would supersede the Aborigines, whose extinction was, by definition, inevitable.[8] While generally associated with racism, evolutionary theory was also applied to classes within a nationality, and to business practices. As one exponent of this theory, Henry Keylock Rusden, wrote in 1876:

> The survival of the fittest means that might — wisely used — is right. And thus we invoke and remorselessly fulfill the inexorable law of natural selection (or of demand and supply), when exterminating the inferior Australian and Maori races...The world...would be incalculably better still, were we to apply the same principle to our conventional practice, by preserving the varieties most perfect in every way, instead of actually *promoting the non-survival of the*

fittest by the propagation of the impudent, the diseased, the defective and the criminal.[9]

These ideas were actively promoted in prewar Western Australia.

Gender differences were evident in the discrimination that women suffered. Women were almost completely excluded from the world of business, industry and politics. Although granted the vote in 1899, they were not permitted to stand for parliament for another twenty-one years. In the workforce, irrespective of class or skill, they were almost invariably lower paid, were poorly represented in the union movement, and performed more menial jobs than men did.

Class and ideology were important determinants in the existing power structures in prewar Western Australia. The problem of defining 'class' in Australian society is a complex exercise that has been addressed by a number of historians.[10] The English historian E.P.Thompson regarded 'class' as an 'historical phenomenon' rather than a 'structure' or a 'category', which entailed the 'notion of historical relationship. Like any other relationship, it is a fluency which evades analysis if we attempt to stop it dead at any given moment and anatomize its structure.'[11] Australian historians Connell and Irving have also shown the fluidity of class relationships by stating that their entire 1982 work on the subject was 'a contribution to the definition of class'.[12] Earlier, they had defined an Australian 'ruling class' as being a long-established, property-owning elite who enjoyed the support of the government, and who ruled by controlling economic production, by preserving a power structure that protected its privileges, and by creating a 'veil of ideas that seem to come from society as a whole, and seem to represent a consensus of opinion'.[13]

Western Australian society during the period 1914–26 displayed some parallels with Connell and Irving's 'ruling class', although the propertied class generally consisted of people who had accumulated their wealth overseas or in the Eastern States rather than in Western Australia. In prewar society in Western Australia, there was a network of propertied men who owned real estate, business, industrial and commercial interests. Many of them attended the same clubs, belonged to the masonic fraternity, and held high church office, usually in Protestant denominations. Many held directorships on local boards of British- or Eastern States–owned firms and financial institutions, and served in government and on the Perth City Council, the Chambers of Commerce and the Fremantle Harbour Board. These patterns of privilege were not significantly changed by the war or its aftermath. Merchants and pastoralists remained the wealthiest income groups, and membership of the Weld Club remained the crown of social achievement.

The relationship between class and imperial ideology is central to this book. The propertied members of Western Australian society were usually fervent supporters of the British Empire and all that it represented. This is perhaps ironic, for the State occupied a very humble place in the imperial scheme. Australia was an unequal partner in economic and military agreements with Britain, and Western Australia was a very minor State, having a small population and virtually no industrial base.

Loyalty to Empire was to cause especial hardship to the working classes in the years to come. Stuart Macintyre has defined the 'working class' as being the majority of society, who were paid on a weekly, daily or even hourly basis, and further divided this class into skilled and unskilled, tradespeople and labourers, and 'rough' and 'respectable'.[14] These divisions were evident in the Western Australian working class.

It was the middle class, including professionals, salaried staff and business owners, that was the most prominent in the economic and political decision-making processes. While Macintyre has observed that the term 'middle class' suffers from the 'grave disadvantage that it uses status rather than economic function as the basis of classification', it remains a useful term for those 'white-collar' workers and capitalists who, by lack of wealth or status, cannot be classified as ruling class.[15] The majority of the middle class and the 'respectable' members of the working class held views of morality, and aspirations, such as to the ownership of property, that were similar to those of their higher socioeconomic counterparts. Many saw education and entry to the professions as rungs by which to climb the social ladder; nevertheless, for most, the progress was limited. As this book shows, there were certain doors that remained closed to all but the elite.

The impact of the Great War was also experienced differently according to one's class. Businessmen — especially shippers and pastoral company executives — profited financially during the war and gained much prestige by participating in fund-raising and recruiting campaigns. The pro-conscription campaigns of 1916 and 1917, which were organized largely by members of the ruling and middle classes and some of the conservative members of the labour movement, were successful in achieving a large 'Yes' majority in Western Australia in both referenda, despite the rejection of conscription elsewhere in Australia. This success encouraged some conservative politicians to employ the same organizing tactics in party fund-raising as they had used in the pro-conscription campaigns. In 1916, the first attempt was made to organize fund-raising for the Liberal Party, and the WA Consultative Council was formed in 1925.

For the working classes, however, the impact of the war was generally devastating. Many soldiers — the majority of whom had been labourers, or industrial, primary or transport workers — returned to vastly changed life circumstances.[16] Even the trades unions showed a remarkable reluctance when it came to retraining their disabled members after the war.

The fact that a well-defined class structure did exist in Western Australia during the period 1914–26, and contributed to social and political tensions, belies claims that this State was a harmonious, united community where consensus reigned. In fact, these two terms, 'consensus' and 'community' — never defined in the works of those historians who argue the consensus line most strongly — are concepts that are as complex as 'class'. A broad sociological definition states that consensus exists in a society when the majority of the decision-makers are in agreement regarding 'the *allocations of authority, status, rights, wealth and income, and other important and scarce values about which conflict might occur*', and have considered themselves to be a unified group.[17] This definition would appear relevant if applied to most politically stable countries; for a nation to function with even reasonable efficiency, a certain degree of consensus is necessary, although some scholars disagree.[18]

When applied to Western Australian historiography, however, consensus develops a much more precise meaning than merely the existence of sufficient cooperation to enable a society to function in the most rudimentary manner. The late Sir Paul Hasluck was perhaps the most powerful exponent of consensus in Western Australian history, as this extract from his autobiography shows:

> [P]erhaps the Perth in which I grew up...was a very decorous and mannered society, perhaps even a backwater of colonial gentility...There were marked social gradations in Perth, not so much of wealth as of family connections. I would not attempt to set down a table of precedence but, as I remember it, doctors, lawyers, and clergymen held positions superior to accountants, dentists and pharmacists and they in turn were higher than tailors and mercers, and they were above grocers, butchers and bakers. *Yet at the same time it was an open society with a strong emphasis on opportunity for all.* The manual worker's son could aspire to be a doctor and be accepted. The barrier he faced was not so much social as the problem of financing his education. We all did believe that we lived in a land of opportunity and equality and we had no grievance about anything. The social gradations tended to bring respect for one another rather than snobbish exclusiveness. One does not despise a kettle because it is not a Dresden teapot.[19]

Hasluck's phrase 'social gradations' was the closest he ever came to acknowledging that there was a class structure in Western Australia. Although denying that wealth was the basis for these 'gradations', he then classified status largely in terms of education and earnings (the one exception, in the latter case, being clergymen). Thus, the 'manual worker's son' is said to have faced economic, rather than social, barriers if he wished to take up a profession. Hasluck also seems to have assumed that, because social mobility was possible, there was no inequality in the society of his youth.

This passage on the 'decorous and mannered society' of Perth is in stark contrast with Hasluck's description of the world he encountered while doing police rounds as a young journalist — a world of brothels, escaped lunatics, and murderers — yet he did not acknowledge that contrast.[20] His apparent ignorance of the depth of inequality in Western Australian society was even more remarkable because he was the son of Salvation Army officers whose work exposed him to poverty and despair during his childhood and youth. However, his denial was in keeping with the views held by a majority of members of the WA Historical Society.

Two academic historians, Geoffrey Bolton and Frank Crowley, also wrote of consensus, social harmony and community solidarity characterizing Western Australian society. In a new Introduction to the 1994 edition of *A Fine Country to Starve In*, Bolton notes that when he wrote the book in 1972, he

...would have seen Western Australia as an illustration of
Gramsci's concept of *egemonia*, the techniques by which the ruling
classes maintain a hold over public opinion by presenting a
mythology or upholding a tradition which the majority of people
can be brought to accept and even internalise as their own. Consensus
was the dominant Western Australian myth in the 1920s and
1930s, disseminated by leaders of opinion in that community, but
tacitly or explicitly accepted by many, and probably most, of its
citizens.

Furthermore, Bolton accepts that the decade from 1911 to 1919
'was a period of unusual conflict and disharmony in Western
Australian society'.[21] However, he continues to stand by his interpretation
of Western Australian society during the Great Depression.
Social harmony is central to that interpretation, and Bolton

Sir Paul Hasluck
Brothels, escaped lunatics and murderers had no place in the 'decorous and
mannered society' of Perth in the 1920s, where young Hasluck was a reporter
on the staff of the *West Australian* and a founding member of the Royal
Western Australian Historical Society.
[Courtesy Royal Western Australian History Society, R1733]

gives a number of examples, including similarities in political views among citizens:

> Good Western Australians disliked extremes in politics, kept on friendly terms with their rivals, and never rocked the boat...Controversies occurred, of course, but they were kept within limits: they were family rows.[22]

The present writer, however, believes that Jenny Gregory's statement that 'as in the eastern states, early twentieth century Western Australia was a heterogeneous rather than a homogeneous society and that this heterogeneity was marked by division and considerable conflict' is a truer description of circumstances during the period 1914–26.[23] In examining the impact of the Great War, the present writer has found that 'the horrors of war' were not soon forgotten. The war's impact on Western Australian society and politics forms a part of the rich, varied, exciting and controversial tapestry that was the experience of men and women who lived through the years described by one of the State's former Premiers — himself a conservative — as 'the most anxious time in our national history'.[24]

1   Those that have been written include M. Lake, *A Divided Society: Tasmania During World War I*, Melbourne, 1975; and R. Evans, *Loyalty and Disloyalty: Social Conflict on the Queensland Homefront, 1914–18*, Sydney, 1987.

2   S. Welborn, *Lords of Death: A People, a Place, a Legend*, Fremantle, 1982.

3   See *Journal and Proceedings of the Western Australian Historical Society* (subsequently *Early Days*), vol. I, part 1, and subsequent issues.

4   (Sir) H. Colebatch (ed.), *A Story of a Hundred Years: Western Australia in 1929*, Perth, 1929.

5   F.K. Crowley, *Australia's Western Third: A History of Western Australia*, London, 1960, p. 236.

6   G.C. Bolton, *A Fine Country to Starve In*, Nedlands, first published 1972, references are to 1994 edn, p. 5; and 'A Local Identity: Paul Hasluck and the Western Australian Self Concept', *Westerly*, no. 4, December 1977, pp. 71–77.

7   G.D. Snooks, 'Development in Adversity, 1913 to 1946', in C.T. Stannage (ed.), *A New History of Western Australia*, Nedlands, 1981, pp. 237–266.

8   For a detailed analysis of the effects of this theory on Western Australian Aborigines, see I.M. Crawford, 'Aboriginal Cultures in Western Australia', in Stannage, *A New History*, pp. 5 ff.

9   Cited in C.D.W. Goodwin, *Economic Enquiry in Australia*, Durham (USA), 1966, p. 332 (emphasis added).

10   See, for example, R.W. Connell and T.H. Irving, *Class Structure in Australian History: Documents, Narrative and Argument*, Melbourne, 1980, p. 1; S. Macintyre, *The Oxford History of Australia, Volume 4: 1901–1942. The Succeeding Age*, Melbourne, 1986; and *The Labour Experiment*, Melbourne, 1989.

11   E.P. Thompson, *The Making of the English Working Class*, London, 1978 edn, p. 9.

12   Connell and Irving, *Class Structure*, p. xi.

13   R.W. Connell and T.H. Irving, 'Yes, Virginia, There is a Ruling Class', in H. Mayer and H. Nelson (eds), *Australian Politics: A Fourth Reader*, Melbourne, 1976, pp. 82–83.

14   Macintyre, *Oxford History*, pp. 47–48. The term 'respectable' was essentially a moral judgment, but was based on economic fact; for example, those who could afford shoes for their children were more 'respectable' than those who could not.

15   Macintyre, *The Labour Experiment*, p. 8.

16   For a statistical analysis of the trades of members of the 10th Light Horse, and the 11th and 12th Battalions, see Welborn, *Lords of Death*, Table Seven a), p. 193.

17   E. Shils, 'The Concept of Consensus', in D.L. Sills (ed.), *International Cyclopedia of the Social Sciences Vol. 3*, London, 1972 edn, p. 260 (emphasis added).

18   See for example, L. Lipsitz, 'The Study of Consensus', in Sills, *International Cyclopedia*, pp. 269–270.

19   P.M.C. Hasluck, *Mucking About: An Autobiography*, Melbourne, 1977, p. 126 (emphasis added).

20   ibid., pp. 106–108.

21   Bolton, *A Fine Country*, p. xviii.

22   ibid., p. 5.

23   J. Gregory, 'Introduction: Western Australia Between the Wars: The Consensus Myth', in J. Gregory (ed.), *Studies in Western Australian History XI: Western Australia Between the Wars, 1919–39*, Nedlands, June 1990, pp. 15–16.

24   Lefroy to Collier, 21 April 1924, in Premier's Department File 229/24, State Archives of Western Australia, Acc. 1496.

'The "Triumph" of Civilisation'
Ben Strange 'celebrated' the outbreak of the 1914–18 war with this unusually
frank comment in the *Western Mail* of 7 August 1914.
[Courtesy West Australian Newspapers Limited]

Chapter One

KEEP THE OLD FLAG FLYING

Western Australian society before the Great War

West Australians received the news of Britain's declaration of war against Germany quietly. The WA Council of Churches had organized a day of prayer for the political situation in Europe on Tuesday 4 August 1914, coincidentally the very day on which the declaration of war was made. People gathered to pray at the Congregational Church building in St Georges Terrace, opposite one of the major newspaper offices. Many remained on the church steps until well after midnight on that first night of the war, hoping to receive news of developments in Europe, half a world away.

'Australians are not built of hysterical material', commented the *Sunday Times*.[1] This assessment contrasts with accounts of how the news of war was received both in the Eastern States of Australia and among the other protagonist nations. 'Australians', wrote the historian Lloyd Robson, many years later

> had made their minds up and were ready and indeed terrifyingly willing to go to war. Their only anxiety was that Britain would not. Australians were all decked out, but what if there were no place to go?[2]

Bill Gammage's comment that 'great wars were rare, and short, and many eagerly seized a fleeting opportunity' similarly indicates an aggressive eagerness to be part of the conflict.[3] According to Michael McKernan, the Australian attitude to war was as to a sporting contest in which 'the home team, the Empire, invariably excelled'.[4]

In Perth, *Truth* revealed its journalistic independence from such attitudes by condemning the 'monstrous display of jingoism' by the *London Times*. It preferred to dwell on the 'titanic struggle' ahead, and on Australia's responsibility as a nation. On the other hand, quietness did not indicate a lack of enthusiasm for, or loyalty to, the cause of the Empire. While saying that there was more excitement at a football match than at the recruiting booths as men volunteered 'without a murmur', *Truth* declared, 'Westralia is proud of her sons...sturdy members of the good old stock...such as won at Waterloo and Trafalgar', thus firmly establishing the link with Empire in the public mind. The *Westralian Worker*, while leaving its readership in no doubt that capitalists had caused the conflict and stood to profit from it, was certain that Australia's duty was 'to defend her heritage' and 'to assist the mother country in her hour of need'.[5]

The *West Australian*'s editorial of 6 August presented a strong image of social harmony and unity of purpose throughout the nation:

> Australia, far distant as it is from the centre of the conflict, will inevitably be shaken severely by the clash of nations in the northern hemisphere...As a member of the family of Empire the Commonwealth comes automatically into the struggle to render the fullest aid our resources will permit, or the need of the Motherland demands. No shadow of doubt rests upon the loyalty of the Australian people. In a moment political factions have become obliterated, the tumult of partisans' voices stilled, and a united nation stands prepared to do its duty...[6]

Some newspapers presented graphic images of the realities of war. In the conservative *Western Mail*, Ben Strange's full-page cartoon, entitled 'The "Triumph" of Civilisation' (page 26), spoke powerfully of the futile bloodshed of warfare.[7] The editor of the *WA Record*, the paper of the State's Catholic community, wrote of the 'purposeless breaking of human hearts', the 'splashing of blood and brains', 'the utter abandonment of God's laws', and the 'empty ring of glory'. The editorial concluded by drawing attention to the irony of the Irish situation, observing that 'if England had hearkened to Ireland's just claims for self-government to-day she might be reckoning on close upon one million of Ireland's martial sons honourably to defend the Empire'.[8] However, the overall impression created by contemporary newspaper reports — whether conservative or labour, church or secular — was one of a quiet, determined, unified people desiring to do their duty for the British Empire.

What was the nature of Western Australian society at the outbreak of World War I?

At the beginning of 1914, the State's population was approximately 323,000, or 6.33 per cent of the national total, making it the least populous in the Commonwealth, except for Tasmania. Census figures for 1911 show that approximately 38 per cent of the population lived in the metropolitan area. The other main population centres were Albany, Geraldton and Kalgoorlie, with the agricultural area, which extended from north of Geraldton to east of Merredin and Esperance, containing 35.5 per cent of the population, and the goldfields, 22 per cent. Only 2 per cent of Europeans lived in the north-western and northern areas of the State.[9]

The population was overwhelmingly British in origin, approximately 15 per cent having been born in Britain or Ireland. There were, however, a number of significant minorities, including a 2,000-strong German-born population resident in the State in 1911, and some 1,300 'Austro-Hungarians'. Germans and Austrians continued to emigrate to Australia until the outbreak of the war.[10]

Physical isolation was very real. In an age before radio and the Trans Continental Railway, the latter being opened in 1917, communications were by cable and ship. A journey by sea from Adelaide took three days. Despite these difficulties, however, the Western Australian business and commercial world had considerable links with the Eastern States, Britain and, to a lesser extent, other overseas countries.

Political parties, especially Labor, also communicated extensively with the outside world. In February 1914, for example, the State Executive of the Australian Labor Federation (ALF) carried a resolution protesting against a recent declaration of martial law in South Africa.[11] The following September, the ALF Eastern Goldfields District Council petitioned the Prime Minister of New Zealand on behalf of Harry Holland, a trade unionist who had been imprisoned as a result of his involvement in industrial trouble in the dominion. The fact that Holland had already been released in July illustrates the difficulty of communication over long distances, rather than West Australians' ignorance of events in the outside world.[12] The interests of ALF member Don Cameron were wide-ranging, and Christmas cards from Frank Hyett, General Secretary of the Victorian Railways Union, and from the Association of Operative Plasterers in Brisbane indicate some of his numerous correspondents in the labour movement in the Eastern States.[13]

Speakers visited Western Australia from time to time, sometimes en route to England. Tom Mann, a British socialist who was one of the leaders of the Victorian Socialist Party, had a particularly successful tour in 1904.[14] The ideas of American socialists, such as Daniel de Leon, Jack London, Eugene Dibs, Vincent St John and W.E. Trautmann[15], were widely disseminated in the State by local socialists Montague (Monty) Miller, Mick Sawtell and Norman Jeffrey. Miller was a regular contributor to *Direct Action*, the Sydney-based paper of the Industrial Workers of the World (IWW), so an exchange of ideas from west to east also occurred, but to a lesser extent.[16]

These men were activists whose ideological lifeline was dependent on ideas and support from interstate and overseas, but how aware of events outside their State were ordinary members of the community? Awareness and the ability to communicate with the outside world were largely dependent on one's location in the State, and were aided by the spread of tramways and telephone lines throughout the metropolitan area and in some of the major country towns. The opportunity for education was boosted with the opening of The University of Western Australia in 1913. The university began humbly in temporary buildings, known locally as 'Tin Pan Alley', in Irwin Street, central Perth. Eight professors, three lecturers and 182 students were distributed among the three faculties of Arts, Science and Engineering. Enrolments far exceeded expectations, indicating an eagerness on the part of the local population for education and the broadening of knowledge.[17]

Perth, Fremantle and the goldfields were well served by the local presses. Apart from the conservative *West Australian*, *Western Mail* and *Kalgoorlie Miner*, there were more radical newspapers such as the *Fremantle Herald*, the *Westralian Worker*, and *Truth*, and Christian denominational papers including the *Western Methodist* and the *WA Record*. The large country towns also had their own local newspapers. The major papers allotted considerable space to interstate and overseas news. A regular reader would probably have been as familiar with events and Members in the British House of Commons as with those in the Western Australian Parliament. Despite a strongly conservative bias, these papers provided a window to the outside world.

The stance of the major newspapers appeared to reflect the thinking of the majority, for West Australians were regarded as being generally conservative in outlook and fiercely loyal to the British Empire, of which they saw themselves as an integral part. Even the Labor Premier John Scaddan remarked in the Legislative Assembly, on the day after war was declared, that 'every citizen was only awaiting an opportunity to prove his loyalty and do his part to maintain the Empire'. The Leader of the Liberal Opposition, Frank Wilson, stated that the Empire was entering upon a 'most thrilling phase of its national existence'. He was sure that Australia, and the State particularly, would be loyal to the Empire 'even to the extent of the last shilling and the last man'.[18]

Imperialism was a powerful ideology with far-reaching influence. Western Australia was economically, militarily and emotionally dependent on Britain, and emphatically upheld the beliefs of Empire. But the situation in Western Australia was by no means unique. Love of Empire ran strong in most Australians in 1914, although it sometimes manifested itself in strange ways. As W.K. Hancock put it, 'those who are most intensely British [frequently] have a special dislike for the English'. He concluded that 'it is not impossible for Australians, nourished by a glorious literature and haunted by old memories, to be in love with two soils'.[19] In a similar vein, Gammage believed that Australians saw themselves as distinct from the British when the two were compared, but 'British' when the comparison was with 'Boers', 'Germans' or 'French'. Australians, he claimed, desired partnership with Britain rather than an unequal, dependent relationship, and saw their participation in the war both as a means of security that would ensure Britain's support in later conflicts and as a way of achieving equality as a nation. At the outbreak of war, therefore, race, nation and Empire played an important part in the rush to enlist.[20]

Imperialism, however, could never create the cohesive force in Australian society that British historian John MacKenzie asserted was apparent in Britain around the turn of the century. MacKenzie wrote that the impact of imperialism within Britain itself was so great that it should 'be studied as an essential part of British history'. He identified several related ideologies that originated in the latter part of the Victorian era, and which came to permeate all aspects of British life in the period. These were militarism, devotion to royalty, identification and worship of national heroes, and 'racial ideas associated with Social Darwinism'.[21]

Renewed militarism, devotion to royalty and 'racial ideas

associated with Social Darwinism' were particularly prevalent in Western Australian society before the outbreak of the Great War. During the South African war, at the turn of the century, there had emerged a popular myth that West Australians were 'more loyal' than other Australians. Two thousand of them had applied to enlist in the first South African contingent, compared with 1,200 from South Australia, which had twice the population.[22] But Western Australia had a higher masculinity ratio than any other State, a factor that also contributed to the State's high enlistment figures in World War I.[23] Loyalty, therefore, cannot be gauged by the number who enlisted, without such factors as the composition of the population being taken into account. Likewise, Ernest Scott's observation that the 'Western Australian goldfields were outstanding' in furnishing recruits must be set against the background of a declining mining industry and increasing unemployment.[24]

The role played by the Christian churches and the education system as vehicles of British imperialism was also significant. Religion was an important part of the lives of the majority of West Australians in the prewar years. Although census figures cannot be construed as indicating active adherence to one of the Christian denominations or to other faiths, few people at that time described themselves as 'atheists', 'agnostics' or 'freethinkers'. These numbers were very small indeed beside the overwhelming majority who claimed allegiance to one of the main Christian denominations.[25]

Protestant religion enjoyed a particularly high profile in the community, with sermons by leading clerics being frequently printed in the *West Australian* and thus gaining a wider audience. While there were exceptions, the Protestant clergy generally preached a message of loyalty to King and Empire as much as to God. The extent and fervour of their beliefs were most clearly evident after the outbreak of war. On the morning of 16 August 1914, Canon Robert Moore, preaching at St John's Church, Fremantle, managed to find a parallel between Jesus lamenting over Jerusalem and the present state of the Empire. He said that it was

ever God's plan to call nations and individuals to bear witness for Him...There is no question about the tremendous vocation of our Empire. There can be little doubt of our shortcomings. Is this to be the fire of purification or the fire of destruction? So much depends on us, for the nation is made up of individuals.

On the same evening, Moore asked his parishioners:

> Is it peace at any price, so we suffer no loss, or is it honourable peace, that no matter what it cost will have made the world better by vindicating honour and justice and truth and opening the way to further evangelisation?[26]

Moore's message was one of certainty about the role of the Empire as an instrument of God's will; individuals, on the other hand, were weak and wavering and needed to purify themselves by sacrifice.

This extremely conservative theology was echoed in various forms in the other Protestant churches. It was the practice of the Methodists and Presbyterians at their annual conferences to pass a resolution assuring the reigning monarch of their 'unswerving loyalty and devotion to the Throne and Person of His Glorious Majesty the King'.[27] While the Irish Catholics of Western Australia were unable to commit themselves so wholeheartedly, the *WA Record* expressed plenty of patriotic pride and was anxious to stress that Irish Catholic Australians would not shirk but would play their part in defending the Empire.[28]

Another way in which the Christian denominations exerted considerable influence, especially among the poor and powerless sections of the community, was in the provision of charity. The Anglican, Roman Catholic and Salvation Army churches ran a number of institutions such as orphanages, 'native' missions or schools for Aboriginal people, and industrial schools or other houses of correction. In 1912, an estimated 600 children were accommodated in Anglican and Catholic orphanages in or close to the metropolitan area.[29]

At the other end of the social scale, the churches provided high-quality teaching establishments for the sons and daughters of the well-to-do. Both private and State schools were particularly effective instruments for inculcating in young minds the military traditions of the British Empire. A.E. Williams, a State school teacher, noted that, prior to 1912, British history was dominant in all levels of education, and 'Australian history was left to the whim of the examiner'. Even in the Perth Chamber of Commerce examinations, the Commercial History of England, rather than Australia, was the major focus.[30] The WA Leaving Examination papers contained numerous examples of British imperialist values. The paper for which students sat in November 1914 consisted of questions related entirely to militarism, the Empire and the British economy. Perhaps understandably, war did not serve to lessen the content of military history in examination questions. The majority of Leaving Examination History questions during the 1914–18 period centred around war and Empire. In 1918, for example, only one of the eight questions dealt with a non-militaristic topic — freedom of speech — but even this was seen as an essentially British liberty not enjoyed by peoples outside the Empire.[31]

Empire Day was celebrated in schools on 24 May every year. Frequently on these occasions, an influential member of the community would visit the school and speak to the children on a topic designed to stir patriotic sentiments, such as 'the part played by individuals in the building of the nation'. Failing the presence of a local dignitary, it was the head teacher's duty to prepare a lecture. Even the smallest country schools held a ceremony that included flying and saluting the Union Jack.[32]

Thus, through the Christian churches (in particular the Protestant denominations) and the education system, the ideology of Empire dominated the culture and learning experiences of the people, and two of MacKenzie's ideologies related to imperialism — renewed militarism and devotion to royalty — were spread with considerable efficiency. Similarly, MacKenzie's reference to imperialism as 'an ideological cluster...which came to infuse and be propagated by every organ of British life' is largely true of the State during that period.[33]

Another of MacKenzie's related ideologies — perhaps the most pernicious, and certainly the most damaging to a minority of the State's population — was the propagation of Social Darwinism, which by 1914 had long undergirded the fabric of Western Australian society. Social Darwinism encompassed various theories of 'progress', whether in terms of eugenics, economics or race extermination. A number of influential men in Western Australia subscribed to these theories. J.H.L. Cumpston, a eugenicist, served on the Board of Health from 1906 to 1910.[34] Others who embraced these ideas were Charles Harper, founding proprietor of the *West Australian* and the *Western Mail*, founder of the educational institution that later became Guildford Grammar School, and a member of both Houses of Parliament; and J.S. Battye, the State Librarian, Director of the Museum and Art Gallery, and holder of influential posts in the Methodist Church, the masonic fraternity and The University of Western Australia.[35] Battye wrote of the Aborigines:

> Religious sense, as we understand the term, is practically absent, and [the Aborigine] seems to have no perception of conscience or moral responsibility...Those actuated by a desire to civilise the natives are baffled by their ineptitude and lack of intelligence. The missionary finds his efforts to plant Christianity upon them futile on account of the absence of a moral and spiritual nature; the pioneer is compelled to recognise and often use their unerring instinct in matters of bush craft, but requires to be ever on guard against their ingrained treachery...

Battye admitted that the Aborigines had been 'dispossessed'. Musing on the problems faced by the government in caring for their 'material welfare', he remarked:

> No doubt the rapid diminution in numbers caused by the spread of civilisation and the adoption of some civilised vices will in many cases lead to absolute extinction, and so solve some of the difficulties.

Battye clearly espoused Darwinian views, concluding that 'the mental characteristics of the native are comparatively of low order. His intelligence is narrow and his reflective faculties are largely undeveloped.'[36]

Social Darwinian views were held across the political spectrum and influenced government policy and individual attitudes. Both governments and individuals conspired to force Aborigines out of their communities and their livelihoods and onto reserves. In 1912, the State Executive of the ALF resolved 'that the employment of Aborigines on private property should be banned'. R.H. Underwood, the Labor Minister in charge of Aboriginal Affairs in 1914, appointed as Protector of Aborigines A.O. Neville, 'a man thoroughly convinced of the desirability of segregating Aborigines on reserves'. Only those Aborigines employed in the northern pastoral industry and as inmates of Christian missions remained outside the Protector's authority.[37]

As well as being expressed in a most harsh and overt way

towards the Aborigines, racism was practised more subtly against other non-British inhabitants of the State. The severity varied, depending on the birthplace of the persons involved or, more crudely, the colour of their skin. Although xenophobia was heightened in wartime, it had been evident in Western Australia, as elsewhere in the nation, ever since European occupation. One historian, John Rickard, has suggested that the concept of 'White Australia' promoted the main focus for Australia's national spirit.[38] The Immigration Restriction Act, which was one of the earliest pieces of legislation passed by the Federal Parliament in 1901, was supported by both sides of the House.

Non-European workers were totally unacceptable to Labor, and it was also against the party's principles to patronize businesses that employed 'Asiatic' labour.[39] In October 1913, the Scaddan State Labor Government attempted to pass legislation aimed at limiting 'foreigners' working in Western Australian mines, to 10 per cent of the workforce. When Liberal Opposition Leader Frank Wilson objected, the *Westralian Worker* reported, his 'smug suggestion...that only in Australia are foreigners hampered brought forth a stinging reply from the Premier'. Capitalists posed as patriots, said Scaddan, while in effect they preferred foreign workers whom they could employ for below-award wages and conditions.[40]

On occasions, the general and continuous suspicion with which Anglo-Australians regarded European immigrants flared into anti-alien campaigns. One such occasion occurred in the winter of 1911, when several Russians were arrested at Kellerberrin and charged with conspiracy. It was feared that one of the prisoners, August Maren, was in fact the anti-tsarist revolutionary 'Peter the Painter'. As the charges were apparently baseless, the Russians were eventually released after serving two months in prison. The Perth press commented not on the injustice of imprisoning the Russians for so long without trial but on the need to screen intending emigrants more thoroughly, especially with regard to their nationality. Despite the lack of evidence, the State Labor Government used the case of August Maren as an excuse to tighten restrictions on emigration to Western Australia, thus resulting in discrimination on the basis of culture, as well as colour.[41]

From the point of view of one of the 'foreigners', Dalmatian-born Anthony Splivalo, Kalgoorlie in 1913 was a community 'plagued by allergies to non-Britishers'. Splivalo astutely observed:

> Many Australians bemoaned the money the foreign miners and
> woodcutters took out of the country. They were mystified as to
> how these ordinary workers managed to save enough money
> within three or four years to return to their native lands compara-
> tively rich men. I often heard it said in contemptuous tones that the
> only way they could do this was by 'living on the smell of an oil
> rag' — that is, by limiting their living expenses to a mere subsist-
> ence level. But while Australians bemoaned the money these men
> removed, I never heard anyone complain about the immense
> rewards English investors in mining and other industries were
> taking out of Australia. Even the goldfields tram system belonged
> to English investors.[42]

Splivalo's observations reveal another important feature of life in
prewar Western Australia: economic dependence upon Britain. In
1913, 60 per cent of Australia's imports came from the United
Kingdom, and 44 per cent of the country's exports went there.[43]
Western Australia was similarly dependent on Britain, and, like
the rest of the nation, the overwhelming majority of the State's
exports were primary products. Almost 100 per cent of wool, over
50 per cent of wheat, one-third of the exports of flour, and sizeable
quantities of other primary products, such as timber, went to the
United Kingdom. Imports from there were valued at approximately £1,500,000, in comparison with £281,500 from 'Other Commonwealth Countries' and £771,500 from 'Foreign Countries'.[44]

Political and economic ties with Britain created a class of businessmen who were dependent on the imperial structure for their
power and influence in the community. These were the directors
and partners of British-owned finance companies and businesses,
and those who benefited from the prevailing trading patterns. As
these same men frequently held office in the conservative political
parties (Liberal or Country Party), they exerted considerable economic and political control over the community, in the context of
the State's subordinate role within the British Empire.

British and Eastern States investment in Western Australia was
extensive, especially in the banking and insurance industries. Of
the six banking houses operating in Perth in 1912, only the Western
Australian Bank was locally owned, although it was also the
largest. British-owned insurance companies in the city included
the Commercial Union, among whose local directors were George

Shenton, prior to his death in 1909, F.H. Piesse MLA, and the lawyer Septimus Burt. Interstate insurance companies, such as the AMP Society and the Mutual Life Assurance Company, also had considerable stakes in the west.

Overseas or interstate firms dominated other trades and industries, too, but to a lesser extent. Of these, the most influential in controlling the economy were Dalgetys, Elders, and the shipping firms.[45]

Dalgetys was established in Western Australia in 1889, with Sir Edward Horne Wittenoom, Legislative Councillor for the North West, as its Chairman of Directors. Wittenoom also was a director on the boards of Millars Karri and Jarrah Company, Australian Estates and the Western Australian Bank, and owner of White Peak Station. Other board members were similarly influential in the community, but despite this, the local management was granted very little autonomy — as is suggested by their title, 'Local Board of Advice'. Even the decision to extend small amounts of credit to customers was made by the London Board of Directors.[46] The other major stock and station agency, Elder Shenton and Company, commenced in 1903 when Elder Smith of Adelaide merged with a local firm established by George Shenton.[47] The shipping trade was dominated by the WA Shipping Association, which claimed to comprise virtually all of the importers in the State, despite having closed its membership in 1901, when some sixty-five individuals and firms had joined.[48]

The State depended heavily on its primary products, wheat in particular. Flour was the basis of the fortunes amassed by several settler families during the second half of the nineteenth century, notably the Forrests, the Padburys and the Shentons. In 1912, Walter Padbury's Peerless Flour Mills, at Guildford, milled over 100,000 bags of corn for local consumption and for export to the Eastern States and Europe. The war did not diminish trade; on the contrary, in 1917 the value of flour exports overseas and to the Eastern States was £421,743, compared to a 1914 figure of £157,467.[49] Primary producers also provided an extensive market for locally made goods. Large commercial businesses, such as D. and J. Fowler and W.D. Moore and Company, sold tools and equipment for the landowner.[50]

Pastoralists were central to the State's economy, not only as producers and consumers but also as one of the highest tax-paying groups.[51] The importance of pastoralism and agriculture had increased from 1903 as the State's other major primary industry, mining, declined. According to popular myth, the pastoralists, or 'squatters', were heroic figures who scratched a living from the hostile earth. Walter Padbury typified the myth of the 'rags to riches' pioneer. In the words of Bolton, Padbury 'could [not] have had a more difficult start...He was a homeless orphan in a hostile land...He worked as a builder's labourer, servant, roustabout, barman and shepherd' before eventually becoming 'the colony's first millionaire'.[52]

But Walter Padbury was exceptional. Most of Western Australia's biggest landholders did not come from penniless pioneering stock, nor even from the 'gentry' who arrived in the colony's early years. Rather, they were comparatively recent arrivals of the 1880s and 1890s. Thomas de Pledge, who built his palatial home, 'Craigmore', on Kings Park Road in West Perth, owned the 950,000-acre Yanrey sheep station in the Onslow district. He was a gentleman farmer from Durham, England, not an impecunious selector who gouged a living out of the virgin bush and acquired wealth by dint of hard work and thrift. Likewise, Daniel Mulcahy, the proprietor of the 772,000-acre Milly Milly Station, and owner of 'Knocknagow', a grand home in East Fremantle, was an Irish merchant with a private school education. His business interests included eight hotels. Neil McNeil, whose grand home overlooked a fine sweep of lawn and some of Perth's most beautiful river views at Peppermint Grove, was a timber merchant from Victoria. Other members of the State's propertied class just prior to the Great War included mining entrepreneurs and shipping company proprietors.[53]

In stark contrast, living conditions for low-income groups were often appalling. As late as 1919, the *Fremantle Herald* described 'fetid dens' and 'filthy slums' that were deemed worse than anything in Sydney, Melbourne or Adelaide. The paper revealed that there were two-roomed dwellings, each room 8 foot by 10 foot (2.4 metres by 3 metres), with no baths, coppers or troughs, and one even without doors, at the corner of Point and Cantonment Streets in Fremantle. Near the convent in Adelaide Street could be found three-roomed dwellings with no wash-houses and no yards. In Mouat Street there was a 'cow yard', where six houses were served by only one tap and one sanitary convenience. These dwellings were rack-rented for 10s a week, by 'respectable' citizens whom the paper named. And the *Herald* claimed that these cases were a very small proportion of the substandard rental properties in Fremantle.[54]

In between the extremes of the palatial homes of landowners and the fetid slums of Fremantle, however, there was a huge range of metropolitan housing. Jenny Gregory's study of the middle-class suburbs of Claremont, Nedlands and Dalkeith showed that the residents, motivated by the 'British concepts; the gentry ideal and the yeoman model', determined the nature of their suburbs and the quality of housing therein. The social image they created was maintained and developed by succeeding generations of residents, thus establishing solidly middle-class suburbs with a high standard of housing.[55]

The political system also emphasized existing inequalities by favouring wealthy men who were long-standing residents of the State. The property franchise and the plural voting system enabled large landowners to secure greater representation in parliament than they would have had under a more equitable system. Although Western Australian women were granted the vote in 1899, they were not permitted to stand for either House of Parliament until 1920. Legislative Assembly candidates were males, of at least twenty-one years, who had lived in the State for twelve or more months, while the minimum age for a Legislative Council candidate was thirty, and his required term of residence in the State, at least two years. The 1900 Payment of Members Act ensured that all parliamentarians were paid a basic salary of £200, and this, together with the abolition of all property qualifications, had enabled the Labor Party to gain government in the Lower House in 1904. Labor's failure to obtain a majority in the Upper House was related to the distribution of Legislative Council seats, which were heavily weighted to favour rural and regional voters, and to the retention of a property franchise for voters. As late as 1911, voters had to be in possession of a freehold estate worth at least £50, or a property that attracted a minimum annual rental of £17.[56]

Labor enjoyed more success in the Lower House. A Labor government took office under the leadership of John Scaddan in 1911. The major conservative party, the Liberal Party, under the leadership of coal mine owner and metropolitan company director Frank Wilson, was in opposition in the Lower House until the third year of the Great War.[57] The Liberal Party had arisen at the turn of the century, out of the political ferment that followed Sir John Forrest's departure from State politics. Between 1903 and 1910, several non-Labor extra-parliamentary organizations had formed, broken up, and amalgamated. Sir John was to maintain an influence over State politics in the last two decades of his life. He was president of the Liberal League formed in 1910, arguably the 'direct ancestor' of the Liberal Party. The Liberal League flourished. By 1912, it had some ninety-seven branches and a membership of around 8,000. The League had a constitution and a detailed platform that emphasized loyalty to the Crown and the British Empire, maintenance of a 'White Australia', free enterprise, and some broad social and industrial reforms aimed at protecting children and establishing wages boards. Conservative politicians, including colleagues of John Forrest, and pastoralists were prominent among the league's office bearers, as well as younger men such as Harold Boas and T.A.L. Davy, later founders of the Argonauts Civic and Political Club and the WA Consultative Council (see Chapter 8). By 1911, the name 'Liberal Party' was entering common usage.[58]

Prior to the 1911 elections, the Liberal Party had received most of its support from the Wheat Belt farmers, as the party's emphasis was on developing rural areas, encouraging immigration, and undertaking public works (with the notable exception of the Esperance Railway, which the party feared would take trade away from Fremantle). When the Liberals lost the 1911 election, ten of the sixteen seats they retained in the fifty-seat Lower House were in the Wheat Belt. Ironically, the grievances of these very same farmers were to result in the formation of the Country Party, whose existence ruined the Liberals' chances of getting power, or retaining it unaided, for the next few years. In 1912, a Farmers' and Settlers' Association (FSA) was formed after a group of Wheat Belt farmers met to consider demands made upon them by the Rural Workers Union. The Country Party, established at a conference of the association the following year, was also supported by small graziers, dairy farmers and orchardists. It made its electoral debut in 1914, winning two seats in the Upper House and eight in the Legislative Assembly. From the start, the party was embarrassed by the influence of 'St Georges Terrace farmers' on its membership and policies.[59]

Apart from gaining prestige in conservative politics, members of the propertied and professional classes established and maintained privileged social links through their membership of churches, clubs and the masonic fraternity. Religious faith and church commitments were important features of the lives of many businessmen. Albany Bell, whose name was later to become synonymous with 'sweating' in the catering industry, is said to have been the first convert to the Church of Christ in Western Australia, in 1891. The church regarded him as a devoted servant who 'was always prominent in the work and who liberally contributed to many Christian enterprises which lacked finance', and rewarded him with the distinction of being Conference President four times between 1902 and 1936.[60] Ernest Allnutt, a Commissioner of the Fremantle Harbour Trust, Managing Director of D. and J. Fowler, and Chairman of Directors of the WA Shipping Association, was also a member of the Dean and Chapter of the Anglican Cathedral and a lay reader. Carl Lescen, manager of the State Savings Bank, was the son of a Lutheran pastor and a foundation officer of the Evangelical Lutheran Church. Lescen was to need all his faith in order to survive the crisis that befell him in 1916, when he was removed from his position on suspicion of being 'disloyal' (see Chapter 2). Prominent Roman Catholics included E.J. Hayes, brewer and Perth City Councillor, and James Brennan, proprietor of the House of Brennan Drapery Emporium.[61]

Sectarian tensions ran deep in the religious, social, political and economic life of the State, affecting even the privileged members of society. The Loyal Orange Order, founded in Western Australia in 1887, had quickly established lodges in a number of metropolitan suburbs and also in several country centres. The annual Orange Parade, on 12 July, which involved several of the Protestant denominations, included the preaching of sermons warning against the 'threat' of Catholicism and stressing the strength of links between Protestantism and Empire. Although parades in Perth and Fremantle were orderly and peaceful, a number of violent incidents occurred during marches on the goldfields in 1897, 1901 and 1904.[62] The ubiquitous masonic fraternity was also prohibited to Catholics. Although divided into a number of lodges, its membership — 4,000 in 1912 — spanned a wide variety of professions, trades and Protestant denominations, and various shades of political opinion, but its values were invariably conservative. Members of the Master Builders' profession, architects, insurance company directors, financiers, and merchants were prominent among the membership of the various lodges.[63]

Social clubs also espoused conservative values and held to a rigidly observed class structure. The most exclusive was the Weld Club, whose 350-odd members included Archbishop C.O.L. Riley, Chief Justice Sir Henry Parker, Sir John Forrest, Sir Winthrop Hackett, proprietor of the *West Australian*, and pastoralists such as A.H. Drake-Brockman and C.J. Lee Steere.[64] The club provided accommodation for country members visiting Perth, and a venue for entertaining business associates and male friends. Other examples of the club's selectivity included its rejection of a request by its own president, Sir Henry Parker, to accommodate a visiting judge from Queensland, when it was discovered that he was a judge of the District Court rather than of the Supreme Court as the members had first supposed. On another occasion, an objection was made, unsuccessfully, against the election of Professor David, a member of one of Shackleton's Antarctic expeditions, to the membership 'on the ground that it might cause a precedent for admitting University Extension lecturers'.[65]

The WA Turf Club was the most exclusive sporting association, sharing members with the Weld Club, one or other of the masonic orders and the Royal Perth Yacht Club. Turf Club members either came from founding families whose values had shaped the society, or aspired to the social position enjoyed by the colonial gentry. Intermarriage among the membership and their kin added to the club's exclusiveness. The WA Trotting Club and the WA Cricket Association occupied less elevated positions on the social ladder, catering for businessmen of lesser standing, such as James Brennan, and would-be members of the 'old colonial gentry'.[66] Australian Rules football, on the other hand, drew a following from a much wider section of the populace.[67]

All of these clubs had an exclusively male membership, and women attended only as guests. The female equivalent to the Weld Club was the Karrakatta Club, which was founded in 1894 and enjoyed the patronage of Ladies Forrest and Onslow. Many women would have been prohibited from joining the club by the expensive membership fee of a guinea and an annual subscription of 30s, and in any case would have found it difficult to overcome the social barriers to mixing with members of the gentry. Despite having taken a leading role in the women's suffrage movement during the 1890s, the Karrakatta Club was proud of its conservative values. In 1914, members were horrified at Dr Roberta Jull's proposal to send a vote of sympathy to the British suffragettes.[68]

Also active were the Women's Christian Temperance Union (WCTU), with a largely middle-class membership, and several Labor women's organizations such as the WA Organisation of Labor Women and the Goldfields Women's Club.[69] While the WCTU membership seemed largely out of touch with the vast majority of women, whose concerns were centred around raising large families and working long hours for very little pay, the Labor women's groups were often far more radical in matters of social reform than their male counterparts were, as was exemplified in resolutions put forward at the 1915 Interstate Labor Conference. The Burswood Women's ALF asked the conference to affirm the advisability of bringing domestic servants under the Conciliation and Arbitration Act. The Goldfields Women's Club requested that women be made Justices of the Peace and be allowed to sit on the Bench at Children's Courts, and that children of widows not be sentenced for a first offence. It also suggested that private hospitals be compelled to have at least one male warder always on duty; that straps for tying down patients be abolished and straitjackets be used only in extreme cases; and that night shifts cease in the mines.[70] These concerns show that women within the labour movement were prominent in demanding reforms, especially in matters affecting the welfare of the family, and also give a glimpse of the harshness of life, especially on the goldfields, during this period. In particular, the resolution regarding the use of straps and straitjackets suggests a high incidence of mental illness in the community. Important though these issues were, the resolutions were all struck off, perhaps because they were raised by women members.

Predictably, cultural institutions also reflected class distinctions. Libraries in the metropolitan area were justly proud of their collections. The Perth and Fremantle Literary Institutes boasted collections of 8,000 and 12,000 books, respectively, yet the imposition of subscription fees prohibited poorer citizens from membership. The Public Library, which had opened in 1887, was free and was well patronized, as were the Museum and Art Gallery. From 1911, these three bodies were managed by one committee headed by J.S. Battye, the State Librarian.[71] The conservative tastes of his committee appear to have dominated the selection of art, literature and items of material culture. If the paintings bought for the Art Gallery — works by McCubbin, Buvelot and Pitt-Morison, for example — 'fostered a pastoral myth'[72], the Museum displays also were typically selective. There was little that conveyed the experiences of working people, and especially of urban workers. In this, however, the Museum simply reflected a trend evident elsewhere in Australia and other parts of the Western world at that time. The acceptable face of Western Australian culture and history was thus determined by a small elite, among whom J.S. Battye was particularly prominent.

The importance of a few leading citizens in the relatively small community is ably illustrated in Paul Hasluck's portrait of J.W. Hackett, proprietor-editor of the *West Australian*:

> [Hackett was] a member of the Legislative Council, Chancellor of the University, a confidant of premiers, a delegate of the Federal Conventions, president of the Public Library, Museum and Art Gallery, chancellor of St. George's Cathedral, and a KCMG as well as editor of the newspaper. In his day and as long as his influence lasted, it was natural to look to the morning newspaper for leadership or support in any cause for the good of the community. Its standing and influence and its stature as an institution were great.[73]

Hasluck enshrined privilege as being beneficial to 'the community', for whom there was a 'common good', never questioning the ability or right of so powerful and privileged a person to determine what was 'good' for others.

In contrast to the exalted position of the few such as Hackett, the majority of West Australians subsisted on the daily labour of their hands, and enjoyed only the power that could be got from unionization and from being able to cast a vote for the Labor Party. Most pay packets did not extend to relaxation and entertainment. By 1912, almost 41 per cent of the State's male workforce belonged to a union, a figure that compared favourably with the Commonwealth average of 44 per cent, especially considering the youth of the Western Australian union movement.[74]

The major source of employment for women was domestic service, an occupation which, along with many other female occupations, was non-unionized.[75] There were, however, approximately 8,500 women working in industrial trades. In 1900, Mamie Swanton founded the Coastal Tailoresses' Union, with the support of Jessie McCallum from the Eastern Goldfields Tailoresses' Union. After years of fighting for an improvement in the conditions under which women and girls as young as ten years laboured in tailoring sweatshops, Swanton was granted a hearing by the Trades and Labor Council. Her evidence was quoted in the Legislative Assembly in 1906: children working seventy hours a week in shifts of twelve to fifteen hours around the clock; women on piecework being paid 3s 6d for making a dozen shirts; and no proper apprenticeship system or chance to become skilled and thus demand higher wages. The labour movement was surprisingly reluctant to deal with these issues.[76]

Working women had to battle against numerous prejudices, many of which came from within their own class. In December 1913, the *Westralian Worker* printed an article on 'Women in the Factory'. The writer claimed that 'excessive employment' of women was responsible for keeping the male basic wage down; that in Victoria, where the largest number of women factory workers was employed, the male basic wage was £78 11s per annum, compared to £123 93s in Western Australia, which had the highest wage. The ratio of female to male workers in the west was said to be only 23.54 to 100, compared with a Commonwealth figure of 36.09 and a Victorian figure of 54.09. The fact that the percentages of women in employment in both South Australia and Tasmania were lower than in Western Australia, and that the male basic wage in those States was also lower was ignored by the writer, who then went on to press a second point: that 'coincidental with the expansion of woman's economic sphere is the decline in the birthrate and the admitted tendency towards race deterioration'.[77]

Among the male workforce, union officials found that rural workers were the most difficult to organize, because of their isolation, and consequently their conditions of employment and pay were usually poor. Early in 1914, a dairyman described his situation at Narrogin. He worked for sixteen hours a day, rising at 4.00 a.m. and finishing at 7.00 or 8.00 p.m., for 30s a week and his keep. His tasks included milking sixteen cows, delivering the milk twice daily, washing the cans, and fetching the cows from a distance of one and a half miles (2.4 kilometres).[78]

Working conditions were frequently dangerous, especially for labourers and miners, as two items in a January 1914 issue of the *West Australian* illustrate. Thomas Arbuckle, a lumper, was injured when he was struck on the head by a piece of coal while removing cargo from the *Yankalilla* at Fremantle Wharf. Arbuckle suffered a brain haemorrhage, and at first his chances of recovery appeared 'slight', but two days later the paper announced that he had made 'some improvement'. The Fremantle Lumpers' Accident Book lists 109 accidents for the year 1914, although there is little indication of the seriousness of most injuries. The second accident recorded in the newspaper was suffered by James McNeill, a machine man, who was critically injured when working on a stope at the Ivanhoe Mine. He was believed to have been using a steel drill, instead of the usual wooden bar, for tamping a hole. A charge exploded, driving the 9 foot 6 inch (2.9 metre) drill through his shoulder. McNeill also lost two fingers of his left hand, and suffered a broken wrist, bruises and abrasions, and an injury to his right eye.[79] McNeill was one of the 857 casualties (including twenty-six deaths) suffered by miners in 1914, a total that had steadily increased since 1905, even though numbers employed in the industry had decreased.[80]

Prior to 1910, the union movement had won a number of reforms for male workers, by using either direct action or arbitration. In the late 1890s, there was a wave of strikes involving members of the carpenters, plasterers, builders' labourers, bookmakers, lumpers, furniture trades and railway workshops unions. Of these, the most significant for future industrial relations was the 1899 strike by the militant Fremantle Lumpers Union (FLU), founded a decade earlier to protect the waterside workers from exploitation. The strike was sparked when the powerful WA Steamship Owners' Association attempted to crush the union by instituting full freedom of contract, reducing rates of pay and increasing the working day from nine to twelve hours. The introduction of strike breakers caused violent scenes on the Fremantle Wharf. After five bitter weeks, the considerable community support for the lumpers, together with concern from businessmen fearing financial losses, prompted a demand for the issue to be solved through arbitration. It was the first time in the State's history that arbitration had been used to settle an industrial dispute, and the strike set a precedent for the introduction of an industrial arbitration system. The FLU succeeded in gaining recognition by the employers, although the latter retained the right to employ non-union labour.[81]

The Arbitration Court was formed in Western Australia in 1901, as a result of the Conciliation and Arbitration Act passed the previous year. Ironically, this Act, which necessitated the existence of the union as the workers' representative, was passed when trades unions were still illegal. This anomaly was corrected by the passage of the Trade Union Regulation Act in 1902. Under the terms of the Conciliation and Arbitration Act, all disputes between employers and employees first had to be brought before a Board of Conciliation, of which there were three in Western Australia. If agreement could not be reached between the parties, the dispute went before the Arbitration Court, which consisted of three members — a president, who was also a judge of the Supreme Court, an employers' representative, and a workers' representative — each of whom were required to stand for re-election every three years. During the years 1914 to 1926, the workers' representative was William Somerville.

Housed in the original 1837 Court House, the Arbitration Court was severely hampered by a lack of resources. As late as 1921, Somerville wrote to Alexander McCallum, State Secretary of the ALF, complaining of the 'shabby, mean treatment' meted out by the National Party Government. The court's officers worked in crowded conditions, with inadequate staff, furnishings or books to cope with an ever-increasing volume of business.[82]

Despite the existence of the arbitration system, industrial strife remained a feature of Western Australian life, partly because the new court did not always adjudicate to the benefit of the worker. A six-month strike by timber workers in 1907 actually resulted from an Arbitration Court decision to reduce some award rates. Timber workers and their families lived on very low pay, in appalling conditions in isolated bush settlements, often without even basic facilities. In the 1907 strike, they were eventually forced to accept their employers' conditions.[83]

Apart from the recognition of trades unions and the foundation of the Arbitration Court, the labour movement was strengthened in 1901 by the formation of a political party, called the State Parliamentary Labor Party, as a result of the first WA Trades Union and Labor Congress in Kalgoorlie two years before. Many of the planks of the congress's platform — such as payment of Members of the Legislative Assembly, redistribution of seats on a population basis, compulsory arbitration, and adult suffrage — had been achieved by the outbreak of the Great War.[84]

The Western Australian labour movement had a number of distinct features. Unlike in other States, the political and industrial wings were combined in the ALF, a body that existed from 1907 until the 1950s, although it was renamed the WA Division of the Australian Labor Party (ALP) in 1919. The ALF consisted of a policy-making General Council, a State Executive, and ten District Councils made up of delegates from the unions and political branches of the party within each district. The District Councils had greater powers than in other States, partly in recognition of the difficulties of organizing in a large area with a scattered population, but also because of the strength of the goldfields labour movement and the development of significant centres of party organization such as Midland Junction and Fremantle.[85] While the joint industrial–political structure was unique and largely determined the ideological character of the ALF in Western Australia, the national labour movement had, early in the twentieth century, adopted similar methods of political action and arbitration to achieve the aims of better pay and working conditions. An extensive debate in the Eastern States about whether the Labor Party should embrace socialism and about the extent of state ownership of capitalist enterprise — both of which created confusion in interpreting party policy — was also carried on within the Western Australian labour movement. Members on both sides of Australia disagreed over the extent to which socialism could be effectively introduced to achieve reforms within the existing capitalist framework.[86]

The ideology of leading members of the ALF was never uniformly moderate at any time during the period 1914–26. While outspoken in his attempts to gain reforms for his fellow workers, Alexander McCallum tended to place his faith in the more moderate methods of arbitration and political action, whereas his colleague, Don Cameron, strongly favoured socialist objectives. Philip Collier was initially a militant, but his ideology became increasingly moderate after the war. McCallum, the Adelaide-born son of a labourer, had arrived in Perth in 1898 at the age of twenty-one. His militancy developed in the West, where he worked as a bookbinder in the Government Printing Office, and was a member of the Bookbinders and Paper Rulers Industrial Union. He quickly gained a reputation for hard work and dedication to the labour movement.[87] Cameron, a Victorian, also came to Western Australia as a young man, and became a labour activist as a result of his experiences as a printer's apprentice at the *Coolgardie Miner* in the 1890s.[88] Collier was founding Secretary of the Political Labor League in Victoria before he moved to the west with his wife, Catherine, in 1904, but he, too, developed as a labour militant on the goldfields.[89] Cameron's, McCallum's and Collier's ideological development within Western Australia belies the belief of some scholars that labour militancy and, in particular, socialism were imports that gained virtually no following in the west.[90]

Labor leader John Scaddan held more conservative views. The son of a miner, Scaddan was born in South Australia in 1876, migrated to Victoria with his parents, and then, at the age of twenty, came to Western Australia. He also experienced life on the goldfields, yet his ideology contained elements of both socialism and conservatism. From 1911 to 1916, Scaddan led a government that introduced legislation to benefit workers, and set up State trading concerns. However, historians have differed in assessing the socialist nature of Scaddan's government. Neither Gibbney nor Robertson regarded the creation of State enterprises as a serious attempt to establish a system of socialism, the former arguing that previous administrations had set up such ventures where public needs were not being met by private enterprise. Although the Scaddan Government attempted to legislate a number of reforms, including State-owned housing for workers in the lower income brackets, a graduated income tax, extension of the arbitration system, provision of maternity allowances, and abolition of State school fees, much of this legislation was rejected in the conservative-dominated Upper House.[91]

Despite the espousal of socialist ideology by labour leaders such as Cameron and Collier, socialist groups enjoyed only sporadic and limited success in the early years of the century. The Social Democratic Federation (SDF) was founded in June 1901 and operated from premises in Hay Street, Perth. Its aim was to establish an independent Commonwealth with collectively owned land and capital, and 'direct popular control of legislation and administration'. The SDF had its own column in the *Westralian Worker* and conducted a lively Sunday program in Perth, with afternoon meetings on the Esplanade and evening lectures in the Mechanics Institute. Both activities were well attended, especially when Monty

Alexander McCallum
Secretary of the WA State Executive of the ALF and of the ALF's Metropolitan
District Council from 1914 to 1921, McCallum was absolutely dedicated to the
labour cause. He suffered a nervous breakdown, resulting from overwork and
illness, in 1916.
[Courtesy Battye Library]

Miller, the white-haired 'veteran of the Eureka Stockade', was
speaking. Even in his eighties, Miller was impressive both in
appearance and speech. Tall and commanding, with burning eyes
and a wide moustache, he was gifted with a fine, resonant voice

and spoke fluently, quoting from a wide variety of sources, including Burns, Emerson, Herbert Spencer, and J.S. Mill.[92]

Tasmanian-born Miller, who was regarded as the father of the SDF, was in his late fifties, with a lifetime's experience of labour activism behind him, when he arrived in Western Australia. He was influenced by the ideas of freethinkers and rationalists such as George Jacob Holyoake, Thomas Cooper and Robert Owen. In his 'Labor's Road to Freedom', which was published at the end of his life in 1920, he argued that the failure of the workers to overthrow capitalism had resulted mainly from an absence of the 'right application of invincible power that resides within themselves'. The bulk of the work consisted of an account of the history of the labour movement since the 1890s strikes. Miller was unconvinced that political government could ever free the workers from their disabilities; the perversion of justice in the courts in order to convict some of the 1890s strikers, and the inability of Labor politicians to remain true to their class once they had achieved government suggested otherwise. He wrote: 'Political promises of future legislative enactments to improve the conditions of labor...became the chief feature in the "make believe" policy [of Labor governments]'.

Miller embraced and preached the ideology of the IWW, a number of branches (or 'locals') of which had been formed in Western Australia, chiefly at Fremantle and at Boulder on the goldfields, before the war. The IWW message was that workers should organize into One Big Union (OBU); that unity would strengthen their cause. It advocated direct action, having no faith in arbitration or in parliamentary action. Miller was a member of the IWW from the commencement of its activity in Australia and was the first Chairman of the organization's headquarters in Melbourne.[93] The activities of the IWW during the war are discussed in more detail in Chapter 2.

Miller also advocated teaching the principles of industrial unionism, instead of bible instruction, in schools, and condemned the 'narrow-minded spirit of craft unionism' that kept women out of the labour movement.[94]

The 'craft' unions were among the oldest in Western Australia, and consisted of members of well-established 'crafts' or 'trades', such as locomotive engine drivers and firemen, compositors, bakers, butchers, tobacco twisters, and so on. The FLU was the first to differ markedly from these craft unions in that it drew its membership from the ranks of unskilled labour. The General Workers Union (the predecessor of the Australian Workers Union in Western Australia) was similar, except that it included mine workers. Craft unions tended to be elitist and conservative, hence Miller's observation about the exclusion of women; other trades unions were larger and more militant. All, however, were exclusive of non-Europeans.[95]

The socialists functioned by the efforts of a small core of deeply committed people such as Miller, Cameron, Mick Sawtell and Harry Leighton. In its first year, the SDF gained 100 members, but by the end of 1903 the organization was in recess. The wider appeal of socialism is difficult to assess. A debate between the SDF and the North Western Society[96] in October 1901, on the subject of 'Socialism versus Private Enterprise', was well attended and the socialist speakers loudly applauded. One of the speakers for the socialist point of view was the Reverend G.D. Buchanan, a frequent debater on the subject of Christian socialism.[97]

A small group of socialists existed, and remained, within the labour movement, although they were frequently dismayed by what they saw as its meekness and its tolerance of the status quo. To some labour members, the difficulty in socialism gaining a following in the west was partly because of the arbitration system but largely because of the strength of craft unionism, which prevented any plans to reorganize unionism along industrial lines. In June 1910, Don Cameron expressed his frustration with the Fremantle Branch of the ALF, as follows:

> Between elections we do absolutely nothing in the shape of educational and propaganda work...[P]rominent unionists seem to think that they can be the best of friends socially, and even on election day were not above having a social glass with the licensed victuallers' nominee...[98]

Cameron was by this time a leader of the socialist movement in Western Australia, and was a frequent public speaker and a regular contributor to the *Westralian Worker* on both local and international matters. Writing in this newspaper on 5 January 1912, he observed bitterly that

> the dawn of the New Year makes another epoch of the development of our present capitalistic system more perfect, the workers

bound more securely than ever, the strengthening of the chains of industrial despotism.

In the same article, he referred to the Conciliation and Arbitration Act as 'a piece of devilish human ingenuity, so effective and economical, the intellectual drug that seeks to obliterate the real objective of democracy...'.[99] It was this type of disillusionment that drove some members of the labour movement to join the IWW.

Despite the talks on the Esplanade and the debates and lectures at the Mechanics Institute, it is probable that most people outside of the labour movement had limited access to socialist ideas, whereas the ideology of Empire was spread by literature and education, and from the pulpits of the Christian churches, so that it was heard and seen by almost everyone. The labour movement's most noticeable presence in the community — apart from strike action — was during the annual parades to celebrate the Eight Hours Movement (from 1891) and May Day (from 1897).[100] These had a strong ideological significance and were evidence of the solidarity of the labour movement. Some of the most elaborate processions were on the goldfields, and the banners that survive from this period attest both to the skills of the British and Western Australian craftspeople who made them and to the strength of union pride and organization.[101]

Western Australian society at the outbreak of World War I was diverse, displaying tensions generated by class, gender, and ideological and economic differences and inequalities. It cannot be regarded as especially harmonious and consensual. By their nature and their activities, the majority of social, economic and political groups within the Western Australian community in 1914 implicitly or overtly espoused British imperialist ideology, and the conservative values of the propertied and professional classes were dominant. While other studies have shown that such domination was by no means restricted to the west, elsewhere the existence of consensus has not been argued as strongly. There was, naturally enough, a commonly held sense of identity as being Western Australian, created in part by physical isolation and by the difficulty and expense of traversing distances in order to be heard and seen by the remainder of the nation. Feelings of isolation and of being ignored by the Eastern States undoubtedly fostered a collective identity, but such an identity was not proof against divisiveness within society. Participation in the war was to deepen existing tensions and reveal the potential for conflict.

1 *Sunday Times*, 9 August 1914.
2 L.L. Robson, *Australia and the Great War, 1914–1918*, Melbourne, 1974 edn, p. 21.
3 W.L. Gammage, *The Broken Years: Australian Soldiers in the Great War*, Canberra, 1974, p. 7.
4 M. McKernan, *The Australian People and the Great War*, Melbourne, 1980, pp. 1–2. Of the situation in Europe, Arthur Marwick wrote: 'Germany's declaration of war on Russia and France seems to have been greeted with the same kind of hysterical enthusiasm with which crowds of ordinary people in every country demonstrated that there really was a "will to war" in pre-1914 Europe'. A. Marwick, *War and Social Change in the Twentieth Century: A Comparative Study of Britain, France, Germany, Russia and the United States*, London, 1974, p. 25.
5 *Truth*, 8 August 1914; *Westralian Worker*, 7 August 1914.
6 *West Australian*, 6 August 1914.
7 *Western Mail*, 7 August 1914, p. 32.
8 *WA Record*, 8 August 1914, p. 12.
9 *Year Book of Western Australia* [hereafter *Year Book*], 1915; *Pocket Year Book of Western Australia, 1919; Commonwealth of Australia — Census* [hereafter *Commonwealth Census*], 1911, vol. II, pp. 364 ff; *Official Year Book of Western Australia, 1957*, vol. 1 (New Series), pp. 72–75. The population figures for major country centres in 1911 were as follows: Albany, 3,700; Geraldton, 3,500; and Kalgoorlie, 13,500.
10 *Commonwealth Census, 1911*, vol. II, pp. 164–165; *Statistical Register of Western Australia* [hereafter *Statistical Register*], 1914, part I, p. 8.
11 State Executive of the ALF (WA) — Minutes Books (hereafter SE Minutes), State Archives, Acc. 1573A, vol. 1, 2 February 1914.
12 SE Minutes, vol. 1, 7 September 1914, 21 September 1914.
13 Don Cameron Papers. Collections are held in State Archives of Western Australia, Acc. 2675A, and the National Library, Acc. MS 1005.
14 V. Burgmann, *'In Our Time': Socialism and the Rise of Labor: 1885–1905*, Sydney, 1985, p. 168.
15 L.G. Churchward, 'The American Influence on the Australian Labour Movement', *Historical Studies of Australia and New Zealand*, vol. 5, no. 19, November 1952, p. 266.
16 See, for example, V. Williams (ed.), *Eureka and Beyond: Monty Miller, His Own Story*, Perth, 1988, pp. 55–61. Norman Jeffrey is also mentioned in Churchward, 'The American Influence', p. 268, footnote 43.
17 A.R. Feeney, The History of The University of Western Australia to 1932, Claremont Teachers College essay, 1959, State Archives of Western Australia, Acc. Q378.9411 FEE. The university's early history is recorded in F. Alexander, *The Campus at Crawley: A Narrative and Critical Appreciation of the First Fifty Years of The University of Western Australia*, Melbourne, 1963.
18 Cited in the *Kalgoorlie Miner*, 6 August 1914. Wilson's phrase, interestingly, was borrowed from a speech by the Federal Labor leader, Andrew Fisher.
19 W.K. Hancock, *Australia*, London, 1961 edn, pp. 50, 51.
20 Gammage, *The Broken Years*, pp. 1–6. For another theory regarding Australian nationalism, see D. Cole, '"The Crimson Thread of Kinship": Ethnic Ideas in Australia, 1870–1914', *Historical Studies*, vol. 14, 1971, pp. 511–525.

21   J.M. MacKenzie, *Propaganda and Empire: The Manipulation of British Public Opinion, 1880–1960*, Manchester, 1984, p. 2.

22   R.M. Andrew, Western Australia and the Boer War: A Colony's Response to a Crisis of the Empire, BA Hons dissertation, University of Western Australia, 1974, pp. 17, 143.

23   J.R. Robertson, 'The Conscription Issue and the National Movement in Western Australia, June 1916 – December 1917', *University Studies in Western Australian History*, vol. III, no. 3, October 1959, p. 46. The percentage of Western Australia's population that enlisted was 10 per cent, compared with a national average of 8.5 per cent.

24   *Commonwealth Census, 1911*, vol. II, pp. 5 ff; E.D. Scott, *Australia During the War: Vol. XI of the Official History of Australia in the War of 1914–1918*, C.E.W. Bean (ed.), Sydney, 1936, p. 404.

25   *Commonwealth Census, 1911*, vol. II, pp. 856–857. Out of a population of 282,000, around 10,000 in the 1911 Census refused to specify their religious allegiance, while fewer than 800 regarded themselves as 'freethinkers' or 'agnostics', and a mere seventy-one described themselves as 'atheists'. In comparison, the five major denominations are listed as follows: 109,500 Anglicans, 56,600 Roman Catholics, 26,600 Presbyterians, 34,300 Methodists and 6,200 Congregationalists. With regard to numbers of worshippers, Anglican communicants in the Perth Diocese at Easter 1912 numbered 4,600; Presbyterian attendance in three presbyteries averaged 4,500, and Methodist full membership numbered 4,600. *Year Book, 1914*, pp. 109 ff. (The largest non-Christian group was the Jewish synagogue with 1,850 members in the metropolitan area and an estimated 500 elsewhere in the State.)

26   Canon Robert Moore, Papers, Sermons and Addresses, 1914, in Canon Robert Henry Moore Papers, State Archives of Western Australia, Acc. 1210A.

27   See, for example, *Methodist Church of Australia, Western Australian Conference Minutes, 1913–22*, Minutes of the 1915 Conference.

28   *WA Record*, 8 August 1914, p. 12.

29   *Year Book, 1914*, p. 109. For information on industrial schools, see State Archives of Western Australia, PR 4106. Industrial schools were corrective homes set up either by churches or by the government.

30   A.E. Williams, A Survey of the Content of History and Citizenship in Western Australian Schools: 1829–1954, BEd dissertation, University of Western Australia, 1957, pp. 20–21.

31   *University of Western Australia, Public Examinations, 1915–16, 1919, 1920*, passim. On freedom of speech, see, for example, W. Murdoch, *The Struggle for Freedom*, Melbourne, 1911. This textbook was used in Western Australian high schools.

32   WA Government, Education Department, School Journals: Boyup Brook, 24 May 1914, 24 May 1916; Ardath, 24 May 1916, State Archives of Western Australia, Acc. 1203/37. Mr Brown, of the Commercial Bank, spoke on the topic mentioned, at Boyup Brook Junior High School, in 1914.

33   MacKenzie, *Propaganda and Empire*, p. 2.

34   M. Roe, *Nine Australian Progressives: Vitalism in Bourgeois Thought, 1890–1960*, St Lucia, 1984, p. 119.

35   This discussion of Battye's and Harper's ideas is based on C.T. Stannage, *Western Australia's Heritage: The Pioneer Myth*, Nedlands, 1985; and *The People of Perth: A Social History of Western Australia's Capital City*, Perth, 1979, pp. 225–226; P. Garrick, 'Two Historians and the Aborigines: Kimberly and Battye', in T. Stannage and B. Reece (eds), *Studies in Western Australian*

History VIII: European–Aboriginal Relations in Western Australian History,
December 1984, pp. 111–130; *Australian Dictionary of Biography* [hereafter
ADB], *Vol. 4, 1851–1890*, Melbourne, 1972, entry for Charles Harper; and *Vol.
7, 1891–1939*, Melbourne, 1979, entry for J.S. Battye.

36   J.S. Battye, *Cyclopedia of Western Australia*, Perth, 1912, vol. I, pp. 46, 48.
      Darwinian theories regarding Aborigines are also discussed in I.M. Crawford,
      'Aboriginal Cultures in Western Australia', in C.T. Stannage, *A New History
      of Western Australia*, Nedlands, 1981, especially pp. 9–11.

37   G.C. Bolton, 'Black and White after 1897', in Stannage, *A New History*, pp.
      137, 139. Government and church administration of Aboriginal people in
      Western Australia is also the subject of P. Biskup, *Not Slaves, Not Citizens:
      The Aboriginal Problem in Western Australia, 1898–1954*, St Lucia, 1969;
      and A. Haebich, *For Their Own Good. Aborigines and Government in the
      Southwest of Western Australia, 1900–1940*, Perth, 1988.

38   J. Rickard, *Australia: A Cultural History*, London, 1988, p. 116.

39   SE Minutes, vol. 1, 19 January 1914.

40   *Westralian Worker*, 3 October 1913.

41   F.G. Clarke, *Will o' the Wisp: Peter the Painter and the Anti-tsarist Terrorists in
      Britain and Australia*, Melbourne, 1983, pp. 89–114.

42   A. Splivalo, *The Home Fires*, Fremantle, 1982, pp. 37, 39–40.

43   S. Macintyre, *The Oxford History of Australia, Volume 4: 1901–1942. The
      Succeeding Age*, Melbourne, 1986, p. 127.

44   *Statistical Register, 1914*, part IV, pp. 5 ff.

45   Battye, *Cyclopedia*, vol. I, p. 701; *Statistical Register, 1927*, part III, p. 9;
      Twentieth Century Impressions of Western Australia, Perth, 1901, pp. 401 ff.,
      478–481.

46   See Dalgetys Papers, N.G. Butlin Archives of Business and Labour, File
      100/3/2, Minutes of Meetings, 1905–26, for Local Directors; also File
      100/3/7/8, Correspondence of Manager and London Secretary, London
      Secretary to Leeds, 26 February 1915, Circular to Branch Managers, 19
      August 1914.

47   Battye, *Cyclopedia*, vol. I, pp. 665, 994. The firm became Elder Smith again in
      1918.

48   See F. Broeze, '"A Great Frankenstein": The Western Australian Shipping
      Association 1894 to 1906', in F. Broeze (ed.), *Studies in Western Australian
      History XIII: Private Enterprise, Government and Society*, Nedlands, 1992, pp.
      49–62.

49   G.C. Bolton, *Alexander Forrest: His Life and Times*, Melbourne, 1958, p. 6;
      J. Nairn, *Walter Padbury: His Life and Times*, Padbury, 1985, p. 142; T. Joll,
      '1901 to 1930', in P. Firkins (ed.), *A History of Commerce and Industry in
      Western Australia*, Nedlands, 1979, p. 47; Battye, *Cyclopedia*, vol. I, pp. 682 ff.
      For flour milling outputs, see *Statistical Register, 1914*, p. 53, and *1917–18*, p. 75

50   Battye, *Cyclopedia*, vol. I, pp. 682 ff.

51   *Commonwealth Census, 1911*, vol. III, part XII, p. 1290; *Commonwealth Census,
      1921*, part XIV, pp. 1084 ff; *Statistical Register, 1927*, part II, p. 8. In the 1911
      Census, slightly over 4,000 males and a mere 114 females got their income
      from pastoralism; in 1921, these figures were 4,723 and 110, respectively, but
      only 433 people were actually classified as pastoralists in government
      statistics for 1923–24, and they paid an average of £250 tax per head.

52   G. Bolton, 'Introduction', in Nairn, *Walter Padbury*.

53   Battye, *Cyclopedia*, vol. II, pp. 121–131, 389. Neil McNeil was an engineer
      who moved to Western Australia from Victoria in 1883, became involved in
      a number of business ventures, and formed a syndicate that 'took over' the

timber industry from the Jarrahdale Company. He also owned 13,000 acres at Mt Barker. See Battye, *Cyclopedia*, vol. II, pp. 289–293.

54   *Fremantle Herald*, 10 October 1919.

55   J. Gregory, The Manufacture of Middle-Class Suburbia: The Promontory of Claremont, Nedlands and Dalkeith within the City of Perth, Western Australia, 1830s to 1930s, PhD thesis, University of Western Australia, 1988.

56   R. Gore, The Western Australian Legislative Council, 1890–1970: Aspects of a House of Review, MA thesis, University of Western Australia, 1975, pp. 11–15, 32–33.

57   Other Members of the Opposition included landowners, company directors, and businessmen such as F.C. Monger, A.N. and A.E. Piesse, and — in the Upper House —E. Mayo Clarke, H.P. Colebatch, Sir J. W. Hackett, E. McLarty and Sir E.H. Wittenoom.

58   See D.W. Black, 'The Liberal Party and Its Predecessors', in R. Pervan and C. Sharman (eds), *Essays on Western Australian Politics*, Nedlands, 1979, especially pp. 191–192; B.K. Hyams, 'Western Australian Political Parties: 1901–1916', *University Studies in History and Economics*, vol. II, no. 3, pp. 11 ff.; B.D. Graham, 'The Place of Finance Committees in Non-Labour Politics, 1910–1930', *Australian Journal of Politics and History*, vol. 6, July–December 1959, p. 46.

59   L. Layman, 'The Country Party: Rise and Decline', in Pervan and Sharman, *Essays on Western Australian Politics*, pp. 159–163; Hyams, 'Western Australian Political Parties', pp. 56–61; D.W. Black, 'Party Politics in Turmoil, 1911–1924', in Stannage, *A New History*, p. 385. 'St Georges Terrace farmers' was a derogatory title given by working farmers to business and professional men who owned farms, the inference being that these men were not 'real farmers' and did not have farmers' interests at heart. The influence of 'St Georges Terrace farmers' in the Country Party increased from 1915 under the domination of FSA President A.J. Monger. Monger was a member of a wealthy pioneering family in the York area and at one time was active in the Liberal League. He also held directorships of a number of farming companies.

60   D.A. Jackson, A History of the Churches of Christ, Graylands Teachers College essay, 1959, State Archives of Western Australia, Acc. Q286.69 JAC, p. 4; A Brief History Compiled for the Jubilee of the Perth Churches of Christ, typescript, 1940, held at State Archives of Western Australia, Acc. Q286.63 CHU, p. 63.

61   Battye, *Cyclopedia*, vol. I, pp. 429, 619, 703, 729.

62   A. Gill, '"To the Glorious, Pious and Immortal Memory of the Great and Good King William": The 12th of July in Western Australia, 1887–1930', in L. Layman and T. Stannage (eds), *Studies in Western Australian History X: Celebrations in Western Australian History*, April 1989, pp. 77–79.

63   Battye, *Cyclopedia*, vol. I, passim. Examples of influential members of the masonic fraternity included Harold Boas, J. Talbot Hobbs and C.L. Oldham (architects); Herbert Hocking (stockbroker); J.G. Pottenger (Director of National Mutual Life Insurance); J.F. Conigrave (Director of Fremantle Building Society); and Harry Boan (merchant).

64   *Weld Club, List of Members for 1912*, held in the State Archives of Western Australia, Printed Records.

65   T.S. Louch, *A History of the Weld Club (1871–1950)*, Perth, 1964, p. 86.

66   B. Stoddart, 'Sport and Society, 1890–1940: A Foray', in Stannage, *A New History*, pp. 656–658.

67   Battye, *Cyclopedia*, vol. II, p. 394.

68 For an account of the WCTU, see G. Reekie, 'With Ready Hands and New Brooms: The Women who Campaigned for Female Suffrage in Western Australia, 1895–1899', *Hecate*, vol. VII, no. 1, 1981, pp. 24–35.

69 ibid., p. 32.

70 SE Minutes, vol. 2, 20 February 1915.

71 *Year Book, 1915*, p. 164; Stannage, *The People of Perth*, pp. 320–323.

72 Stannage, *The People of Perth*, p. 320.

73 P.M.C. Hasluck, *Mucking About: An Autobiography*, Melbourne, 1977, p. 89.

74 I.H. vanden Driesen, 'The Evolution of the Trade Union Movement in Western Australia', in Stannage, *A New History*, p. 370.

75 *Commonwealth Census, 1911*, vol. III, p. 1290; *Commonwealth Census, 1921*, vol. XIV, p. 1084.

76 L. Layman and J. Goddard, *Organise! A Visual Record of the Labour Movement in Western Australia*, Perth, 1988, p. 223; J. Williams, *The First Furrow*, Perth, 1976, p. 46.

77 *Westralian Worker*, 19 December 1913. There are considerable problems with the figures quoted in this article. The *Commonwealth of Australia Official Year Book, no. 13, 1920*, p. 1066, quotes 'weighted average nominal weekly rates for male workers' as follows: Victoria, 54s 7d; Western Australia, 62s 10d (that is, annual wage rates of approximately £145 and £161, respectively); while the *Victorian Year Book, 1913–14*, p. 800, states that the Victorian average minimum wage 'under the Award as at 31.12.13' (that is, a year earlier than the *Commonwealth Year Book* figures) was £2 16s (or 56s).

78 State Executive of the ALF (WA) — Correspondence Files, State Archives of Western Australia, Acc. 1688A, File 147.

79 *West Australian*, 7 January 1914, 9 January 1914; see also Fremantle Waterside Workers (Lumpers), Accident Book, 1914, N.G. Butlin Archives of Business and Labour, Acc. N28/317, 6 January 1914 and for the whole of 1914.

80 *Statistical Register, 1914*, part VII, p. 9.

81 vanden Driesen, 'Evolution of the Trade Union Movement', pp. 363–366.

82 ibid., pp. 373–374; Battye, *Cyclopedia*, vol. 1, p. 372; Somerville to McCallum, 14 September 1921, in William Somerville Papers, State Archives of Western Australia, Acc. 472, File 18.

83 Williams, *The First Furrow*, pp. 47–48.

84 D. Mossenson, Gold and Politics: The Influence of the Eastern Goldfields on the Political Development of Western Australia, 1890–1914, MA thesis, University of Western Australia, 1952, pp. 154–157; vanden Driesen, 'Evolution of the Trade Union Movement', p. 378.

85 For works on the development and structure of the labour movement in Western Australia, see, for example, Black, 'Party Politics in Turmoil', pp. 381–405; or H.J. Gibbney, 'Western Australia', in D.J. Murphy (ed.), *Labor in Politics, 1880–1920*, St Lucia, 1975, pp. 343–383.

86 J.R. Robertson, 'The Internal Politics of State Labor in Western Australia, 1911–1916', *Labour History*, no. 2, May 1962, pp. 49, 50, 52. Robertson remarked that both the 'Parliamentary and non-Parliamentary sections' of the movement 'believed in the advisability and the efficacy of political action' and that, as a result, strikes were few. See also S. Macintyre, *The Labour Experiment*, Melbourne, 1989, pp. 33–34.

87 See entry for Alexander McCallum in *ADB, Vol. 10, 1891–1939*, Melbourne, 1986, pp. 209–211; also *Westralian Worker*, 7 August 1914.

88 *ADB, Vol. 7, 1891–1939*, Melbourne, 1979, entry for D.J. Cameron, pp. 533–535.

89 *ADB, Vol. 8, 1891–1939*, Melbourne, 1981, entry for Philip Collier, p. 70. See also Lloyd Ross, *John Curtin: A Biography*, Melbourne, 1977.

90 See, for example, Gibbney, 'Western Australia', p. 378: 'the Western Australian Labor movement before 1921 was thus a mildly reformist body, with no profound feeling of class consciousness, which was only lightly touched by the more radical currents generated in the east'.

91 ibid., p. 366; Robertson, 'Internal Politics', p. 58; *ADB, Vol. 11, 1891–1939*, Melbourne, 1988, entry for John Scaddan.

92 *Westralian Worker*, 26 June 1901, 8 November 1901; Williams, *The First Furrow*, p. 40. An eye-witness description of Miller is cited in E.C. Fry (ed.), *Rebels and Radicals*, Sydney, 1983, p. 188.

93 For accounts of IWW activity, see, for example, I. Bedford, 'The Industrial Workers of the World in Australia', *Labour History*, no. 13, November 1967, pp. 40–44; P.J. Rushton, 'The Revolutionary Ideology of the Industrial Workers of the World in Australia', *Historical Studies*, vol. 15, 1972–73, pp. 424–446; V. Burgmann, '"The Iron Heel": The Suppression of the Industrial Workers of the World During World War I', in Sydney Labour History Group, *What Rough Beast? The State and Social Order in Australian History*, Sydney, 1982, pp. 171–191; I. Turner, *Industrial Labour and Politics: The Dynamics of the Labour Movement in Eastern Australia, 1900–1921*, Canberra, 1965; and F. Cain, *The Wobblies at War: A History of the IWW and the Great War in Australia*, Melbourne, 1993. Most of these accounts give only passing references to IWW activity in Western Australia. The only published accounts that deal with the Western Australian IWW in any detail are Williams, The *First Furrow*; Fry, *Rebels and Radicals*, ch. 12; and Cain, *The Wobblies at War*, pp. 146–152.

94 V. Williams, *Monty Miller*, pp. 50–51. For other accounts of Miller's life and experiences in Western Australia, see Fry, *Rebels and Radicals*, ch. 12; and Williams, *The First Furrow*. See also M. Miller, Labor's Road to Freedom, typescript, State Archives of Western Australia, Acc. 1461A/40, especially pp. 3, 5, 10, 15, 21, 43, 44.

95 vanden Driesen, 'Evolution of the Trade Union Movement', pp. 355 ff.; and Layman and Goddard, *Organise!*, pp. 29 ff.

96 The North Western Society was probably a pastoralists' organization.

97 Burgmann, *'In Our Time'*, p. 170; *Westralian Worker*, 25 October 1901, 8 November 1901.

98 Don Cameron Papers, State Archives of Western Australia; *Westralian Worker*, 13 June 1910.

99 *Westralian Worker*, 5 January 1912.

100 The Eight Hours Day was usually held at the end of the year — October or December. May Day was celebrated as well as, or instead of, the Eight Hours Day, from 1897 in the goldfields and from 1901 in Perth. Both celebrations flagged during World War I, and in 1921 May Day replaced all the previous celebrations, including Proclamation Day. See Layman and Goddard, *Organise!*, pp. 201 ff.

101 ibid., ch. 1 (the surviving banners, held in the WA Museum, are shown in this book); Williams, *Monty Miller*, p. 52.

Chapter Two

WAR RAGE

Concepts of loyalty and disloyalty

By the end of December 1914, over 4,000 West Australians had enlisted, making the State's initial commitment to the war an impressive one.[1] There were, of course, numerous motives for joining up. For example, one study found that the rural Beverley and Toodyay communities, with their close affinity with Britain, large proportion of British-born, and long appreciation of imperial ideals, saw their involvement in the war in imperial terms. This motivation was not so apparent in the Murchison, a unionist, labour-dominated community with a strong Irish component, which was inspired by the brave deeds of Australians fighting at Gallipoli and elsewhere in Europe.[2] Nevertheless, all three communities contributed extensively to the war effort. Thus, 'loyalty' could be expressed in widely differing ways and for various reasons.

Love of empire was of vital importance to the war effort, ensuring Australia's speedy offer of assistance. The WA Recruiting Committee adopted the motto 'Western Australia will keep the old flag flying yet', underneath which sailed a black swan carrying a Union Jack in its beak.[3] Even those who deplored displays of jingoism rarely hesitated to state that Australia's 'national responsibility' was to fight side by side with Britain. When newspapers such as *Truth* eventually began to criticize the war itself, it was not imperialism that came under attack but 'profiteers'.[4] In mid-1915, John Norton, the Melbourne-based editor of *Truth*, came close to exposing the motivations behind the war when he launched a lengthy attack on the 'perfidious, putrid politicians' and 'prosy, prolix, plate-pushing, penny-pinching, pelf-pursuing, pulpit-preachers of the Wesleymethody wowser-type' who criticized the 'slackers' and 'shirkers' while taking good care to keep themselves well away from the 'Minotaur maw of war'.[5] Yet even while condemning the action at Gallipoli as a senseless slaughter, Norton was not specific in his attack, failing to state that Australia should have no part in the war. Perhaps his reticence owed more to fear of censorship and of the possibility of being charged with prejudicing recruitment, under the War Precautions Act, than to lack of conviction.

A major concern of the Labor Caucus at the outbreak of the war was not so much the adequacy of Western Australia's response to the Empire's needs, but the ability of the party to win the October 1914 State election. Labor emerged victorious but with a reduced majority.[6] Scaddan's administration was constantly frustrated by the conservative majority in the Upper House, which persisted in blocking Bills and refused to allow the government finance. Opposing ideas about the conduct of the war and about priorities created tensions during proceedings in both Houses of Parliament, and within the political parties. While Labor was naturally the prime target of conservative criticism regarding the conduct of the war, there is some evidence of division among the Opposition. The resignation, in March 1915, of Country Party leader James Gardiner, purportedly on the grounds of ill health[7], appears to have smoothed the way for a closer working relationship between the two non-Labor parties, but problems still remained.

Even within Caucus, there was widespread dissatisfaction over government policies. Major issues were 'secret contracts' — in particular, the Nevanas contract for construction of the State-owned Wyndham Meatworks — and the Referenda Powers Bill. Other causes of disagreement were the questions of whether the government should maintain a policy of preference for unionists when engaging employees outside of the public service, and whether salaries and working hours of government employees should be reduced, owing to the economic climate created by the war.[8]

Nevanas and Company was a private, London-based firm contracted by the government to build the Wyndham Meatworks at an estimated cost of £155,000. The contract was terminated when, according to the Minister for Lands, W.D. Johnson, the company failed to comply with the conditions of the agreement.[9] The Opposition, not satisfied with Johnson's explanation, instigated the setting up of a Select Committee to inquire into matters concerning the contract and its cancellation. The resulting report prompted an

'The "Christian" Easter — 1916'
The rulers of the German, Austrian and Turkish Empires played dice with
human lives, Christ (and humanity) were re-crucified, churches burned — but
no blame was laid at the British Empire's door. From *Truth*, 15 April 1916.
[Courtesy Battye Library]

extensive debate in the Legislative Assembly in November 1915, during which bitter attacks on the government were made by three of its own Members, E.E. Heitmann, E.B. Johnston and G. Taylor.[10] Johnston subsequently left the party, giving Labor a minority in the Lower House and assisting in bringing the government down in mid-1916.[11]

The Referenda Powers Bill, an attempt by the Federal Labor Government to push through a referendum to transfer a number of State powers to the Commonwealth, was bitterly opposed by Liberal Members in both Houses. They argued that men on active service, and farmers, who were most likely to support State rights and to vote against the proposals, would be unable to get to polling booths. One Member, A.J.H. Shaw, went to the extent of accusing the Federal Government of attempting to 'create discord in the trenches'. He continued:

> For them [the Federal Government] the momentous question is not how to aid the Empire in the struggle through which it is passing but whether the States shall hand over to the Commonwealth their right to control trade. At the beginning of the war we were all cheered by and heartened by the words of Mr. Fisher, 'Stand by the Old Country to the last man and to the last shilling'. Our last shilling was evidently very soon spent, for within a few months there was a request from Australia to Britain for a loan of eighteen millions. As for the last man, the Commonwealth Prime Minister is evidently prepared to throw that undertaking overboard for within the last few days he has declared himself against conscription.[12]

The gathering pressures of internal strife and constant attack from the conservative Opposition probably were factors in Western Australia's internment of a disproportionately large number of 'aliens'. Incredibly, 21 per cent of the internees at Liverpool, New South Wales, where a mass concentration camp had been set up, came from Western Australia, despite the fact that only 5 per cent of the State's population was German or Austrian born. This resulted from the policy of mass internment of Austrian Slavs from the goldfields.[13]

One of the internees has left an account of this alarming and humiliating experience. Anthony Splivalo, aged seventeen, was too young to apply for naturalization, although he had lived on the goldfields for six years and his brother was naturalized. In response to an order by the military authorities, published in the

Kalgoorlie Miner, Splivalo and a large number of fellow aliens reported to the Caledonian Hall, in Kalgoorlie, one morning in August 1915. Captain Corbett of Military Intelligence interviewed all present and ordered them to depart immediately for the detention camp on Rottnest Island. Splivalo was shocked. He was refused permission even to say goodbye to his brother and friends, and to collect a change of clothing. He and his fellow Slavs were marched by an armed military escort to the railway station, like so many criminals, while curious crowds watched them pass.[14]

Although this experience fell upon Splivalo like a thunderclap, trouble had been brewing for months. Publicly expressed hostility towards 'enemy aliens', including those who were naturalized British citizens, began at 10.00 p.m. on 5 August 1914 with an act that the *Sunday Times* referred to as 'superlative patriotism'. A group of youths bombarded the coat of arms on the wall of the Austrian Consulate, in St Georges Terrace, with bricks until the caretaker 'removed the offensive symbol'.[15] This was a low-key protest compared, for example, to the riots that occurred in Melbourne when a 300-strong crowd attacked the German Club.[16] Nevertheless, the cost in individual human suffering was considerable.

Immediately after the outbreak of hostilities, the Premier received a cable from the new Prime Minister, Joseph Cook, informing him of the issue of a proclamation from Britain, calling upon subjects of the German and Austro-Hungarian Empires to report themselves to police. Scaddan had already advised the German Consul to cease acting in his official capacity.[17] Military intelligence revealed that, at the beginning of September 1914, there were approximately 1,000 'Austrians', 'Slavs' and 'Italians' employed in the Kalgoorlie mines and firewood companies, and a further 600 were estimated to be working at the more isolated mining settlements such as Gwalia, Youanmi and Meekatharra.

A military detention centre was set up on Rottnest Island to house all German prisoners, under a guard of three officers and fifty other ranks from the 88th Infantry. By 7 September 1914, the Commandant of Military District 5 (Western Australia) advised Scaddan that there were 113 prisoners already lodged at Rottnest Island, a further sixteen at Fremantle, and eighty-seven on ships. Although prisoners from the *Emden*, sunk off the Western Australian coast in September, were not sent to the island, the detainees included merchant seamen from three captured cargo steamers, and men who had served in the German Army Reserve. These latter were thought to be especially dangerous, as they had been trained in the use of arms. The principle was to arrest all single men under thirty-two years who had served as reservists, and who had lived for less than four years in the State. Married men with dependants were not to be imprisoned.[18]

These regulations were established early in the war, before bitterness, engendered by lengthy conflict, propaganda and ever-increasing lists of dead and wounded, obscured normal sentiments of decency and justice towards innocent people who could not help the accident of their birth, and who scarcely could be expected to applaud the killing of members of their own race. Here, one senses an attempt by the Western Australian Government to protect the aliens themselves, as well as the rest of the community. Nevertheless, even the old and infirm did not escape surveillance. The Master of the Old Men's Home recommended that an inmate, a German reservist named Widemann, be transferred to Rottnest Island.[19]

In 1915, the Military Commandant, Colonel Bruche, received a number of complaints from prisoners of war at the Rottnest Island detention centre. One, an Austrian, protested that the Germans were 'treated differently', and that he and his fellow prisoners went about in 'ragged clothes' and worn-out boots. Another internee complained of receiving inadequate treatment for a complaint that seems, from his description of matter-filled blisters and pain in his genitals, to have been a venereal disease, although this was denied by the Medical Officer. A third prisoner wrote, with feeling, that 'savages and blacks could not be treated worse'. He claimed that the internees had to carry wood on their shoulders 'like animals', were constantly under guard, and were, on occasions, 'attacked with bayonets'.[20] Anthony Splivalo complained about the quality of the food. Many years later, he reflected:

> Once behind the wire, we were unable to forage for ourselves and had to be fed, much like the creatures in a zoo. A set quantity of food was issued to every individual, consisting of some beef and mutton, white bread, potatoes that had already begun to sprout, a few limp, leafy vegetables, even fewer onions, and on the rarest occasions, as if by inadvertence, a tomato or two. There was also tea, some sugar and Jones' IXL jam. [21]

Splivalo suffered from the humiliation of his situation as much as from physical hardship.

The military authorities inquired into conditions at the camp, and, as a result, tinned meat was issued to the inmates in place of salt meat.[22] While some of the complaints of brutal treatment may have been exaggerated, there was concern within the Federal Government that prisoners were liable to be victimized and physically abused. In the latter part of 1915, the Governor-General, Sir Ronald Crauford Munro Ferguson, toured some of the camps. He wrote to Senator Pearce, the Federal Minister for Defence:

> The only remaining [concentration] camp, and I cannot [see?] it, which causes me anxiety, is that of WA. Nothing has given me such an uncomfortable feeling, since Colonel H's follies at Rabaul, as the Torrens Island floggings — 4th District Concentration Camp was under incompetent control. What may not happen in the 5th District?...I should therefore feel far more comfortable were that of the 5th broken up as in the other districts...[23]

Shortly afterwards, the prison at Rottnest Island was closed and the internees were moved to the camp at Liverpool. Splivalo, who was among those sent to Liverpool, 'remained pessimistic concerning the sort of life we "foreigners" could expect to have in Australia'. After the war, he emigrated to the United States.[24]

After the outbreak of war, the government received a constant stream of 'information' about various individuals who were suspected of disloyalty. Letters from Kalgoorlie and Albany exemplified this type of complaint. From Kalgoorlie came a report of a 'Mr. Hosback, a German [who] would not become [a] naturalised British subject because it would cost him £2...The other day he was laughing about the Germans mining the Thames.' A 'German' in Albany was said to take regular trips back to Europe. 'I feel convinced he must be in the pay of the German government', wrote a local citizen to the Premier.[25] Despite taking the required measures for the internment of German and Austrian citizens, Scaddan attempted to safeguard the rights of innocent parties. In October 1914, he protested to Senator Pearce after military authorities had searched the house and business premises of Strelitz Brothers, importers and shipping agents. Paul Strelitz, the senior partner, had been a naturalized British subject for over twenty years, and served as Consul for the Netherlands. His brother, Richard, was Consul for Sweden and Denmark. Scaddan pointed out that the search had had a 'seriously detrimental' effect on the Strelitzs' business, and that if the accusations made against the brothers were untrue, Pearce should publicly refute them.[26]

Another recurring theme in complaints received against aliens was that they remained employed, while 'Britishers' were out of work. A typical example was this letter from a Day Dawn resident, signing himself M. Rosenwax, who complained to Scaddan:

> Why should these [Austrians and Germans] not be placed where they can do no harm; they are keeping our own people out of work, and as prisoners of war should be removed from our midst. It is common talk here of them being armed with revolvers. I think we should have special constables sworn in at once...I heard for a fact that in No. 17 on the Fingal Mine there are 20 men working...and only 2 speak English. Put yourself in their place in these troublous times — 2 Britishers down at the bottom with 18 foreigners and they all jabbering in their own lingo. [Is] it fair to our manhood, to our pride, is it just?...Were Austrian or German boats to come into Fremantle tomorrow you, as head of the Government, would seize [them] and place the men under guard...[27]

Indeed, there was considerable unemployment throughout the State at that time. Very early in the war, the ALF State Executive recommended the appointment of a committee, equally representing the Employers' Federation, the Chamber of Commerce, the State Government and the ALF, to consider ways and means of dealing with unemployment arising because of the war situation. The government set up a fund to relieve unemployment, to which Labor Ministers contributed 10 per cent of their salaries monthly. Subscriptions were also invited from the general public.[28] Homelessness in the metropolitan area was so serious a problem that the ALF's Metropolitan District Council asked the Royal Agricultural Society to open the Show Grounds for use as a sleeping place by unemployed men. The District Council also left the Trades Hall unlocked at night, asked the churches to follow their example, and appealed to the Perth City Council to make all sanitary conveniences free of charge. According to official estimates, a little over 6 per cent of the unionized workforce was unemployed, but a truer indication of the extent of unemployment comes from Scaddan's remark to Labor Caucus that if a motion urging the government to show preference to unionists when employing labour were carried, 'about 90 per cent of the unemployed will remain unemployed'.[29]

There was extensive rural unemployment, too. The State Government withheld licences to cut timber on Crown land, throwing a number of timber cutters out of work. Senator DeLargie visited the unemployed workers' camps at Bridgetown, and wired Scaddan, requesting that 'something be done' to offer them relief. In September 1914, the Member for Fremantle North East, W.C. Angwin, received a deputation carrying a petition signed by 345 unemployed men, the majority of whom had held rural jobs.[30]

Despite the public's eagerness to remove aliens from the workforce, supposedly in order to create more jobs for 'Britishers', attempts by the government to generate employment by other means were unsuccessful. Schemes for wage reductions and retrenchments in the public service were greeted with hostility. In April 1915, the government tried to persuade Members of the Legislative Assembly voluntarily to reduce their salaries by about 8 per cent. While some, including Opposition Members, agreed to this, others — even Labor parliamentarians — refused to take part, and the scheme soon foundered.[31] The police reacted angrily to attempts to cut their pay. They claimed that no other police force in Australia had been asked to accept reduced wages, and that never before in Australia had there been 'an attempt to touch the police pay during a time of crisis'.[32] Fire brigade officers also objected to proposed pay reductions, claiming that fires were more prevalent then than ever before and that fire-fighters were '24-hour a day men'. The ALF protested similarly on behalf of teachers.[33]

Naturally, West Australians were not alone in their victimization of enemy aliens. In Queensland, forms of persecution included 'patriotic' street demonstrations in Brisbane, where 'caged effigies of the Kaiser' were borne by participants, and attempts were made to link Germans with Satanism.[34] It is probable that tensions were greater in South Australia, where a much larger proportion of the population was of German origin. A number of cases of suicide in rural South Australia attest to the persecution endured by the German community.[35] Apparently, a similar tragedy lay behind a cryptic paragraph in the *West Australian* of 18 June 1915, which reported that the body of a suicide 'believed to be from Germany' had been found in Kings Park, clutching an automatic revolver.[36]

In May 1915, a movement to purge the public service of German-born staff commenced. Some employees of the Lands and

Surveys Department sent a petition, bearing twenty-two signa-
tures, to the Civil Service Association, requesting a meeting to
consider the 'continued employment of Germans, naturalised or
unnaturalised, in the service of the state and federal governments'.
Among the signatories was a senior civil servant, the Surveyor-
General, Harry F. Johnston. The Secretary of the Civil Service
Association, G.P. Stevens, wrote to Scaddan:

> ...[T]he growing aversion to the continued employment of men
> who, although not openly declaring their pro-German views, are
> believed to have pronounced sympathies with the enemy, is so
> strong, that it is felt some action must be taken. You will note that
> the Public Service Commissioner has no power to move in the
> matter except upon a direct charge under Section 47 of the Public
> Service Act, but my committee is of the opinion that the Act passed
> last Session empowers the Government to dispense with such
> procedure if circumstances arise that make it expedient to remove
> any or all enemy aliens from office during the continuance of the
> war, and I am directed to ask if you would be good enough to take
> the matter into serious consideration.[37]

Stevens was referring to the Public Servants Act, 1915, which
empowered the State Government to remove an employee from
the State public service purely on the grounds of his or her place of
birth or parents' nationality, irrespective of whether the person in
question was 'naturalised or a natural-born subject of the King'.
Any such person might be required to take leave of absence
without pay for an indefinite period. This legislation was regarded
by the government as being necessary for national security, and
was passed in both Houses of Parliament without amendment.[38]
Although Scaddan devoted his attention to individual cases where
he felt justice was not being done, he did not oppose the introduction of the Public Servants Act. He did, however, use it as a reason
for not responding to the demands of extremist groups, stating
that adequate machinery was already in place for removing disloyal public servants from the service of the Crown. Early in 1915,
the Public Servants Act was used to dismiss S.V. Stremple, a
Commonwealth Bank employee, who was accused of having stated
in public that Australia had no right to send men to a war that was
not of its making, and that the various governments around Australia had 'forced' 100,000 men to join up.[39]

Events on the battlefields of the northern hemisphere were the most influential factor in the increasing xenophobia on the homefront. Despite strict censorship of accounts describing the conditions of battle, the daily newspapers were permitted to print lists of the dead and wounded. By mid-1915, their photographs were filling the pages of the *Sunday Times* week after week. More than a quarter of the Australian servicemen at Gallipoli were made up of two Western Australian regiments, the 28th Battalion and the 10th Light Horse. From these, 234 men were killed and 138 wounded on 7 August 1915, in the wasteful and utterly pointless sacrifice of life that was known as the Charge of the Nek. Hugo Throssell, who took part, later referred to it as 'that *fool* charge'.[40] Changes in attitude to the war were evinced by the rate of enlistments and the type of men who enlisted. After the Gallipoli landing, the monthly total of enlistments mounted steadily, peaking with an Australia-wide total of 36,000 in July 1915, which was never exceeded. Another peak occurred in January 1916, when 22,101 men enlisted Australia-wide, but from then on numbers tailed off.[41] By this time, too, a number of Gallipoli veterans were back in Australia and being feted by the media and the public (see Chapter 4). More married men enlisted; indeed, women were encouraged to persuade their menfolk to join the Australian Imperial Force (AIF). Other women enlisted as army nurses.[42] The sinking of the unarmed passenger liner *Lusitania* by a German submarine in May 1915 was also a crucial factor in Australian attitudes to enlisting and to 'enemy aliens'.[43]

Despite the censor's heavy pen, a few glimpses of a humanitarian enemy slipped through, making more astute members of the public aware that the Allies did not have a monopoly on bravery, decency and righteousness. An example was the publication by the *WA Record*, in October 1915, of statements by a Private Mackie, who had returned to Perth after serving at Gallipoli. Mackie reportedly said that the members of Kitchener's army operating at the Dardanelles were 'mere boys, who in danger throw down their rifles, and begin to cry, and who have nothing of the stamina of the soldier'. Mackie also said, 'Do not believe those who say the Turks are cruel'. Yet such statements were often quickly rescinded, as in this case, when the editor of the *WA Record*, Father O'Grady, published an apology for 'thoughtlessly [giving] credit to the statements of one whose nerves must have experienced the shock of the battlefield'.[44]

To further counteract these brief glimpses of another side to the conflict, an increasing number of 'patriotic' groups whipped up public indignation. The All-British Association (ABA), formed in Perth in May 1915 under the leadership of Peter Wedd, a one-time Labor candidate, solicitor C.J.R. LeMesurier, and George Toll, had the specific aim of forcing all 'alien enemy subjects' out of work. In contrast with many patriotic groups, the ABA's members appear to have come almost exclusively from middle and working class backgrounds. All of those with political aspirations had been in sympathy with the labour movement at some stage of their ideological development.[45] Wedd, LeMesurier and Toll exerted considerable influence as founders of the association. They shared similar ideological beliefs, including favouring the conscription of both men and wealth. This position aligned them ideologically with the conservative Labor politicians, several of whom joined the National Party after the 1916 split over this issue (see Chapter 3), as did Wedd. Wedd, an ardent supporter of W.M. Hughes, served in France with the AIF in 1917.[46]

The ABA's zeal in seeking out 'enemy aliens' was quite extraordinary. Although ignored by the *Westralian Worker*, the association was given regular coverage in the conservative press.[47] Its activities included weekend mass meetings in numerous metropolitan and country venues — even at the soldiers' training camp at Blackboy Hill. Speakers attacked the government for 'inaction' in dealing with the problem of the 'enemy in our midst', and demanded the dismissal of 'alien enemy subjects' from the government services. The Premier reluctantly agreed to see an ABA deputation but was annoyed by the members' failure to provide adequate evidence of disloyalty by any German-born public servants. Scaddan pointed out that sons of naturalized Germans were fighting at the front, and asked whether the deputation expected him to turn out on the streets fathers whose sons were laying down their lives for their country. This reasoning was entirely lost on the ABA members. LeMesurier replied that the only religion of Germans was war. Scaddan emphatically declared that his government had already taken all appropriate action for the protection of the State.[48] Considering the large number of persons interned in Western Australia, this statement seems indisputable.

The ill-prepared and unsubstantiated evidence presented by the ABA is indicative both of the hysteria and paranoia prevalent at the time, and of the association's confidence — even arrogance — in believing that so little was required to convict a person of treason. Three cases suffice to show the nature of the 'evidence' that the ABA eventually provided. Whittorff, a locomotive driver at West Perth, was denounced for having 'wiped his feet on a Union Jack in a public bar', for uttering 'disloyal sentiments', and for having belonged to 'a German Club'.[49] Wishart, a painter's labourer at the Midland Railway Workshops, was accused of having stated that it was as good to be under German law as British rule. This piece of information had been sent to the ABA by a person signing himself 'Mr. Bridge Painter'. An unidentified school-teacher at Wickepin was said to be 'trying to spread his German influence among the children by teaching as much of his own convictions as possible'. These convictions apparently included applauding the sinking of the *Lusitania*.[50] Despite the tenuous nature of the 'evidence', Scaddan forwarded these accusations to the Military Commandant, who carried out further investigations but found all the charges to be without foundation.[51]

The ABA did, however, enjoy some success. In January 1916, the manager of the State Savings Bank, Carl Lescen, was removed from his post. Adelaide-born Lescen, of Danish-Polish descent, had become the subject of vicious rumours that he sympathized with the Germans and smuggled letters back to Germany. Scaddan defended him initially, but eventually yielded to public pressure. Although none of the accusations made against Lescen had been substantiated, the ABA agitated for people to withdraw their money from the bank in protest against the manager's continued employment. This, it seems, prompted Scaddan's action in dismissing him.[52] Shortly after Lescen's removal, another public servant, Paul Bennecke of the Lands and Surveys Department, was given six months' leave without pay — the result of an accusation that he was a German spy. His accuser had left the State prior to making the charge 'out of fear of his safety' if he remained in Western Australia.[53]

Lescen's dismissal marked a change in Scaddan's attitude to enemy aliens. The impact of war was now being deeply felt in the State, with its attendant problems of unemployment, poor recruitment, repatriation, bitterness over 'foreign labour', and increasing pressure from the ABA, and similar groups, to intern aliens. Tensions were growing within the Labor Party also, and further pressure was exerted on the government by several metropolitan and country Roads Boards, who sent resolutions expressing anxiety over the continued employment of Germans. The similar wording of the resolutions, which urged the government to 'rid the state of all employees of German extraction, without stopping to enquire whether these German employees are loyal or not', suggests that they may have been copied from a common source, possibly supplied by the ABA.[54]

By early 1916, Scaddan had abandoned all attempts to protect German-born government employees from persecution. He requested the preparation of returns showing all employees who were of 'enemy' birth or descent or 'about whose sympathies with the enemy any reasonable suspicion exists'. The information sought included name; place of birth; date and place of naturalization; and birthplace, and date of naturalization of both parents. Some senior public servants regarded the returns as an imposition. The Commissioner for Taxation responded that all members of his department were employed under the Public Service Act, the only 'foreigner' being a British-born caretaker. The returns revealed that the Education Department employed the largest number of 'Germans', thirty-two, while twenty-one were employed in the Railways, and sixteen in the Public Works Department. Only one of these employees was regarded as having 'suspect loyalties'.[55]

The ABA also devoted its attention to infringements of the Aliens Restrictions Order of 1915, which forbade persons of enemy origin to change their names. At least eight charges were lodged by the ABA; again, all appear to have been groundless. Perhaps the most poignant case was that of William Daebritz, Adelaide-born of naturalized parents, whom LeMesurier accused of having changed his name illegally to 'Davis'. The accusation must have been particularly painful to Daebritz's aged parents, who had lost another son in action at the Dardanelles. Subsequent police investigations revealed that William Daebritz had not changed his name. Since his brother's death, he had made three unsuccessful attempts to enlist, and on each occasion was rejected on medical grounds. It seems, in fact, that Daebritz was such a zealous patriot that he had joined the ABA, but had left the organization after quarrelling with LeMesurier. The accusation appears to have been a petty attempt at revenge.[56]

The ABA began to experience serious setbacks in 1916. Its

tactics were condemned by Colonel Bruche, who complained that the association was more interested in embarrassing the officers of the Defence Department than in assisting the defence of the country.[57] Bruche thought that it would be advisable to frame a regulation under the War Precautions Act, empowering the Minister to intern any person making or publishing a false statement that, in his judgment, was intended to 'injure a member of the naval or military forces, or to embarrass or hamper the military administration'.[58] The ABA denounced Colonel Bruche — himself the subject of an earlier inquiry by the Scaddan Government — and accused him of protecting 'wealthy and influential Germans'. Again, these accusations were unsubstantiated, but the Defence Department accepted the legal opinion of the Crown Solicitor that there was 'nothing in the [ABA's] letters which could be made the foundation of a prosecution for any contravention of the law'.[59]

By June 1916, apart from Lescen's case, Military Intelligence had investigated sixty-six allegations made by the ABA against individuals and businesses, and had interned only one man as a destitute. This may well have been the previously mentioned Paul Bennecke, for the internee was described as having been 'a clerk in the Lands Department'. All of the other accusations were entirely lacking in evidence.[60] In keeping with the situation across Australia[61], the ABA failed to unearth 'disloyal' citizens — a factor that probably contributed to its decline. Furthermore, the ABA experienced legal problems. Late in 1915, nine of its members had formed the All-British Co-operative Society for the purpose of publishing a newspaper, the *All British*. In the first edition, dated 24 December 1915, an article entitled 'German School Teachers' named Cornish-born Henry Shugg, who proceeded to sue for damages. The case came to court in May 1916 and resulted in the ABA being fined £75.[62] The association appears to have ceased functioning in the latter part of 1917, its absence from the December conscription campaign suggesting that it had already disbanded.

The ABA was most successful as a vehicle for imperial war propaganda, which it spread very effectively among already receptive people. By mid-1916, the basic law of British justice — that a person is innocent until proven guilty — had become obscured in a welter of wartime hysteria and hatred. Although most suspects were cleared in police records, the majority of the community probably never knew or cared about the outcome of the inquiries.

After the closure of the Rottnest Island detention centre, detainees were kept at the Fremantle Barracks prior to being despatched to Liverpool. Most had surrendered because they were destitute.[63] Internees' wives received a meagre weekly subsistence allowance of 10s, with 2s 6d for each child. In 1916, Archbishop Clune wrote, on behalf of destitute Slav families on the goldfields, to Captain Corbett, the Officer in Charge of Intelligence, protesting against this 'starvation allowance'. Consequently, the amounts were raised to 15s and 3s for wives and children, respectively.[64]

Destitution was often caused by unionists refusing to work with men whom they regarded as aliens, irrespective of whether these men had been granted work permits by the military authorities. The Fremantle Lumpers Union, for example, debarred men of 'enemy origin'. Far from inspiring working-class solidarity, therefore, the war created divisions among fellow workers.[65] These divisions were to deepen as the conflict progressed, especially after Prime Minister Hughes created 'National' unions as a result of the 1917 lumpers' strike (see Chapter 5).

A change of government in the State in July 1916 served to intensify the persecution. Following a political crisis in which Labor lost its majority in the Lower House, Frank Wilson's Liberals came to power with a majority of one.[66] By November, the Wilson Government had decided to terminate the employment of all public servants of German origin. This decision also affected institutions that were partly or wholly supported by government aid.[67] By the end of 1916, Labor Member of the Legislative Assembly E.E. Heitmann, writing to the Acting Premier, Lefroy, observed that 'under the present rule of the Government, it is not necessary to prove anything beyond [a person] being born in an enemy country'.[68]

Other sections of the community also experienced public persecution. Single men who were regarded as being fit enough for enlistment (even if the military authorities thought differently) were accused of cowardice and disloyalty. The results of the 1915 War Census, which became available in May 1916, revealed the number of men who were willing to enlist either immediately or later. The figures for Western Australia are noteworthy in the light of claims that this State was particularly loyal to the Empire. Of the 49,656 men surveyed, only 6,591 were prepared to enlist immediately, and 9,780 later. Even under the lower physical fitness standards now permitted by the military authorities, only about three-quarters of these were considered fit for military service, based on the information that the men had supplied concerning their health. Over 18,000 men refused to enlist, while the remainder had either already enlisted or been rejected.[69]

During the second half of 1916, further attempts were made to ascertain the number of unenlisted single men employed in government service. Each department was issued with a return form on which staff were required to state why they had not enlisted. Three main reasons emerged: rejection on medical grounds, withholding of parental consent, and family responsibilities. An interesting exception was the Education Department list, on which many staff members were noted simply as 'has not volunteered'. Some were classed as 'exempted', but the grounds were unstated.[70]

The first Western Australian troops arrived in France from Egypt in June 1916. In Flanders, Australian and New Zealand divisions were reorganized into the I and II Anzac Corps, led by two British Generals, Sir William Birdwood and Sir Alexander Godley, both of whom had seen service with the Anzacs at Gallipoli. The Somme offensive, which was to cost so many Australian lives, began on 1 July 1916. On 19 July, at Fromelles, the 5th Australian Division lost 5,533 officers and men. Of these, the West Australians in the 32nd Battalion sustained 700 casualties. A further 17,000 casualties were incurred in taking Pozières in mid-July.[71] With enlistments falling away, the WA Recruiting Committee and the 'patriotic' groups increased their efforts to inspire men to join up — or shame them into it.[72]

With the failure, nationally, of the 1916 conscription referendum, public pressure upon civilian young men increased. During 1917, several deputations from the WA Recruiting Committee visited the Premier, Frank Wilson, asking him to urge the Commonwealth Government to declare vacant all positions held by single, fit men of military age. They stated that recruiting in the metropolitan area was worse than in any other part of the State, a situation that apparently existed throughout Australia. One member, Mrs Taylor, said that women could fill many of the positions left vacant by men who enlisted.[73] Early in July, a meeting of Perth citizens resolved to 'use every endeavour to send every man to the front'. The resolution also asked employers to request each unmarried male worker to enlist immediately, or to produce a rejection badge, or to leave his job. The Perth City Council and six of the largest Perth firms — Boans, Brennans, Charles Moore, Bon Marche, Foy and Gibson, and Economic Stores — enforced the resolution. According to Harry Boan, women had been coming into his shop and abusing male employees for not enlisting. The ALF's Metropolitan District Council wrote to Federal Opposition Leader Frank Tudor and Senator Edward Needham, protesting against the enforcement of 'economic conscription', especially as Prime Minister Hughes had recently denied any knowledge of such instances.[74]

Single civilian males and 'enemy aliens' were not the only victims in the increasing atmosphere of suspicion that gripped the community. Anyone who appeared to be less than wholeheartedly loyal to the cause of the Empire came under attack, socially and politically. The number of Military Intelligence files containing accusations against persons making so-called disloyal statements attests to the prevailing paranoia.[75] One example of victimization occurred in September 1915, when A.W. Stewart, an employee of the Telegraph Department, was reported to the military authorities for allegedly making disloyal utterances. Alex McCallum, State Secretary of the ALF, and Edward Shann, Professor of Economics and History at The University of Western Australia, investigated the case and informed the Minister for Defence that, in their opinion, Stewart was a victim of 'pure tyranny' of a type 'not worthy of a civilised country'. Nevertheless, the unfortunate Stewart was later said to have 'admitted having made use of expressions of sympathy with the Germans'. He was severely reprimanded and transferred to a remote station at Cue.[76] Returned soldiers were not above suspicion, either. In November 1917, the military authorities received seven complaints relating to the actions of a Gallipoli veteran who had been overheard talking in two different hotels in Rockingham. The veteran was said to have stated that if conscription were brought in, he would sooner live under German law. The case remained unresolved.

Even religious groups were suspected of disloyalty. Captain Corbett warned the members of the Hebrew congregation against using any language other than English when speaking on the telephone.[77] Roman Catholics were also a target for accusations of disloyalty, but mostly in connection with the Sinn Fein movement from 1916 onwards. Catholics had been angered by the 1915 War Census, which compelled all individuals and institutions, including the Roman Catholic Church, to register their wealth and manpower resources. There was a growing fear that clergy would be conscripted, as they had been in France. Catholic loyalty to the Empire was increasingly called into question, and in June 1915, the *Sydney Morning Herald* inferred that the papacy favoured Germany. The historian Patrick O'Farrell argued that any disloyalty on the part of Irish Catholics was provoked by the British Government's brutal suppression of the Republican Uprising of Easter 1916. Indeed, three leading clerics, Dr Maurice O'Reilly and Archbishops Kelly and Duhig, changed from positions of 'ardent imperialism' (especially in the former's case), to criticizing British policy in Ireland, as a result of the events of 1916.[78] The influence of prominent Western Australian Catholics, including Archbishop Clune, on both sides of the conscription debate is examined in Chapter 3, along with attempts by pro-conscriptionists to associate their opponents with Sinn Feinism.

The year 1916 also saw the issue of conscription for overseas military service come to the fore, and 'disloyal' anti-conscriptionists were brought into the glare of public notice for the first time. Despite the prewar existence of an Australia-wide pacifist movement, most of the opposition during the Great War was to military conscription rather than to the conduct of the war itself.[79]

Accusations of disloyalty against individuals and organizations continued into the closing stages of the war. In October 1918, the WA Recruiting Committee complained that the ALF flew the red flag at its meetings, in contravention of Regulation 27B of the War Precautions Act.[80] Shortly afterwards, Mrs Foley, a schoolteacher at Pinjarra, was reported to have said that the Fremantle lumpers' strike of 1917 had been justified, that strikes were 'right', and that 'the Citizen Army was enrolled for the purpose of shooting their mates, or rather the returned soldiers'. Although the charge was dismissed on the grounds that it arose as a result of 'bad feeling' between Mrs Foley and the mother of one of her pupils, the seriousness with which it was regarded by the military authorities testifies to the prevailing tension at the end of 1918.[81]

All of these cases involved private citizens. Persons who were known to hold 'disloyal' views, by virtue of their membership of certain organizations, were subject to much greater scrutiny. IWW members were regarded as being 'disloyal' because they opposed the war and advocated non-Empire-based, international industrial unionism, and it was on this basis that the organization was banned. Members, including some in Western Australia, were tried and imprisoned on the grounds that they endangered the security of the nation — action that contained some logic in a time of national crisis.[82] An example of the fear with which the government purportedly regarded the IWW is revealed in a secret cablegram despatched by Senator Pearce to the Secretary of State for the Colonies in London, on 31 August 1917:

> ...For your most [confidential] information. The present state of affairs in Australia is extremely unsatisfactory. As pointed out in my telegram of the 5th March the alliance of Sinn Fein and Syndicalism and IWWism is opposed to the war, has captured Labor Organisations, and although defeated decisively on May 5th in the political arena is now determined to render that victory barren by industrial warfare. [The p]resent strike is a deliberate attempt by those extremists above referred to to prevent Australia doing her duty in the war.[83]

The extent of governmental repression was such that anyone remotely connected with IWW members became subject to investigation, as is demonstrated in the case of Willem Siebenhaar, who organized Monty Miller's defence for the November 1916 trial of IWW members. Dutch-born Siebenhaar, who served as Western Australia's Deputy Registrar-General and Deputy Government Statistician prior to his suspension from duties, had already been under investigation as a suspected enemy subject, because of his 'foreign name'. A socialist by conviction, Siebenhaar had arrived in Western Australia in 1891 in search of a 'more free and democratic' society. He quickly found, however, that Perth was a city 'divided by hate' and in which 'wealth, power and cunning ruled in state'. He felt that he had to 'sacrifice principle and courage to caution and self-interest so as not to starve', and at times remained silent when 'complete candour called for speech'.[84] Siebenhaar analysed his situation late in 1916 in a letter to a relative in Holland, which fell into the hands of the Perth Military Censor:

> In October last year I myself had to suffer to some extent for the War Rage. The Middle Class held the reins of Government, and my friendship for an 84 year old Labour Leader [Miller] was used as a pretext to bring my sentiments of fidelity to the country, in doubt. My book 'Dorothea' was also pulled into it. I naturally came out of it with flying colours, although many typical middle classers are

cutting me, which of course adds to their own shame. The Liberal
Government in their hypocrisy has [sic] found another pretext to
block me in my promotion, and I must wait for better times.[85]

It was clear to Siebenhaar that one's loyalty was judged by one's
politics rather than by actual proof of '[in]fidelity to the country'.
Although restored to his former position and compensated for
suspended pay, Siebenhaar, like Splivalo, was embittered by his
experience of Australian justice, and he retired to Italy in the early
1920s.[86]

Labor leader Don Cameron was also under surveillance from
the military authorities, because of his anti-conscription activities
and his associations with IWW member Mick Sawtell, and T.J.
Miller, Victorian Secretary of the Australian Freedom League.[87]
Cameron's correspondence was censored. In August 1918, Military Intelligence in Perth reported to the federal authorities:

> Cameron is usually prominent in any movement which will
> embarrass the Government or annoy ordinary people. He is
> Secretary to the Plumbers Union and spends all his time in political
> and industrial work, and any new opportunities for mischief are
> eagerly seized by him. He is a tireless correspondent and keeps in
> touch with 'red-raggers' everywhere. His correspondents include
> Betsy Matthias of 'Solidarity', Santamaria of the Italian anti-
> conscription movement...[Melbourne], members of the IWW
> including Mick Sawtell released from gaol 5/8/18 in New South
> Wales, [the] Australian Peace Alliance, [and] Rationalist Societies.
> T.J. Miller...writes to Cameron offering him prohibited
> publications...Cameron was a member of the extreme wing at the
> Perth Labour Congress, 1918. He is at present lecturing and writing
> in favour of flying the Red Flag on the Trades Hall, Perth.[88]

The Military Censor observed that Cameron and Sawtell and
'others of their ilk' regarded the capturing of the returned soldiers'
support as a 'deciding factor in accomplishing their revolutionary
aims, and the most strenuous efforts are being made (and with
some little success in that direction)'. This comment evinces the
fear by military authorities that large numbers of returned soldiers
would adopt the ideology of the labour militants and would be a
deciding factor in bringing about a 'Bolshevik' revolution.

During the war, over 100 IWW members Australia-wide were
sentenced to imprisonment on charges including arson and conspiracy. In December 1916, the Federal Parliament passed the

Unlawful Associations Act, under which legislation membership of the IWW was an offence punishable by imprisonment for up to six months. The most notorious trial was that of the so-called 'Sydney Twelve', in November 1916, all of whom were sentenced to terms ranging from five to fifteen years in prison. Arrests followed in Perth and Broken Hill. Twelve Western Australian IWW members, including Miller and Sawtell, were charged and tried. Justice Burnside offered the defendants two alternatives: two years' imprisonment or to be bound over for the same period to 'be of good behaviour and to keep the peace'. Miller opted for the latter but later broke his bond and was sentenced, at the age of eighty-six, to six months' hard labour in Darlinghurst Gaol, in New South Wales.[89]

In January 1918, a further five members stood trial in the Supreme Court in Perth, on charges of conspiracy under the War Precautions Act. Four goldfields workers — Alfred Callanan, M. Yates, T. Hawken and William Johnstone — were acquitted. T.P. Candish, a member of the Carpenters' Union and of the ALF Fremantle District Council, was found guilty of conspiracy 'with diverse persons unknown', although under the Criminal Code rather than under the War Precautions Act. He served six months in prison.[90] The five men petitioned the Attorney-General, asking for compensation of expenses that they had been obliged to incur while awaiting trial: two months' board at 25s a week. The Attorney-General's office replied that there were no grounds for compensation against the Crown.[91]

In the meantime, Yates had discovered that acquittal by the Supreme Court meant very little when he returned to work on the goldfields. Unable to secure employment, he wrote in desperation to McCallum:

> I haven't earned a penny since Nov. 8th, the day of my arrest. I
> have a wife and six little kiddies to keep. My eldest child is a girl,
> 11 years of age. The others range from 6 years down to 6 months.
> This is a nice position for a man to be in, who has been nothing else
> but a working bullock all his life.[92]

Although the State ALF intervened on behalf of the IWW members, Premier Lefroy declared himself 'too busy' to meet a delegation until after the Easter holidays. The Attorney-General, R.T. Robinson, 'deplored' the victimization of the acquitted men but 'regretted' that he could not control the actions of private employers. Robinson's powerlessness in this matter contrasts starkly with the government pressure that had been exerted on the striking members of the Fremantle Lumpers Union the previous year (discussed in Chapter 5), revealing a considerable difference in National politicians' attitudes to employers and workers. Robinson offered charity to alleviate the 'plight' of Yates and his family. Three years later, Candish attempted, unsuccessfully, to obtain compensation for wages lost during his six months in prison, and afterwards while recuperating from 'inhumane treatment'.[93]

Some of the IWW members succeeded in obtaining employment on the Fremantle Wharf, but were kept under surveillance by the Federation of Employers of Waterside Labour, who regularly submitted lists of the names of wharf employees to Captain Corbett. Alfred Callanan's name attracted the attention of Military Intelligence, but Police Inspector Mann informed Corbett that, as Callanan had been acquitted of charges in the IWW prosecutions, and although he was 'alleged to have a predilection for stirring up industrial strife', Mann knew of no reason 'why his presence on the wharf would be an actual danger to shipping or national interests'. Corbett informed the Federation of Employers accordingly, and Callanan remained working on the wharf, as did William Johnstone, who had been acquitted along with Callanan.

In the period September 1918 to May 1919, Military Intelligence objected to only two of the wharf workers: Mick Sawtell, on the grounds of his IWW membership, and William Peters, who was described as

an old lumper and a well-known agitator...[who] also took a prominent part in the Referendum on the anti-conscription side — he was also one of the ring leaders of the labour trouble at Spencers Brook in April of this year. [94]

The comments regarding Peters, in particular, are evidence of the careful and thorough State surveillance of men who were regarded as agitators or 'troublemakers', not only because of their involvement in industrial action but because they opposed conscription for overseas military service. Compared with those few activists who sacrificed the security of regular employment and risked casting dependent families into destitution, there must have been many workers who held similar views but remained silent because they could not bear the cost of dissent.

'Loyalty', therefore, created deep social divisions, not only between members of different classes, nationalities, religious denominations and political allegiances, but also within classes and parties. The experience of internment or other forms of persecution embittered men such as Siebenhaar, Splivalo and Lescen, and they subsequently left the State. The pressure on 'shirkers' to enlist was the beginning of the great divide between 'returned men' and those who did not join up, which was perpetuated in Australia throughout much of the twentieth century. Roman Catholics were regarded by the more jingoistic Protestants with hostility, and Irish groups were suspected of being cover organizations for Sinn Fein. Conflicting concepts of the meaning of loyalty and patriotism manifested themselves in verbal and sometimes physical violence during the period of the conscription crisis. The turbulent events of the eighteen months from June 1916 to December 1917 caused tensions generated by the escalating bloodshed on the battlefields of the Dardanelles and Europe to flare into open conflict — conflict that was to leave deep wounds and bitterness in Western Australian society.

1   M. McKernan, 'War', Table WR 2-8, 'Enlistments in Australian Services By State, World War I', in W. Vamplew (ed.), *Australians: Historical Statistics*, Sydney, 1987, p. 412.
2   S. Anstey, The Impact of the Great War on the Beverley, Toodyay and Murchison Communities of Western Australia, 1914–17, BA Hons dissertation, Murdoch University, 1980, p. 142.
3   A copy of the letterhead appears in Premier's Department File (hereafter PDF) 106/16. The title of Chapter 1 comes from this source.
4   See, for example, *Truth*, 8 August 1914, 'The World at War'; also 15 August 1914 and 19 September 1914.
5   *Truth*, 10 July 1915.
6   ALF (WA), Parliamentary Labor Party, Caucus Minutes, State Archives of Western Australia, Acc. 1313A (hereafter Caucus Minutes), vol. 1, 1906–15, 20 November 1914; J.R. Robertson, 'The Internal Politics of State Labor in Western Australia: 1911–1916', *Labour History*, no. 2, May 1962, p. 68.
7   *West Australian*, 19 March 1915.
8   Caucus Minutes, vol. 2, especially 4 March 1915, 9 December 1915, 3 February 1916.
9   *Western Australian Parliamentary Debates* (hereafter *WAPD*), vol. 51, 1915, p. 58.
10   *WAPD*, vol. 52, p. 2389.
11   For a brief published account of these events, see Robertson, 'Internal Politics', pp. 69–71.

12   *WAPD*, vol. 51, pp. 1329 ff.
13   G. Fischer, *Enemy Aliens: Internment and the Homefront in Australia, 1914–20*, St Lucia, 1989, pp. 78–79.
14   A. Splivalo, *The Home Fires*, Fremantle, 1982, pp. 57–58. Splivalo referred to Corbett as Major Corbett, but official sources refer to him as Captain Corbett.
15   *Sunday Times*, 9 August 1914.
16   *West Australian*, 6 August 1914.
17   Cook to Premier, 14 August 1914, PDF 302/14, vol. II. See also PDF 302/14, vol. III. Citizens of the Austro-Hungarian Empire were usually referred to in Australia, including in official records such as the *Commonwealth of Australia — Census*, as 'Austrians' or 'Austro-Hungarians'. These terms, in reality, embraced several nationalities.
18   Commander, Commonwealth Military Forces, to Premier, 7 September 1914, PDF 302/14, vol. III; *Western Mail*, 'Illustrated Section', 21 August 1914.
19   Department of Public Charities to Premier's Secretary, 28 September 1914, PDF 302/14, vol. III.
20   Department of the Army (WA), Intelligence Files, Australian Archives (WA), Acc. PP14 (hereafter Intelligence Files), series II, no. PF 640, 'Complaints from POWs'.
21   Splivalo, *The Home Fires*, p. 65.
22   Intelligence Files, series II, no. PF 640.
23   Governor-General to Pearce, 21 October 1915, George Foster Pearce Papers, Australian Archives (Canberra), Acc. 4719, vol. 2, bundle 1, folder 1-2. The incident at Torrens Island is discussed in Fischer, *Enemy Aliens*, pp. 194–198.
24   Splivalo, *The Home Fires*, p. 225.
25   Davidson to Premier, 25 August 1914, PDF 302/14, vol. II; Barwick to Premier, 17 October 1914, vol. III.
26   Scaddan to Pearce, 27 October 1914, PDF 302/14, vol. III. For biographical details of the Strelitz Brothers, see J.S. Battye, *Cyclopedia of Western Australia*, 1912, vol. I, pp. 595–596.
27   Rosenwax to Premier, 17 July (August?) 1914, PDF 302/14, vol. II.
28   State Executive of the ALF (WA) — Minutes (hereafter SE Minutes), vol. 2, 11 August 1914, 7 September 1914; PDF 303/14.
29   ALF (WA), Minutes of the Metropolitan District Council, State Archives of Western Australia, Acc. 1319A, vol. 2, 19 November 1914. According to official statistics, quoted in the *Commonwealth of Australia Official Year Book, no. 9, 1915*, p. 1047, 6.3 per cent of the unionized workforce was unemployed, but the real number may have been much greater. See also Caucus Minutes, vol. 1, 24 November 1914.
30   PDF 303/14
31   'Civil Service and Retrenchment — Proposed Reduction of High Officials, etc. 7.89 per cent [salary] Reduction. Members of the Legislative Assembly', PDF 83/15.
32   *West Australian*, 15 April 1915.
33   *West Australian*, 9 April 1915.
34   R. Evans, *Loyalty and Disloyalty: Social Conflict on the Queensland Homefront, 1914–18*, Sydney, 1987, p. 53.
35   M. McKernan, *The Australian People and the Great War*, Melbourne, 1980, p. 155.
36   *West Australian*, 18 June 1915.
37   Stevens to Premier, 10 June 1915, PDF 188/15.

38   *WAPD, 1914–15*, vol. 50, especially pp. 936–938.
39   Scaddan to Stevens; Scaddan to Public Service Commission, 20 July 1915, PDF 188/15.
40   S. Welborn, *Lords of Death: A People, a Place, a Legend*, Fremantle 1982, pp. 91 ff. See also E.D. Scott, *Australia During the War: Vol XI of the Official War History of Australia in the War of 1914–1918*, C.E.W. Bean (ed.), Sydney, 1936, p. 112.
41   McKernan, 'War', Table WR 2-8, Enlistments in Australian Services by State, World War I, p. 412.
42   I. Turner, '1914–19', in F.K. Crowley (ed.), *A New History of Australia*, Melbourne, 1980 edn, pp. 324–325.
43   R.J.W. Selleck, '"The Trouble With My Looking Glass": A Study of the Attitude of Australians to Germans during the Great War', *Journal of Australian Studies*, no. 6, June 1980, p. 3.
44   Intelligence Files, series 1, box 11, no. 2/2/6.
45   For a more detailed study, see B. Oliver, '"All-British" or "Anti-German"? A Portrait of a Western Australian Pressure Group during World War I', in R. Bosworth and M. Melia (eds), *Studies in Western Australian History XII: Aspects of Ethnicity in Western Australia*, April 1991, pp. 28–39. For a comparative study of anti-German organizations in New South Wales, see D. Coward, The Impact of War on New South Wales. Some Aspects of Social and Political History, 1914–17, PhD thesis, Australian National University, 1974, ch. 4.
46   *Western Argus*, 22 February 1921.
47   See, for example, *West Australian*, 7 June 1915, 16 June 1915; *Sunday Times*, 20 June 1915.
48   *Daily News*, 27 August 1915; and *West Australian*, 2 August 1915. See also notes in PDF 188/15.
49   The 'German Club' was probably the 'Deutscher Verein', which was founded by the German Consul, C.P.R. Ratazzi, in 1900. See Battye, *Cyclopedia*, vol. 1, p. 595.
50   ABA to Premier, 1 September 1915, PDF 188/15.
51   Intelligence Files, series I, nos 17/1/1 to 17/1/19; Acting Director of Education to Premier's Secretary, 8 September 1915; Permain to Premier, 17 September 1915; Statements from Suspected Persons; Wittber to Director of Education, 26 October 1914, PDF 188/15; *Daily News*, 8 October 1915; Wittorff to Scaddan, 21 October 1915, and 'Retention of Germans in Government Service: Result of Enquiries Made into Charges Lodged Against Certain Individuals by the All-British Association', PDF 188/15.
52   PDF 188/15; *West Australian*, 4 February 1916, pp. 1, 7.
53   Premier's correspondence dated 24 February 1916 and 6 March 1916, PDF 188/15; *West Australian*, 3 May 1916.
54   PDF 188/15; Cuballing Roads Board, Minutes Book, vol. 4, 1914–16, vol. 4, 5 February 1916, and Letter Book, vol. 16, 9 February 1916, letters nos 696 and 697, held in the State Archives of Western Australia; Perth Roads Board to Premier, 2 February 1916, PDF 95/16. An interesting aspect of the issue is that the Murray Roads Board passed a motion stating that the dismissal of aliens could safely be left in the hands of the Prime Minister and the Federal Government. Murray Roads Board Minutes, 12 February 1916. (The author is indebted to Mr Ron Richards for this information.)
55   PDF 95/16.

56 See correspondence and police report in Intelligence Files, series I, no. 17/ 1/42. For other cases of this type of victimization, see nos 17/1/33, 46, 51, and 57.

57 Bruche to Secretary of Defence, 29 February 1916, Intelligence Files, series I, no. 17/1/25.

58 Bruche to Secretary of Defence, 14 March 1916, Intelligence Files, no. 17/1/ 33.

59 Fischer, *Enemy Aliens*, p. 130; correspondence in Department of the Army (Victoria), Intelligence Files, Australian Archives (Victoria), Acc. PP14/1, item W216/6/78.

60 Intelligence Files, no. 17/1/57.

61 See, for example, McKernan, *Australian People*, p. 157. McKernan observed that all such allegations uncovered by his research 'proved groundless'.

62 *Truth*, 3 June 1916. A full account of the court case appeared in the *West Australian*, 26 May 1916. The author is grateful to Mr Bill Latter for providing a photocopy of the *All-British*, vol. 1, no. 7, 14 April 1916. No mention of the pending court case appears in this issue.

63 Intelligence Files, series I, box 16, no. 13/5/6, List of Prisoners Held at Fremantle, May 1916.

64 Clune to Corbett, 10 March 1916; Military Commandant, Victoria, to Department of Defence, 11 March 1916, Intelligence Files, series II, no. PF 668.

65 Intelligence Files, no. PF 501, 'List of Fremantle Lumpers whom Local Lumpers had Debarred from Working on Wharves on Account of their Birth (or Supposed Birth), in an Enemy Country'. Some of the twenty-four listed included men who had previously been granted the permits necessary to allow persons of enemy origin to work on the wharves. (See also nos 1/1/ 1, 9 and 17.)

66 SE Minutes, vol. 2, 27 July 1916.

67 Circular, Wilson to Clerk of Parliament, Public Library and Museum, Perth Public Hospital, Children's Hospital, Home of Peace, Lady Lawley Cottage by the Sea, Blind Asylum, Kings Park Board, Karrakatta Cemetery and Fremantle Cemetery Boards, Zoological Society, 3 November 1916, PDF 95/ 16.

68 Heitmann to Lefroy, 9 December 1916, PDF 95/16.

69 Record of Recruiting Check Slips Received and Tabulated by War Census Staff to 6 May 1916, George Foster Pearce Papers, Australian Archives, vol. 4, bundle 3.

70 'Returns of Single Men in Government Service — Whether Enlisted', PDF 210/16.

71 Welborn, *Lords of Death*, pp. 108–111; J. Grey, *A Military History of Australia*, Cambridge, 1990, p. 103; D. Horner, 'The Fight that Changed Australia', *Australian Magazine*, 7–8 August, 1993, p. 10.

72 See, for example, PDF 228/16, for the role of the Women's Commonwealth Patriotic Association, the ABA and the Organisation of Women War Workers League at pro-conscription and recruitment rallies. For recruiting figures, see McKernan, 'War', Table WR2-8, p. 412.

73 'Deputation from the Central Recruiting Committee, Comprising Rev. T. Allen, Cr. Mills, Mr. Lathlean, Sgt. Sharples and Mrs. Taylor, re. Enlistment of Single Men in Service', 14 May 1917, PDF 210/16.

74 'Deputation from the Central Recruiting Committee on 9 [or 10?] July, 1917', PDF 210/16; ALF (WA), State Executive to Metropolitan District Council — Correspondence Files, State Archives of Western Australia, Acc. 1689, no. 53, circular letter, W.E. Bold (Town Clerk) to employees of the Perth City

Council, 19 July 1917, and Metropolitan District Council to Tudor and Needham, 9 August 1917.

75 Intelligence Files, series I, boxes 5 and 6.

76 SE Minutes, vol. 2, 6 September 1915; PMG Department to Senator Needham, 22 December 1915, State Executive of the ALF (WA) — Correspondence Files (hereafter SE Correspondence), File 33.

77 See Intelligence Files, series I, box 6, nos 1/12/169 and 78.

78 P. O'Farrell, *The Catholic Church and Community in Australia*, Melbourne, 1977 edn, pp. 318–322.

79 In fact, the Australian Freedom League, formed by the Adelaide Quakers John Hills and John Fletcher in 1912, and boasting a 55,000-strong membership by 1914, curtailed its activities when war broke out, declaring that it did not wish to hamper the government in any way 'in the discharge of their grave responsibility'. Cited in M. Saunders and M. Sumy, *The Australian Peace Movement: A Short History*, Canberra, 1986, p. 17. See also M. Saunders, *Quiet Dissenter. The Life and Thought of an Australian Pacifist. Eleanor May Moore, 1875–1949*, Canberra, 1993, pp. 86 ff.

80 Intelligence Files, no. 1/12/291.

81 Intelligence Files, series I, box 5, no. 1/9/81.

82 For details of reasons for imprisonment, see, for example, I. Turner, *Sydney's Burning*, Sydney, 1967; and E.C. Fry, *Rebels and Radicals*, Sydney, 1983, ch. 12.

83 George Foster Pearce Papers, Australian Archives, vol. 4.

84 Cited from Siebenhaar's writings and correspondence in N. Segal, *Who and What was Siebenhaar? A Note on the Life and Persecution of a Western Australian Anarchist*, Studies in Western Australian History Occasional Papers no. 1, Nedlands, 1988, p. 7.

85 Cited in ibid., p. 20. In this letter, Siebenhaar was referring to the Liberal Government that took office in July 1916 under the leadership of Frank Wilson. The title for this chapter comes from the phrase used here by Siebenhaar. Siebenhaar was also a poet, and his collection *Dorothea* was published in 1910.

86 Segal, *Who and What was Siebenhaar?*, pp. 7–8.

87 By the end of World War I, the Perth Military Censor had built up an elaborate network of files that he claimed were related to Don Cameron's activities. These files — 'IWWism', 'Industrialism', 'Socialism', 'Rationalism', 'Pacifism', 'Enemy Nationality and Foreigners', 'Revolutionary Ideas', 'Anti-Conscription' and 'Disloyalists' — were listed in a memo, dated 22 November 1918, from the Perth Censor to the Victorian military authorities, a copy of which is held in Department of the Army (Victoria), Intelligence Files, no. V298. The author checked all the available Perth files with numbers corresponding to those listed in the memo, but found no reference to Don Cameron.

88 'Extract from Summary of War Intelligence, No. 24 for the Week Ended 17th August, 1918, 5th Military District: WA 95 Don Cameron', Department of the Army (Victoria), Intelligence Files, no. V298. The 'Solidarity' referred to is probably the militant newspaper of that title, a copy of which (vol. II, no. 33, 15 February 1919) is held in Police Department (WA) File 840/1919.

89 F. Cain, *The Wobblies at War: A History of the IWW and the Great War in Australia*, Melbourne, 1993. Ch. 10 discusses the trial of the Western Australian IWW members. Another account of the Western Australian trial is given in J. Williams, *The First Furrow*, Perth, 1976, pp. 57–63.

90 See SE Correspondence, Files 40, 66 and 177.

91 SE Correspondence, File 166. The petition is published in L. Layman and J. Goddard, *Organise! A Visual Record of the Labour Movement in Western Australia*, Perth, 1988, p. 144.
92 Yates to McCallum, 9 December 1918, SE Correspondence, File 166; also Layman and Goddard, *Organise!*, p. 145.
93 See letters and reports in SE Correspondence, Files 166 and 40.
94 Intelligence Files, series I, no. 1/1/19.

Chapter Three

THE CURSE OF CONSCRIPTION

The referendum campaigns of 1916 and 1917

On 30 August 1916, the Prime Minister, William Morris Hughes, recently returned from a successful trip to Britain and the battle-fields of France, announced that a referendum would be held in October, to ascertain whether the Australian people were in favour of conscripting men for military service overseas for the duration of the present war.[1] Conscription for service within the country during wartime, which had been enacted in Federal Parliament in 1903, had already caused considerable dissension. Hughes, how-ever, believed that the military situation was desperate enough to warrant such a step. In the seven weeks from mid-July, the AIF had sustained 28,000 casualties on the Western Front. The British had lost 60,000 men — killed or wounded — in the first twenty-four hours of the Somme offensive. Recruitments in Australia for June, July and August had totalled less than 17,000, far fewer than the numbers Hughes, while in England, had promised Lloyd George, who was then serving as Minister for Munitions in the Asquith–Bonar Law coalition Cabinet.[2]

Hughes's motives in attempting to introduce conscription in Australia have been the subject of considerable debate among historians. According to Ernest Scott, the pressure to produce reinforcements came from the British Army Council, which 'threat-ened' to break up the 3rd Australian Division then training in England. General Birdwood opposed this action and urged 'that the Australian Government should be given the opportunity of sending increased reinforcements'. Birdwood estimated that 20,000 men were required immediately, followed by three monthly drafts of 16,500 each. The British Army Council accepted these figures and cabled Australia on 24 August, indicating that only this number of recruits would save the 3rd Division from dissolution.[3] However, Australia's Official War Correspondent, C.E.W. Bean,

LIBERAL LURK TO LEG-IRON LABOR.

THERE IS A GENERAL DECLARATION IN "LIBERAL" CIRCLES THAT THE TORIES OF AUSTRALIA, MASQUERADING AS "LIB-ERALS," WILL SUPPORT THE CONSCRIPTION REFERENDUM TO A MAN AND TO A WOMAN. MELBOURNE "ARGUS" HAS COMMITTED THE PARTY DEFINITELY BY ANNOUNCING THAT "THE LIBERAL PARTY WILL FIGHT SOLIDLY BEHIND MR. HUGHES IN THE CAMPAIGN," AND THE "WEST AUSTRALIAN" GLEEFULLY PRINTED THIS DECLARATION. STILL, THERE ARE SOME "LABORITES" WHO CAN'T "SEE THE LIGHT" EVEN YET. THESE PARASITIC POLITICIANS SHOULD FORTHWITH GO WHERE THEY BELONG, I.E., INTO THE "LIBERAL" LEAGUES.

'Liberal Lurk to Leg-Iron Labor'
According to *Truth* (9 September 1916), military conscription for overseas
service was nothing less than a scheme ('lurk') by the 'Tories of Australia,
masquerading as "Liberals"' to gain yet more power over workers.
[Courtesy Battye Library]

believed that it was Hughes himself who threatened to break up
the 3rd Division in order to press for conscription.[4] But Bean
confined his opinion to the pages of his diary.

Other factors influencing Hughes's decision were the pending
introduction of conscription in New Zealand and Canada, and his
personal reactions to scenes in France. He had been touched by the
sight of old men, women and children working in the fields to
replace manpower drained by the defence of Verdun. Hughes had
visited Australian soldiers in hospitals and camps in England, and

he had spoken to men of the 1st Division at Armentières. It was before the Somme offensive and many of the troops were fresh from training in Egypt; others were Gallipoli veterans. Hughes was deeply moved by their fine appearance and their high morale. Perhaps he believed, too, that the conscription of Australia's man-power would entitle the nation to an international voice in the postwar world.[5] Furthermore, as Hughes sailed back to Australia, arriving at Fremantle on 31 July 1916, the 1st, 2nd and 4th Austral-ian Divisions were fighting a month-long battle for the village of Pozières. In the heaviest shelling that they had yet faced, the Western Australian 11th Battalion had been reduced to a 'sorry handful of men who were not killed or wounded'. The three divisions sustained over 24,000 casualties, including 6,741 dead.[6]

The Federal Government could have imposed compulsory over-seas military service as a regulation gazetted under the War Precautions Act, with the consent of both Houses of the Federal Parliament, but Hughes feared a split in the Labor Party over the issue. Labor's attitude to the war was ambiguous. In each State and in the federal party, there were strong factions on either side of the conscription debate. Hughes put the case for conscription to a special meeting of the New South Wales Labor Executive, but, after a long debate, his proposals were rejected by twenty-one votes to five. He continued to flout the will of the conference and was expelled from the New South Wales Labor movement. Labor opposition to conscription was based on the belief that everyone had a fundamental right to the basic civil liberty of bodily freedom. While accepting and supporting compulsory military service in Australia, the majority of the party strongly opposed conscription for overseas service.[7]

Hughes's announcement concerning conscription was by no means unexpected within the labour movement. All of the State Congresses had voted on the issue prior to the end of June 1916. The Western Australian Executive, like the other States, abided by the decision of its State Congress. The difference was that, whereas all the other State Congresses had adopted a policy of 'No Con-scription' and fixed penalties for those who did not follow the party line, in Western Australia a compromise resolution was passed, after several days of discussion.[8]

When delegates met for the ALF State Congress in Kalgoorlie in June 1916, the Federal Government had not enunciated any clear policy on conscription, and this issue was only one of 221 items tabled for discussion. However, the amount of time devoted to the issue indicates that it was already deeply divisive.[9] Don Cameron moved that the Congress oppose the conscription of human life for service outside the Commonwealth and that it instruct affiliated councils and unions to oppose all Labor Members who voted for, or otherwise supported, conscription. Australian Workers Union (AWU) Secretary A.J. Walsh moved a contrary amendment that the Federal Government be urged to legislate that all eligible males between the ages of eighteen and fifty-eight be required to serve overseas. The debate raged over the next three days. Eventually, a compromise motion — that 'in the interests of the defence of Australia and the Empire, this Congress desires to express its confidence in the Federal Executive' — was carried by forty-one votes to twenty-six.[10]

There were two factors that contributed to this compromise being reached. First, the political wing of the ALF was weak at that time, with the Scaddan Government holding only half of the seats in the Lower House. Second, the ALF State Secretary, Alex McCallum, was absent. In April 1916, McCallum's fragile health had collapsed under the strain of the previous two years in a very arduous post. The appointment of an assistant, Andrew Clementson, came too late to prevent McCallum from having to take a rest of at least six months, ordered by his doctor, who diagnosed a nervous breakdown.[11] The State Executive informed the District Councils of the severity of McCallum's illness, and appealed for funds to enable him and his wife to embark on a holiday to the Eastern States. The pro-conscriptionist James Cornell was appointed as Acting ALF State Secretary. Thus, McCallum, instead of campaigning against conscription in the west just prior to referendum day on 28 October, was playing an important 'behind the scenes' role in New South Wales. During his absence, McCallum maintained a confidential correspondence with Don Cameron, in which he revealed the strength of his conviction that conscription was wrong, and his determination to act when he returned to the west:

> What I am writing [to] you now is confidential mainly to give you information to work on. I don't want you to give it out that I have sent you any information for publication. The reason being [that] I am collecting certain information *which I am going to take a stand on*

when I get back and when the movement must take action against certain tyrants or I am going to get out.[12]

Shortly after the 1916 referendum, McCallum wrote to Cameron: 'I defy any living man to reconcile Labor principles with conscription'.[13] There seems little doubt, therefore, that McCallum returned from the Eastern States determined to rid the Labor movement of pro-conscriptionists.

Events in the Eastern States also influenced the course of events. In August, the Victorian police raided the premises of the Melbourne Trades and Labor Council and seized copies of reports and the Anti-Conscription Manifesto from the recent Conscription Congress. Although Senator Pearce's sanctioning of the raid was hotly debated in the WA State Executive, no action was taken on resolutions from the Political Labor League of Victoria, protesting against the Defence Minister's conduct. A motion was carried, asking that Pearce explain his action, and pointing out the need for free speech during the lead-up to the conscription referendum.[14] Both the pro- and anti-conscriptionist members of the State Executive were alarmed at Pearce's heavy-handedness, and expressed the belief that such extreme methods of enforcing censorship were undesirable. On the Executive's behalf, Cornell wrote to Pearce: 'The censorship as put into practice is not in the best interests of Australia and is exasperating to a people who believe in free discussion'.[15]

Cornell wrote to Pearce again in September, reiterating his opinion that the public should have unrestricted access to both sides of the debate. He also drew attention to the arbitrary and inconsistent manner in which censorship was applied. As an example, Cornell cited a resolution passed by the State Executive, protesting against censorship, which was published in the metropolitan afternoon paper, the *Daily News*, but did not appear in the following morning's *West Australian* because it had been censored.[16] In reply, the Department of Defence sent the State Executive a copy of instructions relating to censorship of matters concerning conscription and the forthcoming referendum. According to these instructions, the publication of arguments, resolutions and motions stating the case either for or against, or criticizing or supporting government policy, was 'freely allowed' providing that it was not 'offensive to Great Britain or her allies', that it did not incite people to breach any federal or State law or to 'any sort of strike', or that it did not contravene any of the provisions of the War Precautions Act.[17]

Although both pro- and anti-conscriptionists in the ALF were agreed on the subject of censorship, other issues continued to divide their ranks. One such issue occurred during the visit to Western Australia of Thomas Miller, Victorian Secretary of the Australian Freedom League. The league had been formed in South Australia in 1912 to repeal legislation concerning compulsory military training for boys, and branches had been set up in Sydney, Brisbane, Melbourne and Hobart. Although the league had suspended its operations in 1914 because of the 'strong patriotism' that emerged in Australia at the outbreak of the war, it had already created a group of dissidents experienced in campaigning against conscription. When the 1916 referendum was announced, the league re-formed and campaigned actively for the 'No' vote.[18]

A Western Australian branch of the league was operating at the beginning of the war, but does not appear to have been active in the conscription campaigns, even during Miller's visit. Miller went to Perth with the aim of organizing the anti-conscriptionists and bringing the movement into line with the other States. He spoke at a meeting at Trades Hall on Sunday 6 August, where an Anti-Conscription League (ACL) was formed, with Don Cameron as President and Tom Butler as Secretary. Harry Leighton, an IWW member, and Andrew Clementson also held offices in the organization. Miller attended meetings of the ALF State Executive and the Fremantle District Council, bringing with him from Victoria a copy of the suppressed Anti-Conscription Manifesto that the police had seized in the raid on the Melbourne Trades Hall. The manifesto argued that in Great Britain and France, conscription was used to

> render null and void all the achievements of trade unionism, to destroy customs, rights and practices; to dilute and whittle away — to put unskilled labour in the place of skilled labour; women in the place of men; and children in the place of adults.

Furthermore, 'every subject within the prescribed age' was a 'potential subject of the sword', and conscription was 'in principle an instrument of national defence; in practice it is made an instrument of *working class subjugation*'.[19]

Despite Miller's support and an active leadership, the ACL made little headway, even within the labour movement. Cornell ruled that it was 'out of order' for the ACL to affiliate with the ALF, 'on the ground that the Council had defeated a motion favouring anti-conscription'. On 19 October, the Metropolitan District Council voted overwhelmingly in favour of conscription.[20]

The State Executive was subject to increasing pressure from several Eastern States bodies to make clear its position on conscription. The anti-conscriptionist case was also put by the Midland District Council, and from members within the State Executive itself, such as George Ryce, Cameron and S.W. Munsie.[21] On 2 October, the State Executive reached an impasse. Pro-conscriptionists upheld the decision arrived at by the Kalgoorlie Congress in June, but Ryce moved 'that this Executive declares itself opposed to the conscription of human life'. The Chairman, Peter O'Loghlen, ruled that the Executive had no right to override the decision of the Congress unless instructed to do so by a majority of District Councils. An amendment 'that in the opinion of this Executive it is desirable that all Laborites should vote "No" on October 28th' was moved by P.J. Mooney, Metropolitan District Council and Maylands ALF member, and seconded by Leighton. The original motion was withdrawn, and the amendment became the motion. Munsie and Cameron put forward another amendment:

> that in the opinion of the majority of this Executive, the voluntary system has not failed in conserving the best interests of Australia and that we recommend all affiliated organisations to vote 'No' on the 28th instant.

After a long debate, the amendment was lost by nineteen votes to fifteen. The motion was then put and was tied, sixteen to sixteen; a re-vote resulted in fifteen to seventeen, and the concluding vote was sixteen to eighteen, against. So the Executive was plainly divided right down the middle on the issue, although on this occasion victory went to the pro-conscriptionists by a narrow margin of two votes. Thus ended yet another three-hour meeting at which conscription had been almost the only business discussed.[22]

Two weeks later, however, the anti-conscriptionists were victorious. A motion by Leighton and Watts, supporting an anti-conscription declaration signed by thirty-four Federal Labor Members of Parliament including Senator Needham, and urging the people to vote 'No', was carried by fourteen votes to thirteen. Following this, Cornell resigned as Acting Secretary of the ALF, on the grounds that he could not support the anti-conscription motion and at the same time speak publicly on behalf of conscription.[23] Andrew Clementson was appointed in his place, and one of his first duties as Secretary was to send out the anti-conscription declaration in a circular to all District Councils, urging them to support the Federal Labor Party in its fight to 'save Australia from the continental curse of conscription'.[24]

Despite this setback, the pro-conscriptionists organized a strong and successful campaign. They had in their ranks Labor parliamentarians such as J.E. Dodd MLC, Heitmann MLA, Holman MLA and Underwood MLA; John Hilton, editor of the *Westralian Worker*; Liberal Party leaders Wilson, Lefroy, Colebatch, Sir John Forrest and Sir Walter James; and prominent citizens such as the Mayor of Perth, Councillor Rea, and the Town Clerk, W.E. Bold. Branches of the National Service Referendum Council were formed in Perth and Kalgoorlie in September 1916, and Premier Frank Wilson and Sir John Forrest went on speaking tours to country centres. The council even undertook to arrange transport for city voters, to ensure that 'the referendum would be carried in the affirmative'.[25] The 'Yes' campaign was also aided by the ABA, the Australian Born Committee, the Empire Patriotic League, and other groups of similar ideology.

Women played prominent roles in many of the 'patriotic organizations'. The Organisation of Women War Workers League urged the Premier to press women into service to replace men who 'ought to go to the front', and it accused many women of 'putting up obstacles to prevent men enlisting'.[26] In the two weeks prior to the referendum, a group of female members of the National Service Referendum Council, headed by Dr Roberta Jull, and including Labor women such as Miss Eccles and Mrs Jabez Dodd, organized a door-knocking campaign in the metropolitan area. The women volunteers and some returned soldiers whom they employed visited every dwelling to ascertain whether the householders would vote for or against conscription. Potential 'No' voters, or those who were unsure, were revisited and given literature in an attempt to persuade them to favour conscription.[27] No evidence has been found of a similar campaign by the anti-conscriptionists.

The pro-conscriptionists' cause was also waged across church pulpits. According to Canon Robert Moore, a true Christian would recognize his duty to obey the 'leaders of Empire and Commonwealth' and would enlist. In a later sermon, analysing the failure of the 1916 referendum, Moore blamed the 'enemy influence insidiously playing on every impulse', 'the anarchical element' and 'selfishness revealing widespread *paganism*'. Moore also equated anti-conscriptionists with 'syndicalists, IWW men, and Irish-American Sinn Feiners who are trying to fool the Australian people into rejoicing the evil heart of the Kaiser on October 28th'.[28] Other militaristic preachers included the Methodists C.A. Jenkins, Brian Wibberley and Tom Allen; and John Beukers and S.H. Cox of the Congregational Church. Tom Allen's support of conscription was sufficiently zealous to earn him the epithet of 'bloodthirsty cannibal' from Fremantle Labor Member Ben Jones.[29]

The seemingly unanimous public face presented by the mainstream Protestant churches in the west contrasted with the situation in Victoria and New South Wales, where the Presbyterians and the Methodists feared a split in their denominations if the pro-conscription cause was pursued too aggressively. The conscription issue created dissension at the General Assembly of the Presbyterian Church in August 1916. The Reverend D.A. Cameron, Director of Presbyterian Home Missions, was convinced that Presbyterians were equally divided on conscription. This may have been a factor in the result of the Victorian vote, as Presbyterians were a particularly strong denomination there, whereas they represented less than 10 per cent of the Western Australian population. Apart from being numerically weaker, they do not appear to have had a pacifist or anti-conscriptionist element in this State.[30]

The business and professional communities in Western Australia also strongly favoured conscription. Prior to the referendum, many businesses, as well as the Perth Town Hall, displayed enormous banners urging passers-by to 'Vote Yes'.[31] Several members of the Labor Caucus expressed concern about the extent of 'flag waving' in schools. There were instances of children being kept home from school after having been taunted that their parents, 'like the coon, had no flag', or being asked to write 'one-sided essays'. Some business firms in Perth, such as Foy and Gibson, showed a similarly partisan spirit by granting facilities to Liberal

Conscription banners, 1916
'Yes', proclaimed the pro-conscriptionist banners on Perth's Town Hall and neighbouring businesses in Hay Street. Seventy per cent of the West Australians who recorded a vote in the 1916 referendum agreed with them — but a small majority of Australians voted 'No'.
[Courtesy West Australian Newspapers Limited, ACN 008 667 632]

Party speakers but not to Labor. The Perth City Council, the Railway Officers Association and the WA Teachers Union were among those who publicly declared their support for 'National Service'.[32]

A powerful imperialist ideology undergirded the pro-conscription campaign, as exemplified by the language of the broadsheets: 'Read this, and ACT!'; 'Archbishop Mannix advises that Australia should do no more'; 'Ireland fails to give volunteers to the war'; 'IWW joins in anti-recruiting conspiracy'. The Irish were accused of disloyalty to the Empire; the IWW, of this and the attendant sins of atheism and threatening law and order. Stickers were printed:

> Which? Prussian tyranny or British freedom? Continue fighting for freedom by voting 'yes' on October 28th.

and

> Voluntarism has waned. There is no honourable alternative but voting 'yes' on October 28th.[33]

An Empire Patriotic League leaflet proclaimed, 'Australia's "Yes", Fame! Rise! Success! Australia's "No", Shame! Fall! and Woe!'. The referendum was declared to be 'Our Empire's answer to our Empire's call'. The leaflet concluded with these lines:

> God guard our Empire grand,
> World-wide o'er wave and land, for *Right* to Stand!
> Britons still sway the sea; Britons we're proud to be;
> Britons all one are we, Head, heart, help, hand.[34]

For many groups, the pro-conscription campaign was merely an extension of an aggressive recruiting drive. The WA Recruiting Committee consisted of a number of men, from both sides of politics, who were active for the pro-conscription cause: Jabez Dodd, R.P. Vincent, Senator Buzacott, J. Cornell, Eben Allen, E.E. Heitmann, R. Underwood, and Lieutenant G.A. Burkett, whose name featured in several cases of violence by groups of returned soldiers.[35] After the failure of the referendum, these men carried on their recruiting activities with a renewed zeal. The base of the pro-conscription campaign was therefore much broader than that of the anti-conscriptionists. No voice from the conservative side of politics or society deplored the abuse of civil liberties. Western

Australia faithfully reflected Ernest Scott's assessment that 'the case for conscription was supported by nearly every influential public man in Australia apart from those members of the Labour [sic] Party who declared themselves anti-conscriptionists'.[36]

How did the public respond to the arguments presented by the two sides of the debate? West Australians were anxious about many things in the spring of 1916. The seemingly unending lists of dead and wounded from the battlefields of France were evidence of individual sorrows that ultimately touched almost every household. Notices inserted in the 'Killed in Action' columns of the press provided a public testimony to the grief of friends and relatives. One such, appearing in the *West Australian* three weeks before referendum day, exemplifies many: 'Meyer — killed in action somewhere in France on September 3. Private Edward Martin (Ted) Meyer, the dearly loved friend of Miss Phoebe Laughton, 135 Carr Street, West Perth.'[37] Battlefield casualties served to compound many prevailing tensions: fears that the much-cherished tradition of voluntary enlistment had failed, and that Australia would be found wanting in the Empire's hour of need; fears that conscription was merely a means of undermining the labour movement; genuine doubts about Australia's role in the conflict; xenophobia directed at anyone remotely suspected of being German or disloyal; and anger and frustration born of unrelenting hardships.

In the weeks before polling day, these conflicts were reflected in an increasing number of readers' letters to the major newspapers. John Hilton encouraged debate by throwing open the *Westralian Worker*'s columns for the free expression of opinion on both sides. Readers' contributions were numerous, and varied in sentiment. While R.J. Edmonds, a member of the Federated Miners' Union of Westonia, ridiculed Don Cameron's suggestion that conscription would lead to a 'military oligarchy', the majority of responses were from anti-conscriptionists. W. Trainer, of Boyanup, thought that conscription would merely create confusion; that men who were unwilling to fight because of ideological or other reasons were 'useless and a danger from a military point of view'. Gilbert Foxcroft, of Quindanning, wrote: 'Let the conscriptionists tell us then, if they can, wherein lies the wisdom of handing over our civil liberties to the military machine'.[38]

In marked contrast, the *West Australian*, while publishing some anti-conscriptionist letters, gave most of its space to those favouring compulsory military service. Loyalty was an important theme of the letters from both sides, as were ideas of 'honour' and 'playing the game'. J. Barnes, of North Perth, wrote that 'Voluntaryism has failed to get the score and in order that "our side" should win the "next man in", compulsory service, must knock up the score and win the game'. E.A. Lennon, of Fremantle, urged, 'Let us prove that Australia is still a nation of men [by voting "Yes"]'. Jessie Budge, of William Street, asked:

> Are we going to place an ugly blot on the pages of a national history begun so splendidly, which will brand indelibly the present generation as a parcel of halting, hesitating, half-hearted cowards when decision, daring and swiftness of action are of most supreme importance?

Mary Glover, of Cottesloe, advised women that they would be using the 'No' vote 'as a dagger to strike the boys (our boys) lying wounded on No Man's Land'.[39]

On the day before the referendum, none of the letters appearing in the *West Australian* was against conscription. The *Kalgoorlie Miner*, on the other hand, while zealously pushing the cause of the 'Yes' vote, allowed space to G.W. Millard, who challenged the assumption of the Reverend Petherick at St George's, Boulder, that Christ would vote 'Yes' on the basis of the principle of laying down His life for His friends. Millard contested Petherick's right to use the words 'Greater love hath no man...' in the context of conscription. Jesus's sacrifice, he reminded the *Kalgoorlie Miner*'s readers, was voluntary: 'His power to take up life again unassisted is not possessed by any of the earth's creatures to-day'. What, he asked, of the German Christians with German clergy urging them to do the same? Millard believed that vengeance belonged to the Lord, whose message was very different from Mr Petherick's, and he urged the Christians of Kalgoorlie and Boulder to vote 'No'.[40]

While crowd opposition to pro- and anti-conscriptionists lacked the spontaneity and the organization that were evident in Melbourne, some violent incidents did occur.[41] In September 1916, while speaking on the Esplanade for the anti-conscriptionists, Don Cameron was physically attacked by a large crowd including soldiers. In the Legislative Assembly, Labor Member A.E. Green asked the Premier whether he intended to prevent a recurrence of the incident by granting adequate police protection for speakers at meetings. Green accused Recruiting Sergeant Brennan of inciting the attack on Cameron, but the Women's Commonwealth Patriotic Association of Western Australia and the ABA rose to the sergeant's defence. ABA Secretary LeMesurier claimed that Brennan had been made a 'scapegoat', and added:

> He no more instigated the attack on Cameron than I did and I wasn't there. I wish I had been. We are all equally to blame if it is blameworthy to feel passionately that curs of the Cameron type should be suppressed...[42]

Although most of the meetings in the goldfields centres were quiet and orderly, there was evidence of rising tensions as the 1916 referendum drew near. Michael Cahill, a member of the Eastern Goldfields District Council (EGDC), was charged in the Kalgoorlie Police Court with striking Captain William Tulloch at an anti-conscription meeting on 14 October. A few days later, Senator Buzacott was refused a hearing at Westonia because he would not allow Alfred Callanan to present the anti-conscriptionists' side.[43] And in Fremantle, a pro-conscriptionist meeting on 18 October ended in 'wild disorder'. Clearly, the police anticipated trouble in the metropolitan area on the eve of the referendum. On the night of 27 October, an unruly crowd of about 2,000 soldiers and civilians destroyed several Greek-owned cafes in Perth. A military picket of Light Horse, led by Lieutenant Burkett, took two hours to arrive, and it and the police spent a further half hour removing the rioters. The delay was explained in the Chief Inspector's report to the Police Commissioner: on-duty police had been scattered over the city at various meetings where it was thought disturbances would occur. Twenty-two arrests were made, including those of several soldiers.[44]

The Chief Inspector did not comment on the lateness of the military picket, except to remark that 'the only occasions when acts of lawlessness by soldiers occurred in Perth was when there was an entire absence of pickets from the streets'. Detective Sergeant Mann, who was present during the riot, reported that at first he thought it was a rally in favour of conscription. Lieutenant Burkett, who led the picket, was Secretary of the WA Recruiting Committee and was later involved in breaking up an anti-conscription meeting at which Adela Pankhurst was to speak (see page 113).

Despite deeply entrenched racism in Western Australian

society, few responded to the anti-conscriptionists' 'Keep Australia White' propaganda that was so successful in Queensland, with its history of slave labour in the northern canefields. The arrival of ninety-eight Maltese immigrants in late September 1916 was a far more effective weapon for anti-conscriptionists there than in Western Australia, where none of them disembarked.[45] Likewise, the type of propaganda that portrayed the workers as slaves, exemplified by the *Truth* cartoon 'Liberal Lurk to Leg-Iron Labor' (see page 91), had a greater effect in areas with a large industrial workforce.[46] Anti-conscriptionists, however, attempted to exploit any existing unease that conscripted soldiers would be replaced by 'coloured' or female labour. In an 'Appeal to Women', AWU Secretary Tom Butler, who also served as Secretary of the ACL in Western Australia, argued:

> If our industries are to be maintained under conscription, either you women folk will have to turn to and do laborious toil, or Chinese or Indian coolies will have to be imported. Mr. Hughes, however, has solemnly promise[d] not to allow CHEAP LABOR TO BE IMPORTED into Australia, so therefore women will necessarily be forced from the domestic sphere into the factory, the workshop, the mill and the field.

Furthermore, Butler argued, conscription would smash the labour movement and destroy its hard-won gains.[47] Although copies of this leaflet and other anti-conscriptionist literature were seized by the Western Australian Military Censor, there were no prosecutions. The Minister for Defence directed that no prosecution was to be launched unless the Crown Law authorities were satisfied a conviction would be obtained.[48]

As the pro- and anti-conscriptionists waged their campaigns, recruitment figures across Australia slumped. In July, August and September 1916, enlistments totalled about 21,700, a monthly average of some 7,200 men, or less than half the 16,500 per month that Hughes had so rashly promised Lloyd George.[49] Yet while men who refused to enlist were often victimized, some businessmen who supported conscription, purportedly on the grounds of failing recruitment, saw no contradiction in asking that their own workers remain exempt. For example, the WA Chamber of Mines requested that the Premier avoid calling out specialist tradesmen from the gold mining industry.[50] Likewise, the Methodist Church Conference passed consecutive resolutions supporting the introduction of 'National Service', and advocating an approach to the military authorities to ensure that the needs of the church were not 'endangered' by ministers enlisting in the armed forces. [51]

To participate in the referendum, military personnel had to be enrolled voters of twenty-one years or over, or eligible for enrolment. Soldiers in camp in Australia voted in the subdivision in which they were located at the time of the referendum. The votes of soldiers at Blackboy Hill, for example, were incorporated in the total for Guildford.[52] Whether or not the ballot remained secret was a matter of debate. Several returned soldiers who voted either at the Base Hospital or at Plympton School in Fremantle claimed that they had been asked to place their ballot papers in envelopes marked with their name, number, rank and battalion, before putting them in the ballot box. Conversely, others stated that the 'utmost secrecy' had been taken with regard to the soldiers' votes. The ALF's Fremantle District Council investigated the matter but found no conclusive evidence of the abandonment of secret ballot for service personnel.[53] Soldiers on active service voted on 16 and 17 October, almost two weeks before the Australian poll was taken. According to Bean, Hughes placed great importance upon the soldiers' vote. The poll in France was postponed for a day or two to enable General Birdwood to wire a message to the troops, stating that he wanted the men to vote by their consciences and did not want to influence them in any way. Yet he claimed that he knew, better than they did, the need for reinforcements.[54]

The referendum took place on 28 October 1916. Voters were asked:

> Are you in favour of the Government having in this grave emergency, the same compulsory powers over citizens in regard to requiring their military service, for the term of this war, outside the Commonwealth, as it now has in regard to military service within the Commonwealth?[55]

The complicated and vague wording of the question seemed designed to favour the government, unless voters knew exactly what the powers entailed. West Australians responded by over 94,000 (or almost 70 per cent of those who participated) voting in favour of conscription, and 40,900 against. There were 5,680 informal votes, and some 27,000 enrolled voters did not participate, but the 'Yes' vote still gained a clear majority in each of the five electoral divisions except Kalgoorlie, where almost 48 per cent of the electorate voted in the negative. Murchison was the only one of the fifty-five electoral subdivisions to record a 'No' majority.

Australia-wide, a narrow majority of 72,476 voted against the proposal. Of the individual States, New South Wales, Queensland and South Australia voted 'No', while Tasmania, Victoria, Western Australia and the Federal Territories voted 'Yes'.[56] As shown in Table 3.1, the Western Australian result deviated markedly from those of all other Australian States except Tasmania and the Federal Territories.

Table 3.1   Voting figures for each State in the 1916 conscription referendum[57]

State	'Yes'	'No'
New South Wales	356,805	474,544
Victoria	353,930	328,216
Queensland	144,200	158,051
South Australia	87,924	119,236
Western Australia	94,069	40,884
Tasmania	48,493	37,833
Federal Territories	2,136	1,269
Total	1,087,557	1,160,033
Soldiers' votes (included in above totals)	72,399	58,894

The results of the 1916 referendum in Western Australia were indicative of a society in which conservative power structures were strongly entrenched and well organized. Unlike Labor, the conservatives appear to have been completely united in their support of conscription. The resources commanded by the campaigners, and their reiterated cries to root out shirkers and disloyalists indicate that preservation of the status quo was central to the pro-conscription cause. Bravery and loyalty were interpreted only in the framework of Empire. A similar situation existed only in Tasmania, which recorded a 56.17 per cent majority in favour of conscription, and in the mainly rural Federal Territories, which recorded a 62 per cent 'Yes' vote.[58]

W.M. Hughes, continuing to support conscription, split the federal Labor movement by walking out of a Caucus meeting, with twenty-three supporters.   On 14 November 1916, the

Governor-General commissioned him to form a new Federal Government. Hughes named this government, consisting of his pro-conscriptionist supporters, the National Labor Party, and claimed that it was a 'Win the War' party. He was assured that the Liberals would cooperate in order that he could govern. In January 1917, after much further negotiation with federal Liberal politicians, notably Joseph Cook, William Irvine and William Watt, and with Alexander Peacock, Premier of Victoria, Hughes agreed to head a coalition government that would be called the National Party, consisting of pro-conscriptionist Labor Members and Liberals.[59] This party has been referred to variously as the 'Nationalist' Party or coalition and the 'Win the War Party'.

Anti-conscription Labor Party members began calling for the expulsion of their State and federal pro-conscriptionist colleagues. In December 1916, delegates at an Interstate Congress of the Labor movement voted twenty-nine to four in favour of expelling all federal Members of Parliament who had joined the National Party. Western Australia was the only State to vote against the resolution. Congress's ruling meant that Pearce, Lynch, DeLargie, Henderson, Buzacott and Burchell had automatically severed their connection with the Labor movement when they joined the new National coalition.[60] The majority of the State ALF hoped for a reconciliation now that the conscription referendum had failed.

The ALF did, however, require some explanations. Senator Paddy Lynch and State Opposition leader John Scaddan were both asked to explain remarks they were alleged to have made in speeches during the campaign. In a State Executive meeting on 16 November 1916, Don Cameron remarked that he was no longer a friend of Senator Lynch. He believed that Lynch 'had committed the unpardonable offence of trading with the enemy by vilifying...the movement which gave him political birth'.[61] Speaking at Boulder, Senator Lynch had reportedly referred to the anti-conscriptionists as 'mongrels, Huns, hypocrites, pro-Germans [and] IWW [members who] were being financed by German gold'. Furthermore, he had declared that the Labor parties in Victoria, Queensland and New South Wales were 'rotten to the core'.[62] Similarly, Scaddan allegedly had said that while he was 'in bad company politically' by occupying a platform with Liberal Party pro-conscriptionists, he preferred these men to the company of 'Hun advocates'.[63] When asked for an explanation by the EGDC,

Scaddan denied using these words. His denial was accepted, but the council informed him that his explanation regarding his attitude to conscription was unsatisfactory.[64]

On 10 January 1917, a special meeting of the EGDC, chaired by anti-conscriptionist George Callanan, was called to hear Senator Lynch explain his alleged utterances at the Boulder Town Hall. Lynch denied using the word 'mongrel' but admitted to calling the anti-conscriptionists 'pro-Germans'. He was still of this opinion and believed that his reference to the IWW was correct, because all of that organization's members were anti-conscriptionists. Furthermore, he 'knew but could not make public' the fact that 'German gold was being used to finance the breaking up of the AWU'. Lynch was probably referring to the OBU movement, which began at this time. He reiterated his statement that the Labor Party in the Eastern States was 'rotten to the core' and added that 'in fact "rotten" was too mild a term to use when referring to the official heads of the Labor movement', and that he would repeat this with 'all the emphasis he possessed'. Lynch charged his opponents with having 'violated every principle in the Labor Platform' and having 'scabbed' on the labour movement. He emphatically declared that those who would not support Hughes were 'scabs' on Labor; that those who expelled him and his colleagues from the Federal Labor Party were 'cowardly curs whom he would fight to the last ditch'. In conclusion, Lynch defied the council or anyone else to expel him from the Labor movement. The mood of the meeting was extremely angry. On several occasions, Callanan had to appeal to delegates to refrain from interjecting, and also requested that the Senator desist from making personal attacks. When one EGDC member, J.R. Brown, moved that Lynch's explanation was unsatisfactory, and accused him of lying, the Senator's pugnacious temperament overcame him entirely. He rose from his seat next to the chairman, walked to where Brown was sitting near the back of the room, and hit him. After the two were separated, Callanan ordered the meeting closed.[65]

Lynch and his federal pro-conscription colleagues defended their action in joining the National coalition, on the grounds of 'the fundamental principle of freedom of conscience to members of Parliament upon big national questions which are not provided for in the Labour [sic] Platform'. They argued that, by returning to the 'Official Labor Party', they would be 'bound by the decisions of the

State Executives of the other States'. If they accepted this position, 'neither we nor the electors would ever know where we were, as we should be bound to a policy which may be altered at any moment at the whim of these Executives'. The federal Members of Parliament also claimed that conscription was a logical extension of the Labor platform that supported the Defence Act of 1903, and that it was merely a tool to assist in winning the war. They reminded the State Executive of Fisher's pledge in 1914 that if Labor was returned to power, it would do its utmost to prosecute the war to a successful conclusion.[66]

The anti-conscriptionists now moved quickly. At a Special Congress, held in Perth in March 1917, a majority of 134 to thirty delegates resolved that, although the ALF State Executive could not expel any member for supporting conscription, Messrs Pearce, Lynch, DeLargie, Henderson, Buzacott and Burchell had severed their connection with the ALF by joining the National Party.[67] In other words, the dissenting members were expelled not on the grounds of their pro-conscriptionist beliefs, but because these beliefs allied them with Liberal politicians. Furthermore, the differences of opinion over the conscription issue, which had driven some members into the opposition, were held by McCallum and Cameron to be insoluble. The overwhelming majority reached at the Special Congress indicates the change of attitude to the conscription issue that had occurred among party members since the previous year.

In May, the State Executive took the same action against the State members, declaring Scaddan and the 'rest of the renegades' (that is, the Western Australian State Labor members who had joined the National Party) outside of the Labor movement.[68] Reactions to the absconding State members were perhaps even more bitter than at the federal level. When Heitmann's local District Council, in Geraldton, questioned his membership of the National Party, he stated that Hughes and his followers needed all the support they could get in order to win the war. He believed that anti-conscriptionists were in league with the IWW, which had already captured Sydney and was gaining sympathy among unionists in Melbourne and Broken Hill. Tudor's Labor Party, he felt, was supported by every 'pro-German' in Australia. Heitmann said that he had fought the conscription question with Hughes and it would be 'craven' to desert him. James Hickey, another member of the Geraldton District Council, ridiculed the idea that the IWW had any influence on the referendum. He also objected to Heitmann's charge that those who opposed the idea of a coalition government were not doing their utmost to win the war or were in any way 'less loyal' than Forrest, Vincent, Lovekin and other pro-conscriptionist members of the Liberal Party. Despite several conciliatory attempts by the Geraldton District Council, however, Heitmann refused to change his stance. He was not prepared to stop supporting the National Party coalition. The effort taken by the council to dissuade him from remaining with the Nationals suggests that he was a valued member of the Labor movement, but perhaps it also indicated a fear of political eclipse if the party continued to lose members. As in the goldfields, there was lasting bitterness over the conscription issue in Geraldton. In 1921, Hickey, who had been an active anti-conscription campaigner, wrote to Harold Millington, McCallum's successor as Secretary of the ALF, that he had incurred enemies in 1916 who had 'sworn to be revenged'. He knew that the same people were 'quietly organising today'.[69]

Perhaps the greatest blow to the political wing of the ALF was the loss of its leader, John Scaddan. In April 1917, Scaddan set out his disagreement with the Labor Party in a letter to McCallum:

> [I would be] compelled to give first consideration to the dictates of my national conscience as against my Party conscience...We are called upon to declare our allegiance not to principles but to men and by so doing denounce all others as traitors. I am not prepared to do this.

The State Executive then carried two resolutions expelling from the Labor Party Scaddan and ten other State Members of Parliament: Hudson, Dodd, Mullaney, Thomas, Carpenter, Ardagh, Cornell, Heitmann, Underwood and Taylor. Appreciation was shown to those pro-conscriptionists who had refused to 'rat' on the Labor movement, namely Angwin, Holman, Drew, Wilson and Walker.[70] It has been noted earlier in this chapter that McCallum had privately determined to rid the party of all pro-conscription-ists. The retention of those members who supported conscription but did not leave the party suggests two possibilities: either McCallum decided to remain true to the resolution of the March 1917 Congress, to the effect that no one was expelled on the grounds of conviction, or he simply did not have sufficient support to force the issue. By the time the blood-letting was over, the ALF had lost eleven members of the State legislature, as well as six federal parliamentarians. An additional blow was the landslide electoral victory that the National coalition enjoyed in the Western Australian elections in September 1917. The coalition's thirty-five seats included six held by National Labor candidates, won from the Labor Party.[71]

Bitterness towards members who had joined the National Party was felt years after the conscription issue, and its consequences are traced through the remaining chapters of this book. In a May 1917 Caucus meeting, Scaddan was said to be 'allying himself with the enemies of Labor and actively opposing the duly selected Labor candidates'. His loss must have been especially bitter to those who had looked for the birth of a socialist state in the west. Scaddan, after all, had introduced a variant of state socialism during his two terms as Premier between 1911 and 1916.

The other State Labor Parties suffered similar devastation. Anti-conscriptionists expelled almost half of their pro-conscription colleagues in the New South Wales Parliamentary Labor Party, including the Premier, W.A. Holman. The South Australian Premier, Crawford Vaughan, and twenty-four out of thirty-three Labor Members of Parliament, as well as the Tasmanian Labor leader, John Earle, and three out of twenty-two Victorian Members of Parliament, were also expelled.[72]

The departure of the eleven pro-conscriptionists brought several anti-conscriptionists into positions of influence — in particular, Philip Collier, who was elected party leader to replace Scaddan. Collier was an experienced politician who had held the Lower House seat of Boulder since 1905.[73] Other than Collier, Cameron and McCallum, the anti-conscriptionist who was to exert the greatest influence was a new arrival in the west, John Curtin. McCallum's role in Curtin's appointment as editor of the *Westralian Worker* is yet another indication that he was gathering support against the pro-conscriptionists. Curtin commenced his duties in January 1917, some two months before the pro-conscriptionists were expelled from the party. He immediately adopted an editorial policy of attacking Hughes and the newly-formed National coalition. During the 1917 anti-conscription campaign, the *Worker* was almost entirely devoted to the issue of conscription, with

'The Devil's Dance'
'They've got poor Labor down at last' was cartoonist Rob Shaw's comment on
the National coalition's landslide victory in the State elections of September
1917. Shaw depicted it as a victory for capitalists, church and the conservative
('plute') press — and for the Devil, too? But, according to the accompanying
verse, Labor had God on 'his' side and would rise again. Labor did not return
to power until 1924. From *Truth*, 13 October 1917.
[Courtesy Battye Library]

Curtin using statistics to disprove Hughes's claims regarding the required number of military reinforcements for overseas service.[74]

Throughout 1917, anti-conscriptionists remained active, suggesting that the issue was never considered to have been resolved, despite the failure of the previous year's referendum. There were frequent physical and verbal attacks by civilians and soldiers at Labor and anti-conscription meetings, including one at which the guest speaker was Adela Pankhurst. The ALF had invited Miss Pankhurst to speak at a number of metropolitan and country centres in the southern half of the State in February and March 1917. Despite a protest by the ALF State Executive, the WA Recruiting Committee declined to admonish its Secretary, Lieutenant G.A. Burkett, for his role in breaking up Miss Pankhurst's meeting.[75]

The second half of 1917 saw virtually a repeat of the previous year's events. In the northern summer and autumn, the AIF sustained 38,000 casualties at Passchendaele, amounting to 60 per cent of its force in France, and General Birdwood again asked Hughes for a minimum of 6,100 men per month. With Russia's withdrawal from the war, Britain exerted greater pressure on Hughes's government to provide reinforcements. On 12 November, in keeping with an election promise that his government would not impose conscription, Hughes announced that a second referendum would be held, on 20 December 1917. The question to be put to the electorate was as misleading as the first: 'Are you in favour of the proposal of the Commonwealth Government for reinforcing the Australian Imperial Force overseas?' At the same time, Hughes had all German-born Australians and their children removed from the electoral roll, believing that this step would reduce the 'No' vote by 114,000 votes.[76]

Immediately, the anti-conscriptionists set up a number of bodies such as the ALF Campaign Committee, the Anti-Conscription Finance Committee, and the Citizens (Metropolitan Area) Executive Committee of the ACL. At a special meeting of the State Executive on 12 November, a motion was carried that conscription of human life was 'opposed to the principles of the Labor movement, and [the State Executive] therefore urges all councils, branches and unions in the Federation to do all they can to oppose its adoption'.[77]

It was often difficult for the anti-conscriptionists to procure halls for public meetings. The Town Clerk, W.E. Bold, acting on his own initiative, refused to let the Perth Town Hall for anti-conscriptionist meetings, as did the Perth Literary Institute. The manager of the Star Skating Rink offered his premises for nine nights at £30, but objections, which the anti-conscriptionists believed were instigated by Archbishop Riley, were raised by the trustees of the rink.[78] Despite these difficulties, a hectic speaking program was planned for the metropolitan area, the South West, Geraldton and the Murchison, the Eastern Goldfields and North Coolgardie.[79]

During the campaign, complaints were made against many of the anti-conscriptionists, for 'seditious' utterances. As they had done in 1916, police attended each meeting and made transcripts of speeches, many of which attest to the deep bitterness and division in the community. At a meeting on the Perth Esplanade on 2 December, for example, E.J. Dunn, editor of the Perth edition of *Truth*, declared that the response by Western Australian capitalists to the War Loan was disgraceful. The excuse that most of the large firms had their headquarters in other States did not apply to such institutions and companies as the Western Australian Bank and Boan Bros. And then there were the pastoralists, 'who were now getting 20 pence a pound for the wool that they only got 9 pence a pound [for] before the war'.[80]

Some of the statements that attracted the Military Censor's attention included references by Senator Needham, Don Cameron and W.D. Johnson to the number of military divisions at the battle front. J.J. Simons made controversial remarks about censorship, and claimed that 'black' labour was to be introduced to replace men who were conscripted to fight. He also asserted that

Pearce, the carpenter of Subiaco, at the last referendum came to the goldfields with a picked body of men — 200 — armed with rifles and bullets. The two officers selected to command the force had been at Gallipoli and were selected because they were used to shedding blood.

There was more than a grain of truth in Simons' accusation, for statements were taken from Frederick Gillett, Staff Sergeant Major in charge of the expedition, and one of the two 'Gallipoli veterans', Captain E.T.H. Knight. The other captain, Byth, had returned to the front. Gillett and Knight denied that a guard was supplied for Pearce, that the rifles were loaded, or that the soldiers were supplied with beer. Yet no prosecution was made against Simons.[81] While most of these cases never came to court, because of insufficient evidence, Collier, Curtin and Mrs Foxcroft were all fined, under the War Precautions Act, for making statements prejudicial to recruiting and likely to cause disaffection to His Majesty the King. These fines appear to have been reimbursed by the government at a later date.[82]

At a pro-conscription meeting at Meekatharra in December 1917, a returned soldier, Private Pady, incensed the 200-strong crowd, a majority of whom were miners, by saying that they were the type of men who would allow their wives to be ravished by Germans whom they would then shake by the hand. The crowd responded by howling down the three speakers, Pady, Senator Buzacott and Arthur Mason, a Methodist minister.[83] No complaints were made against the invective used by the speakers, merely against the crowd for disorderliness and against the police — in particular, Sergeant Tuohy — for not controlling it. Tuohy himself observed, 'If a Liberal member had come along to speak, he would have received a fairly good reception but the audiences do not care to hear the views of men who desert them'. He was referring to Senator Buzacott.

The electorate went to the polls on 20 December. This time, the 'No' vote won by a larger margin: 1,181,747 to 1,015,159. As shown in Table 3.2, only Western Australia, Tasmania, the Federal Territories and the AIF recorded 'Yes' majorities, but these were all narrower than in 1916.

Table 3.2   Voting figures for each State in the 1917 conscription referendum[84]

State	'Yes'	'No'
New South Wales	341,256	487,774
Victoria	329,772	332,490
Queensland	132,771	168,875
South Australia	86,663	106,364
Western Australia	84,116	46,522
Tasmania	38,881	38,502
Federal Territories	1,700	1,220
Total	1,015,159	1,181,747
Soldiers' votes (included in above totals)	103,789	93,910

In Western Australia, 65 per cent of those who registered a formal vote were in favour of conscription. In every division of the State, however, a greater proportion of people voted against conscription in 1917 than in 1916, with the swing varying from 3 per cent in Perth to almost 5 per cent in Kalgoorlie, as shown in the Table 3.3.

Table 3.3   Percentage of swing away from 'Yes' vote in 1917 referendum, Western Australia[85]

Electoral division	'No' vote as percentage of formal vote		Swing
	1916	1917	
Perth	26.01%	29.01%	3.0%
Fremantle	29.53%	33.10%	3.6%
Swan	25.51%	29.80%	4.3%
Kalgoorlie	41.94%	46.60%	4.7%
Dampier	30.28%	35.10%	4.6%

As in 1916, military personnel serving overseas voted several days before the referendum. It was of vital importance to the Hughes Government that the troops on active service recorded a majority in favour of conscription, and the franchise was extended to include all members of the AIF on active service, irrespective of age. A further incentive to encourage an affirmative vote was attempted. Early in November, Pearce cabled General Birdwood:

> In view of extreme importance to Empire and Australia that referendum shall be carried this time and in view of experience of how the condition of troops affected their votes on last occasion, it is imperative that they should be kept out of firing line and given best possible conditions until end of year.

Birdwood replied that 'everything possible' was being done. The troops were reportedly 'in good heart after recent successful fighting', and the General thought that this would be 'favourable' to the outcome of the referendum. Perhaps he was correct, for the AIF again voted in favour of conscription by a narrow majority of 52 per cent.[86]

Historians have suggested that several factors contributed to the large 'Yes' majority vote in Western Australia in both referenda. These include the 'moderateness' of the labour movement in Western Australia; the weakness of pressure groups such as the

Australian Freedom League, the Quakers, and the IWW; the influence of pro-conscriptionists Archbishop Clune and Senator Paddy Lynch upon their fellow Catholics; rigid censorship; the 'effective campaign' conducted by the *West Australian* in support of conscription; and the smallness of the State's German population.[87] The first of these — the 'moderateness' of the labour movement — is discussed earlier in this chapter, and in Chapters 5 and 7.[88]

With regard to the influence of other anti-conscription pressure groups, it is certainly true that the Australian Freedom League did not have much support in the west, and that the Society of Friends (or Quakers), the only Christian church with a consistently pacifist doctrine, was virtually non-existent in Western Australia.[89] The IWW, on the other hand, was much stronger than previous scholars have estimated. Although the assertion by IWW member George Strickland that 'in both [referendum] campaigns the IWW took the vanguard in the fight' was as exaggerated as pro-conscriptionist estimates of the group's influence, the Perth Criminal Investigation Department arrested Monty Miller prior to the 1916 referendum, and seized his papers, including issues of *Direct Action* and correspondence with Mick Sawtell. Miller was held in prison without trial for forty days. He and Sawtell were convicted of seditious conspiracy in December 1916 and bound over for two years on a good behaviour bond (see Chapter 2).[90]

It is difficult to gauge the extent of Archbishop Clune's reported influence as a pro-conscriptionist. He was absent from Australia, serving as Chaplain-General to the Catholic members of the AIF, when the first referendum took place. He cabled Senator Pearce that 'whoever believes in the righteousness and justice of the war we are engaged in ought not to hesitate to vote for compulsory service in Australia'. His correspondence with Archbishop Mannix on the issue has since been destroyed.[91]

Senator Lynch's influence is similarly a matter for debate. As has been shown, Lynch made enemies in the labour movement over his pro-conscription stance, yet he held his Senate seat until 1927, despite changing parties — a factor that seems to attest to his personal popularity.[92]

Conversely, there is evidence of strong Irish Nationalist and anti-conscription sentiment among Catholics in Western Australia. Large crowds attended meetings to demonstrate for Home Rule in Ireland and to form a United Irish League. The Mayor of Perth, Councillor Rea, presided over the Home Rule meeting; Rea, a pro-conscriptionist, was proof that not all Irish Nationalists were against compulsory military service for the British Empire. The *WA Record* reflected the very strong pro-Irish sentiment of the State's Catholic community. In the weeks preceding the first conscription referendum, the paper's columns were filled with the aftermath of the Irish Uprising of Easter 1916, material reproduced mainly from London papers and bitterly critical of the British Government's role in Ireland. Father T.R. O'Grady, the *WA Record*'s editor, was an anti-conscriptionist. He used the paper as a forum for his own views, and those of Archbishop Mannix and John Fihelly, the Assistant Minister for Justice in the Queensland Cabinet. O'Grady was obviously impressed by T.J. Ryan's Queensland Labor Government and wrote, 'Queensland can be depended upon to administer the knockout blow to the slavery proposals of the conscription-loving Mr. Hughes'.[93]

Military Intelligence and the local police turned their attention to the Irish Nationalist movement just prior to the second referendum. In November 1917, Inspector Walsh reported to the Commissioner of Police that, according to a trusted source:

> There are about 1500 Sinn Feiners in Perth, and about 2500 in Kalgoorlie and Boulder. The ratio of Sinn Feiners in WA to the whole population is about equal to the other Australian states. If the result of the referendum is 'Yes' the Australian Sinn Feiners will rebel against it and will not submit to conscription in any shape or form.[94]

Intelligence maintained a close watch on persons believed to be Sinn Fein members and on premises where meetings were held. It also attempted to suppress an anonymous inflammatory pamphlet, entitled *The Hun–Hibernihun Alliance*, which linked Irish Republican organizations with the Germans. Despite the nature of the pamphlet, Intelligence regarded the information therein as serious enough to warrant further investigation, and kept a close watch on the *WA Record*, which was regarded as having Sinn Fein sympathies.[95] Perth police were informed of a meeting of Sinn Fein members that allegedly took place in Perth on 4 December 1917, at which

> A member stated that Father Lynch had informed him that the Kaiser had, through the Emperor of Austria, promised the Pope the return of Temporal Power in Rome should the Central Powers win

the War and conquer Italy and *that in consequence every true Catholic's interest should be to assist.*[96]

In the meantime, the Chief Military Censor informed the Prime Minister that 'the Sinn Fein Movement is rapidly developing in, at any rate, Melbourne and Sydney', but the Minister for Defence decided to maintain a policy of restraint.[97] No raids were carried out in Western Australia, although reports of Sinn Fein activity in the State continued throughout 1918 and into the postwar period. This is discussed further in Chapter 6.

Censorship has been regarded as another important factor in determining the outcome of the two referenda.[98] But how effective was censorship in Western Australia? The Military Censor was unable to prevent the circulation of information that was embarrassing to the government, nor of rather more inflammatory pamphlets such as the banned Anti-Conscription Manifesto from Melbourne. The *West Australian*'s silence on many of the anti-conscriptionists' activities cannot always be attributed to the acuity of the censor.[99] The paper imposed its own censorship by running a strong, effective pro-conscription campaign.[100] Its editorial on the day prior to the 1916 referendum was typical: it posed the rhetorical question 'What is the alternative?', and replied, 'There is none except that Australia shall cravenly desert the Empire and its allies'.[101] The censor's pen seems to have had little effect on *Truth*, the exception in the generally pro-conscriptionist media. As early as July 1915, the paper's national editor, John Norton, wrote:

> In sacrifice of men and money, of blood and treasure and in the shape of industrial depletion and depression and social stress and strain, Australia, in proportion to her population has paid not *only more than her share, but also very much more than any other dependency of the Empire, or than the UK itself.* [102]

The casualty figures released at the end of the war were to prove Norton tragically correct.[103] Much of *Truth*'s most powerful anti-conscriptionist propaganda was expressed in cartoon and verse; hence, although open to differing interpretations, it more readily attracted the attention of the casual reader (see, for example, page 120).

Certainly, Western Australia's physical isolation compounded the difficulties of the anti-conscriptionists and aided the censor. In

'The Spectre of Conscription'
Anti-conscriptionist — but loyal to the British Empire — was *Truth*'s message
on 9 September 1916.
[Courtesy Battye Library]

1916, all printed matter still arrived by ship or cable rather than from a greater variety of sources, as in other States. The Trans Continental railway line was completed in May 1917, facilitating the passage of people and mail between east and west, but the distances involved still meant that several days passed between despatch and arrival. Furthermore, there were few arrival points, rather than many as in the Eastern States, theoretically making policing much easier. Yet it is difficult to prove that the system of censorship was harsher and more effective in Western Australia than, for example, in New South Wales, where Tom Barker, the editor of *Direct Action*, was twice imprisoned for printing material regarded by the Crown as being prejudicial to recruiting. In the second instance, he refused to pay the £100 fine and instead served the sentence.[104] Further evidence that censorship was extremely effective in the Eastern States comes from a letter from Alex McCallum to Don Cameron:

> All the Trade Union letters were opened and the telephones tapped. Of course nothing was done to the other mob...Wires between the State Executives giving their decision on censorship was [sic] censored and never delivered. In the end they had to send men from state to state to carry the news.[105]

Even under T.J. Ryan's Labor Government in Queensland, censorship provisions effectively silenced all viewpoints 'in any degree critical of the war effort or the righteousness of the Allied Cause'.[106]

The composition of Western Australia's population has also been regarded as an important determinant in the overwhelming 'Yes' majority. Western Australia had a very small German population. By comparison, the large German population in South Australia definitely influenced the 'No' vote there. A clause of the War Precautions Act that disenfranchised German-born people in the 1916 referendum affected some 4,000 voters in South Australia, but an amendment in 1917 removing from the electoral rolls citizens whose fathers were German-born had an even more profound effect on the 'No' vote — for example, in the Angas electorate, the 'No' vote dropped by 18 per cent.[107]

On the other hand, the high percentage of British-born citizens in Western Australia undoubtedly had an influence upon the outcome of the referenda. An influx of 25,000 British immigrants between 1911 and 1914 brought the proportion of British-born West Australians to almost three times the national average.[108] Another population factor that differentiated Western Australia from the rest of the Commonwealth was its high masculinity ratio. As much of the propaganda of both sides in the conscription debate was aimed at women, and as women were actually blamed for the 'No' majority in Queensland[109], this factor deserves further investigation (see pages 122–123).

Many of the above explanations for Western Australia's overwhelming 'Yes' majority in both referenda suggest that the community was united in favour of conscription, and that the weak anti-conscription campaign — battling against limitations imposed by isolation and strict censorship — failed to dissuade sufficient numbers to record a significant 'No' vote. This is particularly true of Metherell's use of the 'consensus theory' to explain the 'Yes' majority.[110] However, factors that have not previously been examined include the strength of the pro-conscription campaign, the responses made by the community to both sides of the debate, and voting patterns within the subdivisions.

Studies of specific electoral districts yield interesting and varied answers regarding the motivations of individuals in voting for or against conscription. The Beverley–Toodyay residents, according to Anstey's analysis, believed that conscription would force into the army those who had 'shirked their duty' and would alleviate the necessity of recruiting from country areas. The Murchison workers, on the other hand, mostly opposed conscription because they 'feared that its introduction would threaten their jobs and civil liberties'.[111] On the goldfields, the voters exhibited an 'independent' spirit. Despite a strongly pro-conscriptionist press, and the neutral stance adopted by many powerful unions, the 'No' vote in the Kalgoorlie electorate was unexpectedly high.[112] The *Albany Advertiser* and influential citizens in Albany supported the 'Yes' campaign. While John Scaddan encountered no difficulties in speaking on behalf of the pro-conscription cause there, Senator Needham, on the opposite side of the debate, was refused the use of the Town Hall, and his open-air meeting was broken up by a noisy crowd including soldiers.[113] There was a similar situation at Northam, with both local papers and a powerful organizing committee supporting the 'Yes' vote.[114] At the suburban level, the West Guildford community was divided when local parliamentarian Joseph T. Davies, Secretary of the Midland Railway Employees Union, supported Hughes's views on conscription.[115] Many unenlisted men in Subiaco experienced victimization as an 'aggressive patriotic fervour' gripped the suburb.[116]

How do these glimpses of Western Australian society compare with the actual voting figures for each subdivision? Conservative influences were evidently strong, although perhaps a little less pervasive than the 70 per cent vote in favour of conscription would suggest. Although only one subdivision (Murchison) recorded a 'No' majority in 1916, some margins were very narrow indeed. In the Dampier division, for example, Mt Magnet's 'Yes' majority amounted to a mere three votes out of 963 (including sixteen informal votes), and in Cue the majority was only twenty, out of 723 votes. Both these subdivisions recorded a 'No' majority in 1917. At Ivanhoe, in the Kalgoorlie division, 1,226 votes were cast in the 1916 referendum, and the 'Yes' majority was a mere eighteen votes; at Kanowna, 732 votes were cast, and the 'Yes' majority was thirty-seven votes. The highest majority was five to one in favour of conscription in Coolgardie, while Mt Leonora and Mt Margaret recorded two-to-one majorities.

A number of differences are discernible in the 1916 and 1917 voting patterns, as shown in Table 3.4.

Table 3.4   Voter participation in the conscription referenda of 1916 and 1917[117]

Year	Participation of enrolled voters		Gender of WA voters	
	WA	Australia	Males	Females
1916	84%	81%	87%	80%
1917 (civilians)	72%	74%	70%	72.93%
1917 (including military personnel)	83.5%	81%	92%	73.06%

Western Australia's participation rate of almost 84 per cent of enrolled electors in 1916 was exceeded only by Victoria and Queensland. In 1916, no differentiation was made between the votes of service personnel and civilians, whereas in 1917 there was. A greater percentage of females participated in the 1916 referendum than in the 1917 referendum, whereas the opposite was true of civilian males. Is it, therefore, possible to discern relationships between voting patterns and location or gender?

Support for conscription was most solid in the Swan division, in the south-west of the State. Katanning's result of four to one in favour of conscription was fairly typical of the division. Forrest, a Labor seat held by Peter O'Loghlen, was the only subdivision to record a majority of lower than two to one in favour of conscription. It had a predominantly male constituency, many of whom were timber workers. Only half of the 1,539 enrolled male voters and two-thirds of the 789 female voters participated in the referendum. In 1917, when a much higher percentage of voters turned out, Forrest recorded a majority against conscription.

Participation by 50 per cent or fewer of male electors occurred in seven of Dampier's seventeen subdivisions. In comparison with Forrest, there was a direct correlation between low attendance at polling booths and a high 'Yes' vote, most notably in the Broome and Onslow subdivisions, both ten to one in favour of conscription; Derby, five to one; and Roebourne, four to one. Although the referendum was held on a Saturday, the poor attendance — especially of male voters — in many northern country districts suggests that workers in isolated areas were often unable to get to a polling booth. Neither was there the added incentive of compulsory voting. The correlation between low participation by male electors and a high 'Yes' vote might also suggest that women voters were more inclined to favour conscription. This would partly explain the larger 'Yes' majorities in the more densely peopled areas where a greater percentage of the population was female. On the other hand, female voter participation was actually higher in Dampier (almost 80 per cent) and Kalgoorlie (81.5 per cent) than in Perth (77 per cent). Perhaps males in closer settlement areas were more likely to favour conscription than their counterparts in isolated areas were. When one takes into account the prewar masculinity ratio, however, it is impossible to conclude with certainty than either males or females more definitely favoured conscription.

The highest voter participation in the 1916 referendum was in the Fremantle division, where Claremont recorded a six-to-one majority in favour of conscription and all but four of the ten subdivisions recorded a pro-conscription majority of two to one or greater. The smallest 'Yes' majorities were in North and South Fremantle, where concentrations of waterside labourers resided. Such influences were not, however, apparent in Albany and Bunbury, the other major centres of maritime industry, although Geraldton recorded a sizeable 'No' minority of 788 out of 1,654 votes.

The question of why the Western Australian population so overwhelmingly favoured conscription is an extremely complex one that has been too readily explained by historians in the past as evidence of consensus in the State. The evidence uncovered by further study of voting patterns and individual subdivisions suggests that, while farmers in the Eastern States were accused of voting 'No' in order to maintain their labour force, the majority of their Western Australian counterparts resoundingly voted 'Yes', as did people in coastal settlements. Isolation played a role in adding to the general paranoia, influencing people to vote for conscription, and in preventing rural workers from participating in the ballot. It is probable that fear of victimization forced some people to vote for conscription. Factors that were shared with Tasmania — the other State that voted convincingly for compulsory overseas military service — included the powerfully entrenched conservative status quo, with its ideology of Empire; the small size of the industrial workforce; and the lack of a militant majority in the labour organization. Added to these were influences that were experienced everywhere in Australia: the pressures created by anguish over the death or injury of friends and relatives; fear and anger towards enemy aliens, 'shirkers' and others who were regarded as 'not doing their share'; economic hardship; and emotional readjustment. The existence of these factors does not indicate 'consensus' among West Australians; nor does it indicate a 'moderate' labour movement. Events of the months and years to follow were to reveal just how deeply and bitterly divided were the labour movement and the entire community.

1   See, for example, L.F. Fitzhardinge, 'The Little Digger', 1914–1952: William Morris Hughes, A Political Biography, vol. II, Sydney, 1979. Fitzhardinge analyses and to some extent qualifies the 'success' of Hughes's visit to Britain. He states that Hughes's 'sheer personality, pungent phrase, absolute self confidence and the novelty of the performance all no doubt played a part' in his instant popularity. He arrived in Britain at a time of growing disquiet regarding the war's lack of progress, and there was increasing criticism by the British people of the coalition government (p. 77). Hughes's critics, on the other hand, included the Lord Chamberlain, Lord Sandhurst, who was 'disappointed' by him; British Labour men who realized that he 'did not speak for the Australian Labor movement'; and 'those who found his economics crude and dangerous' (p. 93).

2   There are numerous sources on the conscription referenda. This account is based on E.D. Scott, Australia During the War: Vol XI of the Official History of Australia in the War of 1914–1918, C.E.W. Bean (ed.), Sydney, 1936, ch. 9; F.B. Smith, The Conscription Plebiscites in Australia, 1916–1917, Melbourne, 1966; J.M. Main, Conscription: The Australian Debate 1901–1970, Sydney, 1970, chs 1 and 2; and L.L. Robson, Australia and the Great War, 1914–18, Melbourne, 1974 edn, pp. 13–19. For examples of Western Australian opposition to 'boy' conscription, see Australian Freedom League leaflets in Bessie Rischbieth Papers, State Archives of Western Australia, Acc. 'Compac 87'.

3   Scott, Australia During the War, p. 338.

4   C.E.W. Bean, Private Diaries, 9 September 1916, Australian War Memorial, Acc. 3/606, item 59, pp. 10 ff. See also H.V. Evatt, Australian Labour Leader:

The Story of W.A. Holman and the Labour Movement, Sydney, 1954 edn, pp. 303 ff. Evatt believed that Hughes was 'misled' (p. 306).

5   Scott, *Australia During the War*, p. 410. For Britain, see, for example, J.M. Winter, 'Britain's "Lost Generation" of the First World War', *Population Studies*, vol. XXI, 1977, part 3, p. 450; Fitzhardinge, *'The Little Digger'*, pp. 119, 173.

6   S. Welborn, *Lords of Death: A People, a Place, a Legend*, Fremantle, 1982, pp. 113–116.

7   Evatt, *Australian Labour Leader*, pp. 302 ff; F.B. Smith, *The Conscription Plebiscites*, p. 13; Main, *Conscription*, pp. 41–42, 49.

8   State Executive of the ALF (WA) — Minutes Books (hereafter SE Minutes), vol. 2, 7 February 1917.

9   For a detailed discussion of the debate, see B. Oliver, '"Rats", "Scabs", "Soolers" and "Sinn Feiners": A Re-assessment of the Western Australian Labor Movement in the Conscription Crisis of 1916 and 1917', *Labour History*, no. 58, May 1990, pp. 50–52.

10 ALF (WA), Minutes of ALP Special Congress, vol. 18, 1913–28, State Archives of Western Australia, Acc. 1573A/18 (hereafter Congress Minutes), pp. 145–153.

11 SE Minutes, vol. 2, 23 March 1916, 17 April 1916, 1 May 1916; circular, State Executive to District Councils, 4 May 1916, in State Executive of the ALF (WA) — Correspondence Files (hereafter SE Correspondence), File 135. That Clementson suffered a similar collapse two years later attests to the strains of jointly holding the positions of ALF State Secretary and Secretary of the Metropolitan District Council. See Clementson to Metropolitan District Council, 3 May 1918, informing it that his doctor had ordered him to take a complete rest for 'at least a month' because he was suffering from 'insomnia' and 'nervous prostration', SE Correspondence, File 88.

12 McCallum to Cameron, 24 September 1916, Don Cameron Papers, National Library (emphasis added).

13 McCallum to Cameron, 16 November 1916, Don Cameron Papers, National Library.

14 SE Minutes, 21 August 1916.

15 Cornell to Minister for Defence, n.d., SE Correspondence, File 24.

16 Cornell to Minister for Defence, 21 September 1916, SE Correspondence, File 24.

17 Department of Defence to ALF, 29 September 1916, SE Correspondence, File 24.

18 L.C. Jauncey, *The Story of Conscription in Australia*, South Melbourne, 1968 edn, pp. 220, 229; M. Saunders and R. Sumy, *The Australian Peace Movement: A Short History*, Canberra, 1986, p. 17.

19 *West Australian*, 8 August 1916; J. Williams, *The First Furrow*, Perth, 1976, p. 53; SE Minutes, vol. 2, 7 August 1916; ALF (WA), Minutes of the Fremantle District Council (hereafter Fremantle DC Minutes), State Archives of Western Australia, Acc. 1198A, vol. 6, 8 August 1916. For evidence of league activity in 1914, see Bessie Rischbieth Papers.

20 ALF (WA), State Executive to Metropolitan District Council — Correspondence Files, State Archives of Western Australia, Acc. 1689 (hereafter SE/Met. DC), File 27. See letter of introduction for T.J. Miller from the ACL re speaking at State Executive meeting that night, 19 August 1916; also Cameron to Metropolitan District Council, 21 September 1916; SE Minutes, vol. 2, 18 September 1916, 16 October 1916; Metropolitan District Council

Minutes, vol. 2, 19 October 1916; Acting Secretary to Anti-Conscription League, 6 October 1916, SE/Met. DC, File 27.

21 SE Minutes, 18 September 1916, 21 October 1916. The Eastern States bodies included the Anti-Conscription Trades Union Executive in Melbourne; the Australian Freedom League; the Industrial Labor Councils of Queensland, New South Wales, Victoria, Tasmania and Barrier; and the Parliamentary Labor Caucus in Victoria.

22 SE Minutes, 2 October 1916.

23 SE Minutes, 16 October 1916.

24 SE/Met. DC, File 27, 18 October 1916. In the light of this circular, the motion by Johnson and Leighton that 'all officers [of the Executive] be given a free hand on the question of conscription' merely reiterated the decision of the 1916 State Congress and also showed that neither side could gain a power-ful enough majority to oust the other. The title of this chapter comes from this source.

25 Bold to Premier, 14 September 1916, Premier's Department File (hereafter PDF) 228/16.

26 F. Wells to Premier, 25 October 1916, PDF 228/16.

27 For details of the street-by-street campaign, see notebooks in Roberta Jull Papers, State Archives of Western Australia, Acc. 956A, envelope 9.

28 Canon Robert Henry Moore Papers, Sermons and Addresses, 1916, 24 September 1916, 29 October 1916, and newspaper clipping, n.d., text of a letter from Moore to Senator Needham, dated 13 October 1916 (emphasis in original). See also J. Smith, '"Not Peace but a Sword": Religion, War and Empire. Canon Robert Henry Moore: The Church of England and the First World War', in J.M. Tonkin (ed.), *Studies in Western Australian History IX: Religion and Society in Western Australia*, October 1987, pp. 65–82.

29 See, for example, Jenkins' sermon and a resolution by Wibberley in *West Australian*, 5 August 1916; Cox's sermon, *West Australian*, 1 August 1916; *Western Congregationalist* for the writings of Beukers, the magazine's editor; police report of conscription meeting 10 December 1917 in Department of the Army, Intelligence Files, Australian Archives (WA), Acc. PP14 (hereaf-ter Intelligence Files), no. 1/12/198, for Jones's remark concerning the Rev. Tom Allen. Jones added that ministers of religion who advocated conscrip-tion ('these followers of the meek and lowly Nazarine') had 'torn down the image of the Man of Peace, the Man of Sorrow, and had replaced it with a hideous image, half mammon, half Mars and wholly Devil'.

30 A.D. Gilbert, The Churches and the Conscription Referenda, 1916–17, MA thesis, Australian National University, 1967, pp. 100–106; *Commonwealth of Australia —Census* [hereafter *Commonwealth Census*], *1911*, vol. I, pp. 200–201 (27,569 out of a population of 282,114).

31 J. Edmonds (ed.), *Swan River Colony: Life in Western Australia since the Early Colonial Settlement*, Perth, 1979, p. 47.

32 ALF (WA), Parliamentary Labor Party, Caucus Minutes (hereafter Caucus Minutes), vol. 2, 2 January 1917 (for schools), and SE/Met. DC, File 1 (for Foy and Gibson); also *West Australian*, 27 October 1916.

33 Conscription referenda leaflets, printed collection, Australian War Memo-rial.

34 PDF 228/16.

35 See, for example, WA Recruiting Committee to Premier, 28 March 1917, PDF 106/15.

36 Scott, *Australia During the War*, p. 348.

37 *West Australian*, 9 October 1916.
38 *Westralian Worker*, 6 October 1916, 13 October 1916, 20 October 1916, 27 October 1916.
39 *West Australian*, 7 October 1916, 27 October 1916.
40 *Kalgoorlie Miner*, 24 October 1916.
41 J. Smart, 'The Right to Speak and the Right to be Heard: The Popular Disruption of Conscriptionist Meetings in Melbourne, 1916', *Australian Historical Studies*, vol. 23, no. 92, April 1989, pp. 203–219.
42 LeMesurier to Premier, 27 September 1916, PDF 228/16. The account of the incident is taken from material in this file.
43 *Kalgoorlie Miner*, 25 October 1916, 20 October 1916.
44 Chief Inspector to Commissioner of Police, 14 November 1916, Detective Sergeant Mann's Report, 11 November 1916, and Sgt Fee's Report, 10 December 1916, Police Department (WA) File 6047/1916, State Archives of Western Australia, Acc. 430; Perth Police Occurrence Book, vol. 17, 1916, 27 October 1916, 28 October 1916, State Archives of Western Australia, Acc. 838.
45 R. Evans, *Loyalty and Disloyalty: Social Conflict on the Queensland Homefront, 1914–18*, Sydney, 1987, pp. 97–98 ff; A.A. Graves, 'The Abolition of the Queensland Labor Trade: Politics or Profits', in E.L. Wheelwright and K. Buckley (eds), *Essays in the Political Economy of Australian Capitalism*, Sydney, 1980, vol. 4, ch. 2.
46 Prior to the war, Western Australia had the smallest industrial workforce of any State in the Commonwealth. *Commonwealth Census, 1911*, vol. I, Classes of Occupation: Males, p. 351; Females, p. 352; Occupations in Western Australia, vol. III, pp. 1606–1619. Western Australia's industrial workforce was 15.03 per cent of the population, marginally smaller than Tasmania's (15.38 per cent); cf. Victoria, 21.95 per cent, and South Australia, 21.73 per cent.
47 Intelligence Files, no. 2/4/19 (emphasis in the original). See also SE Correspondence, File 18, correspondence between the ALF and the Prime Minister.
48 Intelligence Files, no. 2/2/20.
49 M. McKernan, 'War', Table W2-8, Enlistments in Australian Services by State, World War I, in V. Vamplew, *Australians; Historical Statistics*, Sydney, 1987, p. 412.
50 WA Chamber of Mines to Premier, 6 October 1916, PDF 228/16.
51 *Methodist Church of Australia, Western Australian Conference Minutes*, 1916, p. 332.
52 *West Australian*, 27 October 1916.
53 Fremantle DC Minutes, vol. 6, 31 October 1916, 28 November 1916.
54 The Military Service Referendum Act, 1916 (Australia). Instructions for the Conduct of the Polling in France, Conscription Leaflets, Printed Collections, Australian War Memorial; C.E.W. Bean, Private Diaries, item 61, 15 October 1916.
55 See, for example, Main, *Conscription*, p. 49, for the wording of the question.
56 *Commonwealth Parliamentary Papers*, vol. II, p. 7471; also Main, *Conscription*, p. 73, for informal voting figures.
57 *Commonwealth Parliamentary Papers*, vol. II, p. 7471; also Main, *Conscription*, p. 73; Robson, *Australia and the Great War*, p. 76.
58 M. Lake, *A Divided Society: Tasmania During World War I*, Melbourne, 1975, p. 78; *Commonwealth Parliamentary Papers*, p. 737.

59   C.M.H. Clark, *A History of Australia Vol. VI: The Old Dead Tree and the Young Tree Green*, Melbourne, 1987, pp. 42–43.

60   SE Correspondence, File 68.

61   SE Minutes, vol. 2, 16 November 1916.

62   ALF (WA), Minutes of the Eastern Goldfields District Council, State Archives of Western Australia, Acc. 1704A (hereafter EGDC Minutes), vol. 3, 30 October 1916.

63   *Kalgoorlie Miner*, 21 October 1916, cited in EGDC Minutes, 10 January 1917.

64   EGDC Minutes, 13 November 1916.

65   Se Correspondence File 55.

66   These arguments are set out in two statements to the State Executive and signed by the seven federal Members of Parliament who supported conscription. See SE Correspondence, File 45.

67   Congress Minutes, 20 March 1917, p. 205.

68   SE Correspondence, File 55.

69   Hickey to Millington, 31 October 1921, SE Correspondence, File 149.

70   Scaddan to McCallum, 6 April 1917, SE Correspondence, File 81. This file is entitled 'Rats'. Also McCallum to O'Loghlen, 19 April 1917, in the same file; Caucus Minutes, vol. 2, 9 May 1917.

71   D.W. Black, 'The Liberal Party and its Predecessors', in R. Pervan and C. Sharman (eds), *Essays on Western Australian Politics*, Nedlands, 1979, p. 198.

72   J.R. Robertson, 'The Conscription Issue and the National Movement in Western Australia, June 1916 – December 1917', *University Studies in Western Australian History*, vol. III, no. 3, October 1959, p. 43. See also P. Loveday, 'New South Wales', p. 98, B. Dickey, 'South Australia', pp. 274–275, and H. McQueen, 'Victoria', p. 327, all in D.J. Murphy (ed.), *Labor in Politics: The State Labor Parties in Australia, 1880–1920*, St Lucia, 1975.

73   D.W. Black, The Early Administration of Philip Collier, BA Hons dissertation, University of Western Australia, 1959, pp. 70–71. Collier's parliamentary career spanned almost forty-three years, ending with his death in 1948.

74   D. Sholl, John Curtin at the W*estralian Worker*, 1917–1928: An Examination of the Development of Curtin's Political Philosophy as Reflected in his Editorials, BA Hons dissertation, University of Western Australia, 1975. See especially pp. 10–13.

75   SE Correspondence, File 67; SE Minutes, vol. 2, 5 March 1917; PDF 106/16.

76   Clark, *A History of Australia, Vol. VI*, pp. 66–69.

77   SE Minutes, vol. 2, 12 November 1917.

78   SE Minutes, 19 November 1917, 28 November 1917, 3 December 1917.

79   Minutes of a Conference between the Campaign Committee of the SE and the PLP, 23 November 1917 (in SE Minutes).

80   Police transcript, Intelligence Files, series I, no. 1/12/198.

81   See Intelligence Files, nos 1/12/69, 70, 71, 174, 183, 186, 197, 198, for transcripts of speeches and details of fines.

82   SE Minutes, vol. 2, 8 April 1918. For reimbursement of fines, see SE Correspondence, File 40, case notes re T.P. Candish. An account of Curtin's prosecution appears in L. Ross, *John Curtin: A Biography*, Melbourne, 1977, pp. 61–62. The above information in SE Correspondence, File 40, suggests that Ross's assumption that Curtin's fine was not paid is incorrect. See also SE Correspondence, File 177.

83   An account of this meeting is taken from Police Department File 5903/17.

84   Robson, *Australia and the Great War*, p. 98.

85   See *Commonwealth Parliamentary Papers, 1917–19*, vol. IV, pp. 1471 ff.

86   Pearce to Birdwood, 9 November 1917, and reply, 16 November 1917, George Foster Pearce Papers, Australian Archives, vol. 2, bundle 1; Notice issued by Commonwealth Electoral Officer, London, re. Voting Eligibility of AIF Members in 1917 Conscription Referendum, in Australian War Memorial's Conscription Collection; also Scott, *Australia During the War*, pp. 427–428.

87   J.R. Robertson, 'The Internal Politics of State Labor in Western Australia: 1911–1916', *Labour History*, no. 2, May 1962, p. 49, and 'The Conscription Issue', p. 8; D.W. Black, 'Party Politics in Turmoil: 1911–1924', in C.T. Stannage, *A New History of Western Australia*, Nedlands, 1981, pp. 392–393; Jauncey, *The Story of Conscription*, pp. 230–231.

88   See also Oliver, '"Rats", "Scabs", "Soolers" and "Sinn Feiners"', pp. 48–64. This paper challenged the assertions that the Western Australian labour movement's reactions to the conscription issue were markedly different from those of the movement in the Eastern States.

89   Jauncey, *The Story of Conscription*, p. 230; A.R. Pearson, 'Western Australia and the Conscription Plebiscites of 1916 and 1917', *RMC Historical Journal*, no. 3, 1974, pp. 21–26.

90   Williams, *The First Furrow*, pp. 54, 57–61.

91   D.F. Bourke, *The History of the Catholic Church in Western Australia, 1829–1979*, Perth, 1979, pp. 194–195. The author is indebted to Sister M. Raphael, Archivist at St Mary's Roman Catholic Church Archives, for the information on the Clune to Mannix correspondence.

92   D.W. Black, 'P.J. Lynch', in *Australian Dictionary of Biography, Vol. 10, 1891–1938*, Melbourne, 1986, p. 177.

93   See, for example, *WA Record*, 9 September 1916, for a reprinted editorial from the *London Daily Mail*; also 30 September 1916, 'What We Have in Ireland'; and issues for 16 September 1916, 23 September 1916 and 28 October 1916. For an account of the Easter Uprising in Ireland, see, for example, R. Kee, *The Green Flag: A History of Irish Nationalism*, London, 1972, especially ch. 17.

94   Walsh to Commissioner of Police, 19 November 1917, in Department of Defence File A8911/1, 221, Australian Archives (Canberra).

95   Intelligence Files, series I, no. 1/12/184. According to the Index of Intelligence Files held at the Australian Archives (Perth), only one file refers to 'Irish interned' (1 November 1915). Regrettably, this file has disappeared.

96   Precis of a Police Department (WA) file, 'Sinn Fein Organisation in Western Australia', in File A8911/1, 221 (emphasis in the original).

97   Chief Censor to Prime Minister, 3 November 1917, in Department of Defence (Australia), series A3932/1, item SC417.

98   Pearson, 'Western Australia and the Conscription Plebiscites', p. 24.

99   The anti-conscriptionists used a letter from the censor, J.C. Strickland, to the press, prohibiting publication of 'any reference to the arrival or expected arrival of *Maltese immigrants* in Australia', to prove that conscripted men would indeed be replaced by overseas labour. See Intelligence Files, no. 2/3/19 (emphasis in the original).

100   See, for example, issues of the *West Australian* from 27 July 1916 to 7 August 1916. T.J. Miller's visit to Perth received two very brief notices: his arrival by ship, and a paragraph in 'News and Notes' concerning the foundation of the ACL, which was probably inserted by the league itself. On the other hand, the church services and public meetings conducted to commemorate the second anniversary of the outbreak of war received extensive coverage. On

5 August, for example, the 'patriotic' sermons of Archbishop C.O.L. Riley and the Reverend C.A. Jenkins each received two-thirds of a column of newsprint.

101 *West Australian*, 27 October 1916.
102 *Truth*, 10 July 1915 (emphasis added).
103 See Scott, *Australia During the War*, Appendix 7, 'Comparisons of Casualties'. Australia, 65 per cent of those who served overseas were killed or wounded; New Zealand, 59 per cent; British Isles, 50 per cent; Canada, almost 50 per cent; India, 12 per cent.
104 I. Turner, *Sydney's Burning*, Sydney, 1967, pp. 14–19; also F. Cain, *The Wobblies at War: A History of the IWW and the Great War in Australia*, Melbourne, 1993; Pearce to Acting Secretary ALF, 30 June 1916, SE Correspondence, File 18. See also E.C. Fry (ed.), *Tom Barker and the IWW*, Canberra, 1965.
105 McCallum to Cameron, 24 September 1916, Don Cameron Papers, National Library.
106 Evans, *Loyalty and Disloyalty*, pp. 32–33.
107 P.M. Gibson, 'The Conscription Issue in South Australia, 1916–17', *University Studies in History*, vol. 4, no. 2, 1963–64, pp. 63 ff.
108 Robertson, 'The Conscription Issue', p. 45, stated that at the 1911 Census, the European-born percentage of the Australian population was 11.5 per cent, in contrast to 21.54 per cent in Western Australia, the vast majority having been born in Britain. Robertson argued that although Queensland's percentage of European-born exceeded Western Australia's, the fact that Queensland had been a self-governing State since 1859 influenced the vote there.
109 The effect of propaganda aimed specifically at Queensland women is examined by C. Shute, '"Blood Votes" and the "Bestial Boche": A Case Study in Propaganda', *Hecate*, vol. II, July 1976, p. 20.
110 T. Metherell, The Conscription Referenda, October 1916 and December 1917: An Inward-Turned Nation at War, PhD thesis, University of Sydney, 1971.
111 S. Anstey, The Impact of the Great War on the Beverley, Toodyay and Murchison Communities of Western Australia, 1914–17, BA Hons dissertation, Murdoch University, 1980, p. 144.
112 C. Weckert, The 1916 and 1917 Conscription Referenda in the Electorate of Kalgoorlie, unpublished University of Western Australia research essay, 1976, held at State Archives of Western Australia, Acc. PR 8702, pp. 11–13, 19.
113 D. Garden, *Albany: A Panorama of the Sound from 1827*, Melbourne, 1977, p. 290.
114 D. Garden, *Northam: An Avon Valley History*, Melbourne, 1979, p. 210–211.
115 J. Carter, *Bassendean: A Social History, 1929–1979*, Bassendean, 1986, p. 111.
116 K. Spillman, *Identity Prized: A History of Subiaco*, Nedlands, 1985, pp. 206–207.
117 The table is based on figures in the *Commonwealth Parliamentary Papers, 1914–1917*, vol. II, pp. 737, 747, 875–879.

(From Smith's Weekly.)   **WAS IT FOR THIS?**

'Was It For This?'
The long war was over, peace had dawned; yet, across Australia, doubts
gathered about the extent and meaning of the sacrifice. Had 60,000 Australian
servicemen died merely to line the profiteers' pockets? From *Smith's Weekly*,
6 September 1919, reproduced in the *Fremantle Herald*, 3 October 1919.
[Courtesy Battye Library]

Chapter Four

GRAINS CRUSHED BY THE MILL

Problems of repatriating the troops

The Great War ended on 11 November 1918, almost a year after the defeat of Hughes' second conscription referendum. In the final months of the war, Australian divisions went into action at Villers Bretonneux, where losses amounted to almost 2,500, at Harbonnieres, and on the Hindenberg Line at Bullecourt.[1] Twenty per cent of the AIF's 62,000 casualties in the last year of the war were deaths.

Although this chapter concentrates on the problems posed and faced by returning servicemen, there was also a small number of returned female nurses. At least eighty-five Western Australian nurses served overseas with the Australian Army Nursing Service (4.7 per cent of those listed on the army's incomplete nominal roll). Others joined the Voluntary Aid Detachments. Very little has been written of the experiences of Western Australian nurses on active service, but, like the servicemen, they returned to Australia irrevocably changed in outlook. Archbishop Riley encouraged the nurses to join the returned servicemen's organizations then being formed around Australia. Returned nurses were accepted into the membership of what was to become the Returned Services League (RSL) on the same terms as men, but they also formed their own organizations — for example, in Western Australia, a Returned Sisters Association was formed in 1920.[2]

A major problem facing the Federal and State Governments once the hostilities were over was the repatriation of the AIF. Of the 23,700 Western Australian servicemen repatriated, 15,900 had sustained some kind of injury.[3] The Federal Government was slow to respond to the challenges of repatriation, and early schemes were sadly inadequate. Furthermore, an increasing number of social and political tensions compounded the problems faced by returning servicemen, and placed further stresses on an already fragile society. After the October 1917 revolution in Russia, Bolshevism emerged as a new terror to add to the 'Hun-Hibernian' menace. Returning soldiers found themselves cast in the roles of both upholders and destroyers of law and order, depending on whether they embraced or rejected Bolshevism. The conservative stance of the RSL added to the complexity of the situation, and created divisions between ex-servicemen and the labour movement.[4]

There is little evidence of these pressures and fears in the work of historians who promoted the consensus theory. Crowley's 'western third', for example, was a place of tremendous optimism in 1919. Eligibility for Commonwealth pensions ensured that the 'veterans of the war had no fear that their families would suffer from their physical disabilities'. Furthermore, servicemen were returning to a nation that took 'pride in their achievements' and appropriately recognized 'their rights to preferential treatment during rehabilitation'.[5] More recently, scholars have begun to penetrate the myths surrounding Australia's attitudes to its homecoming heroes. Ellis wrote poignantly of 'the men who saw Peace coming in 1918. Not swashbuckling, bronzed Anzacs...but grains being crushed by the mill.'[6] Lindstrom found that World War I servicemen did build up an idealistic picture of homecoming that was similar to the one presented by Crowley as reality. This superficial image of the society they believed they were fighting to defend 'caused problems upon return; so that for many men the collapse of the image of home was the last straw'.[7]

Although some servicemen had already been repatriated before the landing at Gallipoli in April 1915, it was the influx of wounded after this battle that created pressure on the Commonwealth Government to set up appropriate structures to deal with the problems of rehabilitation. In each State, War Councils comprising prominent citizens were formed, and until August 1917, these bodies were responsible for the actual work of repatriating invalided men. Through local committees, and coordinated by a Federal Parliamentary War Committee, they provided artificial limbs and vocational training, acted as an employment agency for the able-bodied, registered those who desired to settle on the land, and collected funds. The costs of setting up ex-service personnel in business, training them, and providing stock and agricultural implements were met initially by a Repatriation Fund, which was launched, with great fanfare, in Melbourne in February 1916. The Federal Government made a grant of £250,000 to the fund, and the Eastern States–based Baillieu and Hordern business empires contributed £20,000 each, thus adding considerably to their prestige as patriots.[8]

Tensions developed between supporters of the 'charity approach' to the care of returned soldiers, and advocates of a system of government funding, based on public taxation according to income. The problem originated in 1914, when the Federal Government was organizing finance for equipping and paying for the AIF. Senator Millen, then Minister for Defence in the Cook Liberal Government, accepted a proposal that pensions should be met out of patriotic funds — charities such as the Red Cross Funds, the YMCA War Work Fund, and others — which were financed by public donation. Although the Fisher Labor Government rejected this policy and, in December 1914, passed the War Pensions Act to provide for pensions for incapacitated servicemen and their dependants, many other expenses were paid out of patriotic funds. These included supplements to the Separation Allowances paid to soldiers' wives and children. Early in the war, legislation was passed compelling married servicemen to allot at least two-fifths of their pay to their wives, and three-fifths if they had children. The Federal Government made an additional Separation Allowance of 1s 5d daily (or 9s 11d per week) and 4½d per day for each child. This allowance was increased by money from patriotic funds to £1 10s 11d per week for wives and an additional amount for children.[9]

War pensions did not come under the control of the Repatriation Department until July 1920. Before this date, they were the responsibility of the Commonwealth Treasury and were administered by a Pensions Board. A Deputy Commissioner of Pensions was appointed in each State, to determine whether a veteran's health or incapacity had been caused by war service or by a condition from which he had suffered prior to enlistment. An example of the latter was miners' phthisis, which, arguably, would have been greatly exacerbated by battlefield conditions of dust, cold and damp, but which was regarded as not being related to war service. Where a disability was judged to have resulted from war service, the Deputy Commissioner also had to determine its nature and extent, in order to recommend a part or full pension.[10]

In 1917, there were two charitable organizations that gave financial assistance to needy wives or widows of Western Australian servicemen. The WA War Patriotic Fund, a charitable organization that paid the Separation Allowance supplement, was jointly chaired by Hal Colebatch MLC, the Colonial Secretary, and Frank Rea, Mayor of Perth. The committee consisted of Labor and Liberal Members of Parliament, other prominent ALF members such as Don Cameron, and the Mayors of Fremantle and Kalgoorlie. The fund's promoters regarded the care of disabled soldiers as an act of charity rather than as a responsibility that should be borne by the entire community, with those of greater means contributing accordingly. Consequently, the onus was on ex-servicemen to prove that they were incapable of work and that they 'deserved' to receive assistance. Childless dependants were ineligible to apply to the Patriotic Fund. The maximum benefit through this fund for a woman with one child was 38s 6d per week, while 42s 6d was paid for two children, with 2s 6d per week for each additional child. This allowance was comparable to the lower female wage rates. The Repatriation Fund granted assistance to discharged servicemen and the wives and children of deceased soldiers 'on the merits of the case', by advancing cash, or by setting them up in business, or by providing furniture or personal effects. A grant of up to £50 could be made by the local body; larger amounts had to be approved by the Board of Trustees in Melbourne.[11]

In its first twelve months of operation, to 30 June 1916, the WA War Patriotic Fund dispensed £21,846 in relief[12] — which attests to the extent of the need. Australian and New Zealand war pensions did not compare favourably with those of other Allied countries. The highest, the British pension, represented almost 74 per cent of the average weekly wage in the United Kingdom, while Australian and New Zealand pensions were less than 50 per cent of the respective average wages. Nevertheless, federal authorities persisted in the belief that the pensions were sufficient to cover the basic cost of living.[13] In 1916, the average fortnightly pension was £2 7s 4d for incapacitated servicemen and £1 4s 6d for dependants. By 1921, these rates had dropped to £1 13s 10d and 18s 5d, respectively.[14]

Other than pensions, the Federal Government offered only one major source of support for returned servicemen: the Soldier Settlement Scheme, which was established in 1918 to assist able-bodied ex-servicemen to obtain farming land. The RSL, which had influenced the government's decision to establish a land settlement scheme, was permitted a representative on the three-member board whose purpose it was to investigate the availability of land.[15] The scheme was administered in Western Australia by a controller, E.A. McLarty, who was Managing Director of the Agricultural Bank and a Member of the Legislative Council. Intending settlers had to register at his office, acquire a certificate of physical fitness, and demonstrate to the Land Qualification Board that they possessed sufficient farming experience to 'make a go' of it.[16]

Although grazing and pastoral land was available, the scheme was designed to encourage ex-servicemen with little income to take up small blocks of agricultural land, 160 acres (65 hectares) of which was granted free. No payments were required for five years, after which half-yearly instalments of 3d per acre were due, the term of payment to be not less than twenty years from the date of selection. Loans advanced by the Agricultural Bank for improvements were repayable over eight years. The Federal Repatriation Department paid a sustenance allowance of 20s to 30s a week, depending on marital status, with 2s 6d for each child, for the first six months, after which time the farm was expected to provide a living.[17] This policy was particularly impractical on the orchard blocks, as fruit trees took years to mature sufficiently to produce in commercial quantities. In the meantime, the farmers had no income and merely ran up debts with the Agricultural Bank, which they could not repay.[18]

Partially disabled men who were unable to take up selections or return to their previous occupations found that they were poorly served by governments, employers, charitable organizations and even the union movement. Many unionist ex-servicemen must have wondered at the rhetoric of solidarity within the labour movement when they were denied the opportunity of earning a living because they had returned disabled. Overall, the unions showed a definite reluctance towards employing disabled men, including their own members.[19]

In January 1918, Alex McCallum convened a conference of unions to discuss questions of repatriation. Scarcely any of the representatives present could hold out much hope of employing more than a few men, and they felt that placing incapacitated persons would be especially difficult. In a report of the conference,

McCallum recorded his disappointment:

> I am sorry to say that the meeting was not very fully attended...and
> it appears to me that the Officers of the Unions have not grasped
> the seriousness of the situation...A number of [union officials] take
> the view that because a maimed man will not be able to work in
> their industry...the problem does not affect them, to this view I
> dissent [sic]. Take, for instance, the position of the Miners, the
> Navvies, and Timber Workers. These men returned from the war
> minus an arm or leg — they will not be again able to follow that
> class of employment. In my opinion, the Union from which that
> man enrolled owes a debt to him to see that he is able to engage in
> some employment which will supplement his pension, otherwise
> he will be sentenced to live under the poverty line for the rest of
> his days and we will again repeat in Australia what has occurred in
> the older lands of having these men begging at the street corners.

This report prompted considerable discussion, in the State Executive, about the obligations of unions towards repatriated soldiers.
George Ryce warned that the labour movement would have to be
careful to prevent the Federal Government from 'shuffling some of
their responsibilities on the Trades Unions'. A motion was carried,
instructing McCallum to insist, at the forthcoming Repatriation
Conference, 'upon the enforcement of Arbitration Awards applying to an industry into which it is proposed to absorb returned
soldiers'.[20]

The Repatriation Conference was held in Melbourne the following month, with the aim of advising the Federal Government
on dealing with the repatriation and re-employment of disabled
soldiers.[21] The Repatriation Department was prepared to consider
only callings that could be learned in one year (the maximum
period for which it would fund training), and proposed that ex-
servicemen learn branches of trades. While the unions favoured
assisting returned men as much as possible, they baulked at
relieving the government of what they believed was its responsibility. Consequently, there was considerable disagreement over
trainees' wages. The labour representatives stood out for the
minimum wage of £3 per week, plus pension and an allowance for
dependants. The employer representatives wanted the wage to
include pension and allowances. Eventually, a compromise was
reached: the pension of 10s per week was absorbed into the wage,
but not the allowance paid to a wife and children.

This was a notable victory for the labour movement in the light of a contemporary recommendation by the WA State War Council that the government suspend or alter Arbitration Court awards in order to employ returned soldiers. The ALF claimed it was under-represented on the twelve-member War Council (subsequently the State Repatriation Board), for it was permitted only one member — McCallum — and he was not allowed a proxy when he was absent from meetings. The Minister for Repatriation justified the appointment of a sole Labor representative, on the grounds that 'all sections of the community should be represented'.[22] Consequently, the Western Australian labour movement felt that it was being denied an adequate role in determining working conditions for returned soldiers, and capitalized as much as it could on examples of National Party Government inadequacy in meeting their needs.[23]

Repatriation policy had not progressed any further by November 1918. News of the armistice came late to West Australians, even though it had been anticipated for several days. The ending of hostilities finally was announced at about 9.00 p.m. on Monday 11 November. The next day, businesses, shops and schools were closed as parades filled the streets in the metropolis and in country towns. Many of the displays of patriotism included elements of strong anti-German sentiment.[24] The Commonwealth Government planned a series of peace celebrations for July 1919.

The Northam victory celebrations provided the stage from which Hugo Throssell VC chose to announce his new-found socialism. Throssell reportedly said:

> We will never be free of wars under a system of production for profit. The Peace Treaty leaves us at the mercy of a system that makes wars. If we want peace we must do away with the system that produces wars.[25]

The local populace reacted with disgust and disbelief. Throssell's war exploits, real and legendary, had made him a hero not only in Northam but throughout the State and the country. Many spurned him from then on, and blamed his war injuries or the influence of his wife, the novelist Katharine Susannah Prichard, for his radical views. Evidence suggests, however, that Throssell's socialism was inspired as much by his experiences on the battle front and the censorship of those experiences after his return home as by his admiration for his wife. Military surveillance was maintained on the Throssells from 1919 onwards.[26]

Heroic and glorious images of war had been boosted by a series of publications, beginning with the *Anzac Book* and the *Westralia Gift Book* in 1916. The former, using sketches, essays and poems written by the men at Gallipoli, determinedly depicted the humorous side of war. The latter celebrated it with jingoism, such as in Alfred Chandler's poem 'Gallipoli', which ran, 'Our dauntless sons have writ the golden name "Australia" / high on every scarp and rock'.[27] In contrast to the general tone of the *Westralia Gift Book* was Hugo Throssell's own account of the action at Gallipoli.[28] Many documents preserved in archives record soldiers' reflections on the battle front. Far fewer reveal their thoughts on re-adapting to civilian life. In later years, some writers and poets, such as Katharine Susannah Prichard and Vance Palmer, presented a more realistic picture of war. Hugo Throssell took his own life as a result of war neurosis, in 1933. Tragically, Prichard had created a similar background, in her novel *Intimate Strangers*, for the character Greg Blackwood, whose readjustment problems included the disintegration of his marriage, and suicide.[29] Prichard altered the original ending of *Intimate Strangers*, so that Greg Blackwood's suicide attempt failed. Many years later, she told her son of her fear that Throssell had read the original draft and, in his depressed state of mind, had seen himself in the character of Blackwood.[30] Alternative voices such as Prichard's, however, were few and tentative in the early 1920s, when the majority of returned soldiers most desperately needed the assurance that their people at home had even the slightest understanding of the Armageddon experience through which they had passed.

With the war over, the business community that had so zealously donated to patriotic funds and supported recruiting drives now turned to the provision of charity for returned soldiers. Foremost in Western Australia was the Ugly Men's Association (UMA), a group of businessmen who raised funds, established an employment bureau and dispensed relief payments to returned servicemen. In 1919, the organization obtained State Government assistance to set up a training college for unemployed returned soldiers. Premier James Mitchell informed the Prime Minister in September that year that the UMA had 'established a farmers' training school which is providing excellent and most necessary training'. Although the average attendance of 146 students was below the hoped-for 400, the school seemed to be progressing well

Captain Hugo Throssel VC
The external image of the heroic 10th Light Horseman conflicted with inner
doubts. At the victory celebrations at Northam in July 1919, Throssel publicly
declared, 'If we want peace we must do away with the system that produces
wars'.
[Courtesy Australian War Memorial, P0516/05/01]

during 1920. Public subscription raised a total of £3,000 for the school, and the State Government subsidized this amount by £2,000. The Federal Minister for Repatriation approved his department bearing half of the cost, providing that the Western Australian Government officially recognized the school, and ensured that it was satisfactorily equipped and able to give necessary instruction in all branches. Furthermore, it required the State to provide land in a convenient location to enable students to undergo training in farm work, and be responsible for half the running costs. In April 1920, however, the Commonwealth Government reneged on this promise, forcing the school's closure, despite its excellent early results. Of the first year's graduates, 174 had acquired and were farming a total of 286,713 acres (116,119 hectares) of land under the Soldier Settlement Scheme; 235 had received certificates from the Land Qualification Board, sixty-five had found other employment; and a further thirty-seven awaited the outcome of applications for Soldier Settlement blocks.[31]

The ALF's Repatriation Committee proposed a solution for employing able-bodied returned servicemen that was different from those offered by the government or the UMA. It recommended that the State Government embark on a massive public works program, including installing sewerage and drainage, building Workers' Homes, extending spur lines to connect the existing main railway lines, continuing the Bunbury breakwater, and commencing other large-scale schemes such as the Geraldton Harbour, the Canning Reservoir, and the Fremantle Railway Bridge.[32] In 1919, the labour movement had some success when the Commonwealth Government established the War Service Homes Commission and consulted with the relevant unions in order to ensure that wages and working conditions for both ex-service trainees and unionists coincided with recognized awards.[33] At first, it appeared that Labor and National Party members agreed when it came to promoting the State's industries. The philosophy of 'State patriotism' (or buying locally made goods) was a recurring theme in the early postwar years. In 1929, the newly arrived Governor, Sir Francis Newdegate, reminded members of the Perth Chamber of Manufacturers that buying locally was 'not only a patriotic duty' that West Australians owed their State, but 'a matter of self interest' in which they would benefit materially.[34]

By this time, also, the State Government, with federal

assistance, had set up vocational training schools in the metropolitan area.[35] However, the labour movement's battle to encourage the establishment of more secondary industry in the State was far from over. Apart from its difficulties with the National Party and with voluntary and employer groups bent on giving 'charity', the ALF also encountered opposition from the RSL. The indifference of the league's conservative leadership to observing award conditions, and its insistence that preference in employment be granted to all returned men drew hostility from the unions. Further tension was created by the RSL's stance on law and order during the industrial unrest of the early postwar years.

The RSL exerted a greater influence on ex-servicemen than any other contemporary organization. The returned services body in Western Australia was founded in May 1916, to protect and advance the interests of returned men. Its objectives included perpetuating friendship and maintaining standards among ex-servicemen; preserving the memory and records of the fallen; providing for the sick, wounded and needy; and 'inculcating loyalty' to Australia and the Empire. From the beginning, the Western Australian body suffered divisions. Under the RSL's original constitution, officers were elected annually. The divisions in the Western Australian body are evident in the fact that some State Presidents appear to have served for no more than a few months. In the first eight years of its existence, the organization had no fewer than eleven Presidents (three of whom served during 1919), and nine State Secretaries. In 1918, there were two returned soldiers' organizations: the Returned Services League and the Returned Services Association. Affiliation with the Returned Servicemen's Imperial League of Australia (also founded in 1916) was refused until the two local bodies had amalgamated. Hence, Western Australia was the last State association to affiliate, and this occurred in 1919, after objections to adopting the national badge and paying the capitation fee had been overcome.[36]

After national affiliation, the State organization was known as the Western Australian Branch, and sub-branches were those bodies formed in country and metropolitan centres. Originally, full membership was restricted to men who had served with the AIF. This was soon extended to include returned nursing sisters and, later, men who had served in other campaigns but were either physically unfit or too old to undertake military service in the

Great War. Applications for membership were investigated by a Vigilance Committee, which recommended acceptance or rejection to the Executive.[37] Despite the upheavals, the league appears to have enjoyed considerable popularity in the early postwar years. In mid-1919, it boasted sixty-seven branches, of which twenty-one were in the metropolitan area[38], and by 1921, State membership numbered above 5,000.[39]

The issue of labour relations caused another split in the league in December 1919, when Joseph O'Neill and some colleagues from the East Perth Sub-branch of the RSL formed the Returned Sailors' and Soldiers' Association of Australia (RSA) in opposition to the existing body.[40] O'Neill and Maloney, Secretary and President, respectively, of the East Perth Sub-branch, had been expelled from the RSL after sending a telegram to the Federal President in Melbourne, stating that '800 Diggers' were prepared to secede from the league, which they claimed did not work in the interests of the ordinary soldier.[41]

O'Neill was keen to gain labour support, and letters passed between him and McCallum regarding a joint meeting between ALF officials and his organization. He denounced the RSL as 'a brass hat body out to destroy Trades Unionism, or at least to weaken it to such an extent that it will be useless as a fighting factor, in the industrial area'.[42] McCallum forwarded a copy of the RSA's constitution to all District Councils, and in April 1920, the State Executive appointed a three-member delegation to wait on the association 'at an early date with a view to bringing about a better understanding between the Returned Soldier and his fellow unionists'. A meeting arranged for 10 May was postponed, and there is no indication that it ever took place.[43] Nor is it known how long the RSA continued to exist separately from the main body of the RSL. The RSA's founders were no doubt inspired by the success of a similarly militant body, the Returned Soldiers' and Sailors' Labor League of Queensland, which also was formed in 1919 and which claimed that its membership had grown to 1,500 in the first two months of its existence. The Labor League argued that ex-soldiers must join the union movement in order to obtain justice.[44] The RSL–RSA split marked a turning point in the history of the Western Australian returned services organization. From that time, the RSL became increasingly conservative politically, and authoritarian in its structure and ideology.

The RSL's increasing conservatism was evident in its opposition to the labour movement's industrial policies. In December 1919, the New South Wales Parliament passed the Returned Soldiers' and Sailors' Employment Bill, which granted preference in employment to returned servicemen and nurses who had served at the front. The Act provided for the reinstatement of ex-military personnel in previous employment, the appointment of a board to assist returned servicemen in obtaining employment, and the amendment of the Industrial Arbitration Act of 1912 to give them preference irrespective of whether they were unionists.[45] The Western Australian RSL, despite its conservative stance, was not able to force the enactment of similar legislation by the Mitchell Government. In November 1920, Hal Colebatch, then Minister for Education in the Mitchell ministry, stated in the Legislative Council merely that 'where practicable' in future, the government would grant preference in employment to returned men.[46] Eventually, in 1921, the RSL received a government subsidy from the Repatriation Department to establish an employment bureau for returned servicemen. The bureau obtained excellent results in its first year of operation, filling 2,105 of the 2,433 positions offered.[47]

It is not surprising that many returned servicemen joined the league, for it must have seemed their only champion in a bleak and confusing world strewn with shattered dreams. Those who returned whole in mind and body had to compete on the labour market, often with younger, more highly qualified and skilled men. Many suffered discrimination because of incomplete training, interrupted by the war, or incapacitation. The deepening recession compounded the problem, resulting in unemployment increasing until 1922.[48] Faced with few options, and undoubtedly influenced by the ideology of the day, which encouraged the belief that a 'sterling character' was sufficient qualification to be a successful farmer, many ex-soldiers and their families regarded a block of land and the opportunity to be 'one's own boss' as the most desirable alternative.

Meanwhile, the Western Australian ALF continued to lobby the Commonwealth authorities for an increase in pensions. The issues that had arisen during the war remained central to the debate in the early 1920s: pensions were invariably inadequate, and they were dispensed in a very arbitrary way. The attitude of the Commissioner of Pensions Office was expressed bluntly to McCallum in a 1919 letter:

It is an established fact that the blind are capable of being trained for an occupation, and the view is held that in the men's own interests they should be encouraged to take up some profitable employment which by occupying their minds would assist them to refrain from brooding over their misfortunes. It is therefore not proposed to provide for any special increase of pension in these cases.[49]

The ALF also objected to the fact that it was left to the WA War Patriotic Fund to establish a free medical service for the dependants of deceased or disabled servicemen. The Prime Minister's response was that pensions were assumed to be 'sufficient to cover the cost of living'.[50]

Although pensions were inadequate, they were eagerly sought by people with no other means. Sometimes pensions and allowances were refused, or were granted and later cancelled, apparently because of bureaucratic reasons. An example was the case of Mrs E. Parsons, of East Perth. Mrs Parsons suffered a double tragedy when her husband died in October 1917 and one of her sons, Gordon, was killed in action barely six months later. Her other son, Hamilton, who had been awarded a Military Medal, had escaped from a German prison camp, returned to Australia, and re-enlisted for active service. At the time of her appeal, he was in Blackboy Hill Training Camp awaiting embarkation. Mr and Mrs Parsons had depended largely on Gordon for their livelihood. Mrs Parsons had applied for a Separation Allowance of 9s 4d per week when Gordon enlisted, but she was told that she and her husband were ineligible because they received an old age pension. After her son's death, Mrs Parsons learned that the law had been changed and that pensioners could now receive a Separation Allowance. Accordingly, she applied for the allowance from the date of the new legislation until her son's death on 5 April 1918. Although she was in urgent financial need, the Defence Department rejected her claim because it was lodged after Gordon's death; her original application had been verbal and there was no record of it. Furthermore, she was already receiving an old age pension of 12s 6d per week, and a war pension in respect of her deceased son.[51]

The case of Private Charlie McGregor was another example of the arbitrariness of the pension authorities. McGregor, who had served with the 28th Battalion, had sustained a leg wound and was unable to return to his previous occupation of miner. He was granted a weekly pension of £1 18s 9d from 5 May 1916 until 24 May 1917, at which time his pension was cancelled, presumably because he was regarded as being fit for work. He got a job as a cleaner on the railways and worked until his leg gave way. A bullet was extracted, and he was hospitalized for six weeks. The Repatriation Department reluctantly agreed to pay sustenance to his family during the time he was in hospital. Despite repeated pleas by the ALF, however, his pension does not appear to have been renewed.[52]

There were also cases of soldiers who were expected to return to work before their wounds had properly healed. Two such cases were Thomas Campbell and Allen Leopold Fairhead, who were discharged from Fremantle Base Hospital with open wounds. Campbell had sustained a shell wound in the left arm while serving at Pozières. He lost a portion of bone, and underwent three operations after his return to Australia. Fairhead was wounded in the leg, in August 1916, and also spent a considerable amount of time in hospitals in France, England and, on returning to Australia, Fremantle. Both soldiers were surprised when, in December 1917, they were told by the Officer in Charge of Fremantle Base Hospital, Colonel Hadley, that their wounds were 'paltry' and they would be better doing some work rather than 'loafing about'. Campbell was a farm worker, while Fairhead lived with his parents at East Pingelly, so it is probable that he was similarly employed. Both believed they were unfit for work, as their wounds had not healed and still required regular dressing. The medical records of both soldiers reveal that their complaints were justified. When Campbell died in 1950, his wife was granted a war widows' pension on the grounds that the 'severity' of her husband's war wound had 'necessitated three years continuous treatment in hospital' and that it could not be 'disregarded as a cause of the ill-health he suffered for many years prior to his death'. Fairhead suffered permanent partial disablement as a result of his wound. In 1921, his leg was described as having healed 'with some deformity and shortening', and he had to wear surgical boots for the remainder of his life.[53]

Sergeant W.R. O'Keefe, who had served at Gallipoli and in France with the 28th Battalion, returned to Australia suffering from phthisis but was refused a pension because, in the judgment of the authorities, his disability was not caused by 'stress of war'.

O'Keefe was unable to perform manual labour, and at the time he appealed to the ALF he was living in Geraldton with his wife and children 'at the point of starvation'. He had been examined twenty times by Military Medical Officers, only one of whom had declared him fit for work. Unfortunately for O'Keefe, it was this diagnosis that was confirmed by the Principal Medical Officer, Lieutenant Colonel Walden, who refused to recommend a pension. Andrew Clementson took O'Keefe's case to the medical and pension authorities in September and October 1917. The Commissioner of Pensions replied that when O'Keefe was discharged from the AIF, the lesions in his lungs had healed and there was no sign of tuberculosis, but that his case was being reconsidered and a decision would be arrived at when the medical reports were received. Ultimately, Senator Needham intervened on O'Keefe's behalf, and the Repatriation Department agreed to pay O'Keefe a sustenance allowance of £3 5s per week and, if necessary, to arrange and pay for his treatment at the State Sanatorium. He was granted a 60 per cent pension as from 22 November 1917, and was able to work on a casual basis, but he never fully recovered from his disability.[54]

McGregor, Campbell, Fairhead, O'Keefe and Mrs Parsons gained little or no satisfaction from appealing to the pension authorities, even when backed up by the ALF. Nevertheless, by 1921 Western Australian military pensions, at the rate of £1 14s 7d per fortnight and 18s 1d for dependants, were higher than in any other State except New South Wales. Military pensioners and their dependants numbered an astounding 23,235, or roughly 7 per cent of the State's population, reflecting the extremely high cost for West Australians of their participation in the Great War.[55]

There were some returned servicemen, however, who faced even greater injustice, because of racial prejudice or mental disability. In the former category were servicemen of Aboriginal descent. At least 300 Aboriginal soldiers from Queensland, New South Wales and Victoria served in the Great War and, in keeping with the rest of the AIF, about one-third were casualties.[56] The Nyungar community of South Australia has recorded the names of twenty-three of its members who served with the AIF in World War I, five of whom were killed in action.[57] No separate figures are available, but Western Australian Nyungar soldiers also fought and died on the Western Front, for a freedom in which they had no share. Five members of the Kickett family, of Quairading, fought in France, and one was killed in action. In August 1918, John Kickett appealed to H. Griffiths, the local Member, to intercede on behalf of his children, who had been prevented from attending the State school. 'Sir', he wrote, 'I cannot see why my children could not attend [the school] here at Quairading. My People are fighting for Our King and Country.' Kickett's plea was rejected.[58]

Enormous difficulties were faced also by those who returned with socially unacceptable disabilities, such as mental breakdown or venereal disease. Medical specialists of the day were undoubtedly influenced by Social Darwinist theory, which assumed that inherent weakness, rather than exposure to some of the most appalling and stressful circumstances ever known to humankind, was the cause of mental breakdown. In his medical history of the war, A.G. Butler stated that it would

> probably be no exaggeration to affirm that the medical 'problem' of nervous breakdown — at least as seen in the Great War — is only 20 per cent a war problem and *80 per cent a problem of war's aftermath.*

After pondering the 'gravity' of a situation in which 'no effective method has been evolved of preventing the degradation of *potential* neurosis into *actual* neurosis', Butler envisaged the 'insidious onset' of 'unconscious malingering' among returned servicemen in the declining economic circumstances of the nation. He asserted that mental neurosis could be prevented in future conflicts by emphasizing the creation of individual and national character; that is, by developing esprit de corps, or more particularly the 'Anzac or AIF spirit', as 'a morale likely to be proof against most of the shocks of war and peace'. He concluded that 'the *prevention* of psychic breakdown in the normally constituted man is obviously far more important than the patching up of psychic misfits'. Furthermore, Butler stated that the consensus of opinion among Medical Officers of the Repatriation Department was that 'war *per se* cannot be regarded as a "cause" of those various marked states — diseases — that make up the content of "major" psychiatry'. He cited the opinion of C.K. Parkinson, Senior Medical Officer of the Repatriation Commission in Sydney, that

> ...examination of practically all ex-soldiers in New South Wales suffering from insanity or major neurotic disorders, convinces me

that the essential factor in their disablement is a constitutional psychopathic personality.[59]

One of the more perceptive comments from a contemporary medical practitioner was made by Dr F.B. Bird, who stated before a 1918 Senate Select Committee on the Effect of Intoxicating Liquor on Australian Soldiers, 'I think the majority [of returned service-men] are not in their ordinary frame of mind'. Bird advocated the closing of public houses, for he believed that alcohol merely exacerbated the problems of repatriation.[60] Despite his remarks concerning 'psychopathic personality', Butler recognized that the majority of so-called 'shell shock' cases resulted from exhaustion and the constant stress of battle, especially at Pozières, which he described as 'the worst bombardment that ever fell on Australian troops'.[61] Similarly, in a more recent study, Lindstrom has commented:

> [The term] 'shell-shock'...gives a false picture of the nature of stress in war, for it ignores, by the implication of a sudden, singular, violent causal event, the importance of time and accumulated previous experience on a soldier's mind.[62]

It is difficult to estimate the number of 'shell-shocked' soldiers who had returned to Western Australia by the end of the war; nor how many of those who were committed to an institution for the insane remained there indefinitely. Butler estimated that the number of Australian wounded 'shell shock' cases on the Western Front for the years 1916 to 1918 was 1,624. Categories such as 'gassed', 'prisoner of war', and — among the non-battle casualties — 'sick', 'accidentally injured' and 'self-inflicted wounds' no doubt hid other cases.[63]

The Claremont Hospital for the Insane records state that the institution admitted only twenty-two 'military personnel' between June 1917 and December 1920, including Martin O'Meara VC. Of these, only three were 'discharged', eight were transferred to Stromness, a home for 'neurotic cases', and one died. The fate of the remaining ten was not recorded, although it seems likely that they remained at Claremont at least until the end of 1920. Only one patient's insanity was attributed to 'shell shock', and one other was recorded as suffering from the 'strain of active service'. Causes were not stated in most cases, or were recorded as 'unknown'.

Some of the individual case notes, however, give a fuller indication of stress caused by active service. One patient had been in the trenches in France for a week before being wounded in the left knee, after which he 'became strange in manner'. Another who suffered from 'delusions', believing himself to be the Acting Commandant at Karrakatta Barracks, was discharged after undergoing treatment for three months. Yet another had served in Gallipoli, Egypt and France, been 'blown up' at Hooge, and been sent to England, suffering from 'shell shock'. His behaviour was described as 'suspicious', 'delusional', 'resentful' and 'morose'. Five of the patients were classed as being 'suicidal' on admission. The most disturbing behaviour was exhibited by a man whose right leg had been amputated at the thigh. This patient persisted in 'shovelling excretia [sic]' into his wound.[64]

Conditions were poor, indeed appalling, at Claremont, and it is difficult to imagine that inmates would have benefited from their time there. Shortly before the end of the war, Ben Jones, the Labor Member for Fremantle, moved that a Royal Commission of Inquiry be set up. Instead, a Select Committee of the Legislative Assembly was appointed, headed by W.C. Angwin, and with Legislative Assembly Members Angelo, Broun, Jones and Stubbs as committee members. They reported on 11 November 1919, the first anniversary of the Armistice, after holding twenty-two meetings and conducting fifty-five interviews with members of staff and ex-patients. The Select Committee made eight recommendations, including that members of staff who had been dismissed during the lock-out of mid-1919, after defying the isolation rule that had been established during an influenza outbreak (see Chapter 5), be reinstated as vacancies occurred; that food for patients be 'more varied'; that some patients be allowed greater freedom; and that additional attendants be placed on duty at night.[65] While these recommendations, if implemented, undoubtedly would have made small improvements, they would scarcely have affected many of the internees. The hospital was said to be accommodating 400 or 500 patients in excess of its capacity.[66] Yet conditions deteriorated even further.

W.E. Courthope, a solicitor from Goomalling, was confined at Claremont from July 1918 until May 1920. Following his release, he published a pamphlet discussing the facts of his case and the conditions he had witnessed at the hospital, including the brutal treatment of returned soldiers. Courthope alleged that Private Martin O'Meara VC was kept tied down in a 'torturing strait-jacket' for fourteen and a half hours of each day, and that he did not receive any treatment. This was also alleged by an ex-patient who was interviewed by the Select Committee. He claimed that O'Meara was put in a straitjacket at 4.30 p.m. every day and not released until 11.00 a.m. the following day, because there was only one attendant on the ward at night.[67] Courthope claimed that another soldier, Palmer, was 'thrown violently to the ground and heavily knelt on' when he refused to obey orders. Others were said to have been dragged along the floor, punched, thrown heavily and kneed in the stomach. Courthope alleged that Sergeant Jack Boles had died from internal injuries after his ribs were broken by the warders.[68]

The number of psychiatric cases still receiving either temporary or permanent institutional care in 1920 averaged from fifty to sixty. On 1 October of that year, the forty-bed Stromness Hospital for 'Mentals' had twenty-two patients, while the seventy-five-bed Kalamunda Convalescent Home for sufferers of 'war neuroses' averaged thirty-three patients daily.[69] Shell shock was also prevalent among returned soldiers in the community. H.E. Bolton, the President of the Perth RSL, attempted to prevent the firing of a seventeen-gun salute to welcome the new Governor, Sir Francis Newdegate, in 1920, arguing that the salute could not do anyone any good but would do considerable harm to shell-shocked soldiers.[70]

Those servicemen who succumbed to mental illness were accused of weakness, and, if Courthope's allegations were true, some of the severe cases were treated with callous brutality, but the sufferers of venereal disease were subject to far greater scorn and social ostracism. Severe military punishments, such as forfeiting pay during any period of absence from duty occasioned by venereal disease, failed to curb the problem, even though such forfeiture was written in the soldier's pay book. Many a soldier 'lost' his pay book in order to prevent his family discovering his condition. In 1918, punishment was brought into line with the British practice of cutting pay by 2s 6d per day. The policy of returning to Australia every serviceman with venereal disease ceased in October 1915.[71]

Legislation enacted in 1916 made it compulsory for sufferers of venereal disease to notify the medical authorities of their condition.

The Commissioner of Public Health, Dr Atkinson, expressed concern at the disproportionate number of male sufferers (507 as compared to fifty-six females), but he attributed the discrepancy in numbers merely to female reluctance to report such a condition. Fewer than half of the syphilis cases had contracted the disease less than ten years before; therefore, returned servicemen did not account entirely for the disproportionate numbers. Health Department statistics revealed 175 cases among the military forces, but these presumably were still in the services, rather than returned and demobilized men.[72] The setting up of the National Council to Combat Venereal Disease, formed in Western Australia in 1918, with four women among its eleven members, reflected increased social awareness of venereal disease.[73] This was also reflected elsewhere in Australia; for example, in New South Wales, as early as 1915, the State Government set up a Select Committee to investigate the prevalence of venereal disease in the community.[74]

An increase in the divorce rate appears to have been another result of repatriation. Petitions for nullity of marriage received in the Supreme Court in Western Australia rose from seventy-nine in 1918 to 145 in 1919, and remained high in the following years. The number of decrees absolute granted rose from twenty-three in 1918 to 121 in 1919, with high figures being maintained during the first half of the 1920s. In the 1921–25 period, Western Australia had the third highest divorce rate in Australia.[75] The increased number of divorces resulted, to some extent, from changes to the relevant legislation. In 1911, the Divorce Act had been extended to include desertion, drunkenness, conviction for crime, lunacy, and adultery by the husband as causes for dissolving a marriage. A 1919 amendment to the Act, to bring it into line with that of New South Wales, provided two further grounds for divorce: restitution of conjugal rights[76] (formerly punishable by imprisonment), and 'ante-nuptial' incontinence; that is, where a husband discovered that his spouse was pregnant to another man or a where a man was responsible for the pregnancy of a woman, other than his intended wife, immediately preceding his marriage. The amendment also extended the provisions concerning insanity. The Divorce Registers of the Perth Supreme Court reveal that by far the most common causes of divorce during and immediately after the war were desertion and adultery. Bigamy was rarely given as a reason for divorce, and other grounds were uncommon.[77]

In Victoria, the 1915 Marriage Act made it easier for a woman to obtain a divorce on the grounds of desertion. Although the percentage of female divorce petitioners dropped from around 55 per cent in 1918 to just above 40 per cent in 1919, it rose steeply again in 1921–22. The situation in Western Australia was similar, with the number of petitions lodged by women rising from 45 per cent (sixty-seven out of a total of 148) in 1919, to 55 per cent (seventy-four out of 133) in 1923.[78] Without further research, it is impossible to ascertain the extent to which the increase in female petitioners is an indication of social changes brought about by the war. It seems evident, however, that the 1919 alterations to existing divorce laws were in response to the high number of marital breakdowns, caused by the traumas of lengthy separation and the added strain of mental or physical disability upon the husband's return.

Although these legislative reforms made divorce easier to obtain, thus granting women more freedom than they had previously enjoyed, it cannot be argued that the experience of war was normally a liberating one. Women who had worked during the war were expected to give up their jobs so that 'diggers' could be employed. Outraged public opinions were expressed in the Western Australian press when women, rather than making way for soldiers, were actually seen to be taking 'their' jobs. In October 1919, even that radical champion of the oppressed, the *Fremantle Herald*, drew attention to a 'scandal' at the Fremantle Base Hospital, where women were said to be replacing 'diggers' as cooks and other workers. While declaring emotionally that soldiers were being 'thrown on the scrap heap', the newspaper did not consider the irony of its own stance that women, instead, be ousted from jobs in favour of returned servicemen.[79] The social consequences of the Great War, therefore, embraced many areas of life in the postwar community, and, while women and children had not undertaken active service themselves, they found their lives radically altered.

The rise in divorces was accompanied, perhaps surprisingly, by a decline in crime statistics. In 1916, 9,245 males and 2,796 females were charged with an offence, as compared to 6,883 males and 755 females in 1919. The 1916 figures were far higher than in any subsequent year until 1926. A sharp decline in the number of females charged before the courts after the end of the war suggests that the stress of war and the absence or death of partners were factors of greater significance in female criminal activity than, for example, unemployment was.[80]

The absence of violent crime by returned soldiers after the war conflicts with the situation in wartime, when there had been incidents involving servicemen destroying property and breaking up meetings. Several historians have linked the phenomenon of 'digger violence' with the fear of Bolshevism.[81] Violent behaviour by groups of returned soldiers, whose political sympathies were often unknown, triggered fears in the community that a Bolshevik revolution was being engineered by militants and would be carried out by ex-servicemen who were trained in methods of warfare. The military authorities in the Eastern States believed that there was a very real possibility of a revolution breaking out even before the end of the war. In September 1918, Detective Moore, of the Sydney Criminal Investigation Branch, reported to the Commander of Military Forces in New South Wales that, according to a 'trusted informant':

> ...the Australian Labor Party [are] patiently watching [for] their opportunity for a favourable stage of public affairs when a revolution could be brought about with some measure of success, with the object of overthrowing the existing state of Government, and fulfilling the dream of the extreme industrialists in their movement to do away with the capitalist class and obtain possession of all the means of production for themselves...When the time appears ripe, a seizure of arms and ammunition would be arranged, particularly of machine guns, with the help of the soldiers.[82]

Similarly, the possibility of labour militants 'capturing' the vote of returned soldiers was stressed by the Melbourne Military Censor, who concluded a January 1919 report on the Workers Industrial Union[83] with this ominous warning:

> There are roughly 200,000 men to return within the next 18 months, and it will be in that time that the life or death of the One Big Union Scheme will be decided. The writer has an uncanny feeling that this is more than coincidence.[84]

Another Military Intelligence report stated that part of the task of the Sydney-based One Big Union Propaganda League was to link returned soldiers in Queensland with the industrial movement. The report quoted one Corporal Murphy, ex-AIF, as saying at a Propaganda League meeting:

I am for revolution, and when could we have a better opportunity than the present, when all the soldiers are returning and they are trained men. The soldiers are waking up to the fact that they have been exploited. This war is only a war for Capital and Territory. I am glad conscription was defeated, and I was never so pleased as when I heard my brother, who was in charge of a battalion, ordering his men to vote 'No'.[85]

In actuality, despite the majority of the AIF coming from the working classes, few were attracted to socialist movements, including Bolshevism; the vast majority supported conservative, anti-labour organizations such as the RSL.[86] Furthermore, conservative powers were actively advocating the recruitment of returned soldiers to combat socialism. At a secret conference in New South Wales on 18 January 1919, attended by Acting Prime Minister William Watt and the Police Commissioners of New South Wales and Victoria, the Chief of General Staff, J.G. Legge, suggested reorganizing the military forces in order to combat 'revolutionary action'. Legge thought that the most appropriate type of fighting force would be small groups of 'picked men' with machine guns, and 'a few aeroplanes with improvised bombs'. He also advocated recruiting 'special mounted constables'.[87] Although Legge did not specifically state that these recruits should be returned soldiers, there seems little doubt that he referred to men with military training in combat zones. His suggestions were not, however, acted upon by the New South Wales Government.

So-called 'digger violence' was not unique to Australia.[88] A particularly Australian phenomenon, however, was the influence of the RSL in postwar society, and the important role that it played in sanctioning 'digger violence'. Even more than elsewhere in Western Australia, the RSL enjoyed a high profile as the guardian of law and order on the goldfields. In 1919, it was involved in enrolling ex-servicemen as special constables to combat industrial unrest. These special constables were regarded by the government, the military and employers as loyal citizens who were assisting in the upholding of law and order; by comparison, striking union members were, by definition, 'disloyal', even after the crisis of war had passed. Thus, serious attempts were made to marginalize the labour movement. Chapter 5 discusses several examples of this attitude in connection with strikes during the years 1919 and 1921. The fact that these same law-abiding returned soldiers often played a prominent role in such 'unauthorized' violence as the Kalgoorlie race riots did not alter their position as 'loyalists' in the eyes of the authorities or employers.

The dangerously volatile state of Kalgoorlie in 1919 is evident in the fact that race riots began when a group of footballers abused five Italians (three of whom were women) entering a cafe in Hannan Street, on the night of 11 August. In the ensuing brawl, one of the footballers, Thomas Northwood, was stabbed in the buttocks with a kitchen knife and later died from loss of blood. All the ingredients were present to create mob hysteria. The dead man was a returned soldier who, it was readily assumed, had been prepared to sacrifice his life for his country. Furthermore, he was stabbed from behind — regarded as being 'a cowardly attack' — using a weapon that was 'unacceptable in a British community as a means of settling disputes'. The Police Commissioner in Perth advised Inspector Duncan of the Kalgoorlie police to 'use every lawful means to compel the Italians to leave Kalgoorlie and Boulder' and to swear in returned soldiers as special constables 'for the purpose of protecting life and property'.[89]

On the afternoon following the stabbing, the RSL held a meeting and demanded that the assailant be surrendered or they would drive all the Italians out of town. After the meeting, a crowd of returned soldiers and civilians forced its way into every Italian owned or licensed hotel in the centre of town, consumed alcohol without paying for it, and smashed furniture and windowpanes. In most cases, lives were not endangered, but Orsatti, the licensee of the All Nations Hotel in Hannan Street, produced a pistol and would have been kicked to death by the mob but for the brave action of Sergeant Fortescue of the Kalgoorlie police.[90] Italian hotels in Boulder were also attacked, by a 2,000-strong crowd. No arrests were made in either disturbance. Inspector Duncan found that neither returned servicemen nor civilians were prepared to administer law and order impartially while there was the chance of beating up the hated Italians, and he realized that arrests would merely divert mob violence to the police, as it had when a man was arrested at Boulder. He admitted that 'unruly members' of the RSL were 'principally responsible' for the riot.[91]

The RSL also featured prominently in the industrial unrest of November 1919, which is described in Chapter 5. An ALF deputation to the Premier alleged that

> The Soldiers' Institute was the Headquarters of many of the special
> constables, who stacked their arms there. It was called the war
> office. The arms were supplied by the Police to an Institute which
> should have had no part in the dispute at all.

Labor politician A.E. Green MLA alleged that about 700 Italians
had left the goldfields because the Kalgoorlie RSL had made it
unsafe for them to remain there. Green also asserted that two secret
societies were in existence, whose members (presumably returned
soldiers) went armed because they feared trouble with the miners
and the Italians. Another Labor Member, S.W. Munsie, stated that
the industrial trouble would 'not have lasted a day if the Kalgoorlie
[RSL] had kept their noses out of it'.[92]

Relations between returned soldiers and the labour movement
worsened during 1920. At a meeting of the EGDC, on 20 December,
a resolution was passed requesting the Crown Law Department to
'put an end to the disgraceful outrages now being perpetrated on
citizens of this district by mobs of organized hoodlums whom the
police take no steps to check'. Furthermore, the council resolved
that, should no action be taken, the organized labour movement
would arm itself and drill 'for protection against the present
intolerable state of affairs'. The incident that provoked this resolution was the alleged terrorizing of two railway employees by a
group of returned soldiers. Since the attack, the men had been
unable to perform their duties and subsequently had been dismissed by the Railways Department. At the same EGDC meeting,
a resolution was passed to organize a

> squadron of riflemen for the purpose of establishing a Peace or
> Vigilant Society with the object of suppressing the swashbuckling
> pests now posing as patriots and loyalists and from whom no
> decent citizen is safe.

The council further resolved to appoint a five-member committee
with 'experience in forming and training platoons'.[93]

The EGDC Minutes maintained an extraordinary silence on the
matter thereafter, with two brief exceptions. At the first meeting in
January 1921, an objection was raised, unsuccessfully, to a line in
one of the resolutions, which referred to the soldiers being 'aided
and abetted by concurring and conducive police'. And in April, a
resolution was passed that the question of military training be referred to the WA Trades Union and Labor Congress.[94] Meanwhile,

some RSL members continued verbal and physical aggression, provoking Frank Worthy, Secretary of the EGDC, to write in May 1921 to the ALF Secretary in Perth:

> I particularly desire to urge your serious attention to the palpable condonation by the Civil Authorities here of the disgraceful outrages on personal liberty by public threat and intimidation by a section of the RS[L] and a gang of filibustering hooligans who are inciting and using them for personal purposes...No body of persons can indefinitely brook the public taunting, challenges, and threats of rifles and machine guns which these hoodlums are publicly indulging in, even at the Town Hall, and under the Chairmanship of the Mayor of the Town.[95]

His last reference was to the formation of an Empire Loyalty League, at a well-attended meeting in the Kalgoorlie Town Hall on 11 May. The league's aim was 'to protest against the disloyal utterances and actions of certain persons in the Eastern States, as reported in the Press, and again assert our unswerving loyalty to the British Empire'. The 'disloyal utterances' in question had occurred at a May Day demonstration in Sydney, at which the Union Jack was torn to shreds and trampled on. At the Kalgoorlie meeting, where the local RSL was well represented, the Mayor announced that he was entirely in accord with the sentiments of the motion protesting against 'disloyal utterances', and said that his blood 'boiled to think of the grand old flag being insulted in Sydney'.

Harry Axford, President of the Kalgoorlie RSL, said that the league

> banded together for the preservation of loyalty and law and order...Men who had gone to fight on foreign shores were prepared to bear arms for freedom and liberty in their own country. He wished he could be in Sydney next Sunday with the soldiers who were going to give a lesson to forces of disloyalty and disorder...Nothing would please him better than to use a machine gun against the enemies of the state.[96]

Others who contributed to the discussion were Tracey, another RSL member, who declared that the flag 'of Empire' had been burned by 'those creatures who owed their existence to it...[who] were not men and proved they were not by not going to the war', and Councillor J. Reid, who remarked that 'the sooner the people of Kalgoorlie, of Western Australia and of the Commonwealth woke up to the danger the better it would be for the whole community'. According to Councillor Schwan, there were over 900 returned soldiers in Kalgoorlie, and 'every man should join up with the League'.[97] The motion was passed unanimously, as was another motion expressing alarm at the 'disloyal propaganda' preached in Australia, and urging the State Government to legislate for its suppression. The meeting concluded with the singing of the National Anthem and 'Rule Britannia', and rounds of cheers for the Union Jack and Billy Hughes.

An Empire Loyalty League was also formed in Perth, with businesspeople and employers prominent on its committee.[98] According to Harold Boas, an architect who was active in conservative politics, the Empire Loyalty League arose out of a great concern that a 'disloyal element [was] creeping into the life of Australia'.[99] The league's President, Frank Moss, challenged the citizens of Western Australia to ask themselves four questions:

> Is not the maintenance of the Empire the very lifeblood of Australia? Do I believe in the maintenance of the Empire? Is a growing spirit of disloyalty being manifested among sections of the population? Is such disloyalty harmful to the maintenance of the Empire?

The 'truthful' answers to these questions would, Moss asserted, determine the necessity of an Empire Loyalty League.[100] At the well-attended inaugural meeting, Moss also referred to the workers' May Day demonstrations in Sydney, which he regarded as an expression of disloyalty to the Empire. Despite claiming that the league was non-sectarian and non-political, he welcomed the support of the Protestant Federation — a group whose main objective was the fostering of anti-Catholicism — and he attacked the activities of the labour movement.[101]

In its close identification with the Empire Loyalty League, as certainly as by its actions on the goldfields, the RSL placed itself firmly on the side of the 'loyalists' and against the organized labour movement. The extent to which its politics influenced the league's membership is unknown, yet it is evident that, from 1921, RSL membership fluctuated. The General Secretary tried to explain the drop in numbers as owing to the dilatoriness of several branches in sending in returns. In 1922, the membership numbered 3,811, about 1,500 fewer than in the previous year, and by 1923 it had dropped even further to 3,558.[102] Doubtless, the decline in membership was influenced by external considerations. As the years of peacetime went by, bringing new relationships and stresses — marriage, children, mortgages — some returned service personnel may have felt less keenly the need to seek out their fellows, or had less time to do so.

Conversely, the public activities of many leading citizens continued to involve expressions of loyalty and remembrance, such as the Perth Club's Annual Dinner in honour of the Empire. The State Governor, Sir Francis Newdegate, was guest of honour at this dinner several times. J.J. Talbot Hobbs, the Perth architect and distinguished soldier who had risen to the rank of Lieutenant General while serving with the AIF in France, frequently represented the RSL on such occasions. Talbot Hobbs's services were recommended to Newdegate by General Birdwood, who wrote of him, '[He is] brave, straight through and *absolutely loyal*, and if you should want anything done in which he could help, I can recommend him to you most strongly'.[103] Talbot Hobbs and Newdegate kept Birdwood informed of local affairs, such as the 'troubles' among the returned soldiers, to which the latter alluded in a 1920 letter — probably referring to the RSA split.[104] The Governor and the Lieutenant General became firm friends. Both believed passionately in the British Empire and perpetuated the myth that it was 'knit together only with the ties of love and affection', rather than by the determination of those who benefited most from maintaining its military and commercial structures: merchants, shippers, mining magnates, pastoralists, brewers. The efforts of such men consolidated British rule world-wide, and it was sanctified by the sermons of leading Protestant clerics such as Archbishop Riley:

> We have built up, *almost without knowing it*, a vast Empire, not by conquests which had held down a defeated foe, but an Empire knit together by a common origin, common laws, common institutions...[105]

While Newdegate was sufficiently impressed with this sermon to retain a copy of it in one of his scrapbooks, his private correspondence shows that he was well aware of the real forces that bound the Empire together. These consisted, in part, of gathering around him the 'right men' to keep him informed of events in the community.

He maintained strong links with the RSL throughout his four years in Western Australia, attending many of the league's social functions and two State Conferences. The league reciprocated by holding a farewell evening for the Governor before his temporary departure to England in March 1922.[106]

Between 1917 and 1921, the labour movement maintained an aloofness from many such 'patriotic' functions. The Labor Party platform had long included the abolition of the post of Governor and of the Legislative Council[107], and the ALF State Executive declined to be represented in an official capacity at any of the functions connected with the Prince of Wales's visit in 1920. At about this time, Fred Grieve, the Secretary of the Eastern Agricultural District Council (EADC) of the ALF, had informed his affiliated unions and councils that sugar was being sold for an exorbitant price and 'only ladelled [sic] out like miserable rations, and in many cases large families (mostly children) have to forego it on their principle food, PORRIDGE'. He claimed that the local cooperative, owned by 350 Northam railway men, was being starved out by large companies such as Colonial Sugar Refineries, and that five other industrial cooperatives were in a similar situation. Perhaps the ALF members felt too keenly the irony of dining at Government House on 'Oysters Parisienne, *Consomme à la Julienne* and Saddle of Lamb with Red Currant Jelly', while the children of the poorer rural families lived on sugarless porridge. The ALF also declined to join the Empire Loyalty League on the grounds that Labor's policies 'clearly denote that the ALP is a loyal party'.[108]

Returned soldiers were, of course, on both sides of the social and political divisions created by the experiences of the Great War. Extremes of these divisions can, indeed, be seen within one family, the Axfords. The deeply conservative politics of Harry Axford, President of the Kalgoorlie RSL, were not shared by his brother, Thomas Leslie Axford, a Victoria Cross winner. The brothers were both present during the industrial unrest on the goldfields in November 1919 (see Chapter 5), but while Tom Axford supported the AWU miners, Harry Axford sided with the Nationalists.[109]

The social, economic and political impacts of repatriation and the role of the RSL on the Western Australian community, therefore, were considerable.

F.K. Crowley remarked that 'the horrible carnage of war was soon forgotten' in Australia's western third. Yet it was not so. As overseas and in the rest of Australia, the Great War cast long shadows on life and in literature. The British mourned a 'lost generation' of men whom they believed would have been the 'flower of their race': the natural leaders, politicians, philosophers and scholars who had perished on the battlefields of France.[110] Even those servicemen who returned physically or mentally unimpaired faced the problems of re-entering a greatly changed community. One of those changes was the increased militancy of the labour movement, a world-wide phenomenon that was profoundly to affect the structure of society in Western Australia, as elsewhere.

Corporal Thomas Axford VC
The Axford family exemplified the deep social and political divisions of postwar Western Australia. Tom Axford VC was an AWU miner; his brother Harry, President of the Kalgoorlie RSL, supported 'scab' miners in the November 1919 strike on the goldfields.
[Australian War Memorial, P1383/11]

163

1   S. Welborn, *Lords of Death: A People, a Place, a Legend*, Fremantle, 1982, pp. 139–144.

2   J. Bassett, *Guns and Brooches. Australian Army Nursing from the Boer War to the Gulf War*, Melbourne, 1992, pp. 97–98; V. Hobbs, *But Westward Look: Nursing in Western Australia 1829–1979*, Perth, 1980, pp. 65–66.

3   A.G. Butler, *Official History of the Australian Army Medical Services, 1914–18*, 3 vols, Canberra, 1943, vol. III, Table 14; Welborn, *Lords of Death*, p. 160.

4   The Returned Services League was referred to by several different titles and acronyms in the early years of its existence. Here, the initials RSL have been used throughout to refer to the main body, the Returned Soldiers' and Sailors' Imperial League of Australia, and RSA for the splinter group, the Returned Sailors' and Soldiers' Association, which broke away to form a separate organization in 1919.

5   F.K. Crowley, *Australia's Western Third: A History of Western Australia*, London, 1960, p. 198.

6   A. Ellis, The Impact of War and Peace on Australian Soldiers, 1914–20, BA Hons dissertation, Murdoch University, 1980, p. 28. The title of this chapter comes from this source.

7   R.G. Lindstrom, Stress and Identity: Australian Soldiers during the First World War, MA thesis, University of Melbourne, 1985, p. 145.

8   E.D. Scott, *Australia During the War: Vol XI of the Official History of Australia in the War of 1914–1918*, C.E.W. Bean (ed.), Sydney, 1936, pp. 828–830.

9   ibid., pp. 206–207. Appendix No. 12 lists 'Australian Patriotic Funds in the War of 1914–1918'. The Western Australian ones were listed as (p. 886): Red Cross Funds; Soldiers' Parcels & Packets; War Patriotic Funds; YMCA War Work; Sick & Wounded (Australia Day); Victoria League (French Comforts) and (Other); Belgian Relief Funds; Queen Carnival; Ugly Men's Voluntary Workers' Association; War & Unemployment Distress Relief; Sailors and Soldiers Welcome Funds, etc.; War Munitions Co. of WA; Motor Ambulance, etc.; Sandbag Fund; Civil Servants War Distress Fund, etc.; Other Funds (not specified). The total amount raised was £1,188,650.

10   ibid., p. 838; Butler, *Official History*, vol. III, pp. 791–792.

11   'List of Patriotic Associations to which Soldiers' Wives may Apply for Financial Assistance in Case of Distress, 20.7.17', State Executive of the ALF (WA)—Correspondence Files (hereafter SE Correspondence), File 113. For wage rates, see, for example, *Pocket Year Book of Western Australia, 1919*: milliner, £1 10s; tailoress, £1 15s; dressmaker, £1 12s.

12   'List of Patriotic Associations.'

13   Butler, *Official History*, p. 960, Table 63. The Australian pension represented 49.7 per cent; New Zealand, 48.1 per cent.

14   *Department of Repatriation — Repatriation Commission Annual Report for the Year Ended 30 June 1921*, War Pensions — Summary, p. 55.

15   J.R. Duncan, A History of the Returned Services League in Western Australia, unpublished research essay, 1962, held at Anzac House, St Georges Terrace, Perth, pp. 55 ff.

16   Studies of the Soldier Settlement Schemes in the Eastern States have shown the importance of the 'agrarian myth' — the belief that Australia's future lay in primary production — and of the fear that Bolshevism would quickly take root in the idle and discontented minds of the unemployed returned soldiers. Lake pointed to the fact that more emphasis was laid upon individual character — 'sobriety', 'industriousness', and 'honesty' being prized attributes — than upon farming experience. M. Lake, *The Limits of*

Hope: Soldier Settlement in Victoria, 1915–38, Melbourne, 1987, especially pp. 53–54; K. Fry, 'Soldier Settlement and the Australian Agrarian Myth After the First World War', *Labour History*, no. 48, May 1985, pp. 29–43.

17 WA Government, Department of Lands, *Soldier Settlement Guide*, State Archives of Western Australia, Acc. PR 11706.

18 See, for example, J. Slee, *Cala Munda: A Home in the Forest. A History of Kalamunda*, Kalamunda, 1979, p. 140.

19 Correspondence March–April 1916, SE Correspondence, File 193.

20 State Executive of the ALF (WA) — Minutes Books (hereafter SE Minutes), vol. 2, 21 January 1918.

21 The conference was attended by one representative from each of the Trades Halls (except Queensland) and from the Chambers of Manufacturers (except Tasmania); the Minister for Repatriation, Senator Millen; J. McNeill, representing the AWU; and the Chairman, J.B. Holme, Under Secretary for the Department of Labour and Industry in New South Wales.

22 SE Minutes, vol. 2, McCallum's Report on the Repatriation Conference, with Minutes of 4 March 1918; also 8 April 1918, 20 May 1918. Assistant Secretary, ALF, to Secretary, State War Council, 26 February 1918; Asst Secretary to Minister for Repatriation, 26 February 1918, SE Correspondence, File 193.

23 This included publishing letters from disgruntled ex-servicemen. See, for example, Craske to ALF, 4 May 1920, and reply, 2 July 1920, SE Correspondence, File 65. It was planned to publish Craske's letter in the *Westralian Worker*.

24 J. Robison and M. McNair, 'Armistice Day, 1918', in L. Layman and T. Stannage (eds), *Studies in Western Australian History X: Celebrations in Western Australian History*, April 1989, p. 47.

25 *Westralian Worker*, 1 August 1919.

26 R. Throssell, *My Father's Son*, Richmond, 1989, pp. 47, 71–77.

27 *The Anzac Book*, London, 1916; A. Chandler, 'Gallipoli', Writers and Artists of Western Australia, *Westralia Gift Book*, Perth, 1916, facing p. 4. See also B. Bennett, 'War Culture: The *Westralia Gift Book*', in Layman and Stannage, *Studies in Western Australian History X*, pp. 37–46.

28 H. Throssell, 'For Valour', Writers and Artists of Western Australia, *Westralia Gift Book*, pp. 5–11.

29 K.S. Prichard, *Intimate Strangers*, Sydney, 1981 edn, p. 25.

30 R. Throssell, *Wild Weeds and Windflowers: The Life and Letters of Katharine Susannah Prichard*, Sydney, 1982 edn, pp. 68–91.

31 Premier's Department File (hereafter PDF) 150/19.

32 'Report of the Repatriation Committee', n.d., SE Correspondence, File 193.

33 'Conference between Representatives of the Building Trades and Mr. Morrell, War Service Homes Commission, 13.1.20', SE Correspondence, File 193.

34 Chamber of Manufacturers to Repatriation Department, 2 December 1919, PDF 518/19; Sir Francis Newdegate Papers, on microfilm in the State Archives of Western Australia (hereafter Newdegate Papers), Acc. MF1541; Sir Francis Newdegate Scrapbooks, State Archives of Western Australia, Acc. 3297A (hereafter Newdegate Scrapbooks), vol. 2, 26 August 1920 (from *Daily News*).

35 Department of Repatriation to ALF, 25 August 1920, 'List of Vocational Training Schools', SE Correspondence, File 193. The trades taught included bricklaying, plastering, plumbing, panelbeating, blacksmithing, motor

mechanics, fitting and turning, french polishing and boot repairing.

36   RSL Papers (National Library of Australia, Acc. 6609), Series 3 Minutes, Verbatim Report of the Adelaide Congress 15 July 1919, pp. 6 ff, 31–34; box 95, Minutes of a Meeting of the Interstate Executive, 7 September 1917.

37   Duncan, A History of the RSL, pp. 6–17.

38   SE Correspondence, File 82.

39   *RSL Annual Report and Balance Sheet*, 1922, p. 3; Duncan, A History of the RSL, p. 13. See also McKernan, 'War', Table WR 129-138, Membership of the Returned Servicemen's League by State, 1918–1982, in V. Vamplew (ed.), *Australians: Historical Statistics*, Sydney, 1987. Membership for 1918 was listed as 5,400.

40   For a detailed account of these events, see B. Oliver, '"The Diggers' Association": A Turning Point in the History of the Western Australian Returned Services League', *Journal of the Australian War Memorial*, no. 23, October 1993, pp. 29–35.

41   *West Australian*, 10 December 1919.

42   O'Neill to McCallum, 9 April 1920, SE Correspondence, File 82.

43   Correspondence dated 13 May 1920, SE Correspondence, File 82.

44   Returned Soldiers' and Sailors' Labor League, *The Returned Soldiers and the Labor Movement*, Brisbane, 1919, especially pp. 1–5. A copy is held in the Mitchell Library, Sydney. See also SE Correspondence, File 82; R. Evans, *Loyalty and Disloyalty: Social Conflict on the Queensland Homefront, 1914–18*, Sydney, 1987, p. 151.

45   *NSW Parliamentary Debates, Second Series, 1919*, vols 75–78, pp. 476, 541, 547, 2260, 2344, 2476, 2478, 2667, 3379.

46   *Western Australian Parliamentary Debates* [hereafter *WAPD*], *1920*, vol. 2, p. 1525.

47   *RSL Annual Report and Balance Sheet*, 1924, State Archives of Western Australia, Acc. 369.2 RET, pp. 4–5.

48   G.D. Snooks, 'Development in Adversity, 1913 to 1946', in C.T. Stannage (ed.), *A New History of Western Australia*, Nedlands, 1981, p. 246, Table 7.6. Trade union unemployment was estimated at 6.3 per cent in 1920–21, 8.3 per cent in 1922–23, and 4.8 per cent in 1923–24. See also *Commonwealth of Australia — Census* [hereafter *Commonwealth Census*], *1921*, part XIV, Western Australia, pp. 1096–1099, which states that 7,671 males and 1,400 females were unemployed at the time of the census, and of these, 3,132 males and 420 females claimed the reason for unemployment was scarcity of work.

49   Commissioner of Pensions to McCallum, SE Correspondence, File 113.

50   Correspondence between Prime Minister and Clementson, 17 April 1919, 2 May 1919, SE Correspondence, File 113.

51   Correspondence, Parsons to McCallum, Parsons to District Paymaster, McCallum to Defence Department, September–November 1918, SE Correspondence, File 34.

52   McCallum to Deputy Commissioner of Military Pensions, 7 January 1919, SE Correspondence, File 113. Charlie McGregor may have been the 'MacGregor' referred to in PDF 302/21, who, with two other returned soldiers, visited the Acting Premier, Colebatch, on 26 February 1922. This MacGregor stated that, before he enlisted, he was earning £2 per day. When he returned, he was employed in the Railway Department, cleaning in the locomotive branch, but he had been retrenched under the system of 'last on, first off'. He had a wife and eight children whom he had to keep on a

fortnightly pension of £4 12s. As he suffered from heart disease and a bad leg, he could do only light work.

53   Department of the Army (WA), Intelligence Files, series I, no. 1/12/197, statements by Campbell and Fairhead; correspondence and medical reports in Department of the Army, Medical Files (hereafter Army Medical Files), 'Thomas Campbell' R14367 and 'A.L. Fairhead' C22980, held at the Australian Archives (Perth).

54   Clementson to Principal Medical Officer, 29 September 1917, and reply, 4 October 1917, Clementson to Commissioner of Pensions, 5 October 1917, and reply, 29 October 1917, SE Correspondence, File 115; SE Minutes, vol. 2, 7 January 1918, 4 February 1918; correspondence and medical reports in Army Medical Files, 'W.R. O'Keefe' PP863/1, M1125.

55   *Department of Repatriation — Repatriation Commission Annual Report for the Year Ended 30 June 1921*, p. 63, War Pensions, Table B; *Commonwealth Census, 1921*, part II, pp. 49–50. Population: Western Australia, 332,732; South Australia, 495,160; Queensland, 755,972. Western Australia's total of 8,373 incapacitated ex-servicemen was almost twice that of South Australia, and pensioners and dependants combined numbered only 365 fewer than in Queensland.

56   R.A. Hall, *The Black Diggers: Aborigines and Torres Strait Islanders in the Second World War*, Sydney, 1989, p. 1.

57   C. Mattingley and K. Hampton (eds), *Survival in Our Land: 'Aboriginal' Experiences in South Australia Since 1836*, Adelaide, 1988, p. 285.

58   Anon, Nyungar Soldiers, unpublished research essay; and Kickett to Griffiths, 29 August 1918, Education Department File, State Archives of Western Australia, Acc. 4259/14. The author is indebted to Dr Neville Green for this material. See also P. Biskup, *Not Slaves, Not Citizens: The Aboriginal Problem in Western Australia, 1898–1954*, St Lucia, 1969, p. 154.

59   Butler, *Official History*, p. 142 (emphasis added), pp. 143, 145 (emphasis in original).

60   Ellis, The Impact of War and Peace, pp. 56 ff; *The Senate Journals and Sessional Papers, 1917–18–19*, vol. I, p. 459.

61   Butler, *Official History*, p. 104.

62   Lindstrom, Stress and Identity, p. 53.

63   Butler, *Official History*, Table 41.

64   Department of Health (WA), Claremont Mental Hospital Register of Military Personnel, 1917–20, State Archives of Western Australia, Acc. 1120/27.

65   *Western Australia: Parliamentary Papers, Votes and Proceedings*, 1919, vol. 2, 'Report of the Select Committee of the Legislative Assembly on the Claremont Hospital for the Insane', pp. i–ix.

66   *WAPD*, vol. 58, 1918, pp. 369, 538.

67   'Report of the Select Committee of the Legislative Assembly on the Claremont Hospital for the Insane', pp. 58 ff.

68   W.E. Courthope, pamphlet, *Sensational Allegations Against Lunacy Authorities*, 1921, and circular, SE Correspondence, File 132. See also Courthope to Premier, 18 September 1914, PDF 303/194, vol. I.

69   *Department of Repatriation — Repatriation Commission Annual Report for the Year Ended 30 June 1921*, especially pp. 17, 31, 49.

70   *Daily News*, 12 February 1920.

71   Butler, *Official History*, pp. 154, 175, n. 28. See also pp. 174 ff. for a description of the venereal disease 'prison' at Langwarrin, Victoria.

72   *West Australian*, 21 October 1916.

73   *West Australian*, 23 July 1918. The National Council to Combat Venereal

Disease consisted of Dr Atkinson (Chair), Archbishops Riley and Clune, Mesdames Rischbieth, Rapley, Cowan and Jones, Professor Dakin, Messrs Fisher, Ryce and Nicholson.

74   D. Coward, The Impact of War on New South Wales. Some Aspects of Social and Political History, 1914–17, PhD thesis, Australian National University, 1974, p. 161.

75   *Statistical Register of Western Australia* [hereafter *Statistical Register*], *1924–25*, part VIII, pp. 4–5, Transactions in the Supreme Court during the Years 1916 to 1925 Inclusive; M. James, 'Double Standards in Divorce: Victoria 1890–1960', in J. Mackinolty and H. Radi (eds), *In Pursuit of Justice: Australian Women and the Law, 1788–1979*, Sydney, 1979, Table 1, p. 205; also *Commonwealth Census, 1921*, part VIII, pp. 510–517. The 1921 Census records a total of 610 divorced persons (316 males and 294 females) in Western Australia, in comparison with 384 divorcees in South Australia and 487 in Queensland.

76   The granting of divorce on the grounds of 'restitution of conjugal rights' seems to have been intended as a way out for women married to soldiers who, for mental or physical reasons, did not maintain the marriage relationship after returning from the war.

77   Supreme Court of Western Australia, Divorce Registers, State Archives of Western Australia, Acc. 3409, vols 5–7, 1914–24. In 1919, for example, out of 148 cases, only five divorces were applied for on the grounds of drunkenness, and the majority of petitioners were husbands; three for lunacy; and one each for bigamy, restitution of conjugal rights, and nullity of marriage, these three latter reasons all being petitioned for by women.

78   James, 'Double Standards in Divorce', pp. 203–210.

79   *Fremantle Herald,* 3 October 1919.

80   *Statistical Register, 1924–25*, part VIII, p. 6, Distinct Persons Brought before the Courts of Justice, 1916 to 1925. The number of women appearing before the courts dropped from 1,256 in 1918 to approximately 600 for each of the years from 1920 to 1923, and to 574 in 1924.

81   H. McQueen, *From Gallipoli to Petrov: Arguing with Australian History*, Sydney, 1984, pp. 3–7, and 'Shoot the Bolshevik! Hang the Profiteer! Reconstructing Australian Capitalism, 1918–21', in E.L. Wheelwright and K. Buckley, *Essays in the Political Economy of Australian Capitalism*, 5 vols, Sydney, 1980 edn, vol. 2, pp. 185–205; D.H. Rawson, 'Political Violence in Australia', part I, *Dissent*, Autumn 1968, pp. 18–27; Evans, *Loyalty and Disloyalty*, especially pp. 165 ff.

82   Moore to Commandant, 2nd Military District, 30 December 1918, Department of the Army (Victoria), Intelligence Files (hereafter Intelligence Files [Vic]), Australian Archives (Melbourne), no. 479/25/190.

83   The Workers Industrial Union was founded in Sydney in 1919 by Jock Garden, Secretary of the Trades and Labor Council.

84   'Censor's Intelligence Report, Sub. 3, 21 January 1919: Workers' Industrial Union: One Big Union', p. 5, Intelligence Files (Vic), no. V282.

85   'Extract from QB 339 — Week Ended 7 January 1919: One Big Union Propaganda League', Intelligence Files (Vic), no. V282.

86   Evans, *Loyalty and Disloyalty*, p. 154; see also Rawson, 'Political Violence', p. 19. For AIF enlistment by class, see Scott, *Australia During the War*, p. 874, Appendix 6, Occupations of the Members of the AIF: 'Tradesmen and Labourers', 211,704, the next largest group being 'Country', 57,430.

87   Legge to Minister for Defence, 20 January 1919, 'Bolshevism — Special Note for the Minister', Intelligence Files (Vic), no. 479/25/190.

88   See, for example, M. Ferro, *The Great War, 1914–18*, transl. N. Stone, London, 1973 edn, p. 224; and D.M. Kennedy, *Over Here. The First World War and American Society*, New York, 1980, p. 218, for descriptions of the reactions of European and American ex-servicemen.

89   See Police Minister to Italian Consul, 2 September 1919, Police Commissioner to Inspector Duncan, Police Department, File 3871/1919.

90   Sgt. Fortescue's Report, 13 August 1919, Police Department, File 3871/1919.

91   Duncan to Police Commissioner, 13 August 1919, 15 August 1919, Police Department, File 3871/1919.

92   'Deputation from State Executive, ALF, re. Kalgoorlie and Boulder Trouble, 18.11.19', PDF 398/19, pp. 4–6.

93   ALF (WA) — Minutes of the Eastern Goldfields District Council, State Archives of Western Australia, Acc. 1704A (hereafter EGDC Minutes), vol. 3, 20 December 1920.

94   EGDC Minutes, 3 January 1921, 11 April 1921.

95   SE Correspondence, File 78, 14 May 1921.

96   Clipping from the *Kalgoorlie Miner*, n.d., SE Correspondence, File 78.

97   Schwan was almost certainly either Albert or William Schwan, who were involved in the industrial unrest on the goldfields in 1919 and 1920. The name was sometimes spelt 'Schwann'.

98   The league's members included the pastoralists and company director Sir Edward Wittenoom; the mining magnate Claude de Bernales; Perth Chamber of Commerce member C.H. Salmon; and Harold Boas, an architect.

99   H. Boas, Bricks and Mortar, unpublished typescript, Harold Boas Papers, on microfilm in the State Archives of Western Australia, Acc. 881A, p. 156.

100 *Empire Loyalty League: Full Report of the Inaugural Meeting, 3 May 1921*.

101 ibid., p. 5.

102 See *RSL Annual Report and Balance Sheet* for the years 1922, 1923.

103 Birdwood to Newdegate, 9 March 1920, Newdegate Papers, Acc. MF 1541 (emphasis added).

104 Birdwood to Newdegate, 29 March 1920, Newdegate Papers.

105 Newdegate Scrapbooks, vol. 1, 3 June 1920, and a clipping of Riley's sermon, unidentified and n.d. (emphasis added).

106 Newdegate Scrapbooks, vol. 4, 8 March 1922.

107 See, for example, SE Minutes, vol. 2, 14 March 1917, 6 August 1919.

108 ALF to Newdegate, 2 June 1920, SE Correspondence, File 96. SE Correspondence, File 52, for Grieve's information; Newdegate Scrapbooks for the State Banquet Menu, 3 July 1920. SE Minutes, vol. 3, 19 May 1921, for comment on party's loyalty.

109 'Deputation from State Executive, ALF, re. Kalgoorlie and Boulder Trouble, 18.11.19', PDF 398/19.

110 See, for example, J.M. Winter, 'Britain's "Lost Generation" of the First World War', *Population Studies*, vol. XXI, 1977, part 3, pp. 449–466.

'The Modern Canutes'
The evil trio of capitalist, press and church feature once more in Rob Shaw's
post-'Bloody Sunday' comment on the ineptitude of conservative forces trying
to stem the tide of Bolshevism and the OBU movement, while denying the
wharf lumpers their basic rights. Ironically, the lumper is depicted as breaking
down the wall with the War Precautions Act (axe) — legislation that was
passed in order to maintain control over the people. From *Truth*, 10 May 1919.
[Courtesy Battye Library]

Chapter Five

SUFFERING FOR LABOUʀ

Overcoming National unionism

The Great War was over, yet the first year of 'peace' — 1919 — was to prove a troubled one for Western Australia. It opened with an influenza epidemic, and continued with a series of disputes, strikes and two riots. These problems were compounded by the growth of sectarianism, including the formation of anti-Roman Catholic societies such as the Protestant Federation.

The influenza epidemic began on the North American continent and was carried to Europe in 1917, by United States troops entering the war on the Allied side. It reached plague proportions in the unhygienic conditions of European trench warfare, and was carried back to Australia in 1918 and 1919 by the AIF. The epidemic created widespread panic in the community, taking 12,000 lives Australia-wide and over 500 in Western Australia.[1]

In February 1919, Hal Colebatch — Western Australian Minister for Health, and Acting Premier in the absence of Henry Lefroy — incurred federal displeasure by imposing separate State quarantine laws that involved isolating ships for seven days before they could be unloaded, and preventing interstate trains from entering Kalgoorlie. A ludicrous situation developed in which Lefroy, stranded in Melbourne by the epidemic, requested, unsuccessfully, that his deputy put on special trains to repatriate West Australians. On the other side of the Nullarbor, Colebatch steadfastly maintained that an adequate period of quarantine was necessary, to prevent influenza germs being carried into the State (which had experienced few influenza cases), even if it meant detaining the Premier in Melbourne.[2]

In mid-April, two ships, the *Dimboola* and the *Delta*, arrived in Western Australia carrying influenza cases. At about the same time, the Federal Government decided to assume control of all interstate traffic during the continuation of the epidemic, and to impose uniform quarantine regulations throughout Australia. Colebatch, now Premier after Lefroy's resignation, urged Acting Prime Minister William Watt to retain the regulation of seven days' quarantine for ships arriving in port, which the Federal Government had imposed at the beginning of the influenza outbreak. Watt refused, claiming that such a safeguard would mean ships lying idle for an 'indefinite period'. Colebatch received support from the Perth Chamber of Commerce and the FSA. However, when the Fremantle lumpers refused to unload the *Dimboola* for the very reason that it had not been adequately quarantined, the President of the Perth Chamber of Commerce, H.W.D. Shallard, stated publicly that their action was 'subversive to all constituted authority' and that 'the government should take immediate steps to up hold law and order'.[3]

The *Dimboola* incident was the culmination of almost two years of industrial injustice perpetrated by employers on the Fremantle Wharf — an injustice that, like the influenza plague, was directly linked to the war. In August 1917, the FLU had refused to load flour on a ship bound for the Dutch East Indies (now Indonesia), declaring that 'the ships should be used to feed our own people'. This strike coincided with the 1917 General Strike against 'speed-up methods' in New South Wales and Victoria, which involved railway workshop employees, transport workers, coal miners and waterside workers.[4] The Federal Government, regarding the situation as an emergency, immediately recruited workers from the ranks of the unemployed, non-unionists, and 'volunteers' ranging from university students to farmers, and formed 'National' unions, including the National Waterside Workers Union (NWWU). These workers — the 'Nationalists' — were often referred to as 'loyalists' or 'volunteers', because they were said to have volunteered to work for their country in place of the (disloyal) striking unionists.[5] Thus, a further division was created in labour ranks between 'Official Labor' and 'National Labor'.

NWWU workers were employed during the 1917 FLU strike at Fremantle. A heavily armed police force was assembled in the metropolitan area, in anticipation of violence, all leave for police officers was cancelled, and the Central Perth Police Station became an arsenal. It was an offence under the War Precautions Act to prevent or hinder the discharge, loading, coaling or despatch of shipping, or the performance of any industrial operation connected with shipping.[6] A lumper who attempted to prevent Nationalists from working on the wharf could be charged under this legislation. The lumpers, therefore, had few weapons with which to retaliate against legal might, although some businesses in Fremantle were declared 'black' because they were owned or patronized by NWWU members.[7] After striking for fourteen weeks, during which time they held out against the 'government, employers, press, pulpit and public' and, according to the Fremantle ALF, gave the 'finest exhibition of solidarity in Western Australian history', the FLU was forced to capitulate.[8]

In September, members of the Australasian Steamship Owners Federation (ASOF) met in Melbourne to determine the terms of settlement they would demand of the striking waterside workers. They adopted an eight-point plan, the main features of which were employer solidarity ('no domestic rules unless mutually agreed to'); preference to NWWU workers; payment of weekly wages instead of an hourly rate; and employment of foremen who were not members of the FLU or the Waterside Workers Federation.[9] These terms were forced upon waterside workers Australia-wide.

The use of Nationalist workers in other industries caused further disputes. In February 1918, at the Spencers Brook wheat bins, near Northam, AWU workers striking for a wage increase were paid off and replaced by Nationalists. The plate-layers and navvies working on the railway went on strike in sympathy, in compliance with an AWU resolution prohibiting work with Nationalists and 'scabs'. Financed by the AWU, the sacked employees remained at Spencers Brook until two of them were arrested for disorderly conduct after they had abused Nationalist workers, calling them 'bloody scabs' and attempting to attack them with fists and stones. The strike then disintegrated, and the outcome of the dispute is unknown.[10]

In the meantime, violent incidents occurred daily on the Fremantle Wharf. FLU members were bitter at being stood down in favour of Nationalists, and at the resulting hardships endured by their families. Police Inspector Sellenger reported, 'Bitterness will continue as long as the two forces work side by side. It is dangerous work with frequent accidents but now every fall is regarded with suspicion.' The Nationalists had their choice of jobs and did not always answer when called if they did not like the work on offer.[11] A considerable police presence was needed to ensure their protection on the wharves. Every vessel, whether cargo or passenger, had a uniformed constable on board during the entire time it was in harbour, and three other officers patrolling in the vicinity.[12] Despite the heavy policing, the National Employers' Federation complained to Colebatch, then Colonial Secretary, demanding that a police officer be stationed at every hatch while cargoes were being unloaded. The Police Commissioner advised Colebatch that this level of protection would necessitate the employment of more than sixty constables during twenty-four hours and that he would require very good grounds before such heavy expenditure could be justified. He commented further that on a recent visit to Melbourne, where similar industrial problems were being experienced, police were not called onto the wharves unless there was reason to believe that a breach of the peace was likely to occur.[13]

Nevertheless, Sellenger was obliged to advise Sergeant Simpson 'always to have some men in attendance at pick-up times, that is 7.45 a.m., 12.45 p.m. and 3.45 p.m., *no matter what may be transpiring elsewhere*'.[14] Violence was most likely to occur when the lumpers and Nationalists were in immediate competition as they waited to be called up for the day's work. A year after the strike, police were still being stationed at intervals from the railway station to the wharf, to protect the men going to and from work. The armistice that marked the end of World War I was celebrated by a midnight battle between the rival unions in High Street, Fremantle.[15]

Sailing into Fremantle Harbour in April 1919, the *Dimboola* provided the FLU with a long-awaited opportunity to redress the balance. Men who had seen their children go hungry for the past two years were in no mood to compromise. The lumpers not only refused to work on the ship until seven days after the infected cases had been removed, but they also prevented the Nationalists from working, by forming a picket line. By 23 April, some 800 lumpers and large numbers of women were assembling daily at the wharf, and a 2,000-strong procession had marched through the streets of Fremantle.[16]

Colebatch met with representatives from the Perth Chamber of Commerce and the labour movement.[17] He stressed the urgency of restoring business on the wharf, arguing that medical opinion discounted the lumpers' fears of contagion. The 'real enemy', in his view, was 'loss of trade' and 'unemployment'. He believed that the lumpers had only themselves to blame for their present situation, and that law and order must be maintained. The government, he said, would not renege on its obligation to the Nationalists. The employers' representatives continued to demand that the lumpers return to work under the existing conditions. They, too, maintained that the 'pledge' of employment made to the NWWU could not be broken. FLU President William Renton and Rowe, another union official, were equally adamant that the lumpers would not return to work unless the Nationalists were removed from the wharf. Thus, the meeting ended with no compromise from either side.

Colebatch advised the Acting Prime Minister that the police force was inadequate to protect the Nationalists if employers made any attempt to resume work. The wharves were open and, since the withdrawal of the Naval Guard at the end of the war, there was nothing to prevent large crowds from entering the work area. There was much local sympathy for the lumpers, and they were 'strongly supported by certain elements' of the returned soldiers. 'Beyond doubt', Colebatch concluded, any effort to force the position by employing Nationalists would 'provoke bloodshed and grave disorder by widespread industrial trouble'.[18] Watt, however, was as implacable as the employers. He informed Colebatch that both the State and Federal Governments were committed to the pledge they had given to the 'loyalist workers':

> [We] cannot permit [the] influenza epidemic to be used as a weapon to force alterations to existing working conditions. [It is] impossible to send any other ships to Fremantle until the difficulty is overcome. Responsibility does not rest with the Commonwealth Government; *it is a local dispute.*[19]

Colebatch, therefore, was under intense pressure from both the Commonwealth Government and several employers' groups. The Association of Employers of Waterside Labour, the Fremantle Harbour Trust and the State Steamship Service drew up a return-to-work agreement along the same lines as those decided by ASOF in 1917. On 25 April, Shallard advised the Premier that the Overseas Shipping Representatives Association in Sydney would omit Fremantle as a port of call for overseas steamers until the labour position was settled and 'the Nationalists who came to the assistance of the Government and people receive the protection and treatment they are entitled to'. A deputation of representatives from the WA Shipping Association, the Perth and Fremantle Chambers of Commerce, merchants, and the National Employers' Federation urged Colebatch to stand up to the lumpers.[20] On 28 April 1919, the ALF appointed a State Disputes Committee (SDC), to have State-wide control over the dispute. The committee comprised one member each from the Fremantle District Council, the Tally Clerks Union and the FLU; two from the State Executive; ALF President Alex Panton, and Secretary McCallum.[21]

This was a trial of strength. On the one hand, the lumpers were keen to exercise their power, and the *Dimboola* was merely an excuse; on the other, the government was committed to honouring its pledge. Pressure from the Federal Government and employers swiftly mounted around the unfortunate Colebatch until he was persuaded that force was the only viable course of action.

The situation was thus when Thomas Charles Edwards, a forty-one year old lumper, left his home on the morning of Sunday 4 May 1919, to join several hundred fellow FLU members on the Fremantle Wharf. Victorian-born Edwards had spent the past nine years in Western Australia. Married, with three daughters whose ages ranged from two to fourteen years, he had experienced much hardship since 1917. His friends later testified to his sympathy for the 'breadless' and his great desire 'for the betterment of those who had suffered so long in apparently hopeless despair'.[22] Edwards and his fellow lumpers were drawn to the wharf by the news that a party of employers, with volunteer labour, was erecting barricades so that the NWWU members could work on the ships unmolested by the FLU.

When Inspector Mann, of the Perth police, arrived at the scene at 9 o'clock, he found eighty foot police lined up in double formation, facing 'about 300 lumpers'. The lumpers were persuaded by police to leave the wharf, and mounted police threw a cordon across Cliff Street to prevent their re-entry.[23] As in 1917, all police leave had been cancelled some weeks prior to the riot, in anticipation of violence at Fremantle, and reinforcements had been brought in from the country.[24] Despite these precautions, the force was insufficient to stop a crowd of 600 to 700 lumpers re-entering the wharf when they saw launches arriving with volunteer workers. The lumpers began throwing iron bars and other missiles at the police. They also stoned the launches carrying the Premier and some members of the volunteer labour force. The crowd soon

Tom Edwards
Fremantle's martyred working-class hero died at the age of forty-one, of head
injuries incurred in the 'Bloody Sunday' riot on Fremantle Wharf, 4 May 1919.
During his funeral, workers throughout the State observed three minutes'
silence in his honour.
[Courtesy Maritime Union of Australia/Department of History,
University of Western Australia]

swelled to about 1,000 men, women and children, including several returned soldiers in uniform. Mann noticed a one-legged
returned man on crutches.

The battle for possession of the wharf went on for over an hour,
by which time the crowd had increased to three or four times its
previous size. Mann knew that his police could no longer hold the

people back. He and the other senior police officers — Inspector Sellenger, the Police Commissioner, and Chief Inspector McKenna —held a meeting at 'C' Shed, with two ALF officials, Alex McCallum and Ben Jones. After obtaining a guarantee from Colebatch that the lumpers would not be attacked while leaving the wharf, McCallum climbed the footbridge and urged the crowd to leave quietly. At this juncture, a car arrived with ammunition for the police and a sergeant began issuing cartridges to the foot constables. The Riot Act was also read. Remarkably, the angry lumpers did not immediately overwhelm the greatly outnumbered police force, a fact that attests to their genuine desire to remain non-violent and to the trust they placed in McCallum. The Chief Inspector quickly stopped the issue of cartridges, and the volunteer workers and police withdrew. The lumpers then left the wharf and held an impromptu meeting at the O'Connor Monument.[25]

The riot, which came to be known as 'Bloody Sunday', was over, although for the next few days, Fremantle was, to all intents and purposes, controlled by the lumpers. Twenty-six police and seven lumpers had been injured, including William Renton, and Tom Edwards, who sustained a fractured skull while going to Renton's aid. As Edwards lay dying in hospital, a series of riots involving returned soldiers and lumpers rocked Fremantle. On Monday night, a large crowd, several thousand strong, gathered between the Federal Hotel and the post office. Two constables had been set upon in High Street. The armed officers who went to their aid were also attacked and savagely beaten. Again, an extremely dangerous situation was defused by McCallum, who, with Renton and Fremantle Trades Hall Secretary Fred Baglin, drew the angry crowd off to a meeting at King's Theatre, where they managed to keep them entertained with speeches for the rest of the evening.[26]

Tom Edwards died on the night of 7 May. At midnight, Colebatch and Deputy Premier James Mitchell sent for the SDC. Colebatch then announced a new policy for the employment of waterside workers. According to the agreement, the Nationalists would be withdrawn from the wharf; the National Workers Bureau, which had been set up to select workers for each shift and to ensure that NWWU members received preference, was to be abolished; and lumpers would be selected for employment by the foreman, as had been the case prior to August 1917. There was to be no victimization on either side. Pending the Arbitration Court decision on the complaint currently before it, lumpers' and tally clerks' unions were to guarantee continuity of work under the existing award, and the guarantee was to be endorsed by the ALF on behalf of the unions. Any difference of opinion was to be settled by arbitration. The recognized period of quarantine would be seven days for all boats arriving at Fremantle. Government relief was to be given to urgent cases of distress among the lumpers' families[27], and Mrs Jane Edwards and her family would be compensated. The amount finally agreed upon for Mrs Edwards was £686.[28] Shortly afterwards, Colebatch resigned as Premier, and James Mitchell was appointed in his place.

Edwards was buried on Friday 9 May, in ceremonial splendour. Flags in Fremantle flew at half mast; even the vessels in the harbour dipped their ensigns. Throughout the State, public transport and work stopped for three minutes. Shops and hotels in Kalgoorlie closed as a mark of respect. The funeral procession was led by Renton, riding on a black horse, followed by a band playing the dead march. Then came the hearse and several thousand mourners. Every Labor politician who was in the State attended. Apart from a large number of metropolitan unionists, the representation from country centres, such as Westonia, Geraldton, Cue, Northam, Wyndham, Collie, Albany and Leonora, was impressive. The 1,000-strong FLU took pride of place in the procession, along with a group of 300 women, and the principal mourners, Edwards' wife and children and other close relatives.[29] Thus, with dignity and honour was buried a young man who, by a single action, had risen in a day from obscurity to the status of martyr and to immortality as a hero of the working-class movement in Fremantle.

The events that took place in Fremantle in May 1919 were of lasting significance. The industrial victories won by the lumpers as a result of 'Bloody Sunday' took immediate effect, and inspired waterside workers in Melbourne to attempt a similar action, on 21 May. It was mainly the enclosure of the Melbourne wharves and the size of the available police force that prevented the lumpers there from enjoying victory.[30]

Early in 1920, the events of 'Bloody Sunday' and Edwards' death were commemorated by the publication of a pamphlet entitled *The Fremantle Wharf Crisis, 1919*. In just over six months, 500 copies were sold, some to buyers as far away as Tasmania and

Port Pirie. Proceeds went towards building a home for Mrs Edwards and her children.[31] Further proof of the violence of emotions evoked by 'Bloody Sunday' was the Fremantle Harbour Trust's refusal to grant the ALF permission to erect a public memorial to Thomas Edwards, on the grounds that it 'would not be conducive to public harmony'. The Commissioners expressed the opinion that 'the occurrence was a most regrettable one and should not be officially perpetuated'. Undaunted, however, the labour movement erected a commemorative fountain at the Trades Hall in Fremantle. The inscription read:

> This memorial fountain was erected to the memory of Comrade Tom Edwards, working class martyr, who sacrificed his life on the Fremantle Wharf on Sunday, May 4, 1919. 'Greater love hath no man...'[32]

Tom Edwards' martyrdom remained a powerful symbol of Fremantle working-class solidarity. It was invoked, for example, during the fifteen-week strike by workers at the Esplanade Hotel in 1921. This strike was unusual in that it was organized and run by women. Staff alleged that, for months beforehand, they had been harassed by the hotel's housekeeper and manager if they insisted on award conditions. The management was particularly remiss in observing requirements for days off. Eventually, the staff sent for their union Secretary, Cecilia Shelley, to inform her that they would cease work, in a body, unless the housekeeper agreed to discontinue her harassment — which may have meant or in-cluded threats of dismissal, or just making things unpleasant for the workers. While the position was being discussed, the hotel manager dismissed the union steward, Rosemary Clune, allegedly for refusing the serve the clerk with afternoon tea. In fact, it was the bellboy's duty to serve tea; the incident was used merely to prejudice staff in the eyes of the public and other unionists and to trivialize the cause of the strike. When the rest of the staff learned of Rosemary Clune's dismissal, they walked out en masse.[33]

Feelings ran high in the community when Asian labour was introduced to replace the striking women workers. While picket-ing the hotel, Cecilia Shelley was hit in the face and knocked into the street by a 'scab' worker. The Industrial Vigilance Committee[34] published a leaflet condemning this action, and declaring that a conspiracy was afoot to reduce wages and smash unionism. It concluded with the following appeal:

> Two years ago the Lumpers and Workers of Fremantle DROVE
> THE SCABS AND LOYALISTS FROM THE WHARF and decisively
> defeated Colebatch's Scab Battalion. Tom Edwards lost his life in
> the fight for Unionism. Workers, have you forgotten this already?[35]

While the leaflet might be dismissed as extremist rhetoric of the militant fringe of the labour movement, there was enormous public response to the dispute. One Sunday in June, a crowd estimated at between 4,000 and 5,000 people gathered on the Esplanade to protest against Asian labour being used as strike breakers. A similar meeting two weeks later attracted around 7,000.[36]

Cecilia Shelley
A tireless worker for the Hotel, Club, Caterers, Tearooms and Restaurant Employees Union, Shelley paid a high price for her militancy. She was expelled from the labour movement in 1925.
[Courtesy Battye Library, 2749P]

Cecilia Shelley worked tirelessly to achieve union solidarity and to negotiate a satisfactory settlement for her members. She later recalled, 'if there was one person out of the union meeting I never slept. I went after them, because I knew one person could break up the lot.' Shelley felt deeply indebted to Alex McCallum, who encouraged and helped her during the dispute, advising her not to go to the Arbitration Court, for he believed that nothing would be achieved by doing so. Eventually, in mid-August 1921, the hotel management re-entered into negotiations with the SDC, and an agreement was reached whereby the sacked staff were reinstated, either at the Esplanade or in similar employment elsewhere.[37]

The anniversary of 'Bloody Sunday' and of Edwards' sacrifice has become intertwined with the commemoration of May Day in Fremantle. *The Waterside Worker*, a contemporary newspaper, retold the story on the 1937 anniversary.[38] In 1950, the Maritime Unity Committee, an association of the major unions based on the harbour, organized a May Day march to the Tom Edwards Memorial and laid a wreath. Vic Williams celebrated May Day 1952 with a poem that clearly linked Edwards' sacrifice with contemporary events:

> I marched with angry thousands
> On the day Tom Edwards fell,
> For the union was in danger
> And we marched to guard it well.
> We cleared the wharf of blacklegs
> And none could bar our way,
> For millions marched beside us
> In a world-wide Labor Day.
> But now the gathering storm-clouds
> Are black as Menzies' brow;
> The unions are in danger.
> We must be marching now!

A film of the first May Day procession in Fremantle in 1954 gave a prominent place to Mrs Edwards, and to the events of May 1919, while the fifty-fourth anniversary of 'Bloody Sunday', in 1973, was the scene of Paddy Troy's last public address after a lifetime of service to maritime unions in Fremantle.[39]

Finally, in the 1980s, Tom Edwards' sacrifice was given public recognition when his memorial fountain was relocated to King's Square, ironically in front of St John's Anglican Church. At the time of Edwards' death, the rector of St John's was Canon R.H. Moore, pro-conscriptionist, imperialist, and himself a strong believer in the concept of sacrifice, both personal and national.[40]

Perhaps Moore would have preferred that the memorial that was eventually to stand in front of his church, bearing an inscription comparing the subject's actions with those of Christ, should have been raised to a soldier of the Empire rather than to a wharf lumper struck down by police while participating in a 'lawless' action. Yet no soldier and no battle of the Great War have become so integral a part of Fremantle's history as have the 1919 lumpers' strike and its martyred hero, Tom Edwards.

The wider impact of the lumpers' victory was felt in the second half of 1919, with industrial unrest on the goldfields and with the Royal Commission on Nationalist Workers. Between April and November 1919, the situation had completely changed for the 'loyalists'. The victory at Fremantle not only had robbed them of their jobs but had empowered the 'official' labour movement with a new spirit of militancy and solidarity. As the end of 1919 approached, it was increasingly evident that the victories gained by 'official' labour unions had created another group of victims. Matt Price, who referred to himself as the 'organiser of the Fremantle Nationalists', and who claimed to have influenced 'many thousands of men' to join the NWWU during the 1917 strike, could not get a shearing job, because of his activities on the wharf. H. Ellis had been unable to work his passage back to England, because the crew claimed that he was a scab. W.D. Spiers claimed he had been driven from the Fremantle Wharf 'through the wilful treachery' of the State Government. He had been employed for only three weeks in the six months since 'Bloody Sunday'.[41]

Others alleged that they had been assaulted by lumpers.[42] It was obvious that the 'no victimization' clause of the May agreement was not being honoured. There had been some 210 NWWU workers at the time of the riot; since then, only fifty-six had remained in regular employment and ten others had worked 'intermittently'. Several had approached the legal firm of Robinson, Cox and Company for advice prior to seeking government assistance to establish farms. According to this firm, 'many instances of victimisation and intimidation' had occurred, including the case of two men who were refused entry to the police force on the grounds that places were being reserved for returned soldiers.[43]

The Royal Commission on Nationalist Workers commenced at Parliament House on 29 September 1919.[44] Many of those interviewed complained of victimization. As one witness, William

Dunne, observed, '[T]here is no doubt in my mind that as regards a man who is known, it is a case of "once a scab always a scab", and he cannot get work'. Yet the Royal Commissioner remained unconvinced that Dunne was unable to obtain work solely because he was regarded as a scab.[45] The fact that some ALF District Councils had requested from the State Executive the names of 'those who scabbed on Fremantle Wharf' suggests that victimization was actively pursued by sections of the labour movement, and that Dunne and others in a similar situation were not exaggerating their predicament.[46]

The Royal Commission achieved very little. After it concluded early in 1920, the Premier received more letters from NWWU members wishing to have their cases considered, yet he refused to reopen the commission, stating, 'It is impossible to believe that any person concerned was ignorant of the existence of the Commission'.[47] The government's treatment of the Nationalist workers reveals the emptiness of much of the rhetoric of 'loyalty'. Once the NWWU members had become an embarrassment, they ceased to be 'loyalists' who had aided the Empire in its hour of crisis. Instead, their honesty was questioned and they were left unemployed, uncompensated, and unable to fit back into the labour movement as a result of their actions.

Industrial action on the goldfields late in 1919 resulted in another defeat for the Nationalist workers. As tensions mounted, Police Inspector Duncan feared that followers of the 'Official Labor Party' would remove 'National Labor Party' supporters from the mines. Urged on by local employers, Duncan was in favour of forming a Citizens' Protection League to preserve law and order.[48] Inspector Mann, of the Perth police, visited Kalgoorlie and found the town to be very unsettled. If the firewood cutters stopped work, 3,000 to 4,000 men would become unemployed and without means of subsistence. Merchants and storekeepers, fearing looting, had allowed stocks to dwindle. Acute hostility existed between the 'Official Labor Party' and the Nationalists. In Mann's opinion, the men of the former were all extremists who held public meetings in Hannan Street in defiance of a resolution passed by the Kalgoorlie Municipal Council to ban such activities. Kalgoorlie was a deeply divided community. Even some of the police were considered 'disloyal' by their own superior officers as well as by 'responsible members of the community'.[49]

Barely controlled hostilities simmered in the community until the beginning of November, when a group of Nationalist workers attempted to re-register the defunct Coolgardie Branch of the Federated Miners Union (FMU). AWU members classed the FMU as bogus and would not work with its members — a position later vindicated by Justice Rooth of the Arbitration Court, who refused to register a second union in the one industry. Alex Panton, the ALF President, travelled to Kalgoorlie to investigate the unrest and discovered that the town was alive with rumours that arms were being distributed to returned soldiers and that special constables were being enrolled at the Soldiers' Institute. A show of tickets revealed small numbers of the 'bogus unionists' in all of the mines. AWU members persisted in their refusal to work with them.

On 6 November, the AWU miners staged an organized demonstration in which they visited the mines and requested FMU members to join their union. The demonstration, which culminated in the so-called riot at Fimiston Mine, was led by the AWU Mining Branch President, George Callanan, whose brother Alfred, the IWW member, had previously been a lumper, but who by the end of 1919 was also an AWU miner. The large family of Alfred Callanan senior had emigrated from New Zealand, via Broken Hill, arriving on the Western Australian goldfields in the 1890s when George was about fourteen years of age. He began his working life as an office boy on the Horseshoe Gold Mine, but soon after entered his life's occupation as an underground miner at the Lake View Mine. His union activity began early and caused him several periods of unemployment. George Callanan was a devout Catholic and a man of high principle. He had been one of the first to oppose conscription during the Great War, and he remained an outspoken advocate of workers' rights. At Fimiston, Callanan and the AWU Miners' Secretary, William Bradley, urged the use of passive resistance and discouraged violent or abusive behaviour.[50]

Several violent incidents occurred, mostly involving returned soldiers who had been signed on as special constables. Albert and Bill Schwan, Colin Edwards and other returned men were involved in scuffles.[51] At Great Boulder Mine, George Callanan persuaded the manager, Richard Hamilton, to address the men. Hamilton agreed to call a meeting of the Chamber of Mines, to meet a deputation from the AWU. Bradley also spoke to the men, reiterating the need to maintain a non-violent protest. When the mine managers did not keep the 4 o'clock appointment, however, an angry crowd went looking for them, and pushed over the fence in front of the Chamber of Mines office. Despite this, George Callanan persuaded the managers to return to the building, where he and other AWU members attempted to negotiate terms of settlement. After forty-five minutes, an impatient crowd of miners entered the office, forcibly by some accounts, although Callanan himself denied this when he testified in court, claiming that the men had entered through an open door.

Shortly afterwards, fifteen miners, including George and Alfred Callanan, were arrested and charged with disturbing the peace. Of the accused, only Martin Lillis had a previous conviction — for being drunk and disorderly.[52] The testimony of witnesses at the ensuing trial was contradictory on the point of whether returned soldiers had been the victims or the perpetrators of violence. Likewise, there was considerable doubt as to which of the Callanans had incited the miners to violence by remarking, 'You know what to do with them' (referring to the bogus unionists). The police witnesses, however, testified that George Callanan had not used any 'bad language', nor had he advocated violence, whereas Alfred Callanan had been prominent at the Perseverance Mine, 'urging the crowd on and calling non-unionists filthy names'. Much of the evidence for the prosecution and the defence indicated that returned men were regarded with extreme hostility by the AWU miners, because of their 'scab' activities.[53] All of the miners were subsequently acquitted. Prior to Justice Rooth's decision not to register the FMU in the Arbitration Court, the AWU had been preparing to call a general strike that eventually would have extended all over the State. Rooth's decision defused the situation, and was a notable victory for the AWU.[54]

Social and political tensions on the goldfields were to increase when the sectarian Australian Protestant Federation began forming branches there. Active groups at Kalgoorlie and Boulder held regular meetings from 1919 to 1922. Women were active members of the federation and sometimes addressed the meetings, as when a Mrs Smith spoke of the Labor Party as 'the Roman Catholic Party'. The federation was multi-denominational, important roles being taken by clergy of several churches — for example, the Reverend Searle of the Congregational Church; J.H. Lang, a

Wesleyan; M. Marsden and the Reverend Fleming. The records make no reference to the backgrounds, education or occupations of lay members. It seems likely, however, that they represented a fairly wide section of the community, corresponding with the congregations represented, but Mrs Smith's remarks suggest that most, if not all, voted for the conservative parties.

Patriotism and conservative political views featured prominently in the addresses given by members and guests of the Protestant Federation. Topics included the 'menace of Mannix and Company'; 'labour unrest'; 'democracy'; and the 'causes of the war'. The speaker on this last subject attributed the conflict to Catholics using the 'German war lust' as a 'tool to destroy Protestant England'. The Reverend Lang of the Kalgoorlie Wesleyan Methodist Church, speaking on the topic 'Why I am a Protestant', gave two reasons for his religious affiliation: 'principally' because he was a man, and secondly, because he was for an 'undivided Empire' and he 'wished to be loyal and true to the Union Jack under which the nation had so wonderfully progressed and developed'. In 1921, the Reverend Shannon, visiting from Ireland, gave an address on the British Israel Movement, of which he was Vice President. British Israelites believed that the British royal family was descended from the House of David, hence allegiance to the King was a religious as well as a patriotic duty. Conversely, Shannon argued, Catholics were loyal to a different religion and a foreign head of state (the Pope). He also addressed a meeting at Boulder Town Hall on the case against Irish Home Rule. The unrest in Ireland, he stated, occurred because there were two separate nations who would never mix.[55]

Protestant Federation members also explored ideas such as the provision of scholarships or bursaries to give 'smart lads and girls' the fuller education necessary for the higher paid government and civil service positions, in order to counteract the 'Roman Catholic element'. They drew up a list of Protestant traders, presumably in order to boycott Roman Catholic businesses, and thus to divide further an already tense community.

There were, of course, tensions and industrial unrest elsewhere in the State, and it was not only the members of the more powerful and militant unions such as the AWU Mining Branch and the FLU who went on strike. The troubled year of 1919 saw industrial action by the Hospital and Asylum Employees Union during the winter and the Public Service Union in December. In July, some twenty members of the former union were locked out of the Claremont Hospital for the Insane during a dispute over the retention of quarantine after the influenza epidemic.[56] The hospital had been declared isolated by the superintendent, Dr Anderson, and employees were forbidden to leave the grounds, under penalty of dismissal. The staff accepted this order until they discovered that Dr Anderson, his chauffeur, ministers of religion, and tradespeople were entering and leaving freely. Some members then left the grounds and consequently were locked out and were unable to return to their duties.

An ALF deputation waited upon the Colonial Secretary, F. Broun, who was adamant that isolation be retained at the hospital. The ALF accused Dr Anderson of using the dispute to break the union, replacing the locked-out staff with non-unionized returned soldiers. The ALF's Metropolitan District Council Secretary, Andrew Clementson, thought it best to fight for the reinstatement of the men and not to inquire into whether isolation was necessary. Union Secretary E.L. Driver disagreed, arguing that, of the public institutions in Western Australia with no cases of influenza, Claremont was the only one that remained in a state of quarantine. The Colonial Secretary refused to grant an inquiry into the administration of isolation restrictions at the Claremont Hospital for the Insane. He stated that he favoured retaining a system of isolation, even though he knew that it could not be complete, for the risk should be reduced to a minimum. He warned that the 'grave consequences' should an epidemic break out in such an institution justified the measures, despite inconvenience to the workers. His caution may have been justified, as influenza cases were being reported daily in the *West Australian*.

The civil servants, who staged a demonstration for higher pay, on 5 December 1919, were rather more fortunate in achieving their aims. Some 1,200 to 1,500 civil servants, including women and some heads of departments, marched to Parliament House, where they were met by the Premier. Mitchell told them that they should not have left their offices at 4 o'clock, yet he would consider their demand for higher pay to keep pace with the cost of living. The majority accepted this and returned to their desks, but a small group of 'the more youthful and rowdy' members booed the Premier. A few days later, the government granted increments and bonuses to civil servants earning £324 or less per annum. These were rejected as unsatisfactory by a mass meeting of the Public Service Union, and the government was forced to agree to appoint a Provisional Public Service Board to supersede all existing appeal boards. This board would investigate anomalies and grievances concerning salaried officers and teachers employed by the government.[57]

The year 1919, therefore, was a mixture of victory and defeat for unionists, and, in most cases, victories had been won by strike action rather than arbitration. Not surprisingly, more and more members of the organized labour movement began to place their faith in industrial unionism — and its vehicle, the OBU — as the only means of overcoming the immense power of the employer. In Western Australian history, the OBU movement is significant for its commitment to direct action, which showed a declining confidence in the Arbitration Court's capacity to do justice to the worker and to deal impartially with each union.[58]

The main impetus for the formation of an OBU came from the most populous States of Victoria and New South Wales.[59] The Workers Industrial Union of Australia (WIU) was founded in Sydney by Jock Garden, Secretary of the Trades and Labor Council, with the intention of amalgamating with all other unions. Garden believed that only a strong and effective industrial organization, such as the WIU, would be capable of redressing the evils of profiteering and 'economic piracy' that had sprung up during the war, and of ensuring a 'decent livelihood' for workers, and he made a concerted effort to attract returned soldiers to the union.[60] Early in 1919, the All Australian Trade Union Conference met in Melbourne and, after considerable discussion and disagreement, adopted the Preamble and Rules of the WIU, which meant that the delegates would work to implement these in each State. They were not adopted unanimously, however. The South Australian and Western Australian delegates voted against the Preamble, because they felt it was open to too many interpretations. The Preamble stated that class struggle, caused by capitalists owning the means of production, must continue until capitalism was abolished, and this end would be achieved only when workers united in one organization and brought about a system of 'social ownership by the whole community'.[61]

Furthermore, the election of office-bearers threatened to be an extraordinarily protracted and cumbersome affair. The issue of local autonomy also caused considerable debate. Western Australian delegate E.H. Barker queried the structure of the OBU, which appeared to be 'ruled from the top by officials'. He was unconvinced by the opinion that 'only by discipline and control by the officials and strict adherence to their instructions on industrial action could success be achieved'. Such a structure, he thought, seemed to bear little resemblance to democracy.[62] Despite his reservations, however, Barker firmly believed in the concept of the OBU, but others within the Labor movement actively opposed it. F.W. Birrell, President of the Adelaide Trades and Labor Council, produced a leaflet describing the failure of 'One Big Unionism' in Canada and warning that if such methods were adopted in Australia, they must 'surely end in similar industrial disaster', with leaders of the movement being imprisoned.[63]

In Western Australia, the WIU intended to take over the AWU structure to implement OBU, this union being the largest in the State. When the Western Australian ALF gathered for its tenth Labor Congress in June 1919, the delegates agreed on the principle of OBU, but there were serious differences of opinion over which form the organization should take. Some believed that the AWU structure and title should be preserved, while others argued for a completely new organization. Other causes for disagreement included the phrasing of the Preamble that had been carried at the Melbourne conference — in particular, the use of the word 'revolution', with its connotations of violence and bloodshed; the 'American phraseology' that suggested an 'imported movement'; the OBU's insistence on direct action rather than arbitration; its condemnation of craft unionism; and its 'autocratic' constitution. Defenders of the Preamble justified the use of the term 'revolution'. Some delegates, notably the members of the Women's Labor Union, expressed disillusionment with the AWU.

The AWU officials defended their union. Tom Butler reminded the Congress that in the 1890s, the union's founders 'went to jail for their principles, and some were even shot for them'. The AWU had 'borne the brunt of five years of strikes to save unionism in Australia' and had used its funds to fight the 1916 and 1917 referenda campaigns and rid the nation of the 'curse of conscription'. Mick Costello and James Hickey defended the AWU's record in achieving gains for women workers. Others advocated building on the already existing base, rather than abolishing the AWU and beginning anew. Finally, the OBU Preamble was put to the vote and rejected by a large majority[64] — an overwhelming victory for the pro-AWU delegates.

An OBU committee was appointed to draft a constitution and perform general propaganda work.[65] The committee was determined not to make the 'mistakes' of the Eastern States organizations. The Western Australian OBU would be created by a State Industrial Congress and would be the State's sole labour industrial organization. Each section would have specified powers, in order to prevent the organization being controlled by a small group of powerful officials. The greatest advantages of the OBU, however, were seen as its ability to control strikes, to prevent 'blacklegging' and to coordinate pay awards; there would no longer be different rates of pay for similar work, nor inter-union jealousy. Andrew Clementson, the OBU Committee Secretary, wrote a paper that concluded that, whereas the democratic control of industry by the workers was impossible under the old craft union system, the OBU would prepare workers for industrial democracy.[66] In its avoidance of Marxist concepts such as class struggle, seizure by workers of the means of production, and collectivization, Clementson's paper differed from earlier propaganda — for example, that written by Jock Garden.[67] Union members in both metropolitan and country areas began responding enthusiastically to the OBU scheme. By September 1919, eleven OBU organizers were active in sixteen workplaces in the metropolitan area in order to spread the propaganda of industrial unionism, and groups had been formed at Bunbury and Albany.[68]

The turning point of industrial unionism in the west was the OBU Congress held in Perth on 25 May 1920, for it was here that the militant rhetoric invoking revolution was soundly rejected in favour of more moderate objectives.[69] Even attempts to use the name 'One Big Union' failed, and a resolution naming the organization the Workers Industrial Union of Australia, WA Section (WIUWA), was carried.[70] The conference adopted a statement of objectives and a constitution that were virtually identical to those of the AWU.[71] Amendments to open the membership to all workers, irrespective of race or gender, were defeated. The conference also adopted a complex five-tier management structure headed by a fifteen-member Grand Council, to be elected by the entire union membership. The Grand Council was to be the 'supreme authority in the Union', with power to 'veto the actions of any [other] governing body or member'. Its functions included the administration of finances and personnel, and liaison with government bodies. Most significantly, however, it alone could 'enter into an agreement, arbitrate, or declare a strike on behalf of all or any of the members of the union'.[72] The reservations concerning abuse of power, which some delegates had expressed at the Melbourne Conference, went unheeded.

The fate of the OBU was not, however, ultimately decided in conferences and committees in Perth but in one of the AWU's strongholds — the Eastern Goldfields — among the humblest of workers, the Italian firewood cutters. The cutters were unskilled, non-unionized labour whom the companies employed on a piece-work basis, at 11s 6d per day, under very bad conditions. Workers camped along the 64-kilometre Lakeside railway line, living in rough accommodation with their wives and families. The work was extremely dangerous, and serious injuries often occurred.[73] In June 1919, the firewood cutters went on strike for better conditions. They had not had a wage increase for several years, yet the firewood companies justified this by complaining of the falling price of sandalwood, and by claiming that many cutters made over £200 a year and the loaders worked only six hours a day.[74] The strike was ended by the unsatisfactory expedient of fixing the cutters' wages and the cost of stores supplied by the firewood companies at 1916 levels.[75]

By October 1920, when Alfred Callanan (or 'Bull', as he was known) arrived at the main camp on the Kurrawang woodline, with a colleague known only as Scott, the firewood cutters' grievances were sufficient to provoke them into further industrial action. Callanan's motivation for this lone initiative seems to have come from a deep commitment to socialism and industrial unionism. Perhaps he chose the firewood cutters deliberately in order to follow tactics that were typical of the IWW in other parts of the world.[76] In giving his attention to a group of mainly non-British workers, he went against the prevailing policy of the AWU, which had made little attempt to unionize the Slavs and Italians on the goldfields. Callanan addressed the workers at numerous meetings, urging AWU members to leave their union and all to join the 'One Big Union'. He ignored the OBU Congress's decision regarding the union's title, and referred only to the 'OBU', never to the WIUWA. Callanan stated that if the workers joined an OBU, 'in time the same conditions will prevail here as in Russia and other countries where the OBU is in operation and the worker will get his rights'.[77] His speeches were well received.

One evening early in November, Callanan addressed some seventy to eighty men who had assembled at the water tank at Lakeside Number Two Camp. He spoke by the light of a hurricane lantern. Constable Richardson, of the Boulder police, had not come similarly equipped and found it impossible to take notes in the darkness. Nevertheless, he recalled that Callanan

> said that the master class and capitalists had an OBU and they as fellow workers should have an OBU to compete. *Workers should control industry, not masters as they were only parasites on workers.* [This control was] *to be achieved by peaceful revolution.* [The workers] did not want bloody revolution. But if they could not get a *peaceful revolution, well, they must have it.*

Callanan was also reported as saying that in Britain, the OBU was bringing 'Lloyd George's capitalistic government to its knees'. One of the firewood cutters asked Callanan what he thought of the Sinn Fein. He replied that he did not know but he believed they would win with American support. It is hardly surprising that Richardson included this comment in his report, as many attempts were made to link Sinn Feinism and Bolshevism. The 'Britishers' at the camp were reportedly hostile to Callanan and told him that they were satisfied with 'Mick Costello and the AWU'. His class was 'not wanted'. Only three Italians signed up.[78] Even so, by the end of November, 140 of Callanan's 'OBU' workers had gone on strike because the AWU refused to recognize their union.[79] The *West Australian* reported that '80 per cent' of men on the woodlines had joined the new union.[80]

The strike that resulted from the clash between the AWU and the 'OBU' lasted for only a week, but alarmed the goldfields community. The preponderance of Italians among 'OBU' members stirred up racist sentiments that always ran close to the surface in the goldfields community. It was only fifteen months since the Kalgoorlie race riots. Connections were readily made between the 'foreign' workers and 'Bolshevik' ideology, both of which were 'unacceptable' in a 'loyal, British' community. The Mayor of

Kalgoorlie wired Premier Mitchell that the mines were closing down for want of fuel, and that all work would cease before the end of the week. The position, according to the Mayor, was 'most grave'. Harry Axford, the RSL President, sent a peremptory message to Mitchell, demanding immediate government action. Inspector Duncan of the Kalgoorlie police later commented to the Police Commissioner that 'the Returned Soldiers have been eager to take a hand in this matter and deal with the executive of the OBU but I have, so far, successfully persuaded them not to interfere'.[81]

Work resumed on Monday 6 December after the intervention of the Italian Consul, Count Gallo.[82] The strike failed chiefly because Callanan's 'OBU' was regarded by the labour movement as a 'bogus' union, in the same way as the FMU had been in the 1919 strike. The issue was debated at length in the Legislative Assembly. The Labor Opposition was at pains to disown Callanan and his associates, Philip Collier stating that 'no such union as the OBU exists in Australia, and these men have simply formed an organisation they call the One Big Union'.[83] Indeed, the title 'One Big Union' had not been accepted officially in any State. Yet, despite Labor's disowning of Callanan's actions, J.C. Willcock, the Labor Member for Geraldton, vehemently opposed suggestions by Country Party leader Thomas Harrison, Mines Minister Scaddan, and Roebourne Member Frederick Teesdale that criminal proceedings be instituted against the 'OBU' leaders Callanan and Scott. Teesdale even went so far as to suggest such 'solutions' as a firing squad or deportation.[84] Significantly, the debate was conducted almost entirely between Labor and ex-Labor members, and residual bitterness over the 1917 split welled up several times.

In repudiating the 'OBU' activities on the woodlines, there was a precedent within the mainstream labour movement, not only of outlawing a 'bogus' organization, but also of amalgamating unions.[85] The labour movement was, therefore, consistent in its planned procedure for achieving one union. Other factors influenced the ALF's disowning of Callanan and his 'OBU' . The AWU was in a desperate situation financially, brought about by its support of the 1919 strikers, and by the deepening economic crisis. Mines were closing, not temporarily as a result of strike action, but permanently. At the beginning of 1920, 1,000 men had been thrown out of work by the closure of the Gwalia and Lancefield Mines and the reduction of staff at Boulder. More were to follow. In July 1921, Menzies Consolidated, at Coolgardie, closed.[86]

Despite its victory over Callanan's 'OBU' movement, the AWU's political power was to be considerably weakened by the failure of the 1921 shearers' strike, in which organized employer groups triumphed. In 1921, the powerful Western Australian Pastoralists and Graziers Association (PGA) refused to pay shearers the new award of £9 10s per week recommended by the AWU.[87] Instead, the PGA paid only the State award of 30s for 100 sheep shorn, plus keep. Nor would they allow contractors to pay higher rates. The PGA would not negotiate with the AWU or the State ALF, and turned down all suggestions of arbitration.[88] Consequently, the shearers formed strike camps at Pindar, Roebourne, Cue, Carnarvon and elsewhere. The importance of the strike was not lost on the ALF State Executive, which warned that

> Western Australia is being made the battle ground in Australia for a trial of strength between the Pastoralists Association and organised labor. Should the union be unsuccessful in this fight it will prejudice their case which will be heard in the Federal Arbitration Court next month.[89]

Local police enrolled special constables from among the non-unionized station hands and shed employees. AWU members picketed the outskirts of Carnarvon but failed to prevent shearers being transported to stations by road. By mid-July, police reported that shearing was proceeding on all local stations and that everything was 'quiet and orderly'. Most of the working shearers, who belonged to the AWU, had accepted State award rates, but others were still holding out for the new rates.[90] Undoubtedly, the power of the PGA was a major factor in the failure of the strike. In 1925, the pastoralists were still boasting of their success in preventing the new award from coming before the Arbitration Court.[91]

The formation of branches of the Communist Party of Australia (CPA) in the closing months of 1920 may also have detracted from the labour movement's commitment to industrial unionism. Initially, only six people committed themselves to membership of the Western Australian branch of the CPA, including Katharine Susannah (Prichard) Throssell and George Ryce. The latter remained a member of the Labor Party, and his expulsion in 1925 was not related to his CPA involvement. The CPA was racked by dissension throughout its early years and was not a powerful force in Western Australian politics; nevertheless, it provided a vision of hope for a few of the more militant members, such as Cecilia Shelley, who were disillusioned with the Labor Party.[92] This led to a polarization of the labour movement into militants and moderates, the communists (militants) absorbing the ideas of the OBU movement, and the ALP (moderates) increasingly rejecting them.

The reality facing the labour movement by the end of 1921, therefore, was the need to stay united in order to survive. Despite removing the rival unionists from the wharves and the goldfields, the militancy of the previous three years had not gained marked improvements in working conditions. Instead, it had left a legacy of dissension within the movement. Aided by the conservative State and Federal Governments, employer groups still wielded tremendous power. Moderate labour members feared that any splinter group would merely further fracture the working-class movement, and reopen the wounds of 1917. The Labor Party again failed to secure government in the State election of April 1921. Despite internecine strife, the National coalition was returned, with thirty seats in the Lower House.[93]

For his attempt to organize the firewood cutters into an OBU, Alfred Callanan paid a double price: ostracism from the labour movement, and unemployment. His apparent disappearance from the goldfields at the end of 1920 is probably explained by his inability to obtain further work in the mines. In March 1923, Callanan appeared before a Kalgoorlie court on a charge of robbery with violence. He admitted holding staff at the Great Boulder Mine at gunpoint and stealing £520, but claimed that he had done so as a protest against the persecution of himself and others by the National Employers' Federation, and in particular by the Chamber of Mines. This, he informed the court, was what the socialists called 'propaganda by deed'. The Chief Justice, Sir Robert McMillan, who was presiding, said that he had never previously encountered a plea of this nature in all his years at the bar. The jury retired for two and a half hours but could not agree, so Callanan was remanded in custody and the trial was rescheduled to be heard at the Supreme Court in Perth, in April. There, the jury was unanimous in finding Callanan guilty of robbery, and sentenced him to seven years' hard labour, which he served at Fremantle Prison. Justice Burnside, who had presided at the trial of Miller and Sawtell in

1916, reminded the defendant that the maximum penalty for robbery with violence was life imprisonment, thus inferring that Callanan had got off lightly.[94] During 1924, the EGDC asked the ALF State Executive to take steps to obtain Callanan's release, on the grounds of ill health. The tone of Secretary Lawler's letter indicated that, on the goldfields at least, Callanan was no longer regarded as an outcast of the labour movement. The consensus of opinion was that Callanan had 'already been sufficiently penalised for his offence'. Collier, Premier since Labor's victory in the 1924 State election, showed no such forgiving spirit. Two years later, Callanan was still in prison.[95]

George Callanan, who was also a labour militant but who had supported the AWU, died suddenly at the age of forty while undergoing a relatively minor operation in Kalgoorlie Hospital, in December 1923. Callanan had variously occupied the positions of Secretary, President and Trustee of the EGDC, as well as President and Secretary of the AWU Mining Branch. The demands of numerous committee, council, union and street corner meetings had undermined his health and almost certainly contributed to his death. In addition, he had had sole responsibility for five children, his wife having predeceased him by eighteen months, probably while giving birth to their youngest child. The five orphaned Callanan children, aged from eighteen months to sixteen years, were left in the care of George's widowed mother. The labour movement turned out in force to pay its last respects to a man whom its members mourned as a 'stalwart comrade and brother' who had 'suffered much for the cause of Labor'. At the funeral service, the Roman Catholic priest, a personal friend, said that Callanan had 'followed in life the example set by our Lord Jesus Christ' — a remark that painted a different picture of this man who, four years before at Fimiston, had been accused of 'physical abuse', 'incitement to riot' and 'threatening' members of the RSL. Despite its crippling financial problems, the EGDC donated 20 guineas to Callanan's family and obtained free rail passes enabling them to travel to Sydney.[96]

Perhaps as a final irony, the OBU scheme foundered on the very edifice that it had attempted to destroy, in its earlier, more militant form. In May 1924, the Federal Arbitration Court refused to register the 'Australasian Workers Union', as the WIU now called itself. Those who objected to the union's registration included, perhaps

George Callanan
'A stalwart comrade and brother [who] suffered much for the cause of Labor',
Callanan endured periods of unemployment and imprisonment because of his
union activity. He died, aged forty years, of overwork and illness in December
1923, leaving five orphaned children. From the *Westralian Worker*, 4 January
1924.
[Courtesy Battye Library]

predictably, several pastoralists and graziers associations, timber
merchants and sawmillers, and the Commonwealth Steamship
Owners' Association.[97] Less predictably, a total of twenty-four
unions lodged objections. These were mainly craft unions but also
included the Timber Workers Union and the Federated Seamen's
Union. Two reasons were given by the Registrar for the Arbitration
Court's refusal to register the union: first, there was already a
union registered by that name, the AWU; and second, the new
union was an organization of organizations and not an organization of persons.[98]

By 1924, however, the attention of the State ALF, the National
coalition government, and indeed most West Australians had
turned to other problems. The militant wing of the labour movement remained, but its ideology developed in other directions, and
the issue of the OBU was never again to dominate labour politics
in the State.

1   S. Macintyre, *The Oxford History of Australia, Volume 4: 1901–1942. The Succeeding Age*, Melbourne, 1986, pp. 187–188; A. Hyslop, The Last Campaign. World War I and Spanish Influenza in Australia, 1918–1919, unpublished paper presented at the Australian War Memorial History Conference, September 1993; L. Liveris, *The Dismal Trader. The Undertaker Business in Perth, 1860–1939*, Perth, 1991, p. 153.

2   See Premier's Department File (hereafter PDF) 111/19.

3   Correspondence in PDF 111/19.

4   V.G. Childe, *How Labour Governs: A Study of Workers' Representation in Australia*, Melbourne, 1964 edn.

5   Macintyre, *Oxford History*, pp. 170–171.

6   Commissioner of Police to Inspector O'Halloran, 25 August 1917 — lists of weapons and ammunition received. These included fifty-six rifles (twenty-three Winchesters), twenty revolvers, and over 5,000 rounds of ammunition. See also a copy of War Precautions Act, Regulation 40C, all in Police Department, File 4092/1918.

7   See, for example, Statement of Sarah Ward, Proprietor of Tea Rooms at 93–95 South Terrace, Fremantle, Police Department, File 4092/1918.

8   *Australian Labor Federation Fremantle District Council Annual Report, 1917*, p. 2.

9   'Precis of Proceedings at a Conference between Representatives of the Oversea, Interstate and Coastal Companies, held at the Australasian Steamship Owners' Federation (ASOF), Steamship Buildings, 509 Collins Street, Melbourne, on Wednesday, September 19th, 1917', Australasian Steamship Owners Federation, Minutes, N.G. Butlin Archives of Business and Labour (Canberra), Acc. E217, vol. 5, 1915–18.

10 See reports in Police Department, File 780/1918; also State Executive of the ALF (WA) — Correspondence Files (hereafter SE Correspondence), File 52.

11 See for example, Inspector Sellenger to Commissioner of Police, 28 November 1917, Police Department, File 4092/1918.

12 Sellenger to Commissioner, 4 January 1918, Police Department, File 4092/1918.

13 Colonial Secretary to Police Commissioner, 25 January 1918, and reply, 4 March 1918, Police Department, File 4092/1918.

14 Sellenger to Simpson, 18 March 1918 (emphasis added), Police Department, File 4092/1918.

15 Police Report, 16 November 1918, Sellenger to Commissioner, 17 November 1918, Police Department, File 4092/1918.

16 Correspondence, Colebatch to Watt, 17 April 1919, 23 April 1919, PDF 112/19.

17 Typed report (4 pp.) of deputation to Colebatch, 23 April 1919, PDF 112/19.

18 Colebatch to Watt, 23 April 1919, PDF 112/19.

19 Watt to Colebatch, 25 April 1919, PDF 112/19.

20 Shallard to Colebatch, 25 April 1919, Notes re. Deputation, n.d. (28 April 1919?), PDF 112/19.

21 State Executive of the ALF (WA) — Minutes Books (hereafter SE Minutes), State Archives of Western Australia, Acc. 1573A/2, 28 April 1919.

22 *Westralian Worker*, 16 May 1919; also Certified Copy of Thomas Charles Edwards' Death Certificate. A full account of the events of the wharf riot is given in the *West Australian*, 5 May 1919.

23 Inspector Mann to Police Commissioner, 9 May 1919, Police Department, File 2396/1919.

24   Police Department, File 2400/1919. The total number of police used in the operation was stated by Colebatch later to be 'a small force of about 150'.

25   Inspector Mann's Report to Police Commissioner, 9 May 1919, Police Department, File 2396/1919. Only the *West Australian*, 5 May 1919, mentioned the reading of the Riot Act.

26   Sellenger to Police Commissioner, 8 May 1919, Mann to Police Commissioner, 9 May 1919, Police Department, File 2396/1919; *West Australian*, 6 May 1919, for an account of the meeting at King's Theatre.

27   FLU to Colebatch, 5 May 1919, SE Correspondence, File 78.

28   'Report of the Compensation due on the Death of Thomas Edwards, to his Wife and Family', SE Correspondence, File 78.

29   See typed press telegram of Edwards' funeral, copy in SE Correspondence, File 78; also P. Hopper, The 1919 Fremantle Lumpers' Strike, BA Hons dissertation, University of Western Australia, 1975, graveside address and list of prominent mourners, facing p. 41; *West Australian*, 10 May 1919; L. Layman and J. Goddard, *Organise! A Visual Record of the Labour Movement in Western Australia*, Perth, 1988, p. 70.

30   Hopper, The 1919 Fremantle Lumpers' Strike, pp. 47–48.

31   See ALF General Secretary to Grieve, 21 May 1920, and reply, 26 August 1920, SE Correspondence, File 52; Circular to District Councils, 29 April 1920, Balance Sheet to 20 October 1920; Correspondence re. *The Fremantle Wharf Crisis, 1919*, 15 May 1920, 29 May 1920, 11 June 1920, 15 July 1920, SE Correspondence, File 78.

32   Minutes of a Meeting of the State Disputes Committee of the ALF, 20 June 1919, SE Correspondence, File 33.

33   See SE Correspondence, File 33.

34   The Industrial Vigilance Committee (IVC) appears to have been set up (perhaps in 1917) to maintain vigilance over civil liberties and reforms won by the labour movement, which were being eroded by the War Precautions Act (WPA). SE Correspondence File 67 contains correspondence between the IVC and the State Executive, all dated 1917, concerning Labor meetings being broken up by returned soldiers; protests against WPA amendments curtailing the freedom of speech; planning Adela Pankhurst's speaking tour in February and March 1917; and ferreting out the Labor 'rats' (pro-conscriptionists who had joined the National Party). The IVC's Secretary was E.L. Driver, but other office-bearers are not known.

35   SE Correspondence, File 33.

36   SE Minutes, vol. 3, 17 June 1921, 1 July 1921.

37   SE Correspondence, File 33. Also Cecilia Shelley, oral history transcript, Battye Library, Acc. OH 171, pp. 19–26. For a published account of the Esplanade Hotel Workers' Strike, see W. Brady, '"Serfs of the Sodden Scone?" Women Workers in the Western Australian Hotel and Catering Industry, 1900–1925', in P. Crawford (ed.), *Studies in Western Australian History VII: Women in Western Australian History*, December 1983, pp. 33–45.

38   Cited in J. Williams, *The First Furrow*, Perth, 1976, p. 76.

39   Layman and Goddard, *Organise!*, pp. 94, 158–160. A copy of the film is lodged with the State Archives of the Alexander Library, Perth. The first verse of Vic Williams' poem 'For May Day 1952' is quoted from his collection *Into Battle with a Song and Other Poems* (1953), and used with permission. See also S. Macintyre, *Militant: The Life and Times of Paddy Troy*, Sydney, 1984, pp. 131, 214.

40   In May 1919, Moore was actually absent from this post, serving as a chaplain

to the AIF, from November 1917 until August 1919. See J. Smith, '"Not Peace, but a Sword": Religion, War and Empire. Canon Robert Henry Moore: The Church of England and the First World War', in J.M. Tonkin (ed.), *Studies in Western Australian History IX: Religion and Society in Western Australia*, October 1987, p. 65.

41 PDF 130/19.

42 See, for example, G. Edwards (Kalgoorlie) to Secretary WWF, 29 September 1919, re. Brash who Alleged being Assaulted in High Street, Fremantle, SE Correspondence, File 78.

43 Robinson, Cox & Co. to Premier, 12 June 1919, PDF 112/19. R.T. Robinson, Attorney-General, was a partner in this firm.

44 SE Correspondence, File 78.

45 'Royal Commission of Nationalist Workers, 6.10.19', pp. 914–922, SE Correspondence, File 177.

46 ALF Secretary to Baglin, 18 July 1919, SE Correspondence, File 177.

47 Premier to Robinson, Cox & Co., 26 February 1920, 20 March 1920, PDF 130/19.

48 Duncan to Police Commissioner, 25 May 1919, Police Department, File 3032/19.

49 Mann to Police Commissioner, 27 May 1919, Police Department, File 3032/19.

50 *Kalgoorlie Miner*, 8 November 1919. For Callanan's biographical details, see *Westralian Worker*, 28 December 1923.

51 SE Minutes, vol. 2, 17 November 1919; PDF 398/19. For press coverage, see, for example, *West Australian*, 7 November 1919. This report refers to Edwards, a returned soldier, as being 'brutally maltreated by the furious crowd of professed industrial liberators, boots being used and cowardly fists falling about a body that had been flung by its owner into the living rampart of Australians who had held back the hordes of Germany'. For published accounts of these events, see J. Murray, 'The Kalgoorlie Woodline Strikes, 1919–1920: A Study of Conflict within the Working Class', in L. Layman (ed.), *Studies in Western Australian History V: Bosses, Workers and Unemployed*, December 1982, pp. 22–37; and B. Oliver, 'Disputes, Diggers and Disillusionment: Social and Industrial Unrest in Perth and Kalgoorlie, 1918–24', in J. Gregory (ed.), *Studies in Western Australian History XI: Western Australia Between the Wars, 1919–39*, June 1990, pp. 19–28.

52 Police Department, File 579/1920; 'Deputation from the State Executive of the ALF re. Kalgoorlie and Boulder Trouble, 4.11.19', p. 2, PDF 398/19.

53 Supreme Court of WA, Criminal Case File 5006/1920, *Rex v. George Callanan and Others*, 2 March 1920, State Archives of Western Australia, Acc. 3473. The 'Others' were Alfred Callanan, Michael Purcell, Frank Banham, Owen Bannon, Willhelm Dravis (Davis), Charles Heil, Ernest Brown, Mate Yuryevich, Ante Katich, Nicholas Turich, Martin Lillis, John Stewart, Joseph Shelley, D. McAuliffe, and Walter Bowden.

54 Intelligence Section to Premier, 26 November 1919, and 'Dispute between the CMU [FMU] and the AWU, and Others Engaged in the Mining Industry in the East Coolgardie Goldfield', 3 January 1920, PDF 398/19.

55 Australian Protestant Federation, Minutes Book of the Kalgoorlie Branch, 1919–22, State Archives of Western Australia, Acc. 'Comap 57'. The author is grateful to Tom Reynolds, Archivist, for bringing this material to her attention.

56   The following account is taken from ALF (WA), Minutes of the Metropolitan District Council, vol. 3, 25 July 1919; and issues of the *West Australian*, 26 July 1919, 28 July 1919 and 1 August 1919.

57   *West Australian*, 6 December 1919, 10 December 1919, 18 December 1919, 25 December 1919.

58   An example of one of the Arbitration Court's anomalies, the discrepancies in the awards granted to the Amalgamated Society of Engineers and the WA Amalgamated Society of Railway Engineers, was discussed in the *Westralian Worker*, 31 December 1920.

59   *Proposed Scheme for Closer Unionism in Victoria* (1918), SE Correspondence, File 189.

60   J.S. Garden, *The Worker's Industrial Union of Australia, One Big Union Manifesto to Returned Soldiers and Sailors of Australia*, n.d., SE Correspondence, File 189.

61   *Workers' Industrial Union of Australia Preamble, Classification and Rules, Adopted at the All-Australia Trades Union Conference, Melbourne, January 1919*, copy in SE Correspondence, File 189. For a more detailed account of the OBU movement in Western Australia, see B. Oliver, '"For Only by the OBU Shall Workmen's Wrongs be Righted". A Study of the One Big Union Movement in Western Australia, 1919 to 1922', in C. Fox and M. Hess (eds), *Papers in Labour History*, no. 5, April 1990, pp. 1–17.

62   Barker to McCallum, 21 January 1919, SE Correspondence, File 189.

63   F.W. Birrell, *Force and Intolerance Must Fail — Canada's Experience of One Big Unionism*, copy in SE Correspondence, File 189.

64   *ALP (WA Division), Fourth General Council (Tenth Congress) Official Report and Proceedings* (hereafter *Fourth General Council Report*). A copy of the report is held in SE Correspondence, File 200.

65   ALF (WA), Minutes of ALP Special Congress (hereafter Congress Minutes), vol. 18, 1913–28, State Archives of Western Australia, Acc. 1573A/18, Minutes of the 1919 Labor Congress.

66   A. Clementson, *Trade Unionists Unite!*, n.d., copy in SE Correspondence, File 151. See also Circular to District Councils, 29 September 1919, SE Correspondence, File 188.

67   For example, J.S. Garden, *Industrial Unionism. What Is It?*, n.d., and *OBU — We Can and We Will Own the Workshops*, n.d., copies in SE Correspondence, File 189.

68   List of OBU Agents', SE Correspondence, File 189. These were as follows: 'J. Walsh: Railway Men and Carters; ?: Swan Brewery; R. Marshall: Swan Bottling Works, Swan Malt House, Emu Brewery; W. Bourne: Government Printing Office; ?: AWU jobs?; Messrs Cross and Kidd: Car Barn; L. White: Sandover and Co., Perth Tannery; ? Smith: Hoskins Bros; W. Buck: Povey's; A. Hunt: Barker and Moore; R. Rouse: Bon Marche; L. Stringer: Boans; W. Auld: Sayers and McEvoy'.

69   Congress Minutes, 25 May 1920.

70   *Fourth General Council Report*, p. 50.

71   Congress Minutes, 26 May 1920; 'One Big Union: Draft Constitution and Rules', p. 3, SE Correspondence, File 151. The statement was as follows: 'To unite the workers of Western Australia in one organisation, and by the provision and distribution of funds and other means to regulate the conditions of labor, the relations between employers and employees, and workmen and workmen, to replace the present competitive system by one of social ownership of the means of production, distribution, and exchange,

and to advocate the formation of one big union of workers for Australia'.

72   'One Big Union: Draft Constitution and Rules', pp. 2, 4, 5.
73   Lakeside Firewood Company, Letter Book 1919–21, State Archives of Western Australia, Acc. 1364A, especially 10 September 1919, 12 September 1919, 24 October 1919, 8 November 1919, 3 December 1919; 8 March 1920, 1 November 1920. See also J. Murray, The Kalgoorlie Woodline Strikes, 1919–29, BA Hons dissertation, University of Western Australia, 1981, p. 23.
74   Interview between Premier and Representatives of the Federal Companies, 13 July 1919, PDF 203/19. Interview between the Premier and the Kalgoorlie Disputes Committee (G. Callanan, Collier, Armon, Clifford, Lambert, Watts, Worthy), 13 July 1919, pp. 4–5, PDF 203/19.
75   Negotiations between the Disputes Committee, the Mining Companies and the Premier, PDF 203/19.
76   This is suggested by Murray, Kalgoorlie Woodline Strikes, p. 31.
77   Police Department, File 8564/1920. The following account is extracted from police reports dated 20 October 1920, 27 October 1920, 6 November 1920.
78   Constable Richardson's Report, 6 November 1920, Police Department, File 8564/20 (emphasis in the original).
79   Duncan to Commissioner, 6 December 1920, Police Department, File 8564/1920.
80   *West Australian*, 30 November 1920.
81   Correspondence, PDF 576/20; Police Department, File 8564/1920.
82   Gallo to Premier, 4 December 1920, PDF 576/20.
83   *Western Australian Parliamentary Debates*, vol. 63, 2 December 1920, p. 2086.
84   ibid., pp. 2085–2095.
85   In 1915, for example, the majority of members of the Westralian General Workers Union had voted in favour of amalgamation with the AWU. See *AWU, Official Report and Proceedings, 1915*, pp. 15–16. The results of the poll were: 'For, 1230; Against, 240; Informal, 146; giving a majority of 990'. Two years later, the Federal Mining Employees Association voted similarly. See *AWU, Report of the Federal Mining Employees' Conference, 1917*, pp. 45–46. 'In favour, 1,027; Against, 457; Majority, 770.' A copy of this conference report is held in SE Correspondence, File 136.
86   Secretary, AWU, Boulder, to Premier, 22 January 1920, PDF 29/21; ALF (WA), Minutes of the Eastern Goldfields District Council, State Archives of Western Australia, Acc. 1704A (hereafter EGDC Minutes), vol. 3, 18 July 1921.
87   *AWU, Pastoral Industry Conference, Trades Hall, Melbourne, 20.11.20*, on microfilm, N.G. Butlin Archives of Business and Labour (Canberra), Acc. 44 PD5, item 85; *Western Australian Pastoralist and Grazier*, vol. 1, no. 1, 26 January 1925, p. 16.
88   See notes of ALF Deputations to Premier Mitchell, 29 July 1921, 17 August 1921, PDF 342/21.
89   ALF General Secretary's Circular, 17 October 1921, and previous correspondence, SE Correspondence, File 95a. The total amount of donations received from Western Australian unions, other than the AWU, at that date was £350. The Collie Miners sent £300 and the Bunbury Lumpers, £40. See SE Correspondence, File 191.
90   Connell to Sgt Leen, Carnarvon Police, 16 July 1921, and other correspondence, Police Department, File 4403/1921. It is likely that some of these men were 'Nationalists' who had lost their jobs on the Fremantle Wharf and in the gold mines in the FLU and AWU triumphs of 1919.

91 *Western Australian Pastoralist and Grazier*, vol. 1, no. 1, 26 January 1925, p. 16. The PGA Executive included Sir Ernest Lee Steere (President), a member of an early colonial family that traced its ancestry back to the Norman Conquest. Lee Steere was a member of the Weld Club and Chairman of the WA Turf Club. Others on the association's Executive included Sir E.H. Wittenoom, a Director of Dalgetys and of the Western Australian Bank; F.F.B. Wittenoom, also on the Dalgetys Board; and members of other old colonial families such as the Lefroys, the Dempsters and the Forrests.

92 Williams, *The First Furrow*, pp. 84–93.

93 D. Black, 'Party Politics in Turmoil: 1911–1924', in C.T. Stannage (ed.), *A New History of Western Australia*, Nedlands, 1981, Table 12.2. Only seventeen Labor Members of the Legislative Assembly were returned.

94 Supreme Court of Western Australia, Criminal Indictment Register, 1915–36, on microfilm, State Archives of Western Australia, Acc. CONS 3422, pp. 183, 197; also *West Australian*, 18 April 1923.

95 Lawler to Barker, 21 July 1924, 10 October 1924, 17 November 1926, SE Correspondence, File 213; Premier's Secretary to Barker, 13 November 1924, SE Correspondence, File 259.

96 EGDC Minutes, vol. 4, 17 December 1923, 14 January 1924; *Westralian Worker*, 21 December 1923, 28 December 1923, 14 January 1924. Also Police Department, Files 5850/1919 and 579/1920. The title of this chapter comes from the priest's remarks at Callanan's funeral.

97 The PGAs were New South Wales, South Australia, Queensland and the Southern Riverina — but not Western Australia. The Commonwealth Steamship Owners' Association was a combination of ship owners, formed in 1905, in order to register under the Commonwealth Conciliation and Arbitration Act. All members' vessels engaged exclusively in the interstate trade were placed on the association's register. J. Bach, *A Maritime History of Australia*, Sydney, 1982 edn, p. 208.

98 *OBU. Why It Failed!*, Sydney, 1924, AWU Papers, File E15/37/11.

Chapter Six

A PREMIER WITH LAND
TO GIVE AWAY
The National Party and immigration policy

Early in 1922, James Mitchell — Northam farmer, Premier, and recently knighted[1] — went 'home' to persuade two million British people to settle in Western Australia, where there was 'work for all'.[2] Under the mass immigration scheme that became known as Group Settlement, thousands of men, women and children travelled from their homes in Britain to take up farming land on the opposite side of the earth.[3] Most were completely inexperienced in this type of occupation, even in their own country, and much of the land they were to take up was unsuitable for agriculture. Mitchell's visit to England occurred at a time of high unemployment in Western Australia, and this, together with the influx of immigrants, created new social and political tensions in the State.

The Group Settlement Scheme was undergirded by imperial ideology, which encouraged the settlement of far-flung parts of the Empire with a sturdy British yeomanry. Prior to 1914, many British immigrants had been placed on rural blocks by the State Labor Bureau[4], but the need to encourage Britons to emigrate was heightened by the postwar economic slump and resulting unemployment in both Britain and Australia — or so the scheme's proponents claimed. During World War I, several organizations in England had urged Australia to do its 'duty to the mother country' by receiving British emigrants. Immigration was portrayed as beneficial to Australia, enabling it to build up its population and become a 'great nation'. Gloomy images of a Britain in which enlisted men returned to find their places taken by women and children were interspersed with 'populate or perish' theories. Leaflets such as the 'Manifesto to Labour in Australia' argued that more people meant more employment, as they had to be provided with clothing, food, housing and other products, and that 'the placing of every thousand workers in jobs in Australia, which otherwise would be unfilled, means more employment for the future population to supply their needs'.[5]

As unemployment figures rose in Western Australia in the postwar years, ALP opposition to large-scale immigration grew.[6] In July 1921, the ALF Secretary, Andrew Millington, informed fellow Trades and Labor Council Secretaries in the Eastern States that there was considerable unemployment in Western Australia, 'despite the pronouncement to the contrary of our State Premier'. The mining and building industries were both in decline, he said, and immigrants were being 'placed in the country on scandalously low wages on the plea that they are inexperienced and require to be taught farm work'.[7] A motion from the Women's Labor League in the goldfields, protesting against further immigration to Australia until work had been found for the unemployed, was included in the Federal Agenda Paper for the ALP Interstate Conference held in Brisbane at the end of 1921. The ALF's Annual Report stated that, despite the Mitchell Government's 'continuous and emphatic denial', unemployment was increasing. The report urged District Councils to cooperate in supplying accurate unemployment figures, so that the ALF could 'effectively combat the assertion that unemployment is non-existent in this state'.[8]

The British Government failed to share the National Party's enthusiasm for encouraging emigration to Western Australia. It would appear that British Conservatives were apprehensive about rumours of Bolshevik and Sinn Fein activity in Australia. The Governor-General, Sir Ronald Munro Ferguson, had sent pessimistic despatches, warning of mob rule, to London during the 1917 General Strike. Between 1917 and 1921, he was in regular correspondence with Lord Stamfordham, the King's Private Secretary. In 1919, Munro Ferguson contacted the Secretary of State for the Colonies, Lord Milner, asking him to verify press reports concerning the deportation from Britain of 100 Russian Jews accused of being 'Bolshevist propagandists'. He wondered whether similar action could be taken in Australia. Lord Milner's response was not encouraging, and he warned against any attempts to send Russian deportees to the United Kingdom for trans-shipment to Russia.[9]

Events in Australia did nothing to calm the fears of British Conservatives. Early in 1920, the so-called 'Queensland Loans Affair' occurred. E.G. Theodore, who had only recently succeeded T.J. Ryan as Labor Premier of Queensland, embarked upon a program of social change that included such legislative reforms as amendments to the Lands Act so that pastoral lessees had to pay higher rents. A group of pastoralists travelled to England and successfully lobbied the London financial institutions to refuse any further loans to the Queensland Government until the new Act was withdrawn. The loans embargo was still in place when Mitchell sought finance in 1922, although the Theodore Government had by then managed to raise loans on Wall Street. British Conservatives feared that if a Labor Government were elected in Western Australia, it might espouse similarly 'Bolshevik' reforms as those of the Theodore Government.[10]

The Western Australian Governor, Sir Francis Newdegate, was the source of other rumours, especially concerning Sinn Fein activity in the State. Western Australian sectarianism entered the international arena at the end of 1920, in a public controversy involving the Roman Catholic Archbishop, Dr Clune, and Sir Francis Newdegate. While visiting Ireland, Archbishop Clune had become deeply distressed by evidence of the brutality of British rule. He stated to the *Times* in London, 'I say with regret and reluctance that every infamy perpetrated by the Germans during the occupation of Belgium has been repeated and, in some cases, exceeded by the British forces in Ireland'.[11] Clune was invited by the British Prime Minister, Lloyd George, to travel to Dublin and interview the Sinn Fein leaders, in the hope of obtaining a temporary truce prior to opening negotiations. Clune was extremely impressed with the courage of Sinn Fein leaders Michael Collins, Desmond Fitzgerald and Kevin O'Higgins. When Lloyd George referred to them as assassins, the Archbishop corrected him: 'No Sir, not assassins but the cream of their race'. The negotiations failed, but, according to Monsignor McMahon, who accompanied Clune, the phrase 'the cream of their race...circled the globe, and played an important part in bringing about the Peace Conference of July 1921, from which the Irish Free State emerged'.[12] It also raised a furore in faraway Perth, and resulted in the Governor sending several secret telegrams to the British Government.

Newdegate took the unusual step of suggesting to Lord Milner that the Pope be prevailed upon to detain Clune in Rome. Newdegate informed Milner:

Were [Clune] prevented from landing it would raise a storm of protest. Were he to return, it appears equally certain that he would be the centre of Sinn Fein, Roman Catholic opposition to the British Empire...We are now suffering from most serious strikes, and what this State requires is peace and quiet...I would add that religious feeling runs very high here at the present time and we are suffering from [f]ires probably due to Incendiaries and have our three Bridges closely guarded.[13]

Newdegate may have been referring, in this cable, to the recent industrial unrest on the goldfields. The reference to 'guarding the bridges' is much more obscure, and evidence for such action has not been found elsewhere. Lord Milner refused to consider Newdegate's suggestion and reminded him that any recommendation of diplomatic action should come from the Commonwealth Government. The correct procedure would have been for the Governor to communicate with Sir Ronald Munro Ferguson.[14]

Archbishop Clune returned to Perth in February 1921 and, shortly after his arrival, delivered a speech in which he gave his opinion of the situation in Ireland. Undaunted by the previous rebuff, Newdegate sent off another cable to the British Colonial Secretary, informing him of Clune's speech, which he thought would be 'telegraphed all over Australia' and would do much to 'revive the bitterness which has been less apparent since the absence of Archbishop Mannix from these shores'.[15] Clune's statements appeared in the press and resulted in the publication, in March 1921, of an anonymous pamphlet entitled *The Menace to Australia and the British Empire*. The pamphlet consisted of an unsigned message 'To the People of Western Australia — Land of Loyalty and Tolerance' and of extracts from the local, interstate and overseas press on Sinn Feinism. 'Irish Catholics led by the Sinn Fein' were said to be linked with 'revolutionary extremists (many inspired from Petrograd), and German agents', in a conspiracy to bring about the 'downfall' of the British Empire. The author claimed that

So far these enemies have found Australia (particularly loyal Western Australia) poor soil in which to sow their poisonous seed, but they are being emboldened and encouraged...by...anti-British agitation springing up elsewhere — America, South Africa, Egypt and India, for there is no doubt whatever that Sinn Fein has been working assiduously to contaminate the coloured members of the British Empire...[T]hese Sinn Fein Catholics, who hate England fanatically, are working day and night like moles, insidiously

undermining firstly, all Protestants in positions of responsibility
...secondly, all the easy-going agnostics, and finally, working
against and discrediting even the members of their own religious
faith who loyally put their Empire before the Irish or any other
question.[16]

Although it is not known how widely this pamphlet was circulated, the fact that it was able to support its arguments by quoting
the *West Australian* and the *Australian* (the journal of the State RSL)
on the situation in Ireland shows that anti–Sinn Fein sentiment was
strong in Western Australia in the early months of 1921. Despite
the appearance of sectarian literature of this type, Newdegate
seems to have believed that Sinn Fein activity enjoyed little success
after Clune's return from Ireland. Even so, he found a more willing
ear for his accounts of Sinn Feinism when Winston Churchill
succeeded Lord Milner as Colonial Secretary in mid-1921. Churchill regarded Bolshevism, too, as a great evil that flourished not only
in Russia but also in the British Labour Party. Others in the British
Cabinet agreed with him.[17]

In June 1921, Churchill wrote in response to an earlier letter
from the Governor:

I was much interested in your account of the Sinn Fein agitation in
Western Australia and the mischievous speeches of Archbishop
Clune, but I note with satisfaction your assurances that their
propaganda has been without effect on the loyalty of the masses of
the population.[18]

While Churchill and Newdegate appear to have been over-
reacting to the situation, their correspondence must be set in the
context of Archbishop Mannix's activities during 1920 and 1921.
Mannix had also travelled overseas, and in July 1920 was arrested
by the British Navy while attempting to enter Ireland. Large
demonstrations were held in the United States of America and in
Australia, to protest against his arrest. Both Prime Minister Hughes
and the British Government failed in their attempts to persuade
the Vatican to recall Mannix. O'Farrell, recording these events,
commented that the fears expressed by other Australian bishops
that such an action would cause a schism in the church were
exaggerated, but Newdegate's correspondence suggests differently. By the end of 1921, however, with both Clune and Mannix
back in Australia, the situation had quietened sufficiently for

Newdegate to put his prejudices aside and commend the former for his 'wise and kindly words uttered in the Cathedral the previous night', which had been reported in the press.[19]

It is hardly surprising, however, that Newdegate's alarmist telegrams, together with Sinn Fein activities in Ireland, may have created a belief in the British Government that British settlers might not be well received in Western Australia. Britain's postwar reluctance to pursue the immigration scheme also shows that the Mitchell Government was not under pressure to accept immigrants. Why, then, did Mitchell advocate large-scale immigration to Western Australia at a time of increasing unemployment and economic uncertainty? The answer to this question derives both from the State's past history and from the postwar economic situation.

Historically, both Labor and conservative State Governments had favoured the rural sector, rather than minerals or industry, as a means of developing the State[20], and Mitchell, undoubtedly, was encouraged by his past success in settling the Wheat Belt.[21] Prior to a slump in 1923, wheat exports had increased in quantity and value each year. Areas such as Katanning, Cunderdin and Meckering reaped high-yielding harvests and relative prosperity as a result of the increased postwar demand for wheat both in Australia and abroad.[22] While some farms failed, the overall impression was one of prosperity for established farmers and wheat growers, giving credence to the powerful belief that life on the land was 'ideal' and something to which everyone should aspire.[23]

Despite Mitchell's success in developing the Wheat Belt, many of his political colleagues opposed his rural-based policies. The National coalition's brief history had been fraught with quarrels, both internally and with the powerful Primary Producers Association (PPA).[24] Two main issues created dissension among the conservatives: State enterprises and the role of the Country Party within the coalition.

The Nationals had inherited from the Scaddan administration government-owned implement works, sawmills, the State Shipping Service, and other enterprises, but had not disposed of these, despite non-Labor bias against State ownership. Some National Party Members in metropolitan electorates, urged on by employer groups, attempted to put through a series of private Bills to amend the State Trading Concerns Act, to allow the government to sell

State enterprises without having to secure parliamentary approval. Although amendment of the State Trading Concerns Act was a plank in the 1920 National Party platform, it was not achieved before the 1924 election, indicating that the administration was committed 'on paper' to this policy but that there was reluctance to carry it out.[25] The dissension over Mitchell's commitment to rural development became so severe that some seats were contested by two National Party candidates in the 1924 election.[26]

Mitchell was also under attack from another section of the conservative coalition. In 1922, after years of internal discord, the Country Party split into Executive and Ministerial factions. The Country Party's role within the coalition was central to the conflict. Those members who formed part of the National coalition and expressed loyalty to Sir James Mitchell (the Ministerials) disagreed with those who were strongly influenced by PPA President A.J. Monger (the Executives).[27] Monger and other PPA members were concerned that the Country Party had lost its independent identity. In both 1919 and 1921, the government had been reorganized without any prior consultation with the Country Party. Mitchell's continued promotion of policies that favoured the development of primary, rather than secondary, industry incurred the opposition of his colleagues within Liberal ranks. The economic historian G.D. Snooks has criticized these policies as 'unbalanced' and 'unjustified' by the economic circumstances prevailing at the time[28] — a view that appears to have been shared by some of Mitchell's Liberal colleagues.

In addition to contending with party strife, the Premier appears to have been misinformed, through some channels, about the seriousness of unemployment in the State in 1921. Mitchell received conflicting assessments of the extent of unemployment on the goldfields. Richardson, an inspector with the Agricultural Bank, who had been asked to investigate the situation, reported to the Premier early in the year that estimates varied from 1,000 to 1,200 men thrown out of work by the closure of the Gwalia and Lancefield Mines. Although he stated that these miners' prospects of obtaining work elsewhere were 'meagre', Richardson saw few indications of unemployment in Kalgoorlie. When he spoke at a meeting on land settlement, only sixty or seventy miners attended the gathering, provoking the observation that land clearing was not popular unless a daily wage was guaranteed. He saw 'little evidence of acute distress' and accused the unions of 'labouring the point' without providing 'concrete evidence'.[29] In February, Richardson wrote to the Premier, remarking yet again on the 'lack of evidence of distress and idleness'. He observed that miners were now willing to be placed elsewhere, without seeing the significance of the desperation that drove men to take up any available work. As a result of his investigation, Richardson concluded that there was 'no unemployment problem worth considering' and that the position was 'greatly exaggerated by the Labor movement'. At the same time, the AWU Secretary at Boulder was urging Mitchell to give the police authority to issue food to '400 unemployed for two months'.[30] Yet the Premier, it seems, preferred to give greater credence to Richardson's observations — perhaps because, in doing so, he did not have to instigate government action to assist the unemployed.

Mitchell's reluctance to regard unemployment as a serious issue was also evident in his attitude towards the labour deputations that came to him in the winter of 1921, seeking work for the jobless. Two deputations from the Perth Trades Hall, in July, were treated with extreme flippancy, if not contempt, by Mitchell. Rather than address the problems arising from the collapse of rural and mining industries, the Premier preferred to dwell on the 'many stoppages of work during the past few months'. He persisted in the belief that recessions were caused by strikes, and asserted that there was always 'work on the land' for those who wanted it, although the unemployed would find nothing in the city. A deputation from the ALF State Executive on 19 July reminded the Premier that the position was 'very serious', with unemployed people holding large demonstrations in the metropolitan area, and concentrations of out of work miners forming in country towns. The deputation urged Mitchell to institute home building programs, harbour works and railway construction, to combat the housing shortage and to provide employment. Mitchell agreed to discuss with the Minister for Works the prospects for carrying out sewerage works, and to meet with John Curtin, at that time an Executive member of the State ALF, to examine the possibility of establishing an Employment Commission.[31]

The ALF's warnings were not exaggerated. Daily meetings of the unemployed were being held on the Perth Esplanade, with a regular attendance of 400 or 500 people. Speakers from the Trades

Hall declared that it was a disgrace that Mitchell was promising to place immigrants in jobs within twenty-four hours of their arrival in the State, while there were so many unemployed. Hundreds of men would soon be retrenched on the railways.[32]

A further deputation to the Premier, in September, included Legislative Assembly Members Clydesdale and Simons, Edward Needham, Secretary of the ALF Metropolitan District Council, and five men whom Clydesdale described as being 'not red raggers' but 'absolutely genuine cases'. One of them, Fisher, was married with five children. During the winter, he had obtained 'about three months work, broken time, at £2 per week', and had been unable to provide sufficient food and clothing for his family. Another man, Cross, had been discharged from the army six months previously and had obtained only six weeks' work since then. He was married, with four children, and was prepared to do 'anything but clearing'. Before the war, he had worked as a telephone linesman. Cross's reluctance to do clearing work was understandable in the light of the experiences of another member of the deputation, who had cleared red gum for 25s an acre (0.4 hectare). The hardwood timber was so tough that each acre cleared was a week's work.[33] The appalling working conditions of clearing contractors were to be highlighted in September 1922 by a group of men striking in the Newdegate area. They alleged that they had been cheated by the government, which had haggled over the number of acres they had cleared, and that the Lands Department had not given them credit for items of equipment they had returned, such as kit, groceries, axes and blankets.[34]

Even if these cases and the previous deputations were insufficient to dissuade the Premier from his immigration scheme, the figures from the State Labor Bureau ought to have attracted his attention. In 1920, 2,462 men and 750 women applied for work through the bureau, and 2,827 employees were placed in jobs.[35] At the end of 1921, out of over 5,000 applications for work, only 2,252 men and 947 women had been placed. Perhaps even more significantly, employers applied for fewer workers in 1921 than they had in 1920.[36] Furthermore, the State Labor Bureau was able to present Mitchell with a profile of which types of workers were most susceptible to unemployment. In March 1922, for example, 867 men and 334 women applied for work, an increase of 260 over the figures for the same month in the previous year. Over 400 of the men were labourers and 140 were farm hands. A few, such as horsedrivers or barmen, possessed a trade, and only seven were professionals. The majority of women were from one of three groups: laundresses/charwomen, cooks or 'general' workers. All female applicants sought employment in domestic or hotel work; none were professionals.[37]

While unwilling to concede that the labour movement had put a strong case for the need to develop public works, Mitchell was influenced by powerful interest groups such as the PGA, and by advice from Britain concerning the State's interests. The PGA Secretary wrote to the Premier, during the 1921 shearers' strike:

> It is strange that while on the one hand the deputations from the Trades Hall are interviewing you asking for relief work for the unemployed, their supporters are lying in wait at the Ports and Railway Stations, which are closely picketed, endeavouring to prevent men from going into the country to carry out their lawful contracts at high rates of pay.[38]

The PGA's attitude exemplified the absolute refusal of employer organizations to comprehend the importance to trade unionists of maintaining award wages and conditions in a time when many went jobless. Unionists believed that, rather than providing work for more people, sustenance allowances simply undermined previous gains and provided employers with cheap labour. Apart from those expressing employer interests in his own State, Mitchell also followed advice from D.J. Doherty, of the London Wool Exchange, who urged him to visit England, to promote both immigration and trade. Doherty saw the proposed visit as being in the interests of the government, of the Kimberley graziers and of the State generally[39], and his opinion was supported by Western Australia's Agent-General in London, John Connolly, a keen advocate of immigration schemes.[40]

Sir James and Lady Mitchell arrived in London in March 1922. At a luncheon in their honour at the Hotel Cecil, Lord Burnham[41] referred to the immigration scheme as a 'God given opportunity of the British Empire to people its lands with British stock'. Under the Empire Settlement Scheme, jointly financed by British and Commonwealth Government loans, 80,000 British emigrants were to be settled annually in Australia, for two years, with possible extension to 1924. Six thousand farms were to be established in Western

Australia (under what was called the Group Settlement Scheme).[42] The British press heralded Mitchell's advent with accounts of his extravagant promises. 'Room for 100,000 in North West Australia', proclaimed the London *Daily News*. The article quoted a report of conditions in the North West, described as '15 million acres varying from stony hills to magnificent black soil plains', which were 'drought proof'. Similar reports appeared in the Scottish and Irish press.[43] The *Daily Mail* reported on 'A Premier with land to give away', while the *Canadian Gazette* remarked, 'We should not be satisfied with the fact that the white population of this vast Empire is 60,000,000. Sir James Mitchell thinks it should be 150,000,000.'[44] The Premier, in fact, asked for 'two million people', claiming that there was 'work for all in Western Australia'.[45]

Sir James Mitchell
The Northam farmer who became Premier asked for 'two million' British farmers to settle in the South West of the State. Mitchell was an 'old West Australian'. He became the founding President of the Royal Western Australian Historical Society.
[Courtesy Royal Western Australian Historical Society, B768]

Despite his welcome by the press, Mitchell arrived in London to find that the British Government was still reluctant to go ahead with the immigration scheme. Its main concern now was that the scheme would collapse if Labor was returned to office in Western Australia.[46] This caused frantic politicking in Western Australia, with Mitchell attempting to enlist Philip Collier's help in persuading the British Government that the policies of the conservatives and Labor differed very little. He suggested that the Opposition leader should 'come home' in order to convince the British Cabinet that the scheme would not be threatened by a change of government[47], but Collier refused the invitation. He did not wish to arrive in Britain six or seven weeks after the Premier, nor could he support the Premier's claim that the State would absorb 25,000 immigrants a year. Already, he claimed, there were 200 applicants waiting for blocks.[48]

Although Group Settlement proper did not commence until after the Empire Settlement Agreement had been signed, British emigrants were accepted for rural settlement in 1921. These settlers were expected to complete a year's experience working for local farmers before receiving their blocks, but some appear to have been allocated land very soon after arrival. The '200 applicants' to whom Collier referred were English immigrants who had worked their year on the land and were ready to be allocated blocks of their own. In addition, the Mitchell Government had assisted a number of unemployed workers — mainly wheat lumpers and miners who were probably ex-National unionists — to acquire blocks in the South West of the State. The first settlement, Group 1, was established near Manjimup in March 1921, and consisted mainly of the unemployed Western Australian workers. Another early group site, to which English immigrants were sent, was on the Peel Estate.[49]

The Empire Settlement Bill passed its third reading in the House of Commons on 22 May 1922, and the agreement was signed by Churchill and Sir Joseph Cook in July.[50] But even before the agreement was finalized, some press and public reaction in Western Australia had changed from support to opposition. The two main areas of criticism were the terms of the imperial loan and the quality of the immigrants who had already been settled on rural blocks. Concerning the former, the *Sunday Times* editorial of 7 May remarked:

> While Mitchell is talking in London about hundreds of thousands
> of immigrants per annum, and borrowing millions to put them on
> the land, the appalling deficit keeps on mounting up like a pyra-
> mid — an inverted pyramid — that threatens to be an eternal
> monument to his disastrous reign in Western Australia.

The editorial went on to point out that of the £2 million loan, Western Australia would get 'only £95 in each £100, and still pay 5 per cent interest, that is £5,000 per annum', on money that the State did not receive; Victoria, on the other hand, received £98 in each £100.[51] The newspaper's comparison with Victoria is not clear, for immigration to Victoria and all of the other States except Western Australia was controlled by the Commonwealth.[52]

Commenting on the unsuitability of many of the immigrants as farmers, the *Call*, previously a zealous supporter of Mitchell's immigration policy, now declared that the British Government was 'selling us a pup'. The State, it said, wanted 'farmers not city loungers' or 'physically impossibles' or 'hopeless inefficients'.[53] The UMA also complained about the 'quality' of British settlers, especially those who had been settled the previous year in the districts of Hobson's Bay and Omar.[54] This criticism is rather surprising, for the UMA was the foremost non-government pro-moter of assisted immigration from Britain. One wonders why the organization did not take greater care to 'screen' prospective farmers.

Even members of Mitchell's own party had reservations about the scheme. A. Lovekin MLC had written privately to Mitchell, prior to the Premier's departure for England, expressing unease about the conditions of any imperial loan to finance settlers. Lovekin observed that the newly established farms would pro-duce virtually nothing for five years, during which time the State would have to recoup £900,000 interest. Furthermore, with a male workforce of only 105,000 and a 'per capita debt of £5 million', the government was not justified in committing its citizens to a 'fur-ther annual liability of £180,000 for 5 years, and £360,000 per annum thereafter'. Lovekin believed that the British Government should pay for the immigrants until they became self-supporting, as an alternative to feeding them at home.[55]

Perhaps the most disillusioned and critical group of all were the settlers themselves. In March 1922, Florence Burt, of Block 670 on

the Peel Estate, communicated her grievances to the Premier, in a
letter filled with outrage and disappointment:

> You guaranteed employment on arrival, instead of which we were
> literally fighting for a job for over three weeks. Eventually we were
> dumped on a pest-ridden swamp unfit for white women and
> children, and finally the selection, which seems to need some
> explanation, people being under the impression that it is a gift
> instead of £8/10/- and upwards per acre with 7 per cent interest.
>
> The children are hideous sights owing to the pests with which
> we are infested and I myself am a nervous wreck through the
> unsatisfactory conditions I am living under. If prompt action is not
> taken, the bulk of the so-called settlers (there are no real settlers at
> heart) will be all lunatics or suicides...[56]

Florence Burt was one of the 1921 British immigrants who had been
allocated a block prior to the Group Settlement Scheme. The
greatest influx of group settlers commenced in 1923, and, as they
came, so did their complaints. However, none of the criticisms
about the terms of the loan, the unsuitability of English city-
dwellers, and the appalling reality of the 'paradise' to which the
unfortunate immigrants were lured appear to have been given the
slightest heed by the State Government.

Most of the group settlements were located between Busselton
and Augusta, with others near Bridgetown, Manjimup, Pemberton,
Northcliffe and Denmark. Before 1921, the South West was very
sparsely populated. There were no railway lines beyond Busselton
and Pemberton. The main road to Augusta was a track winding
through dense timber, so boggy during the winter rains that it was
impassable in places. Each group was to consist of twenty families.
The men would jointly clear 5 acres (2 hectares), partly clear a
further 25 acres (10 hectares), and erect a cottage on each 160-acre
(65-hectare) block. Then a ballot would be held to allocate blocks
to settlers, presumably in the interests of fairness, so that no one
knew which block was his while he was undertaking the prelimi-
nary work. Before their farms were capable of yielding profit, the
State Government would pay the farmers £3 per week. All settlers,
local and British, joined the scheme under these terms.[57]

In recent years, several studies have been made of Group
Settlement in Western Australia. None has attempted to disguise
the hardships the immigrants suffered, and all have commented to
some extent on the failures and shortcomings of the Mitchell
administration. According to Crowley, the scheme was a disaster,

for about 30 per cent of all immigrant group settlers and 42 per cent of those who were Australian-born had left their holdings by April 1924.[58] Gabbedy, who was extremely sympathetic to the scheme, stated that, by 1928, £8 million had been spent on Group Settlement, and that, because so many farmers had abandoned their blocks, only 1,622 holdings remained of the original 2,442.[59] Gabbedy did not attempt to analyse how or why Mitchell could so confidently 'sell' land he had never seen and the quality of which he was totally incompetent to judge. In conclusion, he agreed with the group settler who wrote that 'Sir James...was not to blame' for the scheme's failures. 'It was one of the finest schemes ever started and if he had been allowed to stay in office [in 1933] everything would have been alright'.[60] The earliest and most critical assessment of Mitchell's policy was that of I.L. Hunt, who concluded that the Group Settlement Scheme foundered because the Premier was 'an autocrat and something of a visionary' who saw himself as the immigrants' benefactor. Mitchell, claimed Hunt, gave virtually no attention to the details of the scheme and, as a result, 'an undertaking that required years of methodical preparation was flung together at short notice'.[61]

Hunt was an even harsher critic of the 'groupies' (as group settlers were usually called), themselves. She stated that few were distressed by their lack of ability to make their blocks viable, because many had no intention of remaining on their holdings, being content to claim weekly sustenance payments and do as little work as possible.[62] While it is probable that some of the immigrants fitted this category, far more were undoubtedly wooed by the idyllic and inaccurate descriptions of rural life in Western Australia, which the State Government circulated in the British Isles. The following is an example:

> Nearly ninety groups have been established since May, 1921, when the first was inaugurated. More than 1,600 individual settlers are working on the groups, and, with their wives and families, form a community of 5,000 souls, clearing, fencing, ploughing, sowing — yes, and harvesting, too, where a couple of years ago was the solitude of primeval forest...[T]he aggregate area of a group [twenty families] is in the neighbourhood of 2,000 acres. The land is carefully classified and surveyed, so as to include only soil suitable to intense culture and dairying...Water is abundant in streams and springs, and the climate is mild, whilst the rainfall is anything from 40 to 50 inches annually...Solitude, that curse of pioneering in other days, is unknown.[63]

The idyllic, rustic image was perpetuated in local press articles such as those penned by 'Politicus' in the *West Australian*, who wrote of schools full of

> 40, 50, 60...happy kids. Youngsters from the tailings dump of Boulder; urchins from the ports; little pommies preserving in their cheeks the glow of Devonshire apples, or importing into factory-stamped pallor the glow of life in God's open spaces.

Here, the images of purity engendered by a rural life, as opposed to the corruption of the city, are as strong as in any nineteenth-century literature; yet even 'Politicus' descended to reality by referring to the settlers' having to stop leaks in their 'temporary' cottages.[64]

At the other extreme from these depictions of rural contentment and prosperity is a satirical poem, written by an unknown author — possibly a 'groupie' — to 'celebrate' James Mitchell's announcement that there were presently '600,000 acres of cultivable land available for selection in the state':

> Half a mile, half a mile, half a mile onward,
> Scattered throughout the State
> Are the Six Hundred
> Acres of Scrubby Plain
> Never a drop of rain
> Miles from the nearest train
> Barren Six Hundred
>   ...
> Sand plains to right of 'em,
> Salt lakes to left of 'em,
> Poison all over 'em,
> Jimmy's six hundred;
> Storms never break the spell,
> Heat like a blast from Hell,
> Dead rabbits, phew! the smell!
> Vainly Jim tries to sell
> Barren six hundred.
>
> Farmers from everywhere,
> Seeing no subtle snare,
> Listen to Jim's 'hot air'
> Re. the six hundred.
> Some who weren't in the 'joke' —
> Fresh from the good 'Old Smoke' —
> Went out and came back broke
> From the Six Hundred.[65]

Mrs Irene Cameron's memory of Group Settlement was far closer to the unknown poet's image. Mrs Cameron, whose family had moved from England, during her childhood, to settle initially on the Peel Estate — Florence Burt's 'pest-ridden swamp' — recalled that 'there wasn't even a blade of grass for a chook to eat'. The uncleared block was too small to graze the fifteen cows normally allotted by the Agricultural Bank, so at first the family received only three. Most of their neighbours had never seen a cow and had to be shown how to milk, and how to harness a horse.[66] Many of the would-be farmers were similarly unskilled. A.E. George, who had served with the British Army as a grenadier during the war and who was a factory worker by occupation, was probably better equipped than many, because he had gained three years' land experience as a boy and knew 'rough carpentering'. He and his wife and child had been in Western Australia two days when they were assigned to a group, in October 1923.[67] Another ex-soldier, H.W. Arms, a tractor mechanic, had no knowledge of carpentry or blacksmithing — he specifically stated he could not shoe a horse — although he had worked in South America for a year, driving a tractor. He arrived in January 1924, with his wife and baby daughter, and was assigned a block the following day.[68] Both of these families arrived in the hot season and had no period of adjustment or acclimatization before facing the gruelling work and primitive conditions of the bush.

On joining the group, each settler signed an agreement stating that he would be prepared to work such daily hours as directed by the foreman, unless his absence was approved. Contracts were signed only by males, wives and families presumably being regarded as under their control. Any man whose work was judged unsatisfactory could be 'retired from the settlement without compensation', although he had the right of appeal to the Group Settlement Advisory Committee.[69] The foreman policed this agreement, sending a monthly report to the Controller of Group Settlement, assessing the progress of each settler as a potential farmer.[70] There seems little doubt that settlers were sometimes victimized by foremen as a result of personal disagreements or animosity. The foreman had the power to dismiss 'troublesome' and 'incompetent' group members. On Group 67, for example, foreman Davey commented of one settler:

> This man is very hard to understand, very fickle minded and
> changeable, suffering from after effects of malaria, and I am afraid
> if there is no improvement in his ways, I shall have to dispense
> with him.

Davey's successor, Newbold, warned another farmer that he would be 'suspended' if he continued to disobey orders, and reported him as having caused 'dissension' among the settlers.[71]

The Group 44 foreman, Parmenter, reported several members as 'agitators', including a man named Thomas, who was the leader of the Progress Association. He and three others were singled out because 'while these men are employed on the Group [it] will be impossible to get the men to work more than an eight hour day'.[72] Parmenter dismissed three settlers from Group 44: one of the 'agitators', A. Jegust, who was also described as being 'very idle', and Mr and Mrs Cory, who were judged to be unfit because of their 'indecent behaviour' and 'idle habits'. The report did not elaborate further. Others left of their own accord; for example C. Burge, who was classified as a 'very good worker', declined to work for 'seven shillings a day'. Thomas was still a member of Group 44 in January 1925, when Parmenter again reported him and four other men — Lord, Fielder, Hodgkinson and Woodvine — as 'agitators'. Woodvine was said to have threatened to take Parmenter's life when the two quarrelled over some furniture that had been left behind by another settler. Parmenter also reported Woodvine as having said that if another 'groupie' named Burgess attempted to work overtime, he would 'burn off his bloody fingers'. The foreman commented further:

> Men of this kind are going to discurage [sic] other settlers that are
> willing to try and make a success on the land. Settler[s] Thomas,
> Woodvine, Lord, Hodgkinson and Fielder are the cause of the most
> trouble on this Group and I don't think there is one of this five
> [who] intends to remain as a settler, if I ask them to work overtime
> on burning off operations, they argue the point for nearly the full
> period they are asked to work and say I have no authority to ask
> them to work overtime remooving [sic] stumps on the location they
> are burning off.

Parmenter asked for a 're-worded circular' stressing the authority of the foreman concerning burning off, removing stumps, and other duties.[73] Obviously, the men were reneging on the terms of the agreement they had signed, but, regrettably, their side of the argument has not been preserved. Nothing is known of their backgrounds, although it is probable that they were accustomed to tactics of union solidarity and regarded the conditions on the groups as exploitative.

By September 1927, of the 'agitators' on Group 44, only the frail Lord remained, and the current foreman praised his work and the condition of his stock and plant. The original twenty holdings on this group had been reduced to seven, by amalgamations, and Lord owned two or three of these blocks. He was aided by his wife and three children, but even these apparently successful settlers left in January 1928.[74] They had been among the original twenty families when the group was established in August 1923, and had laboured for four and a half years, attempting to transform their land into a viable farm. Many of the unsuccessful settlers left debts behind, some of which never were repaid.[75]

As 1922 drew to a close, the British press, which had so uncritically accepted the Group Settlement Scheme during Mitchell's visit earlier that year, began publishing indications that all was not well in the rural paradise of Western Australia. The London *Daily News* reported the case of five emigrants from Hull, who had stowed away on a ship to return to Britain. Western Australia's Agent-General, John Connolly, stated that there was 'no just and reasonable cause' for the men to have returned to their homeland. Indeed, Western Australia had received 'upwards of 20,000 emigrants during the last year' and still the government was asking for more. The British press tended to agree that those who failed to 'make it' had been unsuitable in the first place. The *Liverpool Journal of Commerce* observed, 'Because a fellow has been a soldier and has proved himself to be a good stout fighting man it does not follow as a matter of course that he is a wise man, too'. Similarly, the *Edinburgh Evening News* agreed that settlers of the 'right quality' would be able to rough it, to work very hard, and to set aside trade union rules and regulations.[76] The message was reinforced by an account of a 'successful settler', which received wide publicity throughout the English counties in April and May 1923.[77]

The truth was further obscured by continuing government censorship in Western Australia. On 11 October 1922, the British newspaper the *Cornishman* published a letter from W.G. Nancarrow, a guard on the Mullewa Railway, who warned intending emigrants not to come to Western Australia, because of the high level of unemployment. He had picked up fourteen immigrants who had been left stranded and moneyless by unscrupulous agents. Nancarrow believed that 1922 was the worst year that he had known since emigrating from Cornwall himself almost twelve years previously. Recently, 500 men had been sacked from the railways. He saw more poverty in Western Australia than he had ever seen in Cornwall.[78] Mitchell's Secretary, Shapcott, traced Nancarrow through the Railways Department and demanded an explanation for the letter. The railway guard replied that, although he had written in a fit of indignation after encountering the fourteen immigrants, he had on many occasions given unemployed immigrants food from his own tuckerbox. As a Cornishman, he felt 'very keenly' the plight of fellow immigrants. He believed, however, that since he had written, the position had improved and he hoped it would continue to do so. Nancarrow's knuckles were well and truly rapped by Shapcott, who supposed 'he had not written back to the *Cornishman* to explain the improved conditions'. The letter continued:

> A letter of warning...stands as a perpetual reference. It is hardly considered fair, therefore, that a State servant should publish such a sweeping condemnation of the Government's policy because of a condition which he now admits is temporary, while he refrains from correcting the misimpression thus created. Your letter caused some annoyance at this end as it can scarcely be regarded as a correct representation of the general condition of affairs, and I would suggest the wisdom of not publicly airing your views upon the policy of the Government when your knowledge of the matter is generally very limited.[79]

Similarly, the following September, the Agent-General sent Mitchell a coded cable advising that an 'anonymous Perth correspondent' had informed the English press that there were 1,200 unemployed in the metropolitan area and that these numbers would be boosted by the arrival of 400 emigrants from Britain in the coming week. The Premier cabled a reply that there had been a 'slight slackness' in June and July, owing to exceptionally heavy rains, but no unemployment existed now. Migrants, he asserted, were usually placed immediately. Yet the State Labor Bureau figures from the Perth and Fremantle offices show that on 3 September alone, less than a quarter of over 200 applicants were placed in work. On 28 August, only twenty out of 152 were found employment.[80]

Even the few public works projects embarked upon by the Mitchell Government aroused controversy. Country Party Members protested at a decision to build a tramway in the Perth suburb of Como, declaring that no such work should be commenced without the assent of parliament.[81] Instead, they believed, the government should construct country railway lines, which had been authorized by parliament as far back as 1914, and which were essential to agricultural development. Nevertheless, the government pressed ahead with the construction of the Como tramway, which Scaddan opened on 28 October 1922. After that, the Premier received deputations from various metropolitan councils, asking for tramline extensions to other suburbs.[82]

Despite the tramway project, unemployed people increasingly expressed their discontent at the government's inability to provide work.[83] On 2 June 1922, a group of about 150 men and women gathered in front of the Legislative Council, demanding to see the Acting Premier, Colebatch, who came out to a mixed reception. Police reported that at times the 'temper of the crowd was nasty', and they had to remove some people who had climbed over the palisade. Several women were among the speakers. A few days later, some 300 people marched from the Trades Hall to the Treasury Buildings in St Georges Terrace. Another deputation was sent to see Colebatch. Needham addressed the swelling crowd, telling them that the government had nothing to offer. Most of the men present then went to the Charities Department and waited for two hours. At 4 o'clock, they were informed that only the married men present would be given assistance. The single men were turned away empty-handed. The ALF Unemployment Committee later obtained from Colebatch a scale for relief rations that the Charities Department would allocate to unemployed men with dependants. The ration amounted to 1s per head per day for each man, woman, and child under fourteen, for a maximum period of four consecutive days. Colebatch finally relented to pressure from the ALF delegation and agreed to institute a ration for single men, also, to be issued daily for a maximum of three consecutive days.[84]

Increasingly, police officers were discovering the homeless camped in various parts of the city. On one night alone, in June 1922, police reported fourteen men sleeping around the Esplanade, in a parked lorry, a boat shed, and other places. All declined beds at the Salvation Army Home, declaring that they were 'clean' in their present position and would rather stay there. The police did not move them on or charge them with vagrancy.[85] As the situation became more desperate, some unemployed workers 'scabbed' by accepting lower than award wages. The ALF discovered that men were gardening in Kings Park for 10s a day instead of 13s 4d. A meeting of the ALF State Executive resolved to 'take steps to protect the minimum wage rates' after being informed that 'able-bodied' men were being employed by the War Distress and Unemployment Fund Committee for the same daily rate as the gardeners.[86]

Despite the indignities heaped upon them, the unemployed continued to show that they possessed plenty of spirit. A big crowd demonstrated outside the *Sunday Times* office, protesting against statements made by that newspaper to the effect that 'a large number had been placed in work', and that the Trades Hall was 'enjoying publicity' as a result of exploiting the unemployment situation. The editor agreed to withdraw the offending paragraph from a subsequent issue of the paper. His apology did not satisfy many of the crowd, and they again marched to the newspaper office a few days later and symbolically 'counted out' the *Sunday Times*.[87]

The reactions of the employed to the plight of the unemployed were mixed. One of Perth's citizens, John Hinde of the Esplanade, wrote to Colebatch, observing that 'not half' of the number catered for had turned up at the RSL dinner for the needy. He presumed, therefore, that either 'the distress is not so great as stated' or that 'the Trades Hall officials would not take the trouble to notify the hungry men'. He suggested that the Trades Hall supply the names and addresses of the unemployed to charities, who could contact them directly.[88] An invitation to another charity luncheon, at the Returned Soldiers and Sailors Institute the following week, was accepted by only 100 men. The organizers were reportedly disappointed, as they had catered for four times that number. This provoked a public response from one of the jobless, who wrote to the *West Australian*:

> In reading between the lines it is quite clear that...there are 75 per cent of the unemployed who have too much self respect to parade their unfortunate position before the public. I am a married man

with three children and have been unable to obtain employment for four months, yet I could not lower myself to accept such charity or to march in a procession to the Premier's Office to be a laughing stock of the employed, well-filled, well-dressed and therefore 'don't care' public, or to sit down with a knife and fork before the well-meaning, generous citizens and hear their whispered expressions [of sympathy], 'Poor things, how sad!'.[89]

This letter, signed 'One of Many', inspired a thoughtful response from another reader, who wrote:

We see in your paper each day that work is being found for very large numbers of unemployed but this morning I had to cross over the street to pass the Trades Hall, as there were easily 250 unemployed, in front of the building, and the entrance and corridors were packed.

This man thought that the crowd at the Trades Hall did not represent 'half of those anxious to earn a living'. He concluded that there was 'more genuine want in Perth today than there has been for the last eight years'. He also cited the case of a woman whom he knew, with four children. Her husband's pay had amounted to £2 in seven weeks, and the weekly family income, mainly from the oldest child's earnings, averaged £1. They lived on 'porridge and bread and jam'. This family did not want to march in processions and was 'too proud to let others know their desperate need'.[90]

His observations were confirmed by a letter that Needham wrote to Colebatch, early in July 1922, concerning the acute distress of the unemployed, and the government's unfulfilled promises to secure work for them. In the first three weeks of June, the number of unemployed on the Trades Hall Register had risen from 500 to 900, and only 170 had been placed in work. Needham estimated that '1,100 men' had registered at the State Labor Bureau during the month. It is unclear whether women were included in this total. Needham did, however, draw Colebatch's attention to the fact that women, and even expectant mothers, were homeless on the streets of Perth. In a passage, moving in its eloquence and pathos, he wrote:

Distress and destitution still stalk in the community. Women about to become mothers are in destitute circumstances. Men are sleeping in the basement of the Ritz Hotel in mid-winter with nothing but a blanket and a cement floor...[T]he Distress Committee at Trades

> Hall were assisting cases of impending maternity and issuing
> tickets for bread, saveloys, milk for infants, etc. from a small fund
> donated by sympathetic citizens. This fund is now exhausted.[91]

These are the 'depression' images that one tends to equate with
Perth and other Australian cities in the 1930s. There is nothing of
this in Crowley's account of the 'prosperous' 1920s.[92]

Demonstrations and deputations continued throughout the
winter and spring of 1922. During Mitchell's absence in England,
RSL deputations led by Talbot Hobbs and H.E. Bolton had received
little practical assistance from Colebatch.[93] In September, after
Mitchell's return, over 100 returned soldiers invaded a Cabinet
meeting. They left at the Premier's request but sent six representatives to meet with him later in the day. They told him that the RSL
had been drawing attention to the grievances of ex-servicemen for
months, without success. Some 900 returned soldiers were unemployed, including seventy 'maimed and limbless', they claimed,
and employers did not grant them preference, despite statements
to this effect in the press. The Premier was adamant, however, that
returned men were given preference in government service.[94]
While publicly appearing insensitive to the plight of the unemployed, privately Mitchell was remarkably generous. The Premier's records contain a letter from H. Munday, of Guildford, who
facetiously headed his street address 'Rabbit Warren'. Munday
wrote to Mitchell:

> Could you cause to be sent to the wife a few lying in things, as she
> is expecting any time now. I would not write this to you only I
> have 7 mouths to feed and another little one coming along, and I
> have only been able to command casual work...I had 10 days out of
> work at Christmas and no pay and all these depending on me.
> Could you manage to place me in something permanent on the
> railway line somewhere so as to give the little ones a chance...

Mitchell responded by arranging for Brennans' Emporium to send
a parcel of baby clothes, but whether he was able to secure any
work for Munday is unknown.[95]

In the winter of 1923, a new element entered the discontent of
the unemployed. On 26 July, an angry crowd gathered outside
Parliament House as the Governor, Sir Francis Newdegate, arrived
to open parliament. Police noted the prominence of 'immigrants'
among the demonstrators. Millington, Panton and T.J. Hughes

addressed the crowd, telling them that the Premier was 'too busy to see them'. A man whom police recognized as an immigrant, possibly because of his accent, shouted out, 'Yes, he's too busy stuffing his guts. He gets champagne; we can't even get beer. Let us go in and get the scraps they leave.' Millington said that the demonstrators had better go away, as 'nothing could be done'. Another interjector called out, 'Go away with your tail between your legs'. An Englishman named Frank Lewis, whom the police regarded as a 'principal agitator', threatened to go inside and 'see' the Premier. 'I'd like to see them [the Premier and the Governor?] in Whitechapel. I know who would go away with their tail[s] between their legs. I have seen it many a time. They brought us out here to starve.' Lewis, a hod-carrier from Bristol, had worked at clearing land for 12s 6d per acre (half the prewar rate), and also at his trade. When interviewed by police, he commented, 'Australia is a wash-out. I am getting some papers sent to London showing up immigration which is a wash-out.'[96]

The Mitchell Government, therefore, was faced with numerous problems related to its immigration program and the large number of unemployed in the State. Mitchell's policy of providing employment almost exclusively in rural areas had failed. The imperialist ideology that undergirded his land settlement policies did not take into account the unsuitability of the Australian climate and countryside for close settlement. Consequently, the group settlers, far from conning the government, as Hunt inferred in her criticism of the scheme, were themselves frequent victims of genuine, if unintended, exploitation. Many of those who initially cleared the blocks not only failed to benefit from the fruits of their labour but left owing debts. Apart from the experience gained, they were often worse off than they had been before they started.

The most potentially exploitative emigration schemes, however, were those run by charities such as the Young Australia League (YAL) and the New Settlers League (NSL), and involving the resettlement of boys (and, occasionally, girls). Probably the most successful of these schemes was instituted by an individual, Kingsley Fairbridge, and had been in operation since 1913. Fairbridge's vision also epitomized the concept of a 'sturdy British yeomanry' peopling the Empire. He planned to 'shift the orphans of Britain to the shores of Greater Britain, where farmers and farmers' wives are wanted'.[97] Similar aims were espoused by the organizers of the YAL's Boy Immigration Scheme: Harold Boas, J.J. Simons and A.S. McClintock.[98] Early in 1923, Mitchell accepted the YAL's proposal to 'receive and act as guardian to a number of English boys who would be selected by the Church Lads' Brigade of England'. A conference held at the Palace Hotel, Perth, to discuss details was attended by Sir William Windham and other members of the British Overseas Delegation on Immigration; Clydesdale, representing the NSL and the ALF; Crawcour, State Director of Immigration; and several YAL officers. The YAL proposed to establish a number of 'parents' in metropolitan and country areas near the boys' places of work. Windham's queries, as to who would find employment for the boys and whether any apprenticeships would be offered, do not appear to have been adequately answered. Even so, the scheme was passed by Mitchell in September 1923, and it was suggested that, if the boys were suitably settled, girl emigrants might also be considered. The fact that the scheme did not come to fruition was only because the Labor Government, which took office in 1924, had objections to encouraging immigration when 'local lads' could fill vacancies, and placed it in abeyance.[99]

The other major non-government group involved in immigration, the NSL, was a branch of the UMA, which had been involved in repatriation schemes. Despite Clydesdale, Clementson and Tom Butler serving on its executive, or as ALF delegates, the NSL's schemes also exploited workers. The league provoked ALF indignation by fixing the basic wage for agricultural labourers at 25s a week. The ALF requested that the Mitchell Government establish a tribunal to fix the basic wage of workers in agricultural industries, thus preventing this type of exploitation.[100] This request appears to have been ignored, for, the following year, the NSL announced that 4,197 people (including fifty-seven children) had been placed in positions in agricultural areas, at a weekly rate of 25s for single men and £2 to £2 10s for married couples. The NSL Secretary reported that although there had been a 'large amount of criticism' regarding the type of 'migrant' and the wages paid, 'good men' always had their wages increased as they became more efficient.[101]

A very different story emerged at an ALF conference, where disenchanted immigrants had an opportunity to air their grievances. One immigrant claimed that the Labor Exchange in Britain 'picked out' men to go to Australia. 'If you refuse to go they stop your pay.' He had had to walk 25 miles (40 kilometres) into the bush to reach his first job, and had lasted there only three weeks, his employer claiming he was 'no good'. Wry laughter greeted his assertion that his former employer had wanted an 'experienced farmer' at 25s a week. A Glasgow man said it was costing him £4 5s per week to keep his wife and two children at the Immigrants Home in Fremantle. He had been told about a land flowing with milk and honey, but had found exactly the same here as he had left in Scotland — starvation and misery.[102]

In September 1923, NSL members called on the Premier to present the resolutions that had been passed at their Annual Conference. Some of the deputation members believed the failure rate of immigrants as farmers to be about 20 per cent, although 'less than one per cent' failed as 'citizens'. This comment suggests a revision of the original belief that those who did not succeed as farmers somehow lacked moral fibre. The conference had passed a resolution recommending that the Western Australian Government select more emigrants from the 'country districts of Great Britain'. The Premier raised this matter with the Prime Minister and also with the Agent-General in London, and was assured that emigrants were recruited with the greatest care. At least 80 per cent of prospective emigrants were seen personally by an official of the Migration and Settlement Office before being accepted for an assisted passage.[103]

Perhaps the final irony of the settlement schemes was that, while the unemployed and rural workers competed for jobs with newly arrived immigrants, the WA Employers' Federation was complaining of the lack of skilled artisans in the State. The Master Builders and Contractors' Association claimed that it could employ 250 bricklayers, plasterers and carpenters. Likewise, the Chamber of Mines drew attention to a general scarcity of skilled workers on the goldfields. The Chamber of Manufacturers advised that there were vacancies for eleven furniture workers, forty to fifty clothing machinists, twenty bootmakers, and twelve motor body builders, in industries in the metropolitan area. Although there were unemployed artisans in Britain, the government appears never to have entertained the possibility of sponsoring migrants in any capacity except as farmers.[104] Conversely, in the Eastern States, it appears that skilled British artisans had displaced some local tradesmen. This happened in only four unions in Western Australia. The AWU Goldfields Branch reported that some young farm workers had been replaced by immigrants, thus creating a local labour surplus. Both the Federated Seamen's Union (FSU) and the Amalgamated Society of Engineers (ASE) advised that some fifty of their positions had gone to new arrivals, the ASE specifically stating that 'immigrants who came to this state for the purpose of going on the land' were being employed in place of the union's members in some factories and workshops. Similarly, the Operative Bakers informed the Trades Hall that not only had 'some immigrants joined the Bakers Union' but other non-unionists had obtained work in the country at places which 'could not or would not' employ union labour.[105]

By the end of 1923, therefore, although the unemployment crisis was lessening, James Mitchell's Group Settlement Scheme was disintegrating in a welter of criticism from discouraged immigrants, from disenchanted employers, and from the labour movement, which saw hard-won privileges being whittled away by the reintroduction of poor wages and long hours. The British Government, also, was disappointed by the outcome of the scheme. In the House of Commons in May 1924, Sir John Marriott bemoaned the slow rate of progress under the Empire Settlement Act. While disclaiming any criticisms of His Majesty's Government, he asked the Members present to envisage a situation whereby Britain's one million unemployed were transferred to Australia:

> We should be saved in this country at least £100 million a year in unemployment relief...[I]n Australia they would become consumers of English produce and English manufactures, certainly to the extent of not less than £10 million a year.

From this one-sided view, Marriott diverted only to point out that the scheme benefited Australia because a 'white', 'British' population was desired there. In reality, instead of an expected 80,000 emigrants per annum being absorbed, the entire number sent to all the dominions in two years was approximately 112,000.[106]

Two months prior to Marriott's speech in the House of Commons, the people of Western Australia voted the Labor Party, under the leadership of Philip Collier, into power. In 1922, the British Government had feared that a return to Labor would founder the emigration scheme and plunge the State into socialism. Collier had refused to endorse Mitchell's land settlement policy in order to quiet these fears. As Premier, he now had the opportunity to change that policy, and to attempt to reverse the defeats that Labor had suffered since the onset of the 1920s.

1   Premier's Department File (hereafter PDF) 208/21. Mitchell was knighted in June 1921.
2   *West Australian*, 23 March 1922. Mitchell was quoted from a speech that he gave on his first public appearance in Britain, on 21 March 1922.
3   The actual number is difficult to ascertain, but Crowley states that by 1934, '4,500 heads of families' had passed through the scheme. The vast majority were British. See F.K. Crowley, *Australia's Western Third: A History of Western Australia*, London, 1960, p. 268.
4   See Secretary of the State Labor Bureau to Premier's Secretary, 19 October 1921, PDF 302/21.
5   T. Sedgwick (London) to Secretary, TLC, 24 June 1915, and leaflets (origin unknown), State Executive of the ALF (WA) — Correspondence Files (hereafter SE Correspondence), File 65. For population figures, see *Commonwealth of Australia — Census, 1921*, part I, pp. 5–8. Twenty year olds Australia-wide — males 46,472, females 47,483; twenty-five year olds — males 42,540, females 47,231.
6   G.D. Snooks, 'Development in Adversity, 1913 to 1946', in C.T. Stannage (ed.), *A New History of Western Australia*, Nedlands, 1981, Table 7.6, Trade Union Unemployment in Western Australia, 1919–20, 5.1 per cent; 1920–21, 6.3 per cent; 1921–22, 8.3 per cent.
7   SE Correspondence, File 109.
8   State Executive of the ALF (WA) — Minutes Books (hereafter SE Minutes), vol. 3, 15 August 1921; *ALP (WA Division), Annual Report for the Year Ending 31 January 1922*.
9   See, for example, W. Kendall, *The Revolutionary Movement in Britain, 1900–1921: The Origins of British Communism*, London, 1969, chs 13–15; A. Morgan, *J. Ramsay McDonald*, Manchester, 1987, ch. 3. See also A. Moore, *The Secret Army and the Premier. Conservative Paramilitary Organisations in New South Wales, 1930–32*, Kensington, 1989, pp. 17–18; R. Evans, *The Red Flag Riots: A Study of Intolerance*, St Lucia, 1988, p. 168.
10   For a study of the Queensland Loans Affair, see T. Cochrane, *Blockade: The Queensland Loans Affair 1920 to 1924*, St Lucia, 1989.
11   J.T. McMahon, *The Cream of their Race: Irish Truce Negotiations, December 1920 – January 1921*, Ennis (Ireland), n.d. A copy is held in St Mary's Roman Catholic Church Archives, Perth. The author is grateful to Sister M. Raphael, Archivist, for procuring a copy of this pamphlet. Much of the following account is taken from its pages.
12   ibid., p. 24.
13   Newdegate to Milner, 21 January 1921, Archbishop Clune Papers, St Mary's Roman Catholic Church Archives, Perth (hereafter Clune Papers).
14   Milner to Newdegate, 22 January 1921, Clune Papers.
15   Newdegate to Milner, 19 February 1921, Clune Papers.
16   Anon., *The Menace to Australia and the British Empire*, State Archives of Western Australia, Acc. PR 2777, pp. 1–2.

17   M. Gilbert, *Winston S. Churchill, Vol. IV, 1917–22*, London, 1975, pp. 365–370.

18   Churchill to Newdegate, 15 June 1921, Sir Francis Newdegate Papers, on microfilm in the State Archives of Western Australia, Acc. MF1531 (hereafter Newdegate Papers).

19   Newdegate to Clune, 8 December 1921, Newdegate Papers. See also P.O'Farrell, *The Catholic Church and Community in Australia*, Melbourne, 1977 edn, pp. 340 ff.

20   L. Layman, 'Development Ideology in Western Australia, 1933–1965', *Historical Studies*, vol. 20, October 1982, pp. 234, 236.

21   *West Australian*, 9 January 1922, editorial, including a table of the acreage of new lands prepared for cropping in eight cereal districts, 1914–15 to 1920–21, which showed that in the years 1916–17 (when Mitchell was head of the Agricultural Bank), 362,795 acres were cleared (compared with 293,625 acres in 1915–16, and 115,862 acres in 1917–18). In 1920–21, during Mitchell's premiership, 156,135 acres were cleared (compared with 118,409 in 1918–19).

22   For export figures, see *Official Year Book of Western Australia, 1957*, Statistical Summary from 1829, p. 328. See also M. Bignell, *A Place to Meet: A History of the Shire of Katanning*, Nedlands, 1981, p. 278; J.P. Stokes, *Cunderdin-Meckering: A Wheatlands History*, Cunderdin, 1986, p. 147.

23   See, for example, the images in WA Government, Department of Lands, *The Settler's Handy Pamphlet, 1914, Issued by Direction of the Hon. Thomas Bath, MLA, Minister for Lands* (copy held in the Special Collection of the Reid Library, University of Western Australia, Acc. 333.09941), and similar literature and handbooks of the prewar era.

24   See, for example, D.W. Black, 'The Liberal Party and Its Predecessors', in R. Pervan and C. Sharman (eds), *Essays on Western Australian Politics*, Nedlands, 1979; L. Layman, 'The Country Party: Rise and Decline', in Pervan and Sharman, ibid.; B.D. Graham, *The Formation of the Australian Country Parties*, Canberra, 1966, pp. 178 ff.; B.K. Hyams, 'Western Australian Political Parties: 1901–1916', *University Studies in History and Economics*, vol. II, no. 3, September 1955, pp. 35 ff.

25   D.W. Black, The National Party in Western Australia, 1917–30, MA thesis, University of Western Australia, 1974, p. 275. For a history of the development of State enterprises under the Scaddan Government, see J.R. Robertson, 'The Internal Politics of State Labor in Western Australia; 1911–1916', *Labour History*, no. 2, May 1962.

26   Black, 'The Liberal Party', p. 200.

27   Layman, 'The Country Party', pp. 163–164; D.W. Black, 'Party Politics in Turmoil: 1911–1924', in Stannage, *A New History*, pp. 400–402.

28   G.D. Snooks, *Depression and Recovery in Western Australia, 1928/29–1938/39: A Study in Cyclical and Structural Change*, Nedlands, 1974, especially pp. 25–26.

29   Richardson's Report to the Premier, 4 pp., n.d., PDF 29/21.

30   Richardson to Premier, 16 February 1921, 17 February 1921; AWU Secretary to Premier, 14 February 1921, PDF 29/21.

31   Notes of a Deputation from the State ALF to the Premier, 19 July 1921, PDF 302/21. Notes of the Trades Hall Deputations to the Premier on 9 and 11 July 1921 are also in this file.

32   See reports in Police Department, File 5047/1921.

33   Notes from a Deputation to the Premier, 28 September 1921, PDF 302/21.

34   See SE Minutes, vol. 3, Executive Officers' Meeting, 11 September 1922.

35   This figure includes 991 women, but as that is more than applied for work, it is questionable.

36   Figures of the State Labor Bureau for 1920 and 1921, PDF 302/21. In 1920, 2,455 males and 1,797 female workers were applied for, compared with 2,391 and 1,479, respectively, in 1921.

37   State Labor Bureau figures for March 1922, PDF 302/21.

38   PGA to Premier, 22 July 1921, PDF 302/21.

39   Doherty to Mitchell, 17 November 1921, PDF 541/22.

40   A number of schemes, some controversial, are discussed in correspondence and press clippings in PDF 314/22 and PDF 38/22. These include a proposal by Connolly to establish a settlement of Maltese in the Kimberley region, and another scheme to settle British ex-army officers.

41   Sir Harry Webster Levy-Lawson (1862–1933), proprietor of the *Daily Telegraph*, 1903–28. See entry under Lawson in *Dictionary of National Biography, 1931–40*, Oxford, 1949, pp. 533–534.

42   J.P. Gabbedy, *Group Settlement: Part 1. Its Origins: Politics and Administration*, Nedlands, 1988.

43   *Daily News* (London), 17 January 1922. See also clippings from *Londonderry Standard*, 18 January 1922, *Glasgow Herald*, 20 January 1922, *Accrington Gazette*, 21 January 1922, *Financier*, 23 January 1922, PDF 607/22.

44   *Daily Telegraph*, 22 March 1922, *Daily Mail*, 20 March 1922 (the title of this chapter comes from this source), *Canadian Gazette* (London), 20 April 1922, PDF 607/22.

45   *West Australian*, 23 March 1922.

46   Shapcott to Colebatch, 22 March 1922, PDF 30/22.

47   Mitchell to Collier, 5 April 1922, PDF 30/22.

48   *West Australian*, 8 April 1922; also handwritten notes, n.d., in SE Correspondence, File 109.

49   I.L. Hunt, 'Group Settlement in Western Australia: A Criticism', *University Studies in History*, 1958, vol. 3, part 2, pp. 5–11.

50   *West Australian*, 24 May 1922, 21 July 1922.

51   *Sunday Times*, 7 May 1922.

52   Hunt, 'Group Settlement in Western Australia', p. 7.

53   *Call*, 2 June 1922, PDF 65/22.

54   Premier's Department to Premier, 7 April 1922, PDF 30/22.

55   Lovekin to Mitchell, 17 February 1922, PDF 541/22.

56   Burt to Premier, 14 March 1922, PDF 613/22.

57   Hunt, 'Group Settlement in Western Australia', pp. 9–11.

58   Crowley, *Australia's Western Third*, p. 215.

59   J.P. Gabbedy, *Group Settlement: Part 2. Its People: Their Life and Times — An Inside View*, Nedlands, 1988, p. 321.

60   ibid., p. 484.

61   Hunt, 'Group Settlement in Western Australia', pp. 41–42.

62   ibid., p. 19.

63   Leaflet, *On the Map: The Western State and Group Settlement*, n.d., PDF 658/23.

64   *West Australian*, 11 and 18 October 1922.

65   Group Settlement Papers, State Archives of Western Australia (hereafter Group Settlement Papers), Acc. PR 9322. The poem consists of five verses, of which verses 1, 3 and 4 are quoted.

66   Letters from Mrs Irene Cameron to Mrs Ewen, State Archives of Western Australia, Acc. PR 9662.

67 A.E. George, File 2665/23, Group Settlement Papers, Acc. 724.
68 H.W. Arms, File 3210/23, Group Settlement Papers.
69 Group Settlement Members' Agreement, Group Settlement Papers.
70 The Group Settlement Board consisted of E.A. McLarty (Agricultural Bank Director), and G.L. Sutton and P.G. Hampshire of the Agricultural Department. The Controller of Group Settlement was R.J. Anketell (Gabbedy, *Part 1*, p. 50).
71 Foreman's Reports from Group 67, Peel Estate, 1923–25, Group Settlement Papers.
72 Foreman's Reports, Group 44, September 1923, Group Settlement Papers.
73 Foreman's Reports, Group 44, January 1925, Group Settlement Papers.
74 Foreman's Reports, Group 44, January 1925 to January 1928, Group Settlement Papers.
75 See Group Settlement Papers, Files 2665/23 and 3210/23.
76 *Daily News* (London), 28 December 1922, *Liverpool Journal of Commerce*, 28 December 1922, *Edinburgh Evening Standard*, 29 December 1922, PDF 161/22.
77 See, for example, *Cambridge Chronicle*, 18 April 1923, *Torquay Times*, 20 April 1923, *Dorset County Chronicle*, 19 April 1923, *Coloniser*, May 1923, PDF 616/22.
78 Nancarrow's letter to the *Cornishman*, dated 23 June 1922, PDF 666/22.
79 Correspondence between Nancarrow and Premier's Secretary, 18 December 1922, 4 and 12 January 1923, PDF 666/22.
80 Agent-General to Premier, 5 September 1923, and reply, 13 September 1923; State Labor Bureau figures for 28 August 1923 and 3 September 1923.
81 They were Greig and Mills of the Upper House, and Members of the Legislative Assembly Denton, Latham, Stables, Pickering and E.B. Johnston (ex-Labor).
82 PDF 256/122; also *West Australian*, 13 June 1922, 30 October 1922, 3 February 1923, 26 March 1923, 15 May 1923.
83 The following accounts of demonstrations by the unemployed are drawn from reports in Police Department, File 5047/21.
84 Minutes of ALF 5th General Council, 11th Labor Congress, 9 June 1922. Married couples with children received tea, sugar, meat, milk, butter, jam, oatmeal, sago, flour, potatoes, salt, onions, soap and matches. The single men's ration consisted of 1 pound (454 grams) of bread, 8 ounces (226 grams) of meat, half an ounce (14 grams) of tea and one and a half ounces (42 grams) of sugar daily.
85 Police Report, dated 14 June 1922, Police Department, File 5047/1921.
86 Re Kings Park, see ibid.; also SE Minutes, vol. 3, 20 June 1922.
87 *West Australian*, 20 June 1922; Police Report, 27 June 1922, Police Department, File 5047/1921. 'Counting out' is an Australian colloquial expression referring to a group of people standing around an offending object or person, and counting; it derives from the sport of boxing, in which a boxer is 'counted out' in the ring after being knocked down.
88 Hinde to Colebatch, 6 June 1922, PDF 302/21.
89 'One of Many', Readers' Letters, *West Australian*, 14 June 1922
90 Albert Jones, Perth, Readers' Letters, *West Australian*, 16 June 1922.
91 Needham to Colebatch, 7 July 1922, PDF 302/21.
92 Crowley, *Australia's Western Third*, pp. 199–240.
93 See, for example, 'Deputation of Unemployed Soldiers led by General Sir J.J. Talbot Hobbs to Acting Premier', 3 July 1922, PDF 302/21.

94   For a report of the invasion of Cabinet, see *West Australian*, 25 September
     1922. See also issues on 1, 12, 19 and 26 July 1922 for Readers' Letters, and
     statements by Alfred Sleep, Organisation of Unemployed Returned Sol-
     diers.
95   Munday to Mitchell, 13 January 1924, and n.d., Mitchell to Brennan,
     30 January 1924, PDF 733/1923.
96   Police Reports, 26 and 20 July 1923, Police Department, File 5047/1921.
97   J. Lane, *Fairbridge Kid*, Fremantle, 1990.
98   The following account is based on correspondence and reports in PDF 403/
     22.
99   *West Australian*, 12 July 1926.
100 ALF to Premier, 19 August 1922, SE Correspondence, File 163.
101 Report of the Second Annual Conference of the Country Branches of the
     New Settlers League, 7 August 1923, PDF 57/23; *West Australian*, 13 July
     1923.
102 *West Australian*, 31 July 1923.
103 Report of a Deputation of New Settlers League members to the Premier,
     14 September 1923, Premier to Acting Prime Minister, 1 October 1923, and
     reply, 6 August 1924, Premier to Agent-General, 1 October 1923, PDF 571/
     23. See also SE Correspondence, File 233.
104 See correspondence in PDF 703/23.
105 Correspondence in SE Correspondence, File 233.
106 Extract from *House of Commons Debates*, 28 May 1924, PDF 104/24.

Chapter Seven

A HANDFUL OF MEN AT FREMANTLE

The Collier administration and the seamen's strikes

When the Labor Party returned to government in 1924, the State was just beginning to recover from the social and political impact of its participation in the Great War. The number of workers in employment at last exceeded the 1914 total. The State continued to maintain a high proportion of British- or Irish-born: approximately 20 per cent compared with a national average of 12.5 per cent.[1] By the middle of the decade, this trend was increasing, a factor due mainly to the extensive Group Settlement Scheme. During 1925, 8,800 British subjects arrived in the west and only 2,600 departed. This influx contributed to the rapid growth of the population which, at 2.9 per cent during the years 1923 to 1928, was well above the national average.[2]

The increasing centralization of manufacturing industries in Perth and Fremantle meant that more people lived in an urban environment, 46.5 per cent being located in the metropolitan area, in comparison with 38 per cent in 1911. The goldfields, however, saw a reverse trend. While almost a third of the State's European inhabitants lived in that area in 1901, by 1921 this percentage had decreased to 11.5, largely as a result of the decline of the gold industry. While not attributed directly to the impact of the war, the decline of Western Australia's port cities was regarded by the labour movement as 'evidence of the fell influence of capitalism on economic life'.[3] Another change in the demographic profile of Western Australia was the decline of the masculinity ratio, from 134 in 1914 to 114 in 1921, attributable to the State's war casualties, which were significantly higher than the national average.[4] The increase in both the female population and the number of women in paid employment during the war years affected the composition and needs of the postwar workforce.[5]

During the Collier administration's first eighteen months in

'And It Could Be Vastly Different'
The Labor movement's internal wrangling during the seamen's strikes of
1924–25 amused the conservative press, but was regarded with
disappointment and dismay by the *Westralian Worker* in this front-page cartoon
from 25 January 1925.
[Courtesy *Australian Worker*/Battye Library]

Philip Collier
The goldfields militant who became a moderate Premier headed the first
post-war State Labor Government, which took office in 1924.
[Courtesy Battye Library, 816B/H 7633]

office, its policies had considerable social and political effect on unemployment, immigration and industrial relations. But Collier's electoral victory had been a triumph for Labor moderates. The administration's policies were not always markedly different from those of its National predecessor, thus causing more dissension within Labor ranks. By 1924, some of the key militants of the labour movement were no longer active in the State: Don Cameron and E.J. Dunn had gone to the Eastern States, George Callanan had died, and Alfred Callanan was in prison. Even so, the government was soon put under pressure during the seamen's strikes of 1924–25. A second, potentially disastrous, split in the party was avoided, but two militants — George Ryce and Cecilia Shelley — were expelled.

The State election took place on 22 March 1924, but, because of deferred polls in the Pilbara and Kimberley electorates, the result was not certain until the second week of April. Four parties — Labor, National, and the Ministerial (or Majority) and Executive Country Parties — contested the election. Labor's platform consisted of practical reforms: setting up a State Bank to ensure that rural profits were channelled into State enterprise; developing closer settlement along existing railway lines and water supplies; establishing an 'effective' land tax; setting up an inquiry into the working of the Group Settlements; and developing industry — in particular, base metal industries — to help curb the emigration of West Australians. More uniform procedures in the Arbitration Court were also promised, to remove previous anomalies.[6] The Ministerial Country Party's concerns were mainly rural. Its platform included continuing the assisted immigration scheme, constructing railways in settled areas, establishing bulk grain handling facilities, maintaining the 'White Australia Policy', and granting preference of employment to returned soldiers — evidence of the continuing problems that ex-servicemen were experiencing in finding employment. Ideological 'planks' included fostering a 'spirit of nationhood amongst the Australian people', maintaining 'constitutional government', and upholding the 'integrity of the Empire'.[7] The Executive Country Party's concerns were even more exclusively rural than those of the Ministerials: its platform included a 'conditional-support' strategy, which meant that, on issues that were in the interests of the rural electorate, it would vote with the Labor Party if necessary. Conversely, the Executive

Country Party flatly refused to form a coalition with the National Party.[8]

The National Party similarly promoted the unity of the British Empire and the maintenance of a 'White Australia', and pledged to maintain the 'sovereign rights' of the States and present policies of immigration and development, to promote decentralization, to give preference of employment to returned soldiers, and to adhere to the principles of conciliation and arbitration.[9] The Nationals' campaign centred on Mitchell's popularity and his past achievements in the rural sector, which they believed were sufficient to carry the election. Symbolically, Mitchell commenced his campaign with a tour of the Group Settlements, where he was enthusiastically received. At Group 53, amid the crops of towering sunflowers, Mitchell spoke with considerable fervour: '[T]he scheme is my creation, and I am responsible to the people of this country for it...Years ago I put men like you on the wheat belt.'[10]

The major election issue was expenditure. A vote for Mitchell, the *West Australian* argued, was a vote for 'progress', whereas Labor would simply continue the rash spending begun by the prewar Scaddan Government.[11] Somewhat surprisingly, considering the 'Bolshevik' scare of two or three years previously, Bolshevism was hardly raised as an issue in the 1924 election campaign. When the contemporary situation both in the Eastern States of Australia and in Britain is taken into account, it is difficult to ascertain why conservative politicians and their supporters, the employers' federations and the major newspapers, did not make more of the Bolshevik issue. Yet it was not mentioned by any of the conservative candidates, and was barely touched upon by the press.[12] In marked contrast, the British general election campaign of the same year saw the Conservative Party exploit every possible connection between Ramsay MacDonald's administration and Russian communism, resulting in a devastating defeat for Britain's first Labour Government, after only a few months in office.[13] A significant difference between Western Australia and Britain was that Labor administrations had governed on two previous occasions in Western Australia without radically altering the State's economic basis or status quo. Nevertheless, it cannot be assumed that Bolshevism was a dead issue in Western Australia. Events surrounding the maritime strikes of the next eighteen months would cause many of those who had tentatively applauded Collier's government to dismiss it as weak and as a tool of more militant forces.

Although Collier's party secured a majority of only four seats in the Legislative Assembly, every electoral district except Subiaco registered a swing to the ALP.[14] Labor's greatest support came, predictably, from its traditional stronghold in the goldfields, where twelve Members were returned. The party also gained victory in seven metropolitan seats, with the remaining eight scattered throughout the State. New seats were gained in Fremantle, Guildford, Leederville, Menzies, Bunbury, Albany, the Kimberley and the Pilbara.[15] The *West Australian* attributed the Labor victory to the failure of the Redistribution of Seats Bill in the Legislative Assembly's last session before the election, claiming that the current electoral boundaries took 'no cognisance of the movement of the population' and were 'a travesty'.[16] In reality, this statement was true only of goldfields electorates and does not explain Labor's success elsewhere in the State. Other factors included the outworking of the 1917 Labor split, the schism in the Country Party, and the failure of Group Settlement.

Labor candidates won votes from 'National Labor' members of the National coalition — that is, the so-called 'rats' of 1917. Examples were W.D. Johnson's victory over J.T. Davies in Guildford and Alex Panton's victory over Mullaney in Menzies. In the rural seat of Greenough, the sitting Ministerial Country Party leader, and Minister for Agriculture in the Mitchell Government, H.K. Maley, was defeated by the Labor candidate, M.J. Kennedy. A bitter campaign had been waged between Maley and W. Patrick, an Executive Country Party candidate endorsed by the PPA. The *Geraldton Guardian* pointed out the irony of the high percentage of farmers' votes going to Labor — the highest in the State's history — when Mitchell had borrowed £11 million for rural development. Murray-Wellington, in the heart of the Premier's South West development, had returned the sitting Member, George, by a majority of only fifty votes; Mitchell's own margin in Northam was a mere 147 votes; and even 'blue ribbon' metropolitan seats had been affected by quarrels within the coalition. In West Perth, the conservative vote was divided between the two opposing National Party candidates, Edith Cowan and T.A.L. Davy, although it was still strong enough for the electorate to return Davy. The Nationals also won in Subiaco, even though they fielded two candidates.[17]

Despite campaign bitternesses, Collier included pro-conscription-ists W.C. Angwin and J.M. Drew (who had remained with the party), and anti-conscriptionists J.W. Hickey and Alex McCallum in his eight-member Cabinet, indicating his strong desire to bury any remaining differences of opinion within Labor over the conscription issue.[18]

Edith Cowan
The first woman elected to an Australian parliament, Edith Cowan lost the seat of West Perth in 1924 to National Party colleague T.A.L. Davey — a result of the strife within the conservative coalition. In 1926, she became a founding member of the Royal Western Australian Historical Society.
[Courtesy Royal Western Australian Historical Society, R1141]

The Labor victory was received cautiously by employers. The State Manager of Dalgetys commented favourably, in his June 1924 report to London, that the new government proposed to appoint a Royal Commission into the viability of reviving the mining industry, and would continue the Group Settlement Scheme begun by its predecessor.[19] Yet the pastoralists' President, Sir Ernest Lee Steere, urged the non-Labor Opposition parties to unite. While stressing the apolitical stance of the PGA, Lee Steere warned that

The power behind [the Labor government] may become so strong
that a new factor may arise and thus we should, collectively and
individually, do all in our power to unite the present Opposition
[National and Country parties], endeavour to terminate their
squabbles and be prepared for the day which, though not here
now, may arise at any moment.[20]

The new administration soon met with criticism over the issues
of Group Settlement and unemployment. Emigration from the
United Kingdom had been suspended during the election.[21] Labor
maintained the suspension of the Group Settlement Scheme, although initially it was expected that immigration would recom-
mence in August 1924. In the meantime, Angwin, the new Minister
for Lands, began investigating the cost of the scheme to the State.
He was dissatisfied with a clause in the Empire Settlement Agreement, unique to Western Australia, that stated that the debt charged
to the settler by the State, including supervision expenses, should
not exceed £1,000. Angwin claimed that the State Government
expended approximately £1,700 to establish each group farm and
that the clause would cost the State '£3 to £4 million' if it were not
removed.[22] In August, he announced in the Legislative Assembly
that the State Government would have to find over £10 million in
order to finance the farms, to construct the necessary railways,
roads, drainage, schools and hospitals, and to administer the
existing scheme. He advised Colebatch, who had succeeded John
Connolly as Western Australia's Agent-General in London, to
send no more emigrant families unless instructed to do so. Angwin
told the press that, while he believed an increase in population was
economically necessary, he could not justify the present cost of the
Empire Settlement Agreement to the State.[23]

The resumption of the scheme was further delayed by the
renegotiation of the agreement between the Commonwealth and
Britain. Previously, a separate agreement had been made with
each State, but under the terms of the Commonwealth Agreement
of 1925, all States were, in theory, to enjoy the same conditions.
Angwin, acting as Premier while Collier visited England, attended
an Interstate Conference on Immigration, to discuss the proposed
terms of the new agreement, in February 1925. He returned dissatisfied, believing the less industrialized States would be disadvantaged because a certain quota of non-farming immigrants had to be
accepted, along with those intended for rural settlement.[24]

Throughout the first twelve months of the Collier administration, therefore, immigration slowed to a trickle, with only 'special
cases' being accepted.[25] Initially, it appeared that the Labor Government's policy on settlement would differ markedly from that of
its predecessor, but ultimately this was not the case. Resumption
of the settlement schemes was urged by powerful lobby groups
such as the NSL and the Pioneer Memorial Association, the latter
a group supported by Lee Steere and Talbot Hobbs that advocated
placing British boys in employment with farmers and station
owners. It did not expect that the youths would be paid wages at
first, '...although the idea was that they should be paid what they
were worth, as they gained knowledge of the local conditions'.[26]
The NSL's President, Labor Member of the Legislative Assembly
Alex Clydesdale, did not object to these proposals, even though
they exposed young immigrants to possible exploitation. Despite
Labor's long history of opposing immigration while there were
large numbers of unemployed in the State, Angwin showed a
zeal similar to Mitchell's in getting the land settled. The Group
Settlement Scheme recommenced in April 1925 after the Commonwealth and State Governments had signed the new Commonwealth Agreement.[27] Collier had, in fact, written to the Secretary of
the Royal Colonial Institute shortly after the Labor victory, stating
that he had supported the principle of Group Settlement when in
Opposition and that he would work for the improvement of the
existing scheme.[28]

Unemployment, however, remained a problem for the new
administration, even though it was of a slightly lesser magnitude
than in the Mitchell years, as shown in Table 7.1.

Table 7.1   Trade union unemployment in Western Australia and Australia,
1920 to 1926[29]

Year	WA	Australia	Year	WA	Australia
1920–21	6.3%	9.5%	1921	8.6%	11.2%
1921–22	9.3%	9.9%	1922	10.0%	9.3%
1922–23	9.3%	8.1%	1923	5.7%	7.1%
1923–24	4.8%	7.5%	1924	5.5%	8.9%
1924–25	6.0%	9.8%	1925	6.1%	8.8%
1925–26	6.5%	7.7%	1926	7.2%	7.1%

As in the years of the Mitchell administration, deputations on behalf of the unemployed continued to beat a path to Parliament House. One such deputation of Opposition Members, early in 1925, stated that there were 400 out of work in the Fremantle area, including seventy-one men, mostly with dependants, in 'urgent need of food'. They put the blame for the situation on the poor wool season and the industrial unrest in the port. Angwin agreed that Fremantle depended on the shipping trade and that the industrial unrest had created widespread unemployment that the government was unable to alleviate, despite McCallum's efforts as Minister for Public Works. He then pointed to another problem that was a legacy of Mitchell's land settlement policy. Many of the 953 people who had walked off group farms had settled in Fremantle, believing they could get work for 15s a day.[30] A Trades Hall deputation told Acting Deputy Premier Willcock that 120 unemployed men had attended a meeting there the previous day (3 February). Some had been out of work for four months. Willcock's response was remarkably similar to those of Mitchell and Colebatch in previous years. He blamed the unemployment situation on the entry of 'foreigners' to the State, but said that certain restrictions had since been imposed on entry to Australia. He did not think that much else could be done to relieve the position.[31]

Reforms to wages, working conditions and hours were urgently needed. The State's employment profile had changed considerably during and after the war. When the 1911 Census had been taken, the four main sources of employment for males were industry, farming, mining, and commerce. By 1925, the mining industry was employing only one-third of its 1911 total of male workers. The gold mining industry's decline had been accelerated by a wartime embargo on the export of gold, and by the postwar Mitchell Government's lack of support.[32] In contrast, after a wartime slump, farming had become the State's major occupation, employing some 23,000 males, including group and soldier settlers. The industrial workforce, however, remained well below the 1914 total, even in 1925.[33]

The 1920s did not see the dawning of a 'workers' paradise'. Indeed, union membership increased by only 11,000 between 1913 and 1925. Statistics from the period did not differentiate between male and female unionists, but it can be assumed that greater numbers of females in the workforce ultimately meant more women in the union movement. The numbers of females employed in commercial occupations almost doubled between 1911 and 1921. Even so, the majority of working women remained in 'domestic' occupations or farming. Strangely, although the number of male farmers increased from 16,000 in 1914 to 23,000 in 1925, the total of women thus employed — according to government statistics — remained at around 5,800.[34] The reason for this discrepancy was undoubtedly because, under the postwar settlement schemes, only males were regarded as settlers; their wives and children were discounted.[35] The increase in the numbers of women workers did not ensure better working conditions or wages. As several historians have argued, the establishment of a basic wage was a powerful factor in both excluding women from the workforce and restricting those who were employed to the lowest paid jobs. Thus, categories of employment became gender-based. In fact, both management and unions had exploited and manipulated the division of labour into 'men's' and 'women's' work. The disparity in male and female wages arose from the assumption that a working woman had only herself to maintain, whereas a man supported a wife and children; it totally ignored the circumstances of a mother with dependent children, or a single woman supporting aged or invalid dependants.[36]

Consequently, women either were paid at considerably lower rates than men were, even when they performed the same duties, or they commenced at the same rate but quickly reached a ceiling. Male shop assistants, for example, were paid over £1 per week more than were females doing the same work. A sixteen year old female clerk at Dalgetys received the basic starting rate (£50 in 1920), which was paid to both men and women. By the time she was eighteen years of age, her salary had doubled, but the highest salary paid to female clerks was £140 per annum, whereas the managers (invariably male) were paid up to £800 per annum and were among the highest paid salary earners in the State.[37] The arbitration system did nothing to alleviate the situation. Striking women, especially, were regarded as curiosities, as in the case of the 1921 and 1925 strikes by members of the Hotel, Club, Caterers, Tearooms and Restaurant Employees Union, under the leadership of Cecilia Shelley.[38]

Employers often resented the fact that wages and salaries rose in accordance with the cost of living. At the Annual General

Meeting of the Perth Chamber of Commerce in 1924, J.L.B. Weir remarked that, while trade during the past year had been 'of a prosperous nature', gross profits were not showing the healthiness that might be expected. He ascribed this, in part, to the Industrial Arbitration Scheme, which based wages on the cost of living, irrespective of whether the industry was running at a profit or a loss. Weir suggested that legislators might take this into consideration when amending the Arbitration Bill.[39] Although it is doubtful that Weir supposed a Labor administration would take his advice, his words reflected the often-expressed belief among employers that wages ought to be determined by their ability to pay rather than by the right of the worker to earn a living.

In 1925, Perth had the highest male basic wage — £4 11s — of any capital city in Australia. Some fairly substantial increases in wage rates had been achieved. Even the scandalously low wages of dressmakers and tailoresses had almost doubled since 1918, although they were still earning a maximum of only £2 11s 8d for a forty-four hour week. On the whole, wage rises had accommodated the increased cost of living between 1918 and 1925. According to government statistics, the cost of groceries and food in Perth was high compared with other capitals in 1914, although rent was lower; however, prices in Perth had not risen as steeply between 1914 and 1925 as in some other cities.[40]

Despite previous difficulties encountered in getting legislation passed in the Upper House, Angwin believed that both Houses now approved of the Arbitration Court becoming a Basic Wage Commission. He planned to introduce a Bill to that effect early in 1926, and there was a possibility that legislation could be approved for both basic wage and price fixing.[41] By the end of 1925, the government had achieved significant industrial reforms: new workers compensation legislation that provided higher scales of benefits and, for the first time, enabled claims to be made by sufferers of industrial diseases; preference to unionists; and a forty-four hour week for most government workers. The Industrial Arbitration Bill provided for the appointment of a full-time President of the Arbitration Court, and the establishment of an Apprenticeship Board. These industrial reforms were achieved largely by the efforts of the hard-working Alex McCallum.[42] But industrial legislation was particularly susceptible to amendment while passing through the Upper House. Legislation granting statutory recognition to unions whose members were in the rural and domestic workforce was held up for several years; as a result, apprentices of these unions were not included in industrial awards. The Upper House also imposed numerous amendments on those Bills that it did pass. The 1924 Workers Compensation Bill, for example, underwent twenty-three amendments. The Legislative Council refused to allow payments where worker negligence was involved, and disallowed payments being made to dependants living outside the State. It also refused to approve coverage of employees travelling to and from the workplace.[43] Despite these difficulties, the early achievements of the Collier administration lay in industrial reform.

The Mutilation
of the Master Craftsman's Industrial Coat

'The Mutilation of the Master Craftsman's Industrial Coat'
Without a Labor majority in the Upper House, the Collier Government's industrial and social reforms — many of which were framed by Alexander McCallum — had a rough passage through parliament, often being 'mutilated' by Legislative Councillors. From the *Westralian Worker*, 28 November 1924.
[Courtesy Battye Library]

In gaining acceptance of these reforms in the conservative Upper House, the Labor Government was undoubtedly aided by an improvement in the economic situation. The decrease in the number of immigrants during 1925, increasing investments, especially in the private sector, and the continued expansion of the wheat and wool industries were all contributing factors.[44] Improved communications — in particular, the opening of the interstate railway line during the Great War — had made Western Australia more accessible to travellers and markets. Indeed, the quarrel that had erupted in 1919 over the closure of the railway line in an attempt to prevent influenza spreading to the west indicated that isolation could not be maintained even when desired. Communications were also greatly improved when Wesfarmers founded the State's first radio station, 6WF, in 1924.[45] A notable feature of the economic growth in this period was the development of the stock and station company Elder Smith, whose profits almost doubled between 1923 and 1924, despite serious beef stock losses in the Kimberley, North West, Gascoyne and Upper Murchison districts during the drought year of 1924.[46] Although the State's economy did not experience a growth comparable to Elders' speedy development, there were some encouraging signs of recovery. The value of agricultural production had trebled between 1914 and 1924, and manufacturing output had doubled.[47]

The Collier Government's economic and industrial achievements seem all the more remarkable when set against a background of party strife and strikes. For the Labor Party in government, there was always the tension between governing the State and championing the rights of the worker. The militant wing of the labour movement — which lacked representation in the Collier Government but, nevertheless, remained active in the Western Australian ALF — soon became disenchanted with the administration. The focus of its disillusionment was industrial unrest, and in particular the seamen's dispute that broke out in Fremantle towards the end of 1924, and which was to cause the most severe internal conflict within the labour movement since the conscription crisis.

The seamen's dispute began when the FSU requested an alteration to the federal Navigation Act of 1912–20, to prevent the employment of non-union and immigrant labour on coastal ships. Four ships in the Western Australian coastal trade — *Charon*, *Gascoyne*, *Minderoo* and *Gorgon* — were named as being particularly notorious for this practice.[48] Trading activity at the Fremantle waterfront had already been disrupted by the FLU, which was involved in an Australia-wide overtime dispute that had begun in October. The lumpers refused to work outside the hours of 8.00 a.m. to 5.00 p.m. at the standard rate of 2s 9d per hour, and asked for

3s 9d per hour between 6.30 p.m. and 11.00 p.m., and 4s 6d per hour between 12.00 midnight and 7.00 a.m. According to the non-Labor press, however, the dispute was really over the removal of the Nationalist Free Labor Bureau, which still operated on the Sydney Wharf.[49] The *West Australian* was in no doubt that the present lumpers' dispute was rooted in the events of 1917. In Sydney, the NWWU had continued to be granted preference until 1923, when this practice had been thrown out in an Arbitration Court judgment by Justice Powers, on the grounds that the previous ruling had deprived returned soldiers of their right of preference in employment.[50]

The overtime embargo was lifted on 18 November, but almost immediately a British-owned ship, the *Clan Munroe*, was declared 'black' by seamen at Fremantle, because it had a mostly non-European crew, and because it was under charter to the Australian Commonwealth Line while Australian ships remained idle. The lumpers supported the ban by refusing to unload the *Clan Munroe*. A few days later, the ban widened, and a union picket of twenty or thirty seamen threatened to throw a pilot into the harbour if he boarded the steamer *Raranga*.[51] Both the lumpers' and the seamen's disputes received full support from the *Westralian Worker*, which noted that the Australian Commonwealth Line was to be registered in Great Britain so that Stanley Bruce's Federal Government would not have to pay Australian rates to seamen.[52] The *Worker* commented that the Bruce administration had 'never overlooked anything that would improve the interests of the employers by reducing the status of the workers'. The Australian Shipping Board also came under fire from the *Worker* for granting large salaries to its Chairman and board members. Furthermore, the *Worker* claimed, the net profits of the ten largest shipping companies between 1920 and 1923 had amounted to £5,564,645, and these companies had made 154 per cent on invested capital in five years, or a growth of 31 per cent per annum. 'Who is importunate now?' asked the *Worker*. 'The Seamen's Union or the Profiteers?'[53]

Although the majority of the press criticized the strikes at Fremantle, the *Mirror* printed the seamen's side of the dispute. The FSU alleged that H.B. Larkin, who was both Chairman of the Australian Shipping Board and Manager of the Australian Commonwealth Line, was chartering ships under British registration to defeat the federal Navigation Act. Larkin was said to be a mere puppet of the British-owned Inchcape Shipping Combine.[54] Lord Inchcape owned two Australian shipping lines, AUSN Company and Macdonald Hamilton and Company. AUSN was one of the largest Australian coasting companies, with 27 per cent of the ships and 22.6 per cent of the aggregate tonnage. In the decade 1914–24, Inchcape enjoyed the greatest financial success of its entire seventy-four year history of operations in Australia, its annual profits averaging £45,000 to £50,000.[55] The FSU was not alone in believing that the Inchcape Shipping Combine exercised too much influence over Australian affairs. The *Westralian Worker* accused the Bruce Government of trying to sell the Australian Commonwealth Line to Inchcape.[56] In response to Inchcape's comment that he had 'implicit faith that Mr. Bruce would protect the country from what was more or less Bolshevism', the *Worker* published the following scathing poem:

> While Bolshevism, more or less,
> The floodgates of destruction loose [sic],
> For succor in his deep distress,
> Lord Inchcape looks to Mr. Bruce.
>
> The touching faith that he displays,
> Is not a thing of sudden growth,
> He knows a common interest sways.
> A fellow feeling stirs them both.
>
> For while brigandage, real and stark,
> With Inchcape in a leading role
> Sweeps o'er the country, all may mark,
> That Bruce is with them heart and soul.
>
> So in his latest agony,
> For balm to heal his present pain,
> Again to Stanley Melbourne he
> Has turned, and shall not turn in vain.[57]

The *Worker* also printed an open letter from Randolph Bedford, a Member of the Queensland Parliament, to Lord Inchcape, whom he charged with influencing not only the commerce of the country but also its Federal Government. Bedford referred to Inchcape's 'impudent attempt to advise Australians against Government ownership of ships'. According to Bedford, Inchcape's remarks would help only to defeat the Bruce National Party Government in the next federal election, because 'real Australians' were determined to prevent 'industrial exploitation by foreign shipping companies'. He also accused Inchcape of 'probably' being behind the Associated Ship Owners' threat to tie up 100 Australian coastal ships and lock out 6,000 men.[58]

During the lumpers' overtime dispute, Collier experienced the kind of pressure from the mercantile community that had caused Colebatch to yield during the 1919 strike. A special meeting of the Perth Chamber of Commerce was held early in November. An interstate boat was due that evening with 2,500 tons (2,550 tonnes) of cargo, which it would be impossible to unload by the due departure date unless the lumpers worked overtime. The owners were not prepared to let the boat remain unloaded over Sunday; therefore, it was decided that the cargo would not be discharged but would be sent back to the Eastern States. A delegation from the Chamber of Commerce met with Collier a few days later, but he offered no solutions. In December, a local merchant, H.J. Wigmore and Company, protested about the delay that had occurred the previous month when the *Clan Munroe* was prevented from docking because of 'violence on the wharf'. Wigmores 'trusted that a repetition of this incident will not happen again in Fremantle'. The incident to which the company referred happened when strikers attempted to cut the mooring lines of the *Port Bowen*.[59] Further pressure was added by the WA Employers' Federation, which urged the government to introduce amendments to the existing Industrial Arbitration Act so that any 'breach of the Act, such as cessation of work, would be penalised by the Court'. The federation also decided to ask employers' organizations to consider launching a permanent publicity campaign in all States, to 'educate' the general public as to the 'necessity of the laws of the country being observed and administered'. Such a campaign, it was hoped, would also counteract 'the evil effects of communistic propaganda'.[60]

At the end of November, the complexity of the situation in Fremantle increased when the seamen again went on strike as a protest against the State Government, because the Minister for Works, Alex McCallum, refused to increase rates for dredge and tug workers. McCallum declared that he could not grant special concessions to any section of government employees. The FSU did not comply with the usual practice of referring the matter to the ALF's SDC before commencing its three-week strike, but the seamen returned to work on the basis of conditions recommended by the committee, including a forty-four hour week.[61] During the strike, the arrival in Western Australia of FSU President Tom Walsh created further divisions in the labour movement. The conservative press automatically cast Walsh, the 'communist' union boss, in the role of enemy of the Empire. 'Who Rules Australia?' asked the *Sunday Times*, rhetorically, 'King George or King Tom?' The article began by speculating on the myth that the humblest boy in the Empire could aspire to the highest possible position, except the King's. But Tom Walsh, it claimed, aspired to be more powerful than King George, and, under his 'reign', work would be held up in every port in Australia. In any other country, declared the *Sunday Times*, he would be impeached: 'It is only in Australia that he dare set up his kingship and hurl insolence at the Government'.[62] The *Daily News* trivialized an extremely complex situation by observing that the strike had 'practically developed into a fight between the two wings of the Labor movement...with the Government and the public looking on'.[63] Thus, the non-Labor press watched the struggle, put out by the inconvenience it caused to commerce and industry but amused by the spectacle of Labor tearing itself to pieces by internal wrangling.

When the police intervened, at the recommendation of the SDC, and prevented union pickets from stopping passengers joining the liner *Orcades*, the government was accused of protecting 'scab' labour. The SDC claimed to have supported police action only in enabling passengers for the *Orcades* to embark. It had conferred with the FLU Secretary and had published a decision that the *Orcades* was not 'black'; therefore, the pickets had acted irresponsibly in trying to prevent passengers embarking. The ALF State Executive considered that the time had arrived when it 'must decide whether the Labor movement was to be run by a few rash and unscrupulous people whose sole object is to break and disrupt the Labor movement'. The choice was between supporting 'the terroristic activities of these unknowns' and protecting 'innocent and inoffensive people who were anxious to join the mail boat on its way to England'.[64]

Originally an internal dispute, the issue of whether or not the SDC had protected 'scabs' soon became very public, in the form of a debate in the press between Tom Walsh and SDC Secretary E.H. Barker. Walsh argued that the seamen and waterside workers were involved in

> a struggle with the master class and one phase of this struggle is
> finding an expression here in Western Australia, where we have
> not only to fight the private ship owners but the Government also
> to some extent...

Walsh accused the SDC of creating a situation 'that might easily
lead to bloodshed and the probable death of some of the workers,
as occurred in 1919 when Thomas Edwards met his death', and
claimed the committee was now looked upon as 'enemies of the
working class'.[65] Thus, Walsh neatly reversed the role of the Western Australian ALF. According to him, the Labor Government was
also on the side of the employers. Tom Edwards' name remained
a powerful symbol of working-class solidarity in Fremantle, and
Walsh was clearly indicating that the Collier administration had
betrayed all that Edwards died for.

Barker's reply emphasized that the SDC's authority had been
created by the organized labour movement of Western Australia
for the specific purpose of dealing with industrial disputes that
affected more than one district. The committee was elected by the
membership of the District Councils and had sole authority to
declare doctrine 'black'. It had been requested to intercede in the
dispute between the FSU and the government and other employers, he claimed, and FSU representatives had agreed that there was
to be no interference with ships tying up or releasing while negotiations were pending.[66]

The major newspapers presented the government and the Trades
Hall in a favourable light and gave more space to their arguments
than to those of Tom Walsh and the FSU. The *Daily News* reported
on a packed meeting of lumpers in Fremantle's Palladium Theatre.
McCallum's arrival was accompanied by 'deafening applause',
whereas Tom Walsh received a mixed reception of cheers and
hoots. The crowd responded enthusiastically when McCallum
remarked that the FSU was the only union in Australia to refuse to
contribute to the Lumpers' Appeal in 1919. He accused the FSU
leadership of being 'a handful of men at Fremantle making war on
the Labor movement'. When Walsh rose to reply, a section of the
audience 'counted him out'. At the end of the meeting, a resolution
was carried to the effect that the 'parties get into negotiations
straight away with the object of bringing about a definite settlement of the dispute forthwith'.[67]

Nevertheless, Walsh clearly enjoyed a large following among

the seamen, and the union received wide support within the labour movement.[68] The District Councils and their affiliated bodies were divided over the issue. The EGDC condemned the SDC's action, and demanded that its members resign. The ALF's Collie Branch protested similarly. Conversely, the Fremantle District Council expressed its appreciation of the way in which the SDC had handled the seamen's dispute, as did the Bunbury Branch of the Shop Assistants' and Employees' Union.[69]

The wharf labourers also were divided over the issue of whether to support the seamen's strike. William Mather, Secretary of the Albany Branch of the Waterside Workers Federation, believed that they had been persuaded to support the seamen against their better judgment. In a letter to J. Morris, the General Secretary of the Waterside Workers Federation in Melbourne, Mather confirmed that the Fremantle lumpers had 'almost unanimously agreed to work the *Clan Munroe*', and he accused the FSU of 'exploiting' the situation in Fremantle 'by pure misrepresentation'.[70] FLU President Thomas Fox argued, however, that apart from the issue of immigrant and non-union labour working on coastal ships, the FSU also objected to the Australian Commonwealth Line chartering ships in Europe and signing on crews at rates less than those awarded by the Federal Arbitration Court, and that the FLU supported it for this reason. Even after the seamen's dispute was resolved, the *Clan Munroe* was, in fact, never unloaded at Fremantle, and eventually its owners sent the ship to an 'Eastern' (presumably Asian) port. The *Baron Macleay* suffered similarly, although, according to Fox, its owners were hoping to unload its cargo at an east coast port. Fox exhorted his 'fellow lumpers in the Eastern States' to show solidarity by refusing to unload the ship.[71]

Meanwhile, the FSU committed an act that invoked the hostility of many who had previously been sympathetic. At the end of December, the *Westralian Worker* declined to print a letter from George Ryce. Writing as a member of the FSU Branch Executive, Ryce accused the *Worker* of quoting 'verbatim the lies printed in the capitalistic newspapers against the seamen', and of 'joining in the howl set up by the capitalist press wolves'. Ryce also remarked on McCallum's 'ingenuity in framing a clause to take the last ounce out of the worker's carcase', and referred to the SDC as 'this handful of unauthorised humbugs'.[72] The FSU resolved to declare the paper's editor, Curtin, 'black' for declining to publish Ryce's letter. The union would refuse to take any vessel to sea on which Curtin was a passenger. He was, however, given the opportunity to explain his action and to apologize to the union before the resolution was forwarded to other branches or carried into effect. Curtin replied in the next issue of the *Worker*:

> It is a strange procedure that convicts and sentences a man and then invites him to submit his defence. It is also curious that 'capitalistic press wolves' should remain as white angels while the working class editor should be consigned to perpetual blackness for what the unions declare to be an identical offence.

Ryce's letter, said Curtin, contained 'gross untruths' and libelled the SDC and other members of the labour movement. He noted that Ryce had presented no new phase of the seamen's case as a basis for an agreement with the Minister for Works. The *Worker*, he said, had not suppressed or misrepresented facts, but there was, and always would be, 'a refusal to print mere abuse and scurrilous calumny'.[73] Curtin was deeply shocked and hurt by the incident. Shortly afterwards, he wrote to his friend Frank Anstey, a Victorian Labor parliamentarian:

> I confess that thing has worried me more than anything I have ever had to handle since I have been connected with the paper. It may have been wisest to have published it and let it go; but it is a hell of a wise man who knows everything before the event and has nothing to learn after it. I find no pleasure in being described as a suppressor and in reading how the sailors of the Seven Seas are to look upon me as an industrial Ishmael wherever I may go...[74]

Retribution came upon both Ryce and the FSU within months. On 20 January 1925, the ALF State Executive resolved that the FSU had no authority to declare Curtin 'black' and called upon that body to immediately rescind its resolution.[75] By April, the FSU had made no response, so the State Executive resolved that, unless the FSU complied with its January resolution before the next State Executive meeting, the union and its officers would be declared outside the labour movement. Cecilia Shelley opposed the resolution, unsuccessfully.[76] The State Executive next met on 6 May 1925, by which date no reply had been received from the FSU. During the course of the meeting, Tom Houghton, Secretary of the WA Branch of the FSU, entered the room and handed the General Secretary a letter from the FSU, stating that the resolution referring to Curtin had been 'suspended'. The State Executive's Chairman ruled that, as the January resolution had required the FSU resolution to be 'rescinded' and not 'suspended', the letter was unacceptable. The FSU and its Executive, including Houghton and Ryce, were thus expelled from the labour movement.[77] Ryce was not permitted to speak at a meeting of the Metropolitan District Council two weeks later, on the grounds that, as a member of the FSU Executive, he was considered 'out of the movement'.[78] Surprisingly, although Ryce could not speak, he was not barred from the meeting. Both the EGDC and the Midland District Council objected to the State Executive's action.[79]

The FSU eventually complied by removing from its books the resolution concerning Curtin, and, after reapplication to the Fremantle District Council, was received back into the labour movement. George Ryce remained banned. He was accused by the State Executive of securing admission to SDC meetings by falsely 'representing himself to be a member of the Seamen's Union Executive'.[80] John Curtin had raised this issue previously with Frank Anstey:

> Ryce's membership of the Seamen's Union is, itself, one of the problems of the age. He was here Secretary of the Hotel Restaurant Employees Union and of the Fire Brigades Union, and when the consultation with the Disputes Committee was about to open he came into the room and announced he was an executive member of the Seamen's Union.[81]

The ALF State Executive claimed that Ryce had denied being a member of the FSU Executive, and asked him to attend its next meeting and explain why he should not be expelled from the labour movement for his deceitful action. Only seamen or those employed on harbour or river vessels or in marine transport, decks or stokehold were eligible for membership of the FSU. Men engaging in any other trade or profession would cease immediately to be members. Only financial members were entitled to vote or to hold office. As Curtin remarked in his letter to Anstey, Ryce held office in two other unions. After considerable discussion, during which Ryce's supporters, including Shelley, attempted to have a committee appointed to inquire into his bona fides, the State Executive carried a resolution expelling him from the labour movement.[82]

Shelley, Lawler of the EGDC, and others continued to defend Ryce. In an interview many years later, Shelley claimed that Ryce had not been allowed to defend himself.[83] Her own expulsion from the labour movement, however, appears to have been an unrelated matter, for it followed a State Executive investigation into the workings of the Labor Women's Organisation, which took place in September 1925. The State Executive Minutes referred only to an 'unsatisfactory state of affairs'. Shelley was expelled after she failed to answer a summons to appear before the State Executive and show cause why she should not be expelled from the labour movement.[84] This seems to have been an unduly severe course of action. Shortly before her expulsion, Shelley had been involved in another industrial battle on behalf of her union, the Hotel, Club, Caterers, Tearooms and Restaurant Employees. The dispute centred on the refusal by the Licensed Victuallers' Association to renegotiate their employees' award. The union claimed a wage increase of 5s per week and a forty-four hour week. George Ryce also took a prominent role in this dispute, a factor that probably influenced Shelley's support of him. With McCallum's assistance, the workers finally achieved their pay and reduced hours demands but not the preference clause they had also sought. Shelley remained Union Secretary after her expulsion from the labour movement.[85] The sources fail to shed any further light on the nature of the complaints against her. Even Shelley herself had little to say about the matter when she was interviewed in 1976:

> They had nothing to expel me on, you know. They formed a committee of the Labor Women's Organisation, that's another story, of people to enquire into what went on in the Labor Women's Organisation. Nothing went on there, you know, but I was expelled.[86]

The charges against Ryce, however, were justified. Some years after his expulsion, documents came to light that revealed that Ryce was, indeed, a bogus member of the FSU. In 1928, a power struggle arose between Tom Walsh and Jacob Johnson, the General Secretary of the FSU in Sydney. Johnson published a pamphlet containing evidence of Walsh's dishonest dealings with the union, including faking a membership ticket for George Ryce. The pamphlet contained a letter, purportedly from Tom Houghton to Walsh, stating:

I have fixed up the register and weekly report and the minutes to
make it appear that Ryce did join on that date, so should any
questions be asked from anyone on this matter I will be pleased if
you will make arrangements to see that the above information is
supplied, so as to prevent any mistake and beat Barker and Co. [a
reference to the SDC]. I have exchanged George Ryce's name in
place of a member named George Ross, a good fellow, so to all and
sundry George Ryce's [membership number will be 11,467]...[but]
should appear in the Head Office Register as 11,771, as shown in
the weekly report forwarded by this mail...This will remove the
necessity of two men paying into the one membership number.[87]

Apart from its impact on the local labour movement, the activities of the FSU in the summer of 1924–25 had far-reaching implications for the union Australia-wide. The board of the Australian Commonwealth Line and ASOF, united in their opposition to the FSU, initiated proceedings to deregister the union in the Arbitration Court. In a statement that listed the employers' grievances against the FSU, Admiral Clarkson, a Director of the Australian Shipping Board, claimed that diminishing cargoes and unreasonable union demands were forcing the Australian Commonwealth Line out of business. The line could not continue to operate under the prevailing conditions, in which the unions defied laws made by parliament and were able to make their own laws. Consequently, the Australian Shipping Board concluded that the union leaders and a minority of members were determined to break the line. As further efforts at negotiation were deemed to be useless, the board had taken steps to have the FSU deregistered.[88]

Walsh did not oppose in the Arbitration Court the application to deregister the FSU, but he refused to supply crews to two ships, the *Eromanga* and the *Dilga*, which were laid up in Sydney. The presiding judge, Justice Webb, reluctantly granted the application, and the FSU was deregistered and its award terminated as from midnight on 5 June 1925.[89] Deregistration of the union solved no problems for the ship owners. A week later, the articles of the *Monaro* expired. The ship's owners took out fresh articles, but the crew demanded the conditions of the award that had just been terminated. When these were refused, the men left and the vessel was laid up. The same occurred on other ships as their articles expired.[90] The managers of the Australian Commonwealth Line agreed to employ crew under the award conditions, but other ship owners initially refused, and in some cases employed non-union crews. Several violent incidents occurred, as at Port Adelaide, where an attempt was made by FSU members to scuttle the *Wandana*. Darwin waterside workers refused to unload cargo from the *Kinchella* when it berthed there early in August. Here, as in previous disputes of this nature, returned soldiers were prominent among the non-unionists.[91] The private ship owners were finally forced to meet award conditions, and an agreement was signed between them and the FSU on 6 August. The agreement was to exist for two years, during which time the union agreed to abandon all forms of 'job control', meaning that it would not interfere with the free selection and engagement of crews.[92] Prior to this, the Federal Government had amended the Immigration Act, to legalize the deportation of non-Australian-born persons who were 'found guilty of obstructing the transport of goods'. The amendment was made in order to deport Walsh (who was British) and Johnson (who was Swedish). Both men were arrested and tried, but the government failed to deport them.[93]

Shortly after the agreement had been signed, a further dispute arose, concerning the reduction, by £1 per month, of the wages of British seamen while in Australian ports. The ASOF accused the FSU of instigating the strike.[94] Further violence erupted. Two of the first British ships to be detained at Fremantle were the passenger vessels *Orsova* and *Borda*. The cargo carrier *Apolda*, which was loading timber for the South African Government Harbours and Railways, was held up at Bunbury when its crew unanimously decided to join the strike. The crew of the *Huntress*, however, refused to become involved in the dispute.[95]

By the time the *Demodocus*, of Liverpool, arrived in Fremantle at the end of September, Tom Houghton and the FSU had become well practised at persuading crews to join the strike. The vessel's master, Joseph Sprott, testified that a few hours after it commenced unloading, a large crowd of about 200 strikers appeared on the wharf and persuaded the crew, including the Chinese firemen, to disembark and attend a meeting. Houghton claimed that the Trades Hall had ordered him to remove the crew because FSU officials had been refused permission to speak to them on board that morning.[96] Over the next few days, the crew were permitted to return to their work, although they were frequently called to attend meetings at the Trades Hall. The *Demodocus* was prevented from sailing by a crowd of 150 men, who rushed aboard, withdrew the fires that were ready to be lit in the stokehold, and threatened to wreck the boilers and refrigerating machinery if the ship again attempted to leave port. The ship remained at the wharf for another week, but managed to get away under police protection at 5.00 a.m. on 8 October, despite Houghton urging the crew to 'Jump over the side when they commence to let go. We will get you Australian rates of pay, also the Chinese.'[97]

The State Government adopted a much more militant attitude to this dispute than it had to the one in 1924. The matter of police protection for crews was brought up twice in parliament. In reply to a question from Sir James Mitchell, Minister for Justice J.C. Willcock stated that government policy had been decided on the grounds that police protection would be granted only if the crew was 'willing to take the vessel to sea', and the police role was solely to 'prevent disorder'.[98] Apparently, this policy had been adopted to enable the *Demodocus* to leave port. When the crew of the *Borda* refused to take the ship to sea, however, the government altered its policy to favour the employers. On 2 November, a riot broke out on Fremantle Wharf when the ship attempted to set sail, manned by stewards ('scabs'). The government provided a large contingent of police, to prevent the striking British seamen boarding the vessel. In the ensuing brawl, several police officers were wounded and the Commissioner of Police issued rifles and bayonets.[99] The National Party Member for Fremantle, J.B. Sleeman, and Sir James Mitchell criticized Willcock for not ensuring that the police were armed earlier in the riot.[100]

The successful departure of the *Borda* marked a turning point in the British seamen's strike. During the previous month, British shipping companies had avoided Fremantle, where several of their vessels had been laid up for weeks, and South African Government vessels had ceased calling at Bunbury for timber. After the *Borda* incident, the strike was broken and the ports became hopeful of receiving their normal trade again.[101] The year of strikes had cost the Australian shippers dearly. ASOF estimated that its partners had lost 3,138 days in delays, including 1,613 days in the period between the deregistration of the FSU and the signing of the new agreement with crews. Ninety Australian ships had been involved in these delays.[102] In addition to the inevitable loss of profits through ships being laid up, the shipping companies in Fremantle were presented with an enormous bill from the Harbour Trust, amounting to £15,000.[103]

The *West Australian*'s editorial of 3 November pointed out that the British seamen's strike could certainly have been averted by firm action on the government's part:

> The riot at Fremantle yesterday is evidence of the lengths to which the revolutionaries, encouraged by the flaccidity of our Labour leaders, are prepared to go...The cherished institutions built up by a virile democracy are in imminent danger because the men who had succeeded to a great inheritance have proved too pusillanimous to take their stand against a negligible number of revolutionaries who draw their inspiration from alien lands.[104]

Perhaps, from an employer's point of view, this was an accurate assessment of the government's performance, yet members of the working classes could claim, with equal justification, that Collier had yielded to ruling-class pressure and that his actions had severely damaged the solidarity of the labour movement. By the end of its first two years in office, therefore, the administration had survived eighteen months of almost continuous industrial unrest, with accompanying political and economic problems. Far from the social divisions of wartime being healed and forgotten by the mid-1920s, the events of 1925 showed that, especially on the Fremantle Wharf, old bitternesses lay close to the surface of life.

The period also saw a decline in militancy in the mainstream labour movement. Firstly, there was the practical reality of being in government. As Curtin expressed the matter to Anstey, '[I]t is not solidarity to fight a Labor government in the same way that one ordinarily fights the private capitalist'.[105] This attitude placed the militants in a difficult position. Either they acquiesced with the government against their better judgment, or they opposed it and were accused of dividing the labour movement. Two militants, Ryce and Shelley, paid the penalty. A later attempt to expel T.J. Hughes shows that the ALF State Executive increasingly exerted its powers to control and punish those who spoke out publicly against it.[106] Another form of control was exercised by the *Westralian Worker*, which remained silent on such controversial issues as the expulsion of Ryce and Shelley, the investigation of the Labor Women's Organisation, and even the wharf riot of 2 November 1925. The paper's only concession to this last event was the publication of an article by the Anglican Dean of Melbourne, the Reverend J.S. Hart, supporting the strike of the British seamen.[107]

Suppression of militants did not, however, help to allay the

unease felt by employer groups and conservative politicians towards the labour movement as a whole. The industrial unrest of
1924 and 1925 undermined efforts by the Collier administration to
assuage doubts about its competence to govern the State and about
the sincerity of its rejection of Bolshevism. The *West Australian* had
accused the government of weakness when dealing with 'revolu-
tionaries'. Lee Steere's warning of the need for non-Labor parties
to unite was reiterated by Harold Boas in a letter to a colleague in
mid-1925. Boas warned that the only way to defeat Labor was 'to
fight it with its own weapon — a complete and united political
organisation'.[108] In heeding this warning, members of the National
coalition were to change permanently the face of conservative
politics in Western Australia.

1   *Commonwealth of Australia — Census* [hereafter *Commonwealth Census*], *1921*,
    part II, pp. 49–50, *1933*, part X, p. 734; *Year Book of Western Australia*
    [hereafter *Year Book*], *1957*, p. 74.
2   *Statistical Register of Western Australia* [hereafter *Statistical Register*], *1925*,
    part I, p. 4.; G.D. Snooks, 'Development in Adversity, 1913 to 1946', in C.T.
    Stannage (ed.), *A New History of Western Australia*, Nedlands, 1981, p. 249.
    The Australian average was 2.1 per cent.
3   *Year Book, 1957*, p. 74; D. Garden, *Albany: A Panorama of the Sound from 1827*,
    Melbourne, 1979, pp. 255 ff.; S. Macintyre, *Militant: The Life and Times of
    Paddy Troy*, Sydney, 1984, p. 11; Anon., 'How Capitalism has Impoverished
    Albany', *Westralian Worker Print*, 23 May 1919.
4   S. Welborn, *Lords of Death: A People, a Place, a Legend*, Fremantle, 1982, p. 160;
    Year Book, 1957, p. 80.
5   *Commonwealth Census, 1911, 1921*. The number of women workers rose by
    almost 5,000 in the decade 1911–21, while there was an increase, of slightly
    more than 4,000, in the number of male breadwinners.
6   *West Australian*, 18 January 1924.
7   *West Australian*, 19 January 1924.
8   D.W. Black, 'The Era of Labour Ascendency, 1924–1947', in Stannage, *A New
    History*, p. 408.
9   D.W. Black, The National Party in Western Australia, 1917–20, MA thesis,
    University of Western Australia, 1974, p. 275.
10 *West Australian*, 25 February 1924.
11 *West Australian*, 18 March 1924 (editorial).
12 *Sunday Times*, 16 March 1924, remarked: 'As none of the Labor candidates
    has repudiated the "take and hold" affirmation of the All-Australia Trade
    Union Conference in Melbourne, it would be folly for any anti-revolution-
    ary to vote for Labor. If Labor got into power it must attempt to put that
    policy into operation while it stands on the books.'
13 R.W. Lyman, *The First Labour Government, 1924*, London, 1957, pp. 248–270.
14 The greatest swings occurred in Brownhill Ivanhoe (21.4 per cent), Kimber-
    ley (20.8 per cent), and Pilbara (17.1 per cent).
15 Black, 'The Era of Labour Ascendency', pp. 406–407; see also *West Austral-
    ian*, 24 March 1924.

16   *West Australian*, 24 March 1924.

17   L. Layman, 'The Country Party: Rise and Decline', in R. Pervan and C. Sharman (eds), *Essays on Western Australian Politics*, Nedlands, 1979, Table 7.1, Legislative Assembly Seats Won by the Country Party, 1914–1943; *West Australian*, 19 March 1924.

18   *Western Australian Parliamentary Debates* (hereafter *WAPD*), vol. 70, pp. v–vi; *West Australian*, 24 March 1924, for short biographical sketches of the new Members of Parliament. For Scaddan's Cabinet, see *Year Book, 1914, 1915*.

19   Report to the General Manager, Dalgetys, London, 31 July 1924, in Dalgetys Papers, N.G. Butlin Archives of Business and Labour, File 100/3/33/3.

20   *Western Australian Pastoralist and Grazier*, vol. 1, no. 2, February 1925.

21   Premier to Agent-General, 26 March 1924, Premier's Department File (hereafter PDF) 104/24.

22   Correspondence and newspaper clippings in PDF 104/24.

23   *Daily News*, 15 August 1924.

24   *West Australian*, 11 February 1925; *Daily News*, 16 February 1925.

25   See, for example, Prime Minister to Premier, 16 August 1924, concerning British ex-servicemen and their families who had been trained for settlement in Western Australia, PDF 104/24.

26   *Daily News*, 4 March 1925.

27   PDF 104/24. See also F.K. Crowley, *Australia's Western Third: A History of Western Australia*, London, 1960, p. 215.

28   Collier to Noble, 4 June 1924, PDF 229/24.

29   See Snooks, 'Development in Adversity', Table 7.6, for figures in the three left-hand columns; and G. Withers, A.M. Endres, and L. Parry, 'Labour', in V. Vamplew (ed.), *Australians: Historical Statistics*, Sydney, 1987, p. 152, Table LAB 86-97, Unemployment, Australia, 1891–1974, for figures in the three right-hand columns.

30   Notes of a Deputation on behalf of the Unemployed of Fremantle to Acting Premier, W.C. Angwin, n.d. (January 1925?), PDF 33/25.

31   Trades Hall Deputation to the Deputy Premier, 4 February 1925, PDF 33/25.

32   Snooks, 'Development in Adversity', pp. 239, 254; D.W. Black, 'Party Politics in Turmoil: 1911–1924', in Stannage, *A New History*, p. 403; K. Ludlow, The Coal and Gold Industries in Western Australia and Government Assistance During the 1920s, BA Hons dissertation, Murdoch University, 1980, p. 85.

33   Figures were taken from the *Commonwealth Census, 1911, 1921*, and *Year Books, 1914, 1925*. The 1911 figures were as follows: industry, 24,000; farming, 21,000; mining, 18,000; commerce, 15,000. The industrial workforce in 1925 numbered 18,500.

34   Figures are based on *Commonwealth Census, 1911, 1921*, and *Year Books, 1914, 1925*. The number of females in commercial occupations rose from 2,906 in 1911 to 4,973 in 1921.

35   See Group Settlement Members Agreement, Group Settlement Papers, State Archives of Western Australia.

36   D. Kirkby, 'Arbitration and the Fight for Economic Justice', in S. Macintyre and R. Mitchell (eds), *Foundations of Arbitration: The Origins and Effects of State Compulsory Arbitration, 1890–1914*, Melbourne, 1989. This paper discusses the work of Jenny Lee, Raelene Frances and a number of other feminist historians, on arbitration and the workforce.

37 *Statistical Register, 1921–22,* part IV, pp. 19–22; Dalgetys Papers, N.G. Butlin Archives of Business and Labour, Dalgetys Salary and Wages Records, 100/3/48, also File 100/3/12/2, 'Staff Service Forms' (used with permission). See *Statistical Register, 1921–22,* part II, p. 9, for various income brackets.

38 W. Brady, '"Serfs of the Sodden Scone?" Women Workers in the Western Australian Hotel and Catering Industry, 1900–1925', in P. Crawford (ed.), *Studies in Western Australian History VII: Women in Western Australian History,* December 1983, p. 40.

39 Perth Chamber of Commerce, Minutes of the Annual General Meeting, 29 August 1924, State Archives of Western Australia.

40 *Statistical Registers, 1915, 1925–26,* show union membership in 1913 as 31,291, and in 1925 as 42,000. See also *Year Book, 1957,* p. 337; *Pocket Year Book of Western Australia, 1926,* part III, p. 14.

41 Deputation to the Acting Premier, 2 March 1925, PDF 33/25.

42 Black, 'The Era of Labor Ascendency', pp. 412–413. This legislation is dealt with in greater detail by Black in The Early Administration of Philip Collier, BA Hons dissertation, University of Western Australia, 1959, pp. 35–82.

43 R. Gore, The Western Australian Legislative Council, 1890–1920: Aspects of a House of Review, MA thesis, University of Western Australia, 1975, pp. 207–212.

44 Snooks, 'Development in Adversity', pp. 249–252.

45 K. Smith, *A Bunch of Pirates? The Story of a Farmers' Cooperative, Wesfarmers,* Perth, 1984, p. 2.

46 Elders Balance Sheet and Profit and Loss Account, 1928, File 103/1/9, Elder Smith Papers, N.G. Butlin Archives of Business and Labour. Between 1923 and 1924, Elders' profits almost doubled, from £46,000 to £82,000. See also Manager's Report to General Manager, London, 31 July 1925, File 100/3/33/5, Dalgetys Papers.

47 *Pocket Year Book of Western Australia, 1926,* p. 54, and *1927,* p. 337.

48 FSU to ALP, Fremantle, 7 July 1924, State Executive of the ALF (WA) — Correspondence Files (hereafter SE Correspondence), File 172.

49 *West Australian,* 7 November 1924. See also SE Correspondence, File 224.

50 *West Australian,* 24 November 1924.

51 *West Australian,* 26 November 1924.

52 Stanley Bruce became leader of the federal National–Country Party coalition government after W.M. Hughes was forced to resign in January 1923, at which time the two parties combined to prevent an electoral defeat by the Labor Party. See S. Macintyre, *The Oxford History of Australia, Volume 4: 1901–1942. The Succeeding Age,* Melbourne, 1986, pp. 196–197.

53 *Westralian Worker,* 21 November 1924. H.B. Larkin, Chairman of the Shipping Board, received £3,500 a year.

54 *Mirror,* 29 November 1924.

55 S. Jones, *Two Centuries of Overseas Trading: The Origins and Growth of the Inchcape Group,* London, 1986, pp. 143, 145, Figure 5.2; see also P.G. Griffiths, *A History of the Inchcape Group,* London, 1977, p. 90.

56 *Westralian Worker,* 21 November 1924.

57 *Westralian Worker,* 2 January 1925.

58 *Westralian Worker,* 23 January 1925.

59 Perth Chamber of Commerce, Minutes, 16 December 1924; notes of the PCC Deputation to Premier, 6 November 1924, H.J. Wigmore to Premier, 8 December 1924, PDF 675/24.

60 Perth Chamber of Commerce, Minutes, 16 December 1924,

61 ALF (WA), Parliamentary Labor Party Caucus Minutes, State Archives of Western Australia, Acc. 1313A, vol. 5, 26 November 1924; *Westralian Worker*, 5 December 1924, 12 December 1924, 19 December 1924.

62 *Sunday Times*, 7 December 1924.

63 *Daily News*, 5 December 1924.

64 State Executive of the ALF (WA) — Minutes Books (hereafter SE Minutes), vol. 3, 13 December 1924.

65 *West Australian*, 8 December 1924.

66 *West Australian*, 9 December 1924.

67 *Daily News*, 9 December 1924 (the title of this chapter comes from this source); *West Australian*, 9 December 1924.

68 *Daily News*, 9 December 1924.

69 Lawler to Barker, 14 March 1925, SE Correspondence, File 213; ALF (WA), Minutes of the Eastern Goldfields District Council, State Archives of Western Australia, Acc. 1704A, vol. 4, 15 December 1924; Fremantle District Council to Barker, 21 March 1925, SE Correspondence, File 224; Shop Assistant and Warehouse Employees, Bunbury, to Barker, 12 January 1925, and Collier to Barker, 16 December 1924, SE Correspondence, File 271.

70 Mather to Morris, 1 January 1925; Waterside Workers Federation (Albany) Papers (hereafter WWF), N.G. Butlin Archives of Business and Labour, Acc. T62/11/2.

71 Fox to Waterside Workers Federation of Australia, 6 January 1925, WWF, File T62/11/6, pp. 1–3.

72 *Westralian Worker*, 26 December 1924.

73 *Westralian Worker*, 2 January 1925.

74 Curtin to Anstey, 10 March 1925 (hereafter Curtin to Anstey), p. 3, Lloyd Ross Papers, National Library of Australia, MS 3939, box 38.

75 SE Minutes, vol. 3, 20 January 1925.

76 Minutes of SE Officers Meeting, 17 April 1925, and SE Minutes, 20 April 1925.

77 SE Minutes, 6 May 1925.

78 ALF (WA), Minutes of the Metropolitan District Council (hereafter Metropolitan DC Minutes), vol. 4, 21 May 1925.

79 Lawler to Black (SE), 21 May 1925, SE Correspondence, File 213; ALF (WA), Minutes of the Midland District Council (hereafter Midland DC Minutes), 27 April 1925, 11 May 1925, 8 June 1925.

80 SE Minutes, vol. 4, 1 June 1925.

81 Curtin to Anstey, p. 2.

82 SE Minutes, vol. 4, 1 June 1925, 15 June 1925.

83 Cecilia Shelley, oral history transcript, Battye Library, pp. 28–29.

84 SE Minutes, vol. 4, 21 September 1925, 23 November 1925, 7 December 1925. See also correspondence between Barker and Lawler, 12 December 1925, 29 January 1926, 1 February 1926, SE Correspondence, File 213.

85 Brady, '"Serfs of the Sodden Scone"', pp. 39–42.

86 Cecilia Shelley, oral history transcript, p. 29.

87 Houghton to Walsh, 19 June 1925, in J. Johnson, *'The Crooks' Exposed: Damning Evidence Concerning the Seamen's Union 'Crooks'*, 1928, p. 5, held in Federated Seamen's Union Papers, Australian Archives (Canberra), Acc. A432/1, item 29/415.

88 Undated, untitled document in FSU Papers, N.G. Butlin Archives of Business and Labour, Acc. N38/22, identified by an accompanying letter from Tom Walsh to Hon. A.S. Willis MP, 29 June 1925, as 'a statement by Admiral Sir William Clarkson'.

89 Notes of Proceedings in the Commonwealth Arbitration Court on 5 June 1925, FSU Papers, File N38/43, N.G. Butlin Archives of Business and Labour; ASOF Annual Report, 1925, N.G. Butlin Archives of Business and Labour, Acc. E217/93, pp. 13–16.
90 ASOF Annual Report, 1925, p. 16.
91 FSU Secretary, Port Adelaide, to General Secretary, FSU, Melbourne, 22 July 1925, and clippings from the *Standard* (Darwin), 5 August 1925, FSU Papers, File N38/23, N.G. Butlin Archives of Business and Labour.
92 ASOF Annual Report, 1925, pp. 17–18.
93 ibid., p. 20. Re the unsuccessful prosecution of Walsh and Johnson, see Sir Robert Garran Papers, Australian Archives (Canberra), Acc. A467/1, File 29/4143.
94 ASOF Annual Report, 1925, p. 20; Metropolitan DC Minutes, 13 July 1925.
95 Statements by R. Holland, Master, *Borda*, 7 September 1925; C.G. Matheson, Master, *Orsova*, 7 September 1925; R.S. Williams, Master, *Apolda*, Bunbury, 25 August 1925; G.M. Gowrie, Crew Member, *Huntress*, Bunbury, 28 August 1925, Sir Robert Garran Papers, File 29/4143.
96 Statement by Joseph Lambert Sprott, Master, *Demodocus*, 20 October 1925, p. 1, Sir Robert Garran Papers, File 29/4143.
97 Statement by William Hughes, Quarter Master, *Demodocus*, 20 October 1925, Sir Robert Garran Papers. See also Sprott's statement, ibid., p. 2.
98 *WAPD, 1925*, vol. 72, p. 1460.
99 *West Australian*, 3 November 1925.
100 *WAPD, 1925*, vol. 73, p. 1987.
101 *West Australian*, 3 November 1925.
102 ASOF Annual Report, 1925, Appendix G, pp. 39 ff.
103 *WAPD, 1925*, vol. 73, p. 2380.
104 *West Australian*, 3 November 1925.
105 Curtin to Anstey, p. 2.
106 See SE Minutes, vol. 4, 23 November 1925; Midland DC Minutes, State Archives of Western Australia, Acc. 994, vol. 3, 10 October 1925.
107 *Westralian Worker*, 6 November 1925.
108 Boas to W. Balston, 4 July 1925, in Harold Boas Papers, State Archives of Western Australia, Acc. 948A, File 2.

Chapter Eight

A UNITED FRONT AGAINST THE COMMON FOE
The conservative response

After the 1924 State election, the conservative parties in Western Australia were in disarray. The National Labor Party section of the coalition had suffered particularly heavy losses to the ALP in the 1924 election. H.K. Maley, parliamentary leader of the Ministerial Country Party, also lost his seat and was replaced by Charles Latham.[1] Out of this confusion arose a movement led by Liberal League members Harold Boas, R.T. Robinson and T.A.L. Davy, and other influential men such as Sir Ernest Lee Steere. Despite their previous differences, the National Party and the two Country Parties formed the United Party in March 1925. At the new party's official inauguration, National Party President J.F. Allen hailed it as 'a united front against the common foe'.[2] The 'foe' — the labour movement — greeted the move with considerable derision.[3] The *Westralian Worker* announced that 'Westralian nationalism' was to receive 'eastern money' in order to win seats in the federal election of the following year.[4]

Federally, the National and Country Parties, led by S.M. Bruce and Earle Page, had maintained an uneasy, but necessary, coalition since the November 1922 federal election. The Country Party, with fourteen seats, held the balance of power in the House of Representatives.[5] Bruce and Page saw the Labor victory in Western Australia as providing adequate evidence of the need for ongoing cooperation among the non-Labor parties. Consequently, Bruce asked Harold Boas and Sir Charles Nathan to form a body of prominent businessmen, without active party connections, for the purpose of fund-raising to support 'the political forces opposing Communism and Socialism'.[6] Thus, the WA Consultative Council (WACC) was born. The council aimed to foster and encourage the union of all anti-communist political parties, by providing financial assistance for organization, by presenting only one candidate

'Stanley Bruce and "Westralian Nationalism"'
The *Westralian Worker* (28 November 1924) savagely lampooned the formation
of the United Party in Western Australia, and was quick to draw connections
between it and eastern money.
[Courtesy *Australian Worker* / Battye Library]

(either National or Country Party) for each constituency, and by
endeavouring to ensure that people who were likely to vote for the
conservatives were properly enrolled. The conservative parties
had learned a bitter lesson from the 1924 State election and were
trying to avoid making similar mistakes in the future. Public
education was another important aspect of the WACC's activities;
the council planned to use the press and other means to educate the
people to embrace democracy and eschew communism.[7]

The WACC consisted mainly of professional associations, employer groups such as the Perth and Fremantle Chambers of
Commerce, and traders' and wholesalers' associations. The only
individual member was Sir Walter James.[8] At first, the WACC held
weekly meetings and raised funds through the personal contacts
of each member. Community support was gained by exploiting
fears of communist activity and of 'industrial lawlessness' such as
had characterized the seamen's strikes.[9] Communist influence in
the Australian community in the mid-1920s was greatly exaggerated. For some years, the Western Australian branch of the Communist Party had struggled to develop; indeed, it had survived
only because of the efforts of dedicated individuals such as Joe
Shelley, who sold communist literature on the Perth Esplanade,

and Charley Reeve, a former IWW member, who held Sunday meetings that sometimes attracted hostile crowds.[10] While 1925 saw something of a renaissance of communism, the party's Australia-wide membership in 1928 was estimated to be a mere 250.[11]

Gathering sufficient funds for the campaign was of paramount importance to the conservative parties. While corresponding with businessmen to obtain support for the WACC, Boas wrote:

> The Labor Party in this State has at its command some tens of thousands of pounds with which it carries out its political propaganda and organising work, and the only effective way of preventing it, *with its Socialistic tendencies, getting control of the whole political position*, not only in Western Australia, but throughout Australia, is to fight it with its own weapon — a complete and united political organisation.[12]

While the ALF had, in fact, experienced considerable problems in fund-raising, Boas was correct in recognizing the need for a tighter conservative party structure. Until the mid-1920s, the major difference between Labor and non-Labor campaigns had been the degree of organization rather than the funds available. Even in its darkest hour, immediately after the 1916 conscription crisis, Labor had not suffered a disarray of the magnitude of that experienced by the National coalition after the 1924 election. As McCallum stated, 'No man, or body of men, is big enough or great enough to break the Labor Movement. When it comes to a choice between individuals and the Movement, the individual must go.'[13] The truth of his statement had been demonstrated again and again — in the conscription split of 1917, in the refusal to allow National unionists back into 'official' unions, in the rejection of 'bogus' unions such as the FMU and Callanan's 'OBU', and in the expulsion of George Ryce and Cecilia Shelley. No similar emphasis on solidarity existed in non-Labor parties prior to the 1920s. Theirs was a history of allegiance to individuals, beginning with John Forrest, rather than to a movement. The Country Party split, discussed in Chapter 6, further illustrates the importance of strong personal allegiances among the conservatives, for it centred around two men, James Mitchell and Alex Monger.

In a report to the WACC, Boas and like-minded colleagues criticized the relationship between the Country and United Parties, and their haphazard methods of fund-raising; both parties relied almost solely on members' subscriptions, making no appeal to the general public for funds.[14] The report was particularly damning on the selection of candidates:

> Whilst any Tom, Dick or Harry has the right to submit his nomination to an organisation, and demand that he shall receive the full backing, moral and financial, of any organisation that receives its source of supply from this Council [there will never be a united force]...This obvious lack of party organisation and this looseness of system has, in our opinion, been the means in the past of destroying effectively the power of the anti-labor forces...[15]

In summary, the non-Labor parties had too long adhered to nineteenth-century style politics. The driving force behind the move to reorganize came from Young Liberal League members and founders of the Argonauts Civic and Political Club (see pages 274–278): Boas, Davy, Robinson and Ross McDonald.[16] These men were all powerfully motivated by a sense of the urgent need to combat 'communism'. In a paper addressed to the 'Businessmen of Western Australia', Boas presented a scenario whereby socialists were in power in both Houses of Parliament. Australia would be 'at the mercy of Experimentalists', and 'controlled and governed by Communist Internationals with men of the Tom Walsh type dictating'. Boas warned his audience:

> Make no mistake about the character of the Australian Labor Party today. It is an entirely different organisation to that which was in power prior to the War. Communism, Bolshevism and the extreme Socialists [were] then non-existent. Read its constitution today, headed by the Socialisation of all industry, transportation and exchange.[17]

Boas served as Western Australian Campaign Director for the National and Country Parties in the 1925 federal election.[18] The WACC guaranteed to provide £6,500 to finance the campaign, if the National and Country Parties in Western Australia remained united. Their efforts were rewarded when the Bruce Government was returned with a large majority across Australia.[19] In the west, the conservative victory was absolute, perhaps reflecting on the Collier Government's handling of the seamen's strikes. The National Senators William Carroll, Patrick Lynch and G.F. Pearce were all re-elected, defeating Labor candidates E.H. Barker, Andrew Clementson and J.J. Kenneally. Only one Labor Member, A.E. Green, was successful in retaining his House of Representatives seat, the other four seats going to conservatives.[20]

Harold Boas
Architect, Liberal League member and co-founder of the United Party, the WA
Consultative Council and the Argonauts Civic and Political Club, Boas argued
that the Labor Party had 'no moral right' to the name of party because, by
claiming to represent the interests of the worker, it 'created social divisiveness'.
[Courtesy Battye Library, Perth City Council Collection, 3242B/486]

Electoral victory was not, however, a sufficient incentive to keep the factions together for any length of time. A quarrel broke out between the United and Country Parties over the selection of candidates to stand for the Legislative Council elections in March 1926. The United Party granted endorsement for a candidate to contest South West Province, which was held by F.S. Willmott, former leader of the Ministerial Country Party. As a result, the President of the United Party, J.F. Allen, and two senior party officials, Harold Boas and G.W.J. Cumming, all resigned.[21] Boas stated that the reason for his resignation was 'the destruction of efforts to bring about a permanent union between the non-Socialist parties'.[22]

In the meantime, however, Boas continued his work of re-educating the youth of Western Australia. The Argonauts Civic and Political Club had been founded, significantly, on Empire Day, 24 May 1925. At the club's inaugural meeting, 'loyal and patriotic' speeches were made by the movement's founders and guests, including Harold Boas, Sir William Lathlain, Senator Paddy Lynch, and T.A.L. Davy, all of whom held important positions in the National Party at State or federal level.[23] The title 'Argonauts' was suggested by Davy, and symbolized the group as 'setting forth on a sea of discovery' and its members as being 'pioneers of service'. According to one of the inaugural speakers, the Argonauts were duty-bound to 'see that the serpent of communism was killed'.[24]

Similarly to the WACC, the Argonauts Club was founded as a response, by conservative politicians and businessmen, to the Labor Party victory in the 1924 State election, and to the wave of political and industrial strife that had occurred across Australia in the mid-1920s. Despite the Argonauts' claim to 'political neutrality', the two organizations were closely related, sharing a common leadership, aims and activities.[25] The club's specific aims were to combat a 'disturbing element' in society and to give 'the youth of Western Australia a greater sense of responsibility and loyalty to the state'.[26] Boas, architect, ex-serviceman and an active participant in conservative politics for the past fifteen years, believed that industrial unrest could be prevented by weaning industrial workers away from the ALP, rather than by physical confrontation. The Argonauts organized luncheon clubs, a model parliament, lectures, and 'Industrial Groups' whose aim was to educate workers and acquaint them with the 'dangers of industrial communism'.

From its inception, the Argonauts Club maintained a strongly conservative stance and appears to have attracted young professional men rather than wage earners. Indeed, the emphasis on youth was the most notable difference between the Argonauts Club and other 'patriotic' associations. An editorial in the organization's journal stated:

> We believe that there are no *young men* in Western Australia, if they have the energy and the inclination to think seriously, with the country's good always before them, who can think any other way than rightly.[27]

This emphasis on youth was noted and commented upon favourably by the *West Australian*:

> 'The army of youth! Every year 10,000 young men reaching maturity and marching — where? That's the question we — "the Argonauts" — are asking ourselves,' said Mr. Harold Boas recently to a *West Australian* reporter...Less than three months ago 'the Argonauts' was formed — just half a dozen men headed by Mr. Harold Boas...It [now] has more than 300 members; it has club rooms, dining rooms, library, debating society, its own parliament, educational classes, and a hundred and one other appurtenances.[28]

The club's motto was 'Service' and its badge depicted a hand holding a candle. There were four fundamental principles of service, which members were urged to foster: imperial unity; the development and maintenance of constitutional government and law and order; counteraction of the growth of communism and socialism; and the individual's right to freedom and development.[29] The principles embodied a conservative ideology that encouraged members to be loyal to the British Empire, to accept trade unionism only on the basis of conciliation and arbitration, and to believe in the importance of law and order and the value of individual effort. In espousing industrial and political peace, the Argonauts objected to the use of such potentially divisive terms as 'workers' and 'capitalists'. Instead, they saw employers and employees as having 'mutual interests — both essential to the progress and prosperity of the community'.[30] Socialists were singled out as the major cause of disruption in the community and were barred from membership. Through the pages of the *Argonaut*, Boas stepped up his crusade by remarking that the Labor Party's outlook was 'mistaken' because it classified people by their material possessions — that is, as classes — and that Labor did not, in fact, satisfy the 'requirements of principle necessary to qualify it as a permanent political party'. It had 'no moral right' to the name of party, Boas declared, because, by claiming to represent the interests of the worker, it created social divisiveness. In fact, according to Boas, Labor ideology was 'destructive of the very foundation of our society'.[31]

Membership of the Argonauts was open only to males who subscribed to the objectives of the club, and was divided into four categories: town, country, life and honorary.[32] Only members belonging to one of the first three categories could vote or hold office. Apart from the gender restriction, the organization claimed to accept anyone except socialists. There was no written indication of restriction on the grounds of race or religion. The club was run by a council, elected at the Annual General Meeting, where the President also was proposed and appointed. Councillors initially served for a year, although they were eligible for immediate re-election. Their tasks were to elect the office-bearers (two secretaries and a treasurer); to control the club's finances; to appoint subcommittees when required; to engage, supervise and dismiss staff; to undertake management decisions; and to make, alter or repeal by-laws.[33]

The Argonauts' luncheon clubs were organized in a precise and ceremonial manner. Members and visitors were expected to arrive at 1 o'clock 'sharp', sign the attendance book and pay 1s 6d each. On the sounding of the gong by the chairman of the day, members would stand to attention, face the Lamp of Service at the head of the room, and, with right hand outstretched, palm downwards, declare, 'By this symbol I pledge myself to uphold the ideals for which we stand'. The assembly would then sing 'Land of Hope and Glory' before being seated for lunch. Speakers were carefully selected to reiterate the values of the club and to teach the young audience the principles of sacrifice and devotion to Empire. They included the Marquis of Salisbury, a member of the Empire parliamentary delegation that visited Perth in 1927; conservative politicians such as Dr Earle Page and Senator George Pearce; Dr Battye; and General Sir John Monash, a well-decorated, nationally acclaimed war hero, who — despite his persistent refusals to work outside the constitutional system — was a focus for extreme, conservative groups seeking a high-ranking officer to head a military government that would take power if there were a national crisis.[34] An interesting exception among the Argonauts lunchtime speakers was Miss Freda Bage, both in that she was female and in that she was a delegate of the League of Nations, a organization devoted to maintaining world peace, albeit one supported by Stanley Bruce and other conservatives.[35]

The luncheon clubs were tailored to the lunch hour of young workers in the city centre. Members of both the club and its Industrial Groups were drawn mostly from clerical and other 'white collar' professions. By the end of 1925, Argonauts Industrial Groups had been established in thirty-five firms, including Elders,

Dalgetys and Wesfarmers, in several banks, and in retailers such as Boans, Bon Marche, and Foy and Gibson. There was even an Industrial Group at The University of Western Australia. The existence of Argonauts groups at three motor companies and several merchant firms suggests limited 'blue collar' membership, but these members were more likely to have been managers than mechanics.[36] There is no evidence of Industrial Groups being set up among large concentrations of working-class labourers — for example, in the Midland Workshops, on the Fremantle Wharf, or among the heavy industries at Bassendean. Nor is there evidence of any connection between workers who had belonged to National unions and the membership of Industrial Groups, although several National unionists had been clients of the legal firm of Argonauts co-founder R.T. Robinson, in 1919.

The Industrial Groups were intended to counteract communist influences by organizing workers and teaching them to realize the mutual and interdependent interests of employers and employees. According to the Industrial Groups, industrial prosperity would be achieved not only by good working conditions and wages, but also by loyalty, efficiency and service on the part of the worker. The Argonauts adopted cell group tactics similar to those used by their sworn enemies, the communists. The policy was to select a sympathetic staff member of a particular firm to serve as secretary of the Industrial Group. This man and other congenial members would be enrolled in the Argonauts. Boas claimed that, in the space of a few weeks, Industrial Groups with an aggregate membership of 'roughly 300' had formed in over thirty industrial concerns around Perth.[37]

Despite claiming to be politically neutral, the Argonauts leadership took an active role in the 1927 State elections. Apart from openly criticizing the Labor Party, the club was involved in fund-raising for the conservative (or 'anti-Labor') parties, and supported ten Argonauts members who stood for parliament as conservative candidates.[38] Four of these members — T.A.L. Davy, R.S. Samson, J. McCallum-Smith and C.G. Latham — were victorious. Boas even suggested that the *Argonaut* amalgamate with the WACC's proposed journal, the *Constitutionalist*, as there could be 'no possible question of policy in connection with the matter, *as your objective is identical with that which we ourselves have in view*'.[39]

The Argonauts' membership grew rapidly during the club's

first year of existence, peaked in 1926, and was in decline by the middle of 1927. In the metropolitan area, by the end of October 1925, membership was estimated to be 1,300, while country re- cruiting tours yielded over 150 members in the Great Southern Region alone. At its zenith, in July 1926, the club had 2,000 mem- bers, including those at fourteen country branches. The numbers began to decline soon after this. In his Annual Report, Boas de- scribed 1927 as a 'year of exceptional difficulty'. The luncheon club had closed, and the club's headquarters had moved from the original spacious premises on St Georges Terrace[40] to rooms in Albany Chambers, Barrack Street. Membership had dropped to 700, which was 'beyond the comprehension of the leaders', and Pingelly was the only country branch still active.[41] It appears that members had lost interest in the activities offered. Some may also have found the constant reiteration of the principles of 'discipline' and 'service' irksome. Boas complained to the Argonauts Council that members showed no inclination to keep the luncheon club's premises attractive to visitors, nor did they bother to attend lunch- time addresses. On occasions, he had had to apologize to visitors for the low attendance. Boas concluded that there was 'vast room for improvement in the spirit of service of the members'.[42] His tone was similar to that used by the leaders of other 'patriotic' organi- zations, such as the RSL and the Empire Loyalty League, but, like them, he was appealing to sentiments that had only ever burned strongly in the hearts of a minority. The generation who had lived through and served in the Great War might, with justification, have felt that it had given adequate service and made sufficient sacrifices to last a lifetime. Some members, too, may have objected to the overt political stance of an organization whose activities and rhetoric constantly belied its declared 'neutrality'.[43]

Political conservatives in the middle and late 1920s, therefore, experienced mixed fortunes. Conservative strength in the mid- 1920s inevitably raises the question of whether Western Australian social organization had undergone any significant changes, de- spite the traumatic upheavals of the war experience. Some aspects of Western Australian society in 1926 were remarkably different from 1914; others were surprisingly similar. There was greater independence of thought, hence conservatives encountered diffi- culties when they attempted to reassert their control over a com- munity that they perceived to be falling under the influence of

Bolshevism and industrial unrest. Attempts to 're-educate' the people, especially young workers, to ensure electoral victory for the non-Labor parties at State and federal level, and to exterminate the ideologies of communism and socialism were not always received enthusiastically.

Since the war, a succession of groups, such as the RSL and the Empire Loyalty League, had called upon citizens to show both loyalty and a spirit of sacrifice, while themselves adopting an avowedly 'non-partisan' stance. None had met with enormous success. The WACC, however, was the first openly political conservative organization of this type, and its efforts to reorganize the non-Labor parties indicate an acceptance that Labor was not a passing phenomenon but a formidable and enduring political force.

While young workers and ex-soldiers tended to be unenthused by displays of British patriotism, in some areas, imperialist ideology continued to flourish. Prior to the Great War, the ideology of Empire was spread with particular effectiveness through the education system. By 1926, there were some 51,000 primary school children in the State. The effects of the Great War were deeply felt in schools, both during and after the conflict. By emphasizing the self-sacrifice of those who went to the front, and the obligations of those at home, teachers attempted to draw moral lessons from the conflict, which would leave a lasting impression on their young pupils. Perhaps an even greater impression upon the children was the knowledge that forty-seven of the State's schoolteachers had paid the supreme sacrifice. The war, in fact, had fleshed out the abstract idea that had been Empire prior to the conflict, thereby increasing the spirit of patriotism and imperialism generated by the education system. Imperialist ideology was perpetuated even more zealously by private educational establishments such as Scotch College, where the students were constantly reminded of the sacrifice and heroism of the school's war dead.[44]

Within the broader community, the sentiments of Empire took on a new localized meaning, loosely termed the spirit of Anzac, which was spread by the major Protestant churches and the RSL. Yet, if the spirit of Anzac shone brightly, the spirit of religious faith grew dimmer. Although the majority still considered themselves to be adherents of a religious faith — usually one of the four leading Christian denominations: Anglican, Roman Catholic,

Methodist or Presbyterian — the number of respondents to the 1921 Census who claimed to belong to 'no religion' had increased by 100 per cent since 1911. A further 8,000 persons either objected to specifying their religion or refused to reply.[45] The percentage of Catholics in the community decreased from 22 per cent in 1911 to 18.3 per cent in 1933.[46] Whether many lost their Christian faith during war service is impossible to ascertain without further evidence, but declining figures suggest the growth of scepticism and an increasing reluctance to accept traditional beliefs.

Some ex-servicemen, and others who had suffered bereavement as a result of the conflict may also have resented the glorification of war that continued well into the 1920s as a major theme in the sermons of many of the Protestant clergy. Typical was Archbishop Riley's celebration of Anzac Day in 1924, when he spoke fervently of 'the unity of our Empire, the freewill and loyalty of our soldiers and sailors, the affection and devotion between the Dominions overseas and the Mother Country'. He offered thanksgiving for those who had died at Gallipoli 'for King and Empire in the high cause of freedom and honour'. The following month, Empire Day was celebrated with an Empire Loyalty Demonstration at Fremantle. Governor Newdegate and Sir William Lathlain addressed the crowd. Those present sang a patriotic song, entitled 'Marching Through Australia', which ran, in part:

> Raise the song of Empire and shout from shore to shore!
> Tell of Britain's heroes — their deeds in days of yore!
> Freedom's right they won for us — we'll prize it more and more.
> While we go marching through Australia!

> Chorus: Hurrah! Hurrah! Britannia's sons we are!
> Hurrah! Hurrah! Our Empire wide and free!
> Hands and hearts united with our kindred o'er the sea.
> While we go marching through Australia![47]

These verses contain no hint of the 60,000 Australian servicemen who died in the cause of maintaining British freedom, only the oft-repeated assertion that Australians were indebted to the Empire for the preservation of their freedom. One can only surmise the ways in which many of the returned servicemen reacted to these assertions of the nation's dependence on the Empire's fight-

ing forces for its safety and freedom. Perhaps the majority continued to see Australia and Australians as an integral part of the
British Empire, with their sacrifice contributing to one united
purpose. In reality, Australia was permitted only a lesser, humble
role. This colonial cringe was celebrated in a verse of the National
Anthem, 'God Save the King', which was still sung in Western
Australia during the 1920s:

> Far from the Empire's heart
> Make us a worthy part;
> God save our king!
> Keep us forever Thine
> Our land Thy Southern shrine
> And in Thy grace divine
> God save our King![48]

The range of emotions experienced by returned servicemen,
described in Chapter 4, varied from the imperialist patriotism of
Harry Axford, through the acts of violence perpetrated against
strikers on the goldfields, to the dissent expressed by such men as
the Victoria Cross winners Hugo Throssell and Tom Axford, and
the deliberate pro-Labor stance taken by Joseph O'Neill and other
members of the dissident RSA.

A number of Labor politicians, too, were impatient with the
expression of patriotic sentiment. The Collier Government incurred the displeasure of the RSL by decreeing that, in future, ex-
soldiers would not be allowed to go into State schools to address
the children on Anzac Day. According to Collier, 'outsiders' should
not be permitted to encourage the 'glorification of war' in the
minds of schoolchildren. It was sufficient for teachers, many of
whom had served with the AIF, to address pupils on the history
and outcome of the war and Australia's part in it. The RSL,
however, claimed that the way Anzac Day was celebrated throughout the State evinced the high level of patriotism that was felt in
Western Australia. 'One might as well try to stop the birds singing'
as to prevent West Australians from mourning the Anzacs, it
declared.[49]

Yet the issue was broader than the nature of Anzac Day celebrations. It concerned the role of Western Australia within the British
Empire. The Labor Government was beginning to question the
legitimacy of continuing to foster the fierce patriotism that had

plunged so many Australians blindly into a conflict on the opposite side of the earth. In placing this ban on schools, the Collier administration took an unusually bold stance on the issue of 'patriotism'. Previously, the ALP's attitude had been mainly reactionary, as when the State Executive declined to join the Perth Empire Loyalty League on the grounds that the party's policies clearly denoted that it was loyal.[50] But Collier must have been aware that the inculcation of loyalty to Empire ran far deeper than the annual Anzac Day addresses. He would have had to alter the entire education syllabus in order to institute significant changes to the values taught to schoolchildren.

The ALP and the RSL clashed again over the issue of the construction of war memorials. Early in 1925, the RSL called a meeting to form a committee of 'public spirited' persons, presided over by Sir William Lathlain, to work towards the erection of a war memorial in Kings Park, overlooking the city. The Premier and others believed that a hospital would be a more serviceable and fitting memorial to the fallen. Collier declared that he would not subscribe a penny for the erection of a 'non-utility monument', and that there were already too many 'unsightly piles of stone' throughout the country. Nevertheless, the memorial was funded, as the result of an appeal launched by Archbishop Riley on Anzac Day 1928, and was opened, symbolically and fittingly, shortly after Armistice Day in the centennial year.[51] Perth's war memorial was one of the later monuments to be erected in Western Australia. In the early 1920s, Governor Newdegate had frequently been called upon to open war memorials in country towns and in suburbs of Perth. The first of these monuments was opened in 1921, which indicates a considerable fund-raising commitment on the part of the local residents.[52] At Fremantle, the opening ceremony was performed on Armistice Day 1928, after ten years of sporadic fund-raising and much bickering over whether the memorial should take the form of a public utility or an obelisk. As in Perth, those favouring the 'heap of stone' won the day.[53] The disagreements indicate changing community attitudes to the war and to the ways in which the 'sacrifice' of the dead should be commemorated. Yet anti-imperial feeling, although more widespread than before the war, remained an expression of the minority.

Another aspect of imperialist ideology, Social Darwinism, developed a further virulent strain as a result of the war experience.

Professor A.D. Ross, of The University of Western Australia, observed, in a 1925 address to the Royal Society of Western Australia, that the war had aroused a 'new national spirit in the British nation'. He warned that unless that spirit was maintained, economic recovery and improvement would not occur. Ross went on to describe the war as an 'evolutionary process' in which Australia had attained 'nationhood' without 'any slackening of the bonds of union with the homeland'. The main burden of his address was the need to improve industry by research and by the application of scientific techniques. In it, he neatly combined the concerns of imperialism: industrial progress and profit that would benefit the Empire and strengthen the bonds between Britain and the Commonwealth.[54] In these terms, therefore, war could be seen as beneficial, in the sense that it formed part of the 'evolution' of Australia's development into nationhood.

At the very time at which Professor Ross spoke, however, Australia continued to be disadvantaged by an economic system that benefited the ruling classes of Britain and its dominions but hindered individual industrial development. This was despite the popular philosophy of 'State patriotism' described in Chapter 4, which stated that Australian goods should be given preference over those manufactured in Britain. Every penny spent on Western Australian products, naturally, meant fewer pennies spent on goods manufactured elsewhere in Australia or in other parts of the Empire, but this was never spelled out.

Despite the rhetoric that an era of reconstruction and economic progress was dawning, which would benefit all of society, the income groups that had prospered by 1914 — merchants and pastoralists — remained the wealthiest in the mid-1920s. In 1926, the sheep and wool growing industry made a net profit in excess of £81,000, and its profits continued to increase until the end of the 1920s. Agriculturalists also prospered throughout the decade.[55] Success in business was crowned with social distinction. As in 1914, membership of the Weld Club remained a badge of exclusivity prized by upper echelons of the business community. In 1922, the 300-odd membership consisted of the same prominent pastoralists, judges, lawyers and doctors as previously, but there were more architects, bank officers, and accountants than before the war, and also a few Members of Parliament, some senior civil servants and more university staff.[56] Even so, the club remained an exclusive place where the privileged few entertained friends or stayed while 'in town'.

The privileged members of society also maintained their dominance over cultural pursuits. The interwar years have been described as a period of 'stagnation and conservatism' for the Perth Art Gallery, the Museum and the State Library. The policy of acquiring artworks that maintained the status quo continued, with the purchase of Arthur Streeton's *Barron Gorge*, painted in 1924, and the acceptance, in the centennial year, from George Pitt-Morison of his painting *The Foundation of Perth, 1829*, which was powerfully symbolic of the pioneer tradition. The presence of two Labor men, E.H. Barker and W. Somerville, on the Board of Trustees seems to have had very little influence on the choice of acquisitions.[57]

There were, of course, signs of positive social change by 1926. One such sign was the passage of laws that granted more political and social rights to women. In 1920, legislation had been enacted to allow women to stand as candidates for seats in parliament. During the first decade of the Act's existence, two women served as Members of the Legislative Assembly, and a number of others stood, unsuccessfully, as candidates in elections. Edith Cowan held the seat of West Perth from 1921 until 1924, when, as a result of the inter-party strife in the National coalition, she was defeated by T.A.L. Davy.

The first female Labor Member of the Legislative Assembly was May Holman, who 'inherited' the seat of Forrest, in the State's South West, when her father, John Barkell Holman MLA, died suddenly in 1925. She was the first Labor woman to be elected to the Western Australian Assembly, the first Australian woman to be both a trade union official and a politician, and the first to become an experienced parliamentarian. May Holman brought to parliament fourteen years' experience of working for the labour movement — firstly, as a typist in the Perth Trades Hall; then as a member of the *Westralian Worker* staff; and, from 1918, as Assistant Secretary of the Timber Workers' Union. Despite her considerable ability, however, May Holman never held a portfolio in Collier's Cabinet, a probable indication of the residual prejudice that some Labor men held against women.[58]

May Holman's greatest achievement in parliament may well have been the framing of the Timber Industry Regulation Bill,

May Holman
The first Australian woman to be both a trade union official and a politician,
with fourteen years of pre-parliament experience in the labour movement,
Holman skilfully framed the Timber Industry Regulation Bill in 1926; yet she
never held a Cabinet portfolio.
[Courtesy Battye Library, 3550P]

which became law in December 1926. Timber merchants were
notorious for the appalling working and living conditions that
they forced upon their workers. Holman pointed out that Western
Australia was the last State in the Commonwealth to frame regulations to control conditions in this industry, yet it was the largest
timber producer other than New South Wales. The Act empowered special inspectors to examine, without prior notice, the conditions of plant, machinery and buildings at the mills, landings
and yards; enforced the reporting of serious accidents and fatali-
ties; and required managers and workers to ensure that machinery
and appliances were safe. There were also provisions concerning
dust prevention, sanitary conveniences and adequate housing.[59]

The Timber Industry Regulation Bill stood as a considerable
achievement of the Collier Government, considering that all legis-

lation had to pass through a hostile Legislative Council, where the Opposition held the majority. Other workers in high-risk occupations benefited less from the Collier Government's industrial reforms. The lumpers were an example. The FLU victory in 1919 did not improve working conditions on the wharf. Even two decades later, the work of loading and unloading ships was done mostly by hand, as few Australian ports were mechanized prior to World War II. Despite the hazardous nature of employment, there was still no legislation dealing specifically with the regulation of working conditions and hours. There were cases of men working on freezer ships in light clothing, loading soda ash with bare hands, and working long shifts up to twenty-four hours at a stretch. Many aged prematurely under the physical demands of the labour. The Fremantle Lumpers Accident Book attests to the dangerous nature of the work. There were 126 accidents recorded in 1917, 187 in 1920, and 170 in 1924.[60]

Evidently, many inequalities remained in Western Australia in the mid-1920s. Industries that employed large numbers of women and non-British workers (for example, tea rooms, hotels, restaurants, firewood lines), or workers who were isolated and prevented by distance from organizing effectively (such as domestic servants, farm workers, station hands or shearers) created many problems for union organizers. Aborigines formed an even lower stratum of workers, suffering much discrimination in employment and in other areas of life, being barred from joining unions, and in many cases receiving no pay at all except in kind. Despite the stated intention of employer bodies to improve conditions for their workers in postwar Western Australia, rhetoric and reality were worlds apart. Major factors inhibiting the improvement of working conditions, discussed in previous chapters, included the lack of strength in the union movement, the power of the employer, the reluctance of the conservative Upper House to pass industrial reform legislation in the State Parliament, and divisions among the workers themselves. Even highly organized and politically active unions, such as the Fremantle Lumpers and the Timber Workers, experienced problems in gaining better conditions for their members. The power of the employer extended beyond forming political alliances with non-Labor parties, to assisting the military authorities in maintaining an effective system of vigilance that could prevent a worker gaining employment almost anywhere in the State (as exemplified by the IWW members [Chapter 2] and Alfred Callanan [Chapter 5]).

The fortunes of their representative political parties influenced the power of employers and workers. Conservative and Labor politics over the twelve years from 1914 to 1926 showed diverging trends. Defeat in the State and federal elections, and the 1917 split were severe blows to the labour movement. Yet over the next seven years, while the National coalition retained power but was racked with internal dissension, Labor regained its strength and developed a militancy that resulted in significant industrial victories. The National unions were smashed, and, for a while, the OBU concept received considerable support. After 1921, however, the political wing of the ALF adopted more moderate policies: firstly, in its majority support of the AWU as the vehicle for industrial unionism; secondly, in expelling or disowning Alfred Callanan, George Ryce and Cecilia Shelley; and finally, in the policies and actions of the Collier Government, especially in relation to the maritime strikes of 1924–25.

This book argues that militancy was ultimately crushed in the mainstream labour movement by a two-pronged process of circumstance and design: the removal, by various means, of leading militants, and the burdens of governing, especially with a hostile Legislative Council, limited Labor's will or ability to achieve radical reform. Similar processes occurred in the Eastern States and in South Australia.[61] In each case, part of this process resulted from extreme pressure created by the capitalist status quo. As V.G. Childe wrote scathingly, of the Queensland Labor Government — which had remained staunchly anti-conscriptionist, militant, and in power throughout and after the war in a period when all other Labor governments went into Opposition — it had fallen 'more and more under the thrall of a general capitalist assault'.[62]

In many ways, therefore, the 1920s formed the perfect setting for the birth of a conservative historical association intent upon preserving a selected past. As a result, many years were to pass before anything other than consensus and homogeneity was reflected in the writings of the State's historians.

1   D.W. Black, The National Party in Western Australia, 1917–30, MA thesis, University of Western Australia, 1974, p. 219.
2   Cited in the *West Australian*, 25 March 1925. The title of this chapter comes from this source.
3   *West Australian*, 18 December 1924.
4   *Westralian Worker*, 21 November 1924.
5   I.M. Cumpston, *Lord Bruce of Melbourne*, Melbourne, 1989, p. 23.
6   Notes in Harold Boas Papers, State Archives of Western Australia, Acc. 881A (hereafter Boas Papers), File 1.
7   Notes of the WACC, dated 29 June 1925, Boas Papers, File 2.
8   List of Associations Represented at a Meeting of the WACC, held at 89 AMP Chambers on 11 September 1925, Argonauts Papers, State Archives of Western Australia, Acc. 450A (hereafter Argonauts Papers). Other member organizations (with representatives in brackets) were: Automotive Chamber of Industry (F.D. Sewell); Association of Steamship Owners (A.W. Leonard); the British Medical Association, WA (Dr J.E. Ferguson-Stewart); Commonwealth Institute of Accountants (S.J. McGibbon); Coastal Master Tailors' Union (W. Guttridge); Chamber of Manufacturers (L.B. Bolton); Chambers of Commerce, Perth (H.W.D. Shallard) and Fremantle (S.T. Edwards); Dentists Association of WA (Dr J.A. Campbell-Wilson); Employers' Federation (R.O. Law); Electrical Suppliers and Contractors' Association (H.A.F. Bader); Flour Millers' Association (W. Padbury); Grocers' Association (A.P. Leonard); Institute of Architects (H. Cohen); Institute of Engineers (R. Andrews); Lime and Stone Merchants' Association (H. Snashall); Licensed Victuallers' Association (G.E. Hollingsworth); Master Carriers' Association (Colonel Manning); Metropolitan Undertakers' Association (E. Ledger); Perth and District Master Plumbers' Union (S.W. Hart); Pastoralists' Association of WA (J.H. Church, John Forrest and W. Sanderson); Retail Traders (Sir W. Lathlain KB); Sawmillers Association (R. Bunning); Timber Merchants Association (J. Ainslie); WA Hardware Association (G.R. Preston); WA Caterers Union of Employers (Albany Bell); Wholesale Grocers and Traders (R. Russell); Warehousemen's Association (E.H. Fairley); Wholesale Wine and Spirit Merchants Association (A.B. Bathgate), Sir Walter James KC.
9   Black, The National Party, pp. 231–232.
10 J. Williams, *The First Furrow*, Perth, 1976, p. 91.
11 A. Davidson, *The Communist Party of Australia: A Short History*, Stanford, 1969, p. 12; Williams, *The First Furrow*, p. 95; S. Macintyre, *The Oxford History of Australia: 1901–1942. The Succeeding Age*, Melbourne, 1986, p. 247.
12 Boas to Balston, 4 July 1925 (emphasis added), Boas Papers, File 2.
13 'Manifesto' by Doland and McCallum, State Executive of the ALF (WA) — Minutes Books (hereafter SE Minutes), vol. 2, 7 February 1917.
14 Report to the Members of the Consultative Council, n.d., Boas Papers, File 2.
15 ibid.
16 H. Boas, Bricks and Mortar, unpublished autobiography, Boas Papers, p. 174, mentions Robinson, Davy and McDonald as being 'all active in the Young Liberals, the Liberal and National Party machine and the Argonauts'.
17 Draft of an address by Boas to the 'Businessmen of Western Australia', n.d., Boas Papers, File 2.
18 The National and Country Parties combined to form the United Party only in Western Australia. The federal party remained the National Party until the 1930s.
19 Boas, Bricks and Mortar, p. 147; Cumpston, *Lord Bruce*, p. 59. The election

was held on 14 November 1925 for both Houses of Federal Parliament. In the House of Representatives, the Nationals won thirty-six seats, an increase of eight over their 1923 result, while Labor lost seven seats and the Country Party retained its fourteen.

20 *Commonwealth of Australia Parliamentary Papers, General, 1926–28*, vol. II, pp. 445, 638, 641.
21 Black, The National Party, p. 237.
22 Boas to United Party, 11 March 1926, Boas Papers, File 2.
23 *Argonauts*, vol. 1, no. 1, July 1925, p. 12. For another published account of the Argonauts' activities, see F.G. Clarke, 'The Argonauts Civic and Political Club: An Early Attempt at Industrial Group Organisation in Western Australia, 1925–30', *Labour History*, no. 18, May 1970, pp. 32–39.
24 *West Australian*, 26 May 1925.
25 See, for example, typed draft of H. Boas' Report of the Argonauts Club for the Period Ending 30 June 1927, Argonauts Papers.
26 Boas, Bricks and Motar, pp. 111, 154.
27 *Argonaut*, vol. 1, no. 2, September 1925 (emphasis added).
28 *West Australian*, n.d., cited in *Argonaut*, vol. 1, no. 2, p. 3.
29 'The Policy of the Argonauts', *Argonaut*, vol. 1, no. 2, pp. 2–3.
30 ibid., p. 2.
31 *Argonaut*, vol. 1, no. 3, October 1925.
32 The first two rated the payment of an annual subscription of £1 1s and 10s 6d, respectively; the third of £10 10s; and the last was free.
33 1925 Rules of the Argonauts, Boas Papers, File 2.
34 See, for example, G. Serle, *John Monash: A Biography*, Melbourne, 1982, pp. 468 ff.; also A. Moore, *The Secret Army and the Premier: Conservative Paramilitary Organisations in New South Wales, 1930–32*, Kensington, 1989; M. Cathcart, *Defending the National Tuckshop: Australia's Secret Army Intrigue of 1931*, Melbourne, 1988, pp. 75–100; R. Darroch, *D.H. Lawrence in Australia*, Melbourne, 1981, pp. 32–95.
35 Memo of Proceedings for 'Argonauts' Lunch Club, 23 September 1927, and typed draft of H. Boas' Report of the Argonauts Club for the Period Ending 30 June 1927, Argonauts Papers.
36 'List of Firms where Industrial Groups have been Established', *Argonaut*, vol. 1, no. 5, December 1925, p. 11. The management of the retail firms Boans, Bon Marche, and Foy and Gibson all took an active pro-conscription stance during the war and placed pressure on unmarried male staff to enlist.
37 *Argonaut*, vol. 1, no. 4, November 1925.
38 List in Argonauts Papers.
39 Boas to Chairman of WACC, 16 September 1925 (emphasis added).
40 *Argonauts*, vol. 1, no. 1, July 1925.
41 Typed draft of Boas' Report of the Club for the Period Ending July 1927, Argonauts Papers.
42 H. Boas, Private and Confidential Report to the Argonauts' Council, n.d., Boas Papers, File 2.
43 Even in the 1927 Report, Boas stated that the club preserved an 'attitude of neutrality'.
44 H. Colebatch (ed.), *A Story of a Hundred Years: Western Australia in 1929*, Perth, 1929; D.H. Rankin, *The History of the Development of Education in Western Australia, 1829–1923*, Perth, 1926, pp. 115–116. The author is also grateful to Dr Jenny Gregory, author of a forthcoming history of Scotch College (to be published in 1996), for the information relating to that institution.

45 *Commonwealth of Australia — Census, 1921*, part XIV, pp. 1066–1071. Angli-
    can, 153,000; Roman Catholic, 64,500; Methodist, 39,000; and Presbyterian,
    28,400. Of the non-Christian religions, the Hebrews and the Buddhists had
    approximately 1,000 followers each.

46 D.F. Bourke, *The History of the Catholic Church in Western Australia, 1829–
    1979*, Perth, 1979, p. 199.

47 Unidentified newspaper clippings in Sir Francis Newdegate Scrapbooks,
    State Archives of Western Australia (hereafter Newdegate Scrapbooks),
    vol. 4.

48 See, for example, the program of the 18th Annual Memorial Service for
    South African War Veterans held in Kings Park, Perth, on 22 May 1921,
    preserved in Newdegate Scrapbooks, vol. 3.

49 *Returned Services League Annual Report and Balance Sheet*, 30 June 1924, pp.
    13–14.

50 SE Minutes, vol. 3, 19 May 1921.

51 *Listening Post*, 21 August 1925; J.R. Duncan, A History of the Returned
    Services League in Western Australia, unpublished research essay, 1962,
    held at Anzac House, St Georges Terrace, Perth, pp. 66 ff.

52 Newdegate Scrapbooks, vol. 4, 1921–23. This volume contains numerous
    commemoration programs.

53 J. Moroney, 'Fremantle War Memorial: Patriotism or Civic Pride?', in
    L. Layman and T. Stannage (eds), *Studies in Western Australian History X:
    Celebrations in Western Australian History*, April 1989, pp. 53, 55–56.

54 A.D. Ross, 'Science and Industry', Presidential Address read to the Royal
    Society of Western Australia, 14 July 1925, *Journal of the Royal Society of
    Western Australia*, vol. XI, no. 15, pp. 151–163.

55 *Statistical Registers of Western Australia, 1926–27*; G.D. Snooks, *Depression
    and Recovery in Western Australia, 1928/29–1938/39: A Study in Cyclical and
    Structural Change*, Nedlands, 1974, Tables 3.2, 4.2.

56 T.S. Louch, *A History of the Weld Club (1871–1950)*, Perth, 1964, p. 122.

57 J. Gooding, 'A Gallery for All? The Art Gallery of Western Australia',
    J. Gregory (ed.), *Studies in Western Australian History XI: Western Australia
    Between the Wars, 1919–39*, June 1990, pp. 96 ff.

58 K. White, 'May Holman "Australian Labor's Pioneer Woman Parliamentar-
    ian"', *Labour History*, no. 41, November 1981, p. 110; J. Carter, *Bassendean: A
    Social History, 1829–1979*, Bassendean, 1986, pp. 152–157.

59 *The Statutes of Western Australia. 17 Geo V. 1926*, Perth, 1927, pp. 209–221.

60 S. Macintyre, *Militant: The Life and Times of Paddy Troy*, Sydney, 1984, pp. 65–
    67; M. Tull, 'Blood on the Cargo: Cargo-Handling and Working Conditions
    on the Water Front at Fremantle, 1900–1939', *Labour History*, no. 52, May
    1987, pp. 23–25; Fremantle Waterside Workers (Lumpers), Accident Book,
    1901–27, N.G. Butlin Archives of Business and Labour. The union member-
    ship during this period numbered between 800 and 1,200.

61 See, for example, F. Moss, *Sound of Trumpets: History of the Labour Movement
    in South Australia*, Netley, 1985, pp. 265 ff.

62 Cited in R. Evans, *Loyalty and Disloyalty: Social Conflict on the Queensland
    Homefront, 1914–18*, Sydney, 1987, p. 175.

Chapter Nine

HISTORY FOR POSTERITY

Constructing a Western Australian past

One cold, winter night in 1926, a group of men and women met in a bleak classroom at The University of Western Australia, to form an historical society.[1] It was a significant meeting of carefully selected, socially influential people, including the descendants of such old colonial families as the Cowans, the Roes and the Burts. The presence of Mrs J.B. Roe, the daughter-in-law of Swan River Colony's first Surveyor-General, Captain J.S. Roe, attested both to the brevity of the State's European history, and to the group's determination to give the fledgling society an old colonial respectability. Paul Hasluck remembered that it was a 'conspiratorial gathering', which was anxious to safeguard its history. He was there only because he had been invited by two of the chief instigators of the project, Edith Cowan, and Ivor Birtwistle, editor of the *Western Mail*.[2] Fifty years later, Hasluck recalled the atmosphere of that first meeting:

> They spoke with frankness. They were certainly going to have an old Western Australian as president, and some of them had already spoken to Sir James Mitchell...He was interested and willing to act. They had to fit Dr. Battye in somewhere, because he had control of so many records at the public library. They also wanted Canon Alfred Burton, for he had cornered the market in the Hale and Wollaston Papers...Some other names were mentioned less favourably and discarded...My name was mentioned as one who would be suitable as honorary research secretary...*I was accepted because someone knew who I was.*[3]

Thus the WA Historical Society was founded. Members of the foundation council included J.S. Battye, Professor Shann, Edith Cowan, Mrs J.B. Roe, and Paul Hasluck, while the two Archbishops and the Premier were invited to become the society's patrons.[4]

The formation of a society to collect and preserve the State's historical records indicated that, by 1926, with the centenary of European settlement approaching, West Australians were becoming aware of the value of their identity and heritage as distinct from those of the rest of Australia and of the British Empire as a whole. The formation may have indicated a new pride in Australian achievement and a recognition that Australian interests superseded the interests of the Empire; the type of patriotism, in fact, that was usually associated with the labour movement. Instead, the society developed as an elite group, thoroughly steeped in the traditions of Empire. Elitism was evidenced in its ideology, its membership, the establishment of its headquarters in the exclusive Karrakatta Club, the imposition of an annual subscription of 15s, and its choice of social activities.[5]

The nature of the history that the society perpetuated was also significant. The founding members ensured that the society produced histories that reflected only a narrow range of experience. They had similar perceptions of what was 'important' and what was publicly 'unacceptable'. An attitude developed that those who had been directly concerned with past events were best able to record them, and that 't'othersiders' would not give proper credit to the pioneering families. Furthermore, there was a considerable reluctance to reveal the darker side of the State's history. The convict period, for example, was ignored as if it had never occurred. Hasluck regarded this secrecy concerning persons of convict origin as a kindness.[6] Yet it could be argued that the silence merely continued to deny convicts and their descendants their rightful place in the State's history. The Historical Society concentrated on collecting the reminiscences and documents of the 'respectable' old colonists, indicating that they had no interest in the lower social strata. The absence of labour members from the society, with the notable exception of Philip Collier, also influenced the type of history preserved. Indentured servants, seen only through the eyes of their masters, were 'troublesome' and 'lazy'.[7] Unions received no mention.

Evidence suggests that the academic members of the society, and in particular Dr Battye, held similar perceptions of history to those of the 'old colonists', although there were some disagreements between them. Battye, who arrived from Victoria in 1893 to take up the post of State Librarian, had become a part of Western Australian society and quickly absorbed the outlook and mores of the status quo. Like other Historical Society members, he was anxious to record the struggles of the 'pioneers', and much of his work was devoted to giving them a place of honour in the State's history.[8] He wrote not a word about Aboriginal labour on pastoral stations, nor of the Reverend John Gribble, the Anglican missionary who, a mere forty years before, had showed considerable courage in exposing to public scrutiny the iniquitous treatment of Aborigines in the Gascoyne and Murchison districts.[9] Battye and the 'old colonists' were indeed kindred spirits in their interpretation of Western Australian history. If, as asserted by Hasluck, differences of opinion sometimes created friction between them, these may have been caused more by Battye's inflexible personality than by professional jealousies.[10]

The establishment of an elite group to preserve only a selective history of the State was a deliberate political act on the part of the WA Historical Society. The results of its legacy abound in Western Australian historiography. Social and political divisions were ignored, and historians who argued against the consensual interpretation of Western Australian history were strongly criticized. As shown in the Introduction to this book, Perth in the 1920s was recalled by Paul Hasluck as being a community where a recognized status quo still remained firmly in place. He acknowledged the 'eminence and influence' enjoyed by the *West Australian*, because the paper 'still lived and breathed in the traditions set by Sir Winthrop Hackett and Charles Harper and by Sir Alfred Langler, executor of the Hackett estate'. Ivor Birtwistle, editor of the *Western Mail* — a slightly less exalted but thoroughly respectable publication — was a co-founder of the Historical Society; he conceived the idea and was largely responsible for selecting the committee. Hasluck commented that 'In those days one did not talk of publicity campaigns. One made sure of having support in the right places.'[11]

There are many inconsistencies in Hasluck's depiction of Perth's genteel society. While such values and attitudes still existed, and were particularly popular among the wealthy and powerful, they were increasingly challenged by other values. These challenges had caused members of the Liberal League to sound alarms about the spread of communism and the changing nature of the Labor Party. Perhaps the most significant inconsistency was the 'conspiratorial' way in which the founders of the Historical Society met

Ivor Birtwistle OBE
Editor of the *Western Mail*, Ivor Birtwistle 'conceived the idea of' the Royal
Western Australian Historical Society and was largely responsible for selecting
a founding committee dedicated to safeguarding and selectively portraying
Western Australia's past. 'In those days', reflected Hasluck, 'one did not talk
of publicity campaigns. One made sure of having support in the right places.'
[Courtesy Royal Western Australian Historical Society, B768]

to select members with such care. They recognized that their
beliefs and values were being challenged, and that there were
many facets of their history that they did not wish to make public.

Paul Hasluck's, Frank Crowley's and Geoffrey Bolton's writings all perpetuate the myth of consensus in Western Australia.
Thirty years after the foundation of the Historical Society, Crowley,
then a lecturer in Australian History at The University of Western
Australia and a member of the Historical Society's council, acknowledged the existence of conflicting values and opinions in
Western Australian history. In 1956, he delivered a paper on
'problems in local and regional history', in which he discussed
many of the pitfalls encountered in works by people with little or

no training in history writing. This, he said, resulted in a 'preoccupation with fact' and a lack of analysis. He referred to an 'obsession with the earliest years of pioneering' and to the

> country and local histories with their pedigrees of pioneer landed families, *as though the Australian countryside ever had only one social class of any historical interest and importance*...Although one does not expect the land-owning pioneer to write social and economic history, except in occasional and unconscious flashes, or to be aware that his workmen and his other contemporaries of lesser social importance might have had a characteristic history of their own, *yet most twentieth century local historians seem to be equally unaware of such important realities of the past.*[12]

Despite making this astute observation, Crowley appeared unable to avoid such pitfalls in his own writing. The theme of one of his major histories, *Australia's Western Third*, was economic rather than social development. His chapter on the Great War opens with the remarkable assertion that 'The most important feature of Western Australia's history during the first twenty years of the twentieth century was the development of a large-scale wheat-growing industry'.[13] Crowley virtually omitted industrial strikes, 'shell-shocked' and otherwise permanently incapacitated returned soldiers, the IWW, the Labor Party split, and in fact most of the documentary evidence of working-class participation in, and attitudes to, the war. Whether Crowley did this deliberately or from a lack of documentary evidence is difficult to ascertain. Yet even the casual researcher who looked no further than the pages of that 'pillar of society' the *West Australian* could hardly escape the realization that Western Australia during and after the Great War was a deeply divided society suffering from acute stresses and tensions.

Hasluck's autobiography has already been mentioned as a powerful example of consensus history, and his treatment of the 'marked social gradations' in Western Australian society is discussed in the Introduction to this book. Bolton has commented of Hasluck's analysis that

> the main impression of *Mucking About* is to reinforce the view that would see the Western Australia of pre-1939 as a clannish, *homogeneous* community with a strong sense of its separate identity, particularly in its *lack of some of the complexities and tensions apparent elsewhere in Australia.*

He admitted that he himself had fostered the tendency to 'create a myth of a simpler and more Arcadian Western Australia'.[14] Bolton's description of Perth as a similar society to that remembered by Hasluck is a case in point. He wrote:

> It was a society which for long cherished notions of gentility and a certain Englishness of outlook. Parliament House...was still something of a club where the members were united by *friendship and family ties*...[T]he Labor Party...was less clannish than its opponents, most of its members were 't'othersiders' with a common background in the goldfields or a few small industries. The trades unions behind them were *seldom militant*, and the fiercest disputes of the Australian Labor Party in the Eastern States soon came to rouse only the faintest echoes across the Nullarbor.[15]

Again, this description contrasts strongly with events described in this book.

Several other academic historians have accepted, uncritically, the notions of consensus and parochial narrowness as adequate explanations of Western Australian society during the Great War and the 1920s. Even while rejecting this analysis as being untrue of the following decade, Professor Fred Alexander, in his 'personal appraisal' of Bolton's *A Fine Country to Starve In*, wrote:

> I doubt very much whether there was such a thing as a Western Australian consensus by 1939. If there was, I think it was very different from that of 1929. There was a receptiveness to ideas, and to events outside Western Australia, which *certainly had not been present at the end of that most depressing of all decades in Australian history, the 1920s.*
> *The self-satisfaction and complacency* of that post–Great War decade was no doubt somewhat different in character in the West than in the more industrialised and urbanised states of Eastern Australia. But much the same characteristics were in evidence, *writ somewhat larger, perhaps, in parochialism on the one hand and [in] pleasant good fellowship and easy-going casual friendliness on the other.*[16]

Perhaps Alexander was disillusioned by the disappointments he had suffered in connection with his work for the League of Nations Union. In her study of anti-war organizations in Western Australia during the interwar period, Margaret Brown observed that Alexander was 'discouraged' by the lack of active public support that the peace organizations received from 'the average male citizen'.[17] Interestingly, Brown also initially questioned the consensus approach to Western Australian history, but concluded that, in the context of her study of peace movements, the 'picture of an insular, passive society' could be modified only 'a little'.[18]

A powerful tradition of Western Australian historiography is traceable from the early decades of the century until the 1970s. Beginning with 'gentry' history, it developed concepts of an 'open society' of 'equal opportunity', regardless of class, and a 'strong' and 'parochial' community. This interpretation has even influenced some writers of labour history, most notably John Robertson and David Black. The latter used a 'labour' version of the consensus idea to explain the so-called 'tolerance extended to conscriptionists' by the Western Australian ALF, which he argued

> was a result of the same moderation which enabled the unique integration of its political and industrial wings; this of course was also symptomatic of the lack of a base for industrial trades unionism in a state where only 17 per cent of the value of production was derived from manufacturing...Perhaps it was such an outlook, too, which explained why Justice Burnside did not send to gaol any of the IWW supporters found guilty in 1916 of distributing 'someone else's seditious propaganda' but instead administered a paternalistic reprimand and released the men on bond.[19]

Thus, the consensus notion has been used to substantiate further erroneous assumptions, in this case that the ALF was 'tolerant' towards pro-conscriptionists, and that the IWW members were let off lightly by a paternalistic judge. The material in this book has established a very different reality.

The consensus tradition of Western Australian history writing retains some of its power, despite a sizeable body of modern research that argues the lack of harmony and homogeneity in the west.[20] Yet some conservatives still refuse to enter into historical debate with anyone whose interpretations differ on the nature and content of Western Australian (and Australian) history. In a 1990 review, Hal Colebatch, journalist and son of the conservative politician and editor of *A Story of a Hundred Years*, praised Geoffrey Bolton's *Oxford History of Australia, Volume 5: 1942–1988* for being 'free of the spite and ideological obsessions which have disfigured some recent Australian histories'. Colebatch added:

> [Australia] has had few great dramatic developments — there is nothing in its modern history to compare with, say, the totalitarian

revolutions or the re-birth of Democracy in post-war Germany.
An historian faces a problem in selecting what is *significant* — *and
even what is interesting* — from a vast amount of diverse material.[21]

This damning and inaccurate assessment of the significance of
Australian history could easily have been written by Colebatch's
father, who over sixty years previously concluded his 'bird's eye
view' of Western Australia with a similarly cosy and bland
description:

> Australia is a white man's country in which the conquest of
> nature is comparatively easy. To read Rolvaag's 'Giants in the
> Earth' — that saga of West American colonisation — is to realise
> how much kinder are conditions to the Australian people. A
> hundred years ago the 'Parmelia' brought from the cradle of
> British civilisation, men and women of English, Irish, Welsh and
> Scottish birth. In a new land they have merged more closely with
> each other than in the country of their origin. All have become
> Australians, and their pride as West Australians is complemen-
> tary with an ardent loyalty to Australian nationhood. The end of
> another one hundred years — no matter what vicissitudes of
> fortune may intervene — will find this state great and prosperous,
> the home of a happy and united people, stimulated by high
> tradition, qualified by inherited character, and determined in love
> and patriotism, to hand on to their successors the honest fruits of
> victory.[22]

On the rare occasions when consensus historians have admitted the existence of divisiveness in Western Australian society,
they have always been clear about where the dissent originated.
It came from 't'othersiders' or 'foreigners'. 'Good Western Australians disliked extremes in politics', said Bolton.[23] The conscription crisis contains numerous examples of blame for dissent
being placed on people who originated outside the State. Robertson
claimed that on the eve of the 1916 referendum 'the differences
over conscription had never threatened to become disruptive',
whereas the 'few' who opposed conscription were 'extremists'.[24]
According to Metherell, the 'anti-conscriptionists' attempted to
import 'purge tactics from the eastern states'.[25] Thus, he echoed
the sentiment that 'real Westralians' were not dissidents. This
book argues that many of the most ardent pro-conscriptionists
were either old colonialists, or 't'othersiders' who had established business interests in the State. Similarly, the leaders of
anti-conscription protest, such as Don Cameron and Alex

McCallum, although immigrants to the west in their youth, had developed as militants while in the State.

The book also challenges the idea that the conservative forces were invariably reactionary and defensive; that is, that efforts to maintain the status quo resulted only from the perceived threats of Bolshevism. Instead, much of the evidence from the period suggests that conservative forces were often on the attack. The War Precautions Act, which eroded workers' right to strike and gave preference to 'scab' unions, was reluctantly repealed two years after the end of the war. The RSL's militant — although largely unsuccessful — lobbying for preference of employment for all ex-servicemen, irrespective of whether they were unionists, created considerable tension and hostility between returned soldiers and the labour movement. Employer groups such as ASOF, the PPA, the timber millers, and the firewood companies on the goldfields all were extremely reluctant to improve wages and conditions for their workers. As shown in preceding chapters, postwar industrial awards and reforms were hard won.

In addition to the industrial battles, the political wing of the ALF found itself confronted by more tightly organized and efficiently financed political opponents as the conservatives recognized the value of Labor's disciplined political structures, and emulated them. This book has shown, then, that much Labor militancy was defensive, and much conservative activity, rather than being a rearguard action against the attacks of Bolshevism, was indeed a well-planned strategy aimed at returning industrial and political relations to a status that favoured conservative politicians and employers.

The Great War cast a long shadow. Western Australian society was irrevocably changed. There were the war casualties — over 6,000 dead and in excess of 15,000 wounded. Approximately 7 per cent of the population, including dependants, were in receipt of repatriation benefits. Even the smallest country towns had their war memorials as a perpetual physical reminder — if indeed a reminder was needed — of the cost of sacrifice for the Empire. Each was the focus of displays of mourning every Anzac and Armistice Day. Although the nature of these ceremonies showed that the war had not diminished — indeed, perhaps it had even increased — public displays of loyalty, disillusionment with militarism, and uncertainty about Australia's continuing role in the Empire increasingly found popular expression. Never again would West Australians unite under 'the old flag' to the extent that they had done in 1914.

1	P.M.C. Hasluck, 'The Founding of the Society: Some Personal Reminiscences', *Early Days: Journal of the Royal Western Australian Historical Society*, vol. VIII, part I, 1977, p. 15.
2	ibid.; I.T. Birtwistle, 'Royal Western Australian Historical Society: Recollections of its First Decade (1926–1936)', *Early Days*, vol. VII, part II, 1969–76, p. 40.
3	Hasluck, 'Founding of the Society', p. 16 (emphasis added).
4	Birtwistle, 'Recollections', pp. 40–41; Hasluck, 'Founding of the Society', p. 16.
5	Birtwistle, 'Recollections', p. 40: '[T]he Society began...mapping out a programme of monthly general meetings, council meetings, social gatherings, balls and dances, marking and protection of historical buildings and sites, creation of memorials, publication of journals and proceedings, and so on'.
6	Hasluck, 'Founding of the Society', pp. 13–15.
7	See, for example, Canon Burton, 'The Diary of Anne Whatley', *Journal and Proceedings of the Western Australian Historical Society*, vol. 2, part VII, 1930, p. 26.
8	See, for example, J.S. Battye, *Cyclopedia of Western Australia*, Perth, 1912, vol. II, passim, and *The Development of the Pastoral Industry in Western Australia*, Perth, 1923
9	J.B. Gribble, *Dark Deeds in a Sunny Land, or Blacks and Whites in North Western Australia*, R. Tonkinson (ed.), Mt Lawley / Nedlands, 1987.
10	See, for example F. Alexander's essay on Battye, in *Australian Dictionary of Biography, Vol. 7, 1891–1939*, Melbourne, 1979, pp. 212–213.
11	Hasluck, 'Founding of the Society', pp. 10–11. The *Western Mail*'s role in fostering the powerful myth of a harmonious, Arcadian society even into the 1930s, through the media of art and photography, has been explored in C.T. Stannage, *Embellishing the Landscape: The Images of Amy Heap and Fred Flood, 1920–1940*, Fremantle, 1990.
12	F.K. Crowley, 'Problems in Local and Regional History', *Journal and Proceedings of the Western Australian Historical Society*, vol. V, part II, 1956, p. 21 (emphasis added).
13	F.K. Crowley, *Australia's Western Third: A History of Western Australia*, London, 1960, p. 156.
14	G.C. Bolton, 'A Local Identity: Paul Hasluck and the Western Australian Self Concept', *Westerly*, no. 4, December 1977, p. 75 (emphasis added).
15	G.C. Bolton, *A Fine Country to Starve In*, Nedlands, 1994 edn, p. 4 (emphasis added).
16	F. Alexander, '"A Fine Country to Starve In": Review', *Westerly*, no. 1, April 1973, p. 65 (emphasis added).
17	M. Brown, Western Australians and the World: Anti-War Organisations as a Case Study 1919–39, MA thesis, University of Western Australia, 1981, p. 100.
18	ibid., p. 208.
19	D.W. Black, 'Party Politics in Turmoil: 1911–1924', in C.T. Stannage (ed.), *A New History of Western Australia*, Nedlands, 1981, p. 392.

20   See, for example, J. Gregory (ed.), *Studies in Western Australian History XI: Western Australia Between the Wars, 1919–39*, Nedlands, June 1990.

21   H. Colebatch, 'Review', *West Australian*, 7 July 1990 (emphasis added).

22   (Sir) H. Colebatch (ed.), *A Story of a Hundred Years: Western Australia in 1929*, Perth, 1929, p. 476.

23   Bolton, *A Fine Country*, p. 5.

24   J.R. Robertson, 'The Conscription Issue and the National Movement in Western Australia, June 1916 – December 1917', *University Studies in Western Australian History*, vol. III, no. 3, October 1959, pp. 8, 15.

25   T. Metherell, The Conscription Referenda, October 1916 and December 1917: An Inward-Turned Nation at War, PhD thesis, University of Sydney, 1971, p. 413.

BIBLIOGRAPHY

Note: The abbreviated titles of repositories, as follows, are shown after unpublished archival source materials and some contemporary pamphlets and leaflets:

AA	Australian Archives (Canberra)
AA (Vic)	Australian Archives (Melbourne)
AA (WA)	Australian Archives (Perth)
ABL	N.G. Butlin Archives of Business and Labour (Canberra)
AWM	Australian War Memorial (Canberra)
BL	J.S. Battye Library of Western Australian History (Perth)
ML	Mitchell Library (Sydney)
NL	National Library (Canberra)
RL	Reid Library, University of Western Australia (Perth)
SMA	St Mary's Roman Catholic Archives (Perth)
SA	State Archives of Western Australia

GOVERNMENT SOURCES

Printed

Commonwealth of Australia — Census, 1911, 1921, 1933.
Commonwealth of Australia Parliamentary Papers, General, 1914–1917, vol. II; *1917–1919*, vol. IV; *1926–28*, vol. II.
Commonwealth of Australia Official Year Book, no. 9, 1915; no. 13, 1920.
New South Wales Parliamentary Debates, Second Series, 1919, vols 75–78.
Official Year Book of Western Australia, 1957, vol. 1 (New Series).
Pocket Year Books of Western Australia, 1919–1926.
Department of Repatriation — Repatriation Commission Annual Report for the Year Ended 30 June 1921.
The Senate Journals and Sessional Papers, 1917–18–19, vol. I.
Statistical Registers of Western Australia, 1914–1927.
Victorian Year Book, 1913–14.
Western Australia, Parliamentary Papers, Votes and Proceedings, 1919, vol. 2, 'Report of the Select Committee of the Legislative Assembly on the Claremont Hospital for the Insane'.
Western Australian Parliamentary Debates, 1915–1925.
WA Government, Department of Lands,
    The Settlers' Handy Pamphlet, 1914, Issued by Direction of the Hon. Thomas Bath,

MLA, Minister for Lands (RL).
Soldier Settlement Guide (SA).
WA Government, Education Department, *The Swan Reader, Fifth Book*, 1920 (SA).
Year Books of Western Australia, 1914–1918, 1925, 1926, 1957.

Manuscript

Department of the Army (Victoria), Intelligence Files V282, V298, 430/2/1054, 479/25/190 (AA Vic).
Department of the Army (Western Australia), Intelligence Files, series I and II (AA WA).
Department of the Army (Western Australia), Medical Files R14367, C22980, PP863/1, M1125 (AA WA).
Department of Defence (Australia), series A8911/1, item 221; series A3932/1, item SC417 (AA).
Department of Health (Western Australia), Claremont Mental Hospital Register of Military Personnel, 1917–20 (SA).
Group Settlement Papers (SA).
Police Department (Western Australia), Correspondence Files and Occurrence Books, 1914–22 (SA).
Premier's Department (Western Australia), Correspondence Files, 1914–26 (SA).
Supreme Court of Western Australia (SA),
    Criminal Case File 5006/1820.
    Criminal Indictment Register, 1915–36.
    Divorce Registers, vols 5–7, 1914–24.
WA Government, Education Department, School Journals: Boyup Brook, 1914, Ardath, 1916, and File 4259/14 (SA).

NON-GOVERNMENT SOURCES
Printed

Australian Labor Federation Fremantle District Council Annual Report, 1917.
Australian Labor Party (WA Division),
    Fourth General Council (Tenth Congress), Official Report and Proceedings.
    Annual Report for the Year Ending 31 January 1922.
Australian Workers Union,
    Annual Reports, 1922–26.
    Official Report and Proceedings, 1915.
    Report of the Federal Mining Employees' Conference, 1917.
    Pastoral Industry Conference, Trades Hall, Melbourne, 20.11.20.
Conscription Referendum Leaflets, 1916, 1917 (AWM; SA).
Empire Loyalty League: Full Report of the Inaugural Meeting, 3 May 1921.
Methodist Church of Australia, Western Australian Conference Minutes, 1913–22.
Presbyterian Church of Australia, Minutes of Proceedings of the General Assembly, Western Australia, 1913–15.
Returned Services League Annual Report and Balance Sheet, 1922–24.
University of Western Australia, Public Examinations, 1915–16 to 1920.
Weld Club, List of Members for 1912.
Workers' Industrial Union of Australia Preamble, Classification and Rules, Adopted at the All-Australia Trades Union Conference, Melbourne, January 1919.

Manuscript

Argonauts Papers (SA).
Australasian Steamship Owners Federation,
      Minutes, vols 5–8 (1914–25) (ABL).
      Annual Reports, 1922–25 (ABL).
Australian Labor Federation (Western Australia) (SA),
      Minutes of ALP Special Congress, vol. 18, 1913–28.
      Minutes of the Eastern Goldfields District Council, 1916–24.
      Minutes of the Fremantle District Council, 1915–18.
      Minutes of the Metropolitan District Council, 1914–25.
      Minutes of the Midland District Council, 1914–26.
      Parliamentary Labor Party, Caucus Minutes, 1914–24.
      State Executive of the ALF — Correspondence Files 1–346, 1913–27.
      State Executive of the ALF — Minutes Books, vols 1–4, 1914–26.
      State Executive to Metropolitan District Council — Correspondence Files, 1917–24.
Australian Protestant Federation, Minutes Book of the Kalgoorlie Branch, 1919–22 (SA).
C.E.W. Bean, Private Diaries, 1916, 1917 (AWM).
Harold Boas Papers, including Argonauts Papers, and Bricks and Mortar (unpublished autobiography) (SA).
Don Cameron Papers (SA; NL).
Archbishop Clune Papers (SMA).
Cuballing Roads Board,
      Letter Book, vol. 16 (1916) (SA).
      Minutes Book, vol. 4 (1914–16) (SA).
Dalgetys Papers (ABL),
      Minutes Books, 1905–26.
      Correspondence, 1905–26.
Elder Smith Papers (ABL).
Federated Seamen's Union Papers (ABL; AA).
Fremantle Waterside Workers (Lumpers), Accident Book, 1901–27 (ABL).
Sir Robert Garran Papers (AA).
Roberta Jull Papers (SA).
Lakeside Firewood Company Letter Book, 1919–21 (SA).
M. Miller, Labor's Road to Freedom, typescript (SA).
Canon Robert Henry Moore Papers (SA).
Sir Francis Newdegate Papers, on microfilm, and Scrapbooks, vols 1–4, 1920–24 (SA).
George Foster Pearce Papers (AA; NL).
Perth Chamber of Commerce, Minutes, vols 5–7, 1914–25 (SA).
Returned Services League Papers (NL).
Archbishop C.O.L. Riley Papers (SA).
Bessie Rischbieth Papers (SA).
Lloyd Ross Papers (NL).
Cecilia Shelley, oral history transcript (BL).
William Somerville Papers (SA).
Waterside Workers Federation (Albany) Papers (ABL).

BIBLIOGRAPHY

NEWSPAPERS AND PERIODICALS

Argo, 1926.
Argonaut, vol. 1, nos 1–5 (1925).
Argonauts, vol. 1, no. 1, July 1925.
Daily News, 1914–26.
Fremantle Herald, 1915, 1919.
Geraldton Guardian, 1914, 1924.
Journal and Proceedings of the Western Australian Historical Society (subsequently *Early Days*), 1926–77.
Kalgoorlie Miner, 1914–26.
Listening Post (magazine of the RSL), vols 1–3, 1921–24.
Mirror, 29 November 1924.
Primary Producer, 1924.
Sunday Times, 1914–24.
Truth, 1914–16.
West Australian, 1914–26.
Western Australian Pastoralist and Grazier (magazine of the PGA), vol. 1, nos 1 and 2 (1925).
WA Record (magazine of the Roman Catholic Church in Western Australia), 1914–17.
Western Argus, 1921.
Western Congregationalist (magazine of the Congregational Church in Western Australia), 1916–17.
Western Mail, 1914–26.
Westralian Worker, 1914–26.

CONTEMPORARY BOOKS, PAMPHLETS, LEAFLETS AND ADDRESSES

Anon., *The Menace to Australia and the British Empire*, n.d. (SA).
The Anzac Book, London, 1916.
Battye, J.S., *Cyclopedia of Western Australia*, 2 vols, Perth, 1912.
—— *The Development of the Pastoral Industry in Western Australia*, Perth, 1923.
Birrell, F.W., *Force and Intolerance Must Fail — Canada's Experience of One Big Unionism*, 1919 (SA).
Burton, Canon, 'The Diary of Annie Whatley', *Journal of Proceedings of the Western Australian Historical Society*, vol. 2, part VII, 1930.
Clementson, A., *Trade Unionists Unite!* 1919 (SA).
Colebatch, (Sir) H. (ed.), *A Story of a Hundred Years: Western Australia in 1929*, Perth, 1929.
Courthope, W.E., *Sensational Allegations Against Lunacy Authorities*, 1921 (SA).
Garden, J.S., *The Workers' Industrial Union of Australia. One Big Union Manifesto to Returned Soldiers and Sailors of Australia*, n.d. (SA).
—— *Industrial Unionism. What Is It?* n.d. (SA).
—— *OBU — We Can and We Will Own the Workshops*, n.d. (SA).
Johnson, J., 'The Crooks' Exposed: Damning Evidence Concerning the Seamen's Union 'Crooks'*, 1928 (AA).
McMahon, J.T., *The Cream of Their Race: Irish Truce Negotiations, December 1920 – January 1921*, Ennis (Ireland), n.d. (1921?) (SMA).
Murdoch, W., *The Struggle for Freedom*, Melbourne, 1911.
On the Map: The Western State and Group Settlement.

*OBU. Why It Failed! S*ydney, 1924 (ABL).
Proposed Scheme for Closer Unionism in Victoria, 1918.
Queensland Central Executive of the ALP, *Official Manifesto 'Solidarity or Disruption?'*, *Brisbane Worker Print*, 11 March 1919 (SA).
Rankin, D.H., *The History of the Development of Education in Western Australia, 1829–1923*, Perth, 1926.
Returned Soldiers' and Sailors' Labor League, *The Returned Soldiers and the Labor Movement*, Brisbane, 1919 (ML).
Ross, A.D., 'Science and Industry', Presidential Address read to the Royal Society of Western Australia, 14 July 1925, *Journal of the Royal Society of Western Australia*, vol. XI, no. 15, pp. 151–163.
Throssell, H., 'For Valour', *Westralia Gift Book*, Perth, 1916, pp. 5–11.
Twentieth Century Impressions of Western Australia, Perth, 1901.
Writers and Artists of Western Australia, *Westralia Gift Book*, Perth, 1916.

OTHER BOOKS AND ARTICLES

Alexander, F., *The Campus at Crawley: A Narrative and Critical Appreciation of the First Fifty Years of The University of Western Australia*, Melbourne, 1963.
—— '"A Fine Country to Starve In": Review', *Westerly*, no. 1, April 1973, p. 65.
Bach, J., *A Maritime History of Australia*, Sydney, 1982 edn.
Bassett, J., *Guns and Brooches. Australian Army Nursing from the Boer War to the Gulf War*, Melbourne, 1992.
Australian Dictionary of Biography, 12 vols, Melbourne, 1966–90.
Bedford, I., 'The Industrial Workers of the World in Australia', *Labour History*, no. 13, November 1967, pp. 40–44.
Bell, C., and Newby, H., *Community Studies: An Introduction to the Sociology of the Local Community*, London, 1971.
Bennett, B., 'War Culture: The *Westralia Gift Book*', in L. Layman and T. Stannage (eds), *Studies in Western Australian History X: Celebrations in Western Australian History*, April 1989, pp. 37–46.
Bignell, M., *A Place to Meet: A History of the Shire of Katanning*, Nedlands, 1981.
Birtwistle, I.T., 'Royal Western Australian Historical Society: Recollections of its First Decade (1926–1936)', *Early Days*, vol. VII, part II, 1969–76, pp. 39–56.
Biskup, P., *Not Slaves, Not Citizens: The Aboriginal Problem in Western Australia, 1898–1954*, St Lucia, 1969.
Black, D.W., *Index to Parliamentary Candidates in Western Australian Elections, 1890–1989*, Perth, 1989.
—— 'The Liberal Party and Its Predecessors', in R. Pervan and C. Sharman (eds), *Essays on Western Australian Politics*, Nedlands, 1979, pp. 191–232.
—— 'Party Politics in Turmoil: 1911–1924', pp. 381–405, and 'The Era of Labour Ascendancy, 1924–1947', pp. 406–440, in C.T. Stannage (ed.), *A New History of Western Australia*, Nedlands, 1981.
—— 'P.J. Lynch', in *Australian Dictionary of Biography, Vol. 10, 1891–1939*, Melbourne, 1986, p. 177.
Bolton, G.C., *Alexander Forrest: His Life and Times*, Melbourne, 1958.
—— 'Black and White after 1897', in C.T. Stannage (ed.), *A New History of Western Australia*, Nedlands, 1981, pp. 124–178.
—— *A Fine Country to Starve In*, Nedlands, 1994 edn.
—— 'A Local Identity: Paul Hasluck and the Western Australian Self Concept', *Westerly*, no. 4, December 1977, pp. 71–77.

BIBLIOGRAPHY

—— 'Introduction', in J. Nairn, *Walter Padbury: His Life and Times*, Padbury, 1985.

Broeze, F., '"A Great Frankenstein": The Western Australian Shipping Association 1894 to 1906', in F. Broeze (ed.), *Studies in Western Australian History XIII: Private Enterprise, Government and Society*, Nedlands, 1992, pp. 49–62.

Bourke, D.F., *The History of the Catholic Church in Western Australia, 1829–1979*, Perth, 1979.

Brady, W., '"Serfs of the Sodden Scone?" Women Workers in the Western Australian Hotel and Catering Industry, 1900–1925', in P. Crawford (ed.), *Studies in Western Australian History VII: Women in Western Australian History*, December 1983, pp. 33–45.

Burgmann, V., *'In Our Time': Socialism and the Rise of Labor, 1895–1905*, Sydney, 1985.

—— '"The Iron Heel": The Suppression of the Industrial Workers of the World During World War I', in Sydney Labour History Group, *What Rough Beast? The State and Social Order in Australian History*, Sydney 1982, ch. 8.

Butler, A.G., *Official History of the Australian Army Medical Services, 1914–18*, 3 vols, Canberra, 1943.

Cain, F., 'The Industrial Workers of the World: Aspects of its Suppression in Australia, 1916–1919', *Labour History*, no. 42, May 1982, pp. 54–62.

—— *The Wobblies at War: A History of the IWW and the Great War in Australia*, Melbourne, 1993.

Carter, J., *Bassendean: A Social History, 1829–1979*, Bassendean, 1986.

—— 'Two Historians and Convictism: W.B. Kimberly and J.S. Battye', in C.T. Stannage (ed.), *Studies in Western Australian History IV: Convictism in Western Australia*, December 1981, pp. 68–73.

Cathcart, M., *Defending the National Tuckshop: Australia's Secret Army Intrigue of 1931*, Melbourne, 1988.

The Centenary of Australian Quakerism, 1832–1932, Sydney, 1933.

Childe, V.G., *How Labour Governs: A Study of Workers' Representation in Australia*, Melbourne, 1964 edn.

Churchward, L.G., 'The American Influence on the Australian Labour Movement', *Historical Studies of Australia and New Zealand*, vol. 5, no. 19, November 1952, pp. 258–277.

Clark, C.M.H., *A History of Australia Vol. VI: The Old Dead Tree and the Young Tree Green*, Melbourne, 1987.

Clarke, F.G., 'The Argonauts Civic and Political Club: An Early Attempt at Industrial Group Organisation in Western Australia, 1925–30', *Labour History*, no. 18, May 1970, pp. 32–39.

—— 'A Note on Finance Committees in Western Australian Non-Labor Politics, 1920–26', *Politics*, vol. XII, no. 1, May 1977, pp. 124–126.

—— *Will o' the Wisp: Peter the Painter and the Anti-tsarist Terrorists in Britain and Australia*, Melbourne, 1983.

Coates, R., 'Lenin's Impact on Australia', *Australian Left Review*, no. 24, April–May 1970, pp. 26–31.

Cochrane, T., *Blockade: The Queensland Loans Affair 1920 to 1924*, St Lucia, 1989.

Cole, D., '"The Crimson Thread of Kinship": Ethnic Ideas in Australia, 1870–1914', *Historical Studies*, vol. 14, 1971, pp. 511–525.

Colebatch, H., 'Review', *West Australian*, 7 July 1990.

Connell, R.W., and Irving, T.H., *Class Structure in Australian History: Documents, Narrative and Argument*, Melbourne, 1980.

—— 'Yes, Virginia, There is a Ruling Class', in H. Mayer and H. Nelson (eds), *Australian Politics: A Fourth Reader*, Melbourne, 1976, pp. 81–92.

Crawford, I.M., 'Aboriginal Cultures in Western Australia', in C.T. Stannage (ed.), *A New History of Western Australia*, Nedlands, 1981, pp. 3–34.
Crowley, F.K., *Australia's Western Third: A History of Western Australia*, London, 1960.
—— (ed.), *A New History of Australia*, Melbourne, 1980 edn.
—— 'Problems in Local and Regional History', *Journal and Proceedings of the Western Australian Historical Society*, vol. V, part II, 1956, pp. 19–28.
Cumpston, I.M., *Lord Bruce of Melbourne*, Melbourne, 1989.
Darroch, R., *D.H. Lawrence in Australia*, Melbourne, 1981.
Davidson, A., *The Communist Party of Australia: A Short History*, Stanford, 1969.
Dickey, B., 'South Australia', in D.J. Murphy (ed.), *Labor in Politics: The State Labor Parties in Australia, 1880–1920*, St Lucia, 1975, pp. 229–289.
Dictionary of National Biography, 1931–40, Oxford, 1949.
Edmonds, J. (ed.), *Swan River Colony: Life in Western Australia Since the Early Colonial Settlement*, Perth, 1979.
Evans, R., *Loyalty and Disloyalty: Social Conflict on the Queensland Homefront, 1914–18*, Sydney, 1987.
—— *The Red Flag Riots: A Study of Intolerance*, St Lucia, 1988.
Evatt, H.V., *Australian Labour Leader: The Story of W.A. Holman and the Labour Movement*, Sydney, 1954 edn.
Farrell, F., *International Socialism and Australian Labor: The Left in Australia, 1919–1939*, Sydney, 1981.
Ferro, M., *The Great War, 1914–18*, transl. N. Stone, London, 1973 edn.
Firkins, P. (ed.), *A History of Commerce and Industry in Western Australia*, Nedlands, 1979.
Fischer, G., *Enemy Aliens: Internment and the Homefront in Australia, 1914–20*, St Lucia, 1989.
Fitzhardinge, L.F., *'The Little Digger' 1914–1952: William Morris Hughes, A Political Biography*, vol. II, Sydney, 1979.
Fry, E.C. (ed.), *Rebels and Radicals*, Sydney, 1983.
—— (ed.), *Tom Barker and the IWW*, Canberra, 1965.
Fry, K., 'Soldier Settlement and the Australian Agrarian Myth After the First World War', *Labour History*, no. 48, May 1985, pp. 29–43.
Gabbedy, J.P., *Group Settlement: Part 1. Its Origins: Politics and Administration; Part 2. Its People: Their Life and Times — An Inside View*, Nedlands, 1988.
Gammage, W.L., *The Broken Years: Australian Soldiers in the Great War*, Canberra, 1974.
Garden, D., *Albany: A Panorama of the Sound from 1827*, Melbourne, 1977.
—— *Northam: An Avon Valley History*, Melbourne, 1979.
Garrick, P., 'Two Historians and the Aborigines: Kimberly and Battye', in T. Stannage and B. Reece (eds), *Studies in Western Australian History VIII: European–Aboriginal Relations in Western Australian History*, December 1984, pp. 111–130.
Gibbney, H.J., 'Western Australia', in D.J. Murphy (ed.), *Labor in Politics, 1880–1920*, St Lucia, 1975, pp. 343–383.
Gibson, P.M., 'The Conscription Issue in South Australia, 1916–17', *University Studies in History*, vol. 4, no. 2, 1963–64, pp. 47–80.
Gilbert, M., *Winston S. Churchill, Vol. IV, 1917–22*, London, 1975.
Gill, A., '"To the Glorious, Pious and Immortal Memory of the Great and Good King William": The 12th of July in Western Australia, 1887–1930', in L. Layman and T. Stannage (eds), *Studies in Western Australian History X: Celebrations in Western Australian History*, April 1989, pp. 75–83.

BIBLIOGRAPHY

Gooding, J., 'A Gallery for All? The Art Gallery of Western Australia', in J. Gregory (ed.), *Studies in Western Australian History XI: Western Australia Between the Wars, 1919–39*, June 1990, pp. 96–105.

Goodwin, C.D.W., *Economic Enquiry in Australia*, Durham (USA), 1966.

Graham, B.D., *The Formation of the Australian Country Parties*, Canberra, 1966.

—— 'The Place of Finance Committees in Non-Labour Politics, 1910–1930', *Australian Journal of Politics and History*, vol. 6, July–December 1959, pp. 41–52.

Graves, A.A., 'The Abolition of the Queensland Labor Trade: Politics or Profits', in E.L. Wheelwright and K. Buckley (eds), *Essays in the Political Economy of Australian Capitalism*, Sydney, 1980, vol. 4, pp. 41–57.

Gregory, J., 'Introduction: Western Australia Between the Wars: The Consensus Myth', in J. Gregory (ed.) *Studies in Western Australian History XI: Western Australia Between the Wars, 1919–39*, Nedlands, June 1990, pp. 1–16.

Grey, J., *A Military History of Australia*, Cambridge, 1990.

Gribble, J.B., *Dark Deeds in a Sunny Land, or Blacks and Whites in North Western Australia*, R. Tonkinson (ed.), Mt Lawley / Nedlands, 1987.

Griffiths, P.G., *A History of the Inchcape Group*, London, 1977.

Haebich, A., *For Their Own Good. Aborigines and Government in the Southwest of Western Australia, 1900–1940*, Perth, 1988.

Hall, R.A., *The Black Diggers: Aborigines and Torres Strait Islanders in the Second World War*, Sydney, 1989.

Hancock, W.K., *Australia*, London, 1961 edn.

Hasluck, P.M.C., 'The Founding of the Society: Some Personal Reminiscences', *Early Days: Journal of the Royal Western Australian Historical Society*, vol. VIII, part I, 1977, pp. 7–22.

—— *Mucking About: An Autobiography*, Melbourne, 1977.

Hobbs, V., *But Westward Look: Nursing in Western Australia 1829–1979*, Perth, 1980.

Horner, D., 'The Fight that Changed Australia', *Australian Magazine*, 7–8 August 1993, pp. 8–13.

Hunt, I.L., 'Group Settlement in Western Australia: A Criticism', *University Studies in History*, 1958, vol. 3, part 2, pp. 5–42.

Hyams, B.K., 'Western Australian Political Parties: 1901–1916', *University Studies in History and Economics*, vol. II, no. 3, September 1955, pp. 48–61.

James, M., 'Double Standards in Divorce: Victoria 1890–1960', in J. Mackinolty and H. Radi (eds), *In Pursuit of Justice: Australian Women and the Law, 1788–1979*, Sydney, 1979, pp. 203–210.

Jauncey, L.C., *The Story of Conscription in Australia*, South Melbourne, 1968 edn.

Joll, T., '1901 to 1930', in P. Firkins (ed.), *A History of Commerce and Industry in Western Australia*, Nedlands, 1979, pp. 43–82.

Jones, S., *Two Centuries of Overseas Trading: The Origins and Growth of the Inchcape Group*, London, 1986.

Kee, R., *The Green Flag: A History of Irish Nationalism*, London, 1972.

Kendall, W., *The Revolutionary Movement in Britain, 1900–1921: The Origins of British Communism*, London, 1969.

Kennedy, D.M., *Over Here. The First World War and American Society*, New York, 1980.

Kirkby, D., 'Arbitration and the Fight for Economic Justice', in S. Macintyre and R. Mitchell (eds), *Foundations of Arbitration: The Origins and Effects of State Compulsory Arbitration, 1890–1914*, Melbourne, 1989, pp. 334–351.

Lake, M., 'An Aspect of Tasmanian Patriotism in the Great War: The Persecution of Aliens', *Tasmanian Historical Research Association Papers and Proceedings*, vol. 19, no. 3, 1972, pp. 87–99.

—— *A Divided Society: Tasmania During World War I*, Melbourne, 1975.

——*The Limits of Hope: Soldier Settlement in Victoria, 1915–38*, Melbourne, 1987.

Lane, J., *Fairbridge Kid*, Fremantle, 1990.

Layman, L., 'The Country Party: Rise and Decline', in R. Pervan and C. Sharman (eds), *Essays on Western Australian Politics*, Nedlands, 1979, pp. 159–190.

—— 'Development Ideology in Western Australia, 1933–1965', *Historical Studies*, vol. 20, October 1982, pp. 234–260.

—— and Goddard, J., *Organise! A Visual Record of the Labour Movement in Western Australia*, Perth, 1988.

Lipsitz, L., 'The Study of Consensus', in D. Sills (ed.), *International Cyclopedia of the Social Sciences*, London, 1972, pp. 269–270.

Liveris, L., *The Dismal Trader. The Undertaker Business in Perth, 1860–1939*, Perth, 1991.

Louch, T.S., *A History of the Weld Club (1871–1950)*, Perth, 1964.

Loveday, P., 'New South Wales', in D.J. Murphy (ed.), *Labor in Politics: The State Labor Parties in Australia: 1880–1920*, St Lucia, 1975, pp. 13–125.

Lyman, R.W., *The First Labour Government, 1924*, London, 1957.

Macintyre, S., *The Labour Experiment*, Melbourne, 1989.

—— *Militant: The Life and Times of Paddy Troy*, Sydney, 1984.

—— *The Oxford History of Australia, Volume 4: 1901–1942. The Succeeding Age*, Melbourne, 1986.

MacKenzie, J.M., *Propaganda and Empire: The Manipulation of British Public Opinion, 1880–1960*, Manchester, 1984.

Main, J.M., *Conscription: The Australian Debate, 1901–1970*, Sydney, 1970.

Marwick, A., *War and Social Change in the Twentieth Century: A Comparative Study of Britain, France, Germany, Russia and the United States*, London, 1974.

Mattingley, C., and Hampton, K. (eds), *Survival in Our Own Land: 'Aboriginal' Experiences in South Australia Since 1836*, Adelaide, 1988.

McKernan, M., *The Australian People and the Great War*, Melbourne, 1980.

—— 'Catholics, Conscription and Archbishop Mannix', *Historical Studies*, vol. 17, 1976–77, pp. 299–314.

—— 'War', in V. Vamplew (ed.), *Australians: Historical Statistics*, Sydney, 1987, pp. 410–417.

McQueen, H., *From Gallipoli to Petrov: Arguing with Australian History*, Sydney, 1984.

—— 'Shoot the Bolshevik! Hang the Profiteer! Reconstructing Australian Capitalism, 1918–21', in E.L. Wheelwright and K. Buckley (eds), *Essays in the Political Economy of Australian Capitalism*, 5 vols, Sydney, 1980 edn.

—— 'Victoria', in D.J. Murphy (ed.), *Labor in Politics: The State Labor Parties in Australia: 1880–1920*, St Lucia, 1975, pp. 291–339.

Moore, A., *The Secret Army and the Premier. Conservative Paramilitary Organisations in New South Wales, 1930–32*, Kensington, 1989.

Morgan, A., *J. Ramsay McDonald*, Manchester, 1987.

Moroney, J., 'Fremantle War Memorial: Patriotism or Civic Pride?', in L. Layman and T. Stannage (eds), *Studies in Western Australian History X: Celebrations in Western Australian History*, April 1989, pp. 53–58.

Moss, F., *Sound of Trumpets: History of the Labour Movement in South Australia*, Netley, 1985.

Murphy, D.J. (ed.), *Labor in Politics. The State Labor Parties in Australia, 1880–1920*, St Lucia, 1975.

BIBLIOGRAPHY

Murray, J., 'The Kalgoorlie Woodline Strikes, 1919–1920: A Study of Conflict Within the Working Class', in L. Layman (ed.), *Studies in Western Australian History V: Bosses, Workers and Unemployed*, December 1982, pp. 22–37.

Nairn, J., *Walter Padbury: His Life and Times*, Padbury, 1985.

O'Farrell, P., *The Catholic Church and Community in Australia*, Melbourne, 1977 edn.

Oliver, B., '"All-British" or "Anti German"? A Portrait of a Western Australian Pressure Group During World War I', in R. Bosworth and M. Melia (eds), *Studies in Western Australian History XII: Aspects of Ethnicity in Western Australia*, April 1991, pp. 28–39.

—— 'Disputes, Diggers and Disillusionment: Social and Industrial Unrest in Perth and Kalgoorlie, 1918–24', in J. Gregory (ed.), *Studies in Western Australian History XI: Western Australia Between the Wars, 1919–39*, June 1990, pp. 19–28.

—— '"...For Only by the OBU Shall Workmen's Wrongs be Righted". A Study of the One Big Union Movement in Western Australia, 1919 to 1922', in C. Fox and M. Hess (eds), *Papers in Labour History*, no. 5, April 1990, pp. 1–17.

—— '"Rats", "Scabs", "Soolers" and "Sinn Feiners": A Re-assessment of the Role of the Western Australian Labor Movement in the Conscription Crisis of 1916 and 1917', *Labour History*, no. 58, May 1990, pp. 48–64.

—— '"The Diggers' Association": A Turning Point in the History of the Western Australian Returned Services League', *Journal of the Australian War Memorial*, no. 23, October 1993.

Pearson, A.R., 'Western Australia and the Conscription Plebiscites of 1916 and 1917', *RMC Historical Journal*, no. 3, 1974, pp. 21–26.

Prichard, K.S., *Intimate Strangers*, Sydney, 1981 edn.

Rawson, D.H., 'Political Violence in Australia', part I, *Dissent*, Autumn 1968, pp. 18–27.

Reekie, G., 'With Ready Hands and New Brooms: The Women who Campaigned for Female Suffrage in Western Australia, 1895–1899', *Hecate*, vol. VII, no. 1, 1981, pp. 24–35.

Rickard, J., *Australia: A Cultural History*, London, 1988.

Robertson, J.R., 'The Conscription Issue and the National Movement in Western Australia, June 1916 – December 1917', *University Studies in Western Australian History*, vol. III, no. 3, October 1959, pp. 5–57.

—— 'The Internal Politics of State Labor in Western Australia; 1911–1916', *Labour History*, no. 2, May 1962, pp. 48–75.

Robison, J., and McNair, M., 'Armistice Day, 1918', in L. Layman and T. Stannage (eds), *Studies in Western Australian History X: Celebrations in Western Australian History*, April 1989, pp. 47–52.

Robson, L.L., *Australia and the Great War, 1914–1918*, Melbourne, 1974 edn.

Roe, J., *Social Policy in Australia*, Stanmore, 1976.

Roe, M., *Nine Australian Progressives: Vitalism in Bourgeois Thought, 1890–1960*, St Lucia, 1984.

Ross, L., *John Curtin: A Biography*, Melbourne, 1977.

Rushton, P.J., 'The Revolutionary Ideology of the Industrial Workers of the World in Australia', *Historical Studies*, vol. 15, 1972–73, pp. 424–46.

—— 'The Trial of the Sydney Twelve: The Original Charge', *Labour History*, no. 25, November 1973, pp. 53–57.

Saunders, M., *Quiet Dissenter. The Life and Thought of an Australian Pacifist. Eleanor May Moore, 1875–1949*, Canberra, 1993.

—— and Sumy, R., *The Australian Peace Movement: A Short History*, Canberra, 1986.

Scott, E.D., *Australia During the War: Vol XI of the Official History of Australia in the War of 1914–1918*, C.E.W. Bean (ed.), Sydney, 1936.

Segal, N., *Who and What was Siebenhaar? A Note on the Life and Persecution of a Western Australian Anarchist*, Studies in Western Australian History Occasional Papers, no. 1, Nedlands, 1988.

Serle, G., *John Monash: A Biography*, Melbourne, 1982.

Selleck, R.J.W., '"The Trouble With My Looking Glass": A Study of the Attitude of Australians to Germans during the Great War', *Journal of Australian Studies*, no. 6, June 1980, pp. 2–25.

Shaw, A.G.L., 'Violent Protest in Australian History', *Historical Studies*, vol. 15, no. 60, pp. 545–561.

Shils, E., 'The Concept of Consensus', in D. Sills (ed.), *International Cyclopedia of the Social Sciences, Vol. 3*, London, 1972 edn, pp. 260–266.

Shute, C., '"Blood Votes" and the "Bestial Boche": A Case Study in Propaganda', *Hecate*, vol. II, July 1976, pp. 6–22.

Sills, D. (ed.), *International Cyclopedia of the Social Sciences, Vol. 3*, London, 1972 edn.

Slee, J., *Cala Munda: A Home in the Forest. A History of Kalamunda*, Kalamunda, 1979.

Smart, J., 'The Right to Speak and the Right to be Heard: The Popular Disruption of Conscriptionist Meetings in Melbourne, 1916', *Australian Historical Studies*, vol. 23, no. 92, April 1989, pp. 203–219.

Smith, F.B., *The Conscription Plebiscites in Australia, 1916–17*, Melbourne, 1966.

Smith, J., '"Not Peace but a Sword": Religion, War and Empire. Canon Robert Henry Moore: The Church of England and the First World War', in J.M. Tonkin (ed.), *Studies in Western Australian History IX: Religion and Society in Western Australia*, October 1987, pp. 65–82.

Smith, K., *A Bunch of Pirates? The Story of a Farmers' Co-operative, Wesfarmers*, Perth, 1984.

Snooks, G.D., *Depression and Recovery in Western Australia, 1928/29–1938/39: A Study in Cyclical and Structural Change*, Nedlands, 1974.

—— 'Development in Adversity, 1913 to 1946', in C.T. Stannage (ed.), *A New History of Western Australia*, Nedlands, 1981, pp. 237–66.

Spearritt, P., *Sydney Since the Twenties*, Sydney, 1978.

Spillman, K., *Identity Prized: A History of Subiaco*, Nedlands, 1985.

Splivalo, A., *The Home Fires*, Fremantle, 1982.

Stannage, C.T., *Embellishing the Landscape: The Images of Amy Heap and Fred Flood, 1920–1940*, Fremantle, 1990.

—— (ed.), *A New History of Western Australia*, Nedlands, 1981.

—— *The People of Perth: A Social History of Western Australia's Capital City*, Perth, 1979.

—— *Western Australia's Heritage: The Pioneer Myth*, Nedlands, 1985.

Stoddart, B., 'Sport and Society, 1890–1940: A Foray', in C.T. Stannage (ed.), *A New History of Western Australia*, Nedlands, 1981, pp. 652–674.

Stokes, J.P., *Cunderdin-Meckering: A Wheatlands History*, Cunderdin, 1986.

Swenarton, M., *Homes Fit for Heroes: The Politics and Architecture of Early State Housing in Britain*, London, 1981.

Sydney Labour History Group, *What Rough Beast? The State and Social Order in Australian History*, Sydney, 1982.

Thompson, E.P., *The Making of the English Working Class*, London, 1978 edn.

Throssell, R., *My Father's Son*, Richmond, 1989.

—— *Wild Weeds and Windflowers: The Life and Letters of Katharine Susannah Prichard*, Sydney, 1982 edn.

BIBLIOGRAPHY

Tull, M., 'Blood on the Cargo: Cargo-Handling and Working Conditions on the Water Front at Fremantle, 1900–1939', *Labour History*, no. 52, May 1987, pp. 15–29.

Turner, I., *Industrial Labour and Politics: The Dynamics of the Labour Movement in Eastern Australia, 1900–1921*, Canberra, 1965.

—— '1914–19', in F.K. Crowley (ed.), *A New History of Australia*, Melbourne, 1980 edn, pp. 312–356.

—— *Sydney's Burning*, Sydney, 1967.

vanden Driesen, I.H., 'The Evolution of the Trade Union Movement in Western Australia', in C.T. Stannage (ed.), *A New History of Western Australia*, Nedlands, 1981, pp. 352–380.

Welborn, S., *Lords of Death: A People, a Place, a Legend*, Fremantle, 1982.

Wheelwright, E.L., and Buckley, K. (eds), *Essays in the Political Economy of Australian Capitalism*, 5 vols, Sydney, 1980 edn.

White, K., 'May Holman "Australian Labor's Pioneer Woman Parliamentarian"', *Labour History*, no. 41, November 1981, pp. 110–117.

Williams, J., *The First Furrow*, Perth, 1976.

Williams, R., *Key Words: A Vocabulary of Culture and Society*, London, 1976.

Williams, V. (ed.), *Eureka and Beyond: Monty Miller, His Own Story*, Perth, 1988.

Winter, J.M., 'Britain's "Lost Generation" of the First World War', *Population Studies*, vol. XXI, 1977, part 3, pp. 449–466.

Withers, G., Endres, A.M., and Parry, L., 'Labour', in V. Vamplew (ed.), *Australians: Historical Statistics*, Sydney, 1987, pp. 145–165.

UNPUBLISHED THESES, PAPERS AND ESSAYS

Andrew, R.M., Western Australia and the Boer War: A Colony's Response to a Crisis of the Empire, BA Hons dissertation, University of Western Australia, 1974.

Anon., A Brief History Compiled for the Jubilee of the Perth Churches of Christ, 1940, State Archives of Western Australia, Acc. Q286.63 CHU.

Anon., Nyungar Soldiers, unpublished research essay, Battye Library.

Anstey, S., The Impact of the Great War on the Beverley, Toodyay and Murchison Communities of Western Australia, 1914–17, BA Hons dissertation, Murdoch University, 1980.

Black, D.W., The Early Administration of Philip Collier, BA Hons dissertation, University of Western Australia, 1959.

—— The National Party in Western Australia, 1917–30, MA thesis, University of Western Australia, 1974.

Brown, M., Western Australians and the World: Anti-War Organisations as a Case Study 1919–39, MA thesis, University of Western Australia, 1981.

Coward, D., The Impact of War on New South Wales. Some Aspects of Social and Political History, 1914–17, PhD thesis, Australian National University, 1974.

Duncan, J.R., A History of the Returned Services League in Western Australia, unpublished research essay, 1962, held at Anzac House, St Georges Terrace, Perth.

Ellis, A., The Impact of War and Peace on Australian Soldiers, 1914–20, BA Hons dissertation, Murdoch University, 1980.

Feeney, A.R., The History of The University of Western Australia to 1932, Claremont Teachers College essay, 1959, State Archives of Western Australia, Acc. Q378.9411 FEE.

Gilbert, A.D., The Churches and the Conscription Referenda, 1916–17, MA thesis, Australian National University, 1967.

Gore, R., The Western Australian Legislative Council, 1890–1970: Aspects of a House of Review, MA thesis, University of Western Australia, 1975.

Gregory, J., The Manufacture of Middle-Class Suburbia: The Promontory of Claremont, Nedlands and Dalkeith within the City of Perth, Western Australia, 1830s to 1930s, PhD thesis, University of Western Australia, 1988.

Hopper, P., The 1919 Fremantle Lumpers' Strike, BA Hons dissertation, University of Western Australia, 1975.

Jackson, D.A., A History of the Churches of Christ, Graylands Teachers College essay, 1959, held at State Archives of Western Australia, Acc. Q286.69 JAC.

Lindstrom, R.G., Stress and Identity: Australian Soldiers during the First World War, MA thesis, University of Melbourne, 1985.

Ludlow, K., The Coal and Gold Industries in Western Australia and Government Assistance During the 1920s, BA Hons dissertation, Murdoch University, 1980.

Metherell, T., The Conscription Referenda, October 1916 and December 1917: An Inward-Turned Nation at War, PhD thesis, University of Sydney, 1971.

Mossenson, D., Gold and Politics: The Influence of the Eastern Goldfields on the Political Development of Western Australia, 1890–1914, MA thesis, University of Western Australia, 1952.

Murray, J., The Kalgoorlie Woodline Strikes, 1919–20, BA Hons dissertation, University of Western Australia, 1981.

Robinson, D., A Demographic and Social History of Perth and Suburbs, 1901–1911, MA thesis, University of Western Australia, 1979.

Sholl, D., John Curtin at the *Westralian Worker*: 1917–1928: An Examination of the Development of Curtin's Political Philosophy as Reflected in his Editorials, BA Hons dissertation, University of Western Australia, 1975.

Shute, C.M., Australian Women and the Great War: Aspects of Ideological Change with Particular Emphasis on Queensland, BA Hons dissertation, University of Queensland, 1973.

Weckert, C., The 1916 and 1917 Conscription Referenda in the Electorate of Kalgoorlie, unpublished University of Western Australia research essay, 1976, held at State Archives of Western Australia, Acc. PR 8702.

Williams, A.E., A Survey of the Content of History and Citizenship in Western Australian Schools: 1829–1954, BEd dissertation, University of Western Australia, 1957.